ITALY IN THE AGE OF REASON
1685–1789

LONGMAN HISTORY OF ITALY
General editor: Denys Hay

* Italy in the Age of Dante and Petrarch 1216–1380
John Larner

Italy in the Renaissance 1380–1530
Denys Hay and John Law

Baroque Italy 1530–1687
Eric Cochrane

* Italy in the Age of Reason 1685–1789
Dino Carpanetto and Giuseppe Ricuperati

* Italy in the Age of the Risorgimento 1790–1870
Harry Hearder

* Modern Italy: 1871–1982
Martin Clark

* already published

LONGMAN HISTORY OF ITALY
Volume Five

Italy in the Age of Reason
1685–1789

DINO CARPANETTO
AND
GIUSEPPE RICUPERATI

Translated by
CAROLINE HIGGITT

LONGMAN
London and New York

Longman Group UK Limited
Longman House, Burnt Mill, Harlow,
Essex CM20 2JE, England
Associated companies throughout the world

*Published in the United States of America
by Longman Inc., New York*

First published 1987

British Library Cataloguing in Publication Data

Carpanetto, Dino
Italy in the Age of Reason: 1685–1789.
— (Longman history of Italy; v.5)
1. Italy — History — 1559–1789
I. Title   II. Ricuperati, Giuseppe
945'.07   DG545

ISBN 0-582-48338-7 CSD
ISBN 0-582-49145-2 PPR

Library of Congress Cataloging in Publication Data
Carpanetto, Dino, 1949–
Italy in the age of reason, 1685–1789.

(Longman history of Italy; v. 5)
Bibliography: p.
Includes index.
1. Italy – History – 1559–1789. I. Ricuperati,
Giuseppe. II. Title. III. Series.
DG467.L67 1980 vol. 5 [DG545]   945'.06   86–15174
ISBN 0-582-48338-7
ISBN 0-582-49145-2 (pbk.)

Set in Linotron 202 11/12 Garamond
Produced by Longman Singapore Publishers (Pte) Ltd.
Printed in Singapore

Contents

List of maps and tables vii
Glossary viii
Foreword x

PART ONE   Demography, economy, classes and institutions in
                  eighteenth-century Italy (Dino Carpanetto)

Chapter One   Italian population in the eighteenth century
                  and the role of the towns 2
Chapter Two   The countryside: structural weaknesses and
                  signs of revival 22
Chapter Three   Trade and manufacture. The historiographical
                  problem of the crisis of the seventeenth
                  century 34
Chapter Four   The gradual recovery of the Italian economy in
                  the eighteenth century 45
Chapter Five   Classes and institutions: the hegemony of the
                  nobility and the role of the State 54

PART TWO   Political ideas and pressure for reform in the first
                  half of the eighteenth century (Giuseppe Ricuperati)

Chapter Six   The renewal of the dialogue between Italy and
                  Europe: intellectuals and cultural institutions
                  from the end of the seventeeth century to the
                  first decades of the eighteenth century 78
Chapter Seven   The veteres against the moderni: Paolo Mattia
                  Doria (1662?–1746) and Giambattista Vico
                  (1668–1744) 96
Chapter Eight   Jurisdictionalism, deism and free thought:
                  Pietro Giannone (1676–1748) and Alberto
                  Radicati di Passerano (1698–1737) 106

Chapter Nine	The political proposals of enlightened Catholicism	121
PART THREE	*Reform in the first half of the eighteenth century (Dino Carpanetto)*	
Chapter Ten	Italy in the first half of the eighteenth century: the beginnings of reform	140
Chapter Eleven	The Habsburg-Lorraine model: the Lombardy of Maria Theresa, Tuscany under the Regency and the Duchy of Modena	158
Chapter Twelve	Bourbon Italy: Naples and Parma	179
Chapter Thirteen	Reforms without Enlightenment: the Papal States, the republics and Charles Emanuel III's Piedmont	193
PART FOUR	*Italy from the reforms of enlightened absolutism to the crisis of the* ancien régime *(Dino Carpanetto)*	
Chapter Fourteen	Tuscany in the age of Leopold	210
Chapter Fifteen	The Duchy of Milan under Maria Theresa and Joseph II	223
Chapter Sixteen	Enlightenment and reform in Naples and Sicily	236
PART FIVE	*The political and economic debates of the period of the Enlightenment and reform (Giuseppe Ricuperati)*	
Chapter Seventeen	The Enlightenment in Naples. The school of Bartolomeo Intieri: Ferdinando Galiani (1728–87) and Antonio Genovesi (1712–69)	250
Chapter Eighteen	The Enlightenment in Lombardy: Pietro Verri (1728–97), Cesare Beccaria (1735–94), *Il Caffè*	259
Chapter Nineteen	Jurisdictionalism and Enlightenment: Cosimo Amidei (dates uncertain) and Carlantonio Pilati (1733–1802)	273
Chapter Twenty	The Enlightenment in the Mezzogiorno and the crisis of the *ancien régime*: the school of Genovesi, Pagano (1748–99), Filangieri (1752–88)	284
Chapter Twenty-one	The intellectuals and the State in the crisis of the *ancien régime* in Piedmont	298

PART SIX   *Historians and the Italian Enlightenment*
                  (*Giuseppe Ricuperati*)

Chapter Twenty-two   The *ancien régime* and the Italian
                       Enlightenment: a historiographical problem ..   310

Maps   335
Index   338

List of maps and tables

Map 1. Principal towns and regions   336
Map 2. Political divisions during the eighteenth century   337
Table 1. Italian population 1650–1700 by geographical area   3
Table 2. Italian and European population in the eighteenth
         century   3

Glossary

a livello	Contract where land is let out on a perpetual lease with nominal rent; emphyteusis.
allivellazione	Policy of introducing land letting on *a livello* contracts.
alzamento	Introduction of a new coinage with less silver or gold in it – i.e. coin worth more than the precious metal contained in it.
annona	State organisation and control of the distribution of food.
arrendamenti	Contracted out *fiscali* (cfr.) – customs, gabelles, dues on goods in store, monopolies, public offices – in the Kingdom of Naples.
arrendatori	Collectors of the *arrendamenti*.
catasto	Cadastral register, land register. The census carried out to draw up the register.
ceto civile	Neapolitan social group between the nobility and the commoners, composed of lawyers of various sorts. Part of it was the *ministero togato* (cfr.).
Collegio delle Provincie	Founded in Turin by Victor Amadeus II to train personnel for state service.
Crusca	(=chaff) Name of academy founded in the Renaissance, and still in existence, with the aim of separating good Italian usage from the 'chaff'. It produced a dictionary, first published in 1612, which arbitrated on pure and impure Italian.
donativo	Direct tax, originally guaranteed to rulers by their estates.
emphyteusis	Contract whereby a peasant could use land for a long period or in perpetuity, on condition he maintained and improved the land and paid a low rent in money or kind.

fidecommesso	Legal settlement of property, preventing successors from freely disposing of it.
fiscali	Taxation rights, such as taxes, customs, etc.
Ghibelline	Faction which in the Middle Ages supported the emperor against the pope.
giuspubblicismo	Juridical and political theory which opposed to feudal and private laws the law of the state.
Guelph	Faction which in the Middle Ages supported the pope against the emperor.
illuminista	Follower of the theories of the Enlightenment.
Josephism	Jurisdictional policies carried out by Joseph II.
jurisdictionalism	That body of legal arguments seeking to limit the jurisdiction of the Church in secular affairs.
latifundia	Large privately owned estates in southern Italy.
maggiorascato	System of inheritance where property passes to the nearest male relative.
mezzadria	Share-cropping lease.
mezzadro	Share-cropper.
ministero togato	Neapolitan social group within the *ceto civile* (cfr.), composed of the top ranking state officials.
Perequazione	The great land survey conducted in Piedmont and Savoy by Victor Amadeus II, culminating in the implementing of edicts in 1731 for Piedmont and 1738 for the duchy of Savoy.
Piazza	The six constituencies that sent a representative to the municipal council of Naples. Five of these were nobles, the other a commoner.

To Sara
To Luciana

Foreword

This book is an attempt at a general survey which sets out to document the significant revival in eighteenth-century studies that we have seen in recent decades. Going beyond the limited view of the eighteenth century as the prelude to the Risorgimento, or those views coloured by nationalism which so frequently characterised the approach of historians from Unification to the Fascist era, Italian eighteenth-century studies can now take their place in the European historiography of the Enlightenment. Undoubtedly the starting-point for this fruitful renewal lies in the important studies by Franco Venturi, which began in the 1930s and culminate in the monumental *Settecento riformatore*, still in course of publication. Thanks to this work, in which Venturi combines deep scholarship with wide intellectual interests, it is possible today to recognise the significance for Italy of the Enlightenment and the crisis of the *ancien régime*, and to understand the complex and sometimes contradictory picture of passionate intellectual debate, pressure for philosophical and political change, an energetic desire for reform, the problems in the institutional inheritance, the resistance of the privileged classes and powers, and the oppressive tradition of the past. To Venturi, his culture and his humanity this book owes much. It is a pleasure to acknowledge here our grateful recognition of this debt.

We would also like to thank colleagues of the Department of History of the University of Turin, particularly our friends Massimo Firpo, Luciano Guerci and Enzo Ferrone who have encouraged us with their loyalty and friendship. Our thanks also go to Caroline Higgitt for her translation and to Dr Claudio Rosso and Professor Geoffrey Symcox for their valuable comments on the latter. Finally, we would like to recall the name of Angelo Pressenda, a friend who in the recent months has supported us personally and in our work.

Dino Carpanetto
Giuseppe Ricuperati
Turin, July 1984.

Demography, economy, classes and institutions in eighteenth-century Italy (Dino Carpanetto)

CHAPTER ONE

Italian population in the eighteenth century and the role of the towns

At the beginning of the eighteenth century the population of Italy was, according to the most reliable estimates, roughly 13.5 million. The fall in population caused by famines, epidemics – the plagues of 1630 and 1657 being the most dramatic – and by the wars of the first half of the seventeenth century was followed by a demographic recovery which was also the start of a long period of development. In Italy, as in the rest of Europe, the eighteenth century saw the start of a period of growth which, in alternating phases and different rhythms, has continued up to the present day. This demographic phenomenon was not identical throughout the peninsula. Bearing in mind the great and varied geographical divisions, we see that between the middle and end of the seventeenth century the most consistent contribution to the demographic revival came from the northern regions which had suffered most from the seventeenth-century contraction; there was little movement in central and southern Italy and none at all in the islands (Table 1).

The highest density of population was in the North, with more than 50 inhabitants per sq km. In central Italy it was about 45 inhabitants per sq km, while in the South and the islands the average density went down to about 37 inhabitants per sq km. It should be remembered that northern Italy was one of the most densely populated areas not only in the peninsula but in the whole of Europe. Moreover, this large population was spread over a very wide territory, while elsewhere in the continent high population was generally concentrated in a smaller area. The demographic contribution of the country areas of the Veneto and Lombardy was important in sustaining the level of population, as were the numerous urban settlements; these were generally of small or medium size, with the exception of Venice and to a lesser extent Milan. The territories of mainland Venice in particular were very heavily populated, with about 70 inhabitants per sq km and reaching almost 120 inhabitants in the province of Padua. The principal growth, from its beginning in the second half of the seventeenth century, took place in the agricultural areas, whereas the increase in urban population was not, with rare exceptions, so noticeable.

During the eighteenth century Italy thus participated in the phenomenon

Table 1. Italian population 1650–1700 by geographical area (taken from Bellettini, A. (1979) Aspetti e problemi della ripresa demografica nell'Italia del Settecento, in *Società e storia* 6, p. 822)

(A) Total numbers

Year	1650	1700	1750	1800
Northern Italy*	4,255	5,660	6,511	7,206
Central Italy†	2,738	2,777	3,100	3,605
Kingdom of Naples	2,850	3,300	3,900	4,847
Sicily and Sardinia	1,522	1,456	1,776	2,136
Total	11,366	13,193	15,287	17,794

(B) Percentage variation

Period	1650–1700	1700–1750	1750–1800	1700–1800
Northern Italy*	+ 33.0	+ 15.0	+ 10.7	+ 27.3
Central Italy†	+ 1.4	+ 11.6	+ 16.3	+ 29.8
Kingdom of Naples	+ 15.8	+ 18.2	+ 24.3	+ 46.9
Sicily and Sardinia	− 3.8	+ 22.0	+ 20.3	+ 46.7
Total	+ 16.1	+15.9	+ 16.4	+ 34.9

* Piedmont, Lombardy, Venetian mainland, duchies.
† Grand Duchy of Tuscany, Papal States.

of a growth of population, which took place all over Europe and was to have a bearing on the great economic and social changes of the nineteenth and twentieth centuries. In Italy, however, the levels of growth were much lower than in the rest of Europe (Table 2).

In one century, from 1700–1800, the Italian population increased by more than 4 million, from 13.5 to 17.8 million (a variation of 34.8 per cent, as opposed to an increase of 67.8 per cent over the same period in Europe). The tendency of the population to fall in mainland Italy, more noticeable in the second half of the century, is an indication of the persistence of factors which specifically inhibited economic change in the peninsula. On the other hand,

Table 2. Italian and European population in the eighteenth century (millions) (taken from Bellettini, A. P. 820 (op. cit. in table 1 above)).

Year	Italy	Rest of Europe	Total	Variation (1700=100) Italy	Rest of Europe	Total
1700	13.2	101.8	115.0	100.0	100.0	100.0
1750	15.3	124.7	140.0	115.9	122.5	121.7
1800	17.8	170.2	188.0	134.8	167.8	163.5

3

a comparison of the factors inherent in the demographic development of the eighteenth century shows striking similarities between growth in Italy and in Europe, though, in view of what can be learned from demographic studies, the influence of the rising birthrate is more apparent in Italy. In each case the movement of population varies little, showing a pattern typical of the *ancien régime*. It is rather the lessening of demographic crises which maintains the increase in population. Widespread and severe disasters such as plague, famine and war were now no longer of the same magnitude or frequency as in the seventeenth century. Instead, there was an overall, though slight, improvement in general living and working conditions, in individual and collective hygiene and in sanitation, together with an increased ability of agriculture to support the population growth. Broken down into the different geographical areas of the country, the population figures show more activity in southern and insular Italy than in the central and northern areas. In other words, the tendency of the previous fifty years, when southern Italy had been recovering only slowly from the disasters of the first half of the seventeenth century, has been reversed; and we see the beginning of that demographic preponderance of the South which was also to characterise Italian history in the nineteenth century.

The largest population in absolute terms was in the Kingdom of Naples with, in the mid-eighteenth century, a little under 4 million inhabitants in an area of 106,000 sq km. In a detailed study of the demographic sources in the South, Pasquale Villani has identified the existence, as early as the end of the seventeenth century, of growth in the southern population and he places the period of increased acceleration to the thirty years 1730–60.[1] Naples itself, the heavily populated capital, was untypical with its 300,000 inhabitants; these had been drastically reduced by the plague of 1656 and then restored in the first half of the eighteenth century partly by an influx of people of all classes from the country but also by a constant superiority of births over deaths. A similar expansion in population did not take place in all areas in the South. In Lucania, Molise and Capitanata Foggia there was a consistent increase, while in other areas like Calabria and the Abruzzi the population fell.

This inequality of population distribution which particularly characterises society in southern Italy has few echoes in other parts of Italy. According to the German historian, J. Beloch, writing at the beginning of this century, and the recent research of M. Aymard,[2] demographic trends in Sicily were very similar to those in southern Italy. After an initial twenty years of crisis or stagnation in population growth, resulting from the two famines of 1707 and 1716, there was a rapid expansion from the 1720s onwards. Here too the most consistent growth was in the countryside, while the cities, like Palermo and Catania, expanded but rarely showed any significant percentage increase in population. The increase in the different provinces was not uniform, as seems to be confirmed by the tendency already apparent in the seventeenth century for a greater demographic expansion in the western part of the island, in the provinces of Palermo, Trapani, Agrigento and Caltanissetta. In the eastern part of Sicily, only Catania and its surrounding territory

4

keep up with the average growth of the island as a whole, unlike the provinces of Messina, Syracuse and Enna. In various parts of the interior of the island the population remained stable, on a level with the previous century or only slightly higher. In general the demographic expansion is apparent in the grain- and wine-growing areas, while recession occurs in the areas dependent on silk, livestock and trade with the East.

We have at present only fragmentary information about population patterns in Sardinia but from this it would seem that the island was one of the least populous regions of Italy with, at the beginning of the century, 300,000 inhabitants in an area of approximately 24,000 sq km, and that the population grew in proportion with that of the rest of the peninsula.

Numerically speaking, at the beginning of the eighteenth century the Papal States had the largest population after the Kingdom of the Two Sicilies, with about 2 million inhabitants in an area which was also second in size. Confirming the tendency in mainland Italy for a limited increase during the first half of the eighteenth century, growth in this area was negligible in the first fifty years of the century. Population growth in Tuscany too appears to have started late, while in northern Italy it begins earlier. Similarly in the duchies of central-northern Italy and in the Venetian Republic the increased rate of demographic development is to be found in the second half of the century rather than the first. However, it should be said that quantitive documentation in these areas is very fragmentary.

In Austrian Lombardy statistics derived from taxation reveal instead a consistent growth of population from the seventeenth-century crises up to the 1760s, with a more rapid increase apparent from 1730. In total the increase was in the order of 10 or 12 per cent, with a higher growth in the countryside. As has already been emphasised, this is typical of Italian demographic development, which differs from that of Europe precisely in this concentration of population growth in the country rather than in the towns. One of the few towns to exhibit a contrary tendency is Turin, capital of Savoy, which already in the first half of the century had an intense growth rate, fed by the influx from the countryside. This to some extent can be seen as a consequence of the political and social orientation of Piedmont towards the capital. After the territorial growth resulting from the War of the Spanish Succession, Piedmont had a population of over 1.5 million. Higher still was the population density of Liguria which around the middle of the century was almost 90 inhabitants to the square kilometre.

With a few exceptions, Italian towns show in the eighteenth century population levels which are either stationary or slower in growth than those of the country.[3] This slow movement of the urban population was pushed up by more or less consistent numbers of people moving from the countryside into the towns, often according to seasonal factors. This trickle was to become a flood at the end of the eighteenth and beginning of the nineteenth century. The towns attracted people from the rural areas even though life in the country seemed more secure and food crises were less apparent than in the town, since supplies of necessary foodstuffs were closer to hand. In particular, the areas just outside the towns acted as a pool of labour for the urban centres. On the other hand, there is no clear demographic distinction between town and country: the two areas are closely linked by a process of continuous osmosis. Indeed, the country extended to within the walls of some Italian towns, with market gardens and a peasant class. Many towns drew people from specific areas, who then became more or less established within the town.

In general it can be said that this interpenetration between town and country is less apparent in centres of predominantly commercial activity, and in ports concerned generally with trading and uninvolved for historical and geographical reasons with the agricultural interior. This new physical and political link with the country is underlined too by the townscapes which became more open and spacious, looking increasingly outwards with fewer architectural signs of a rigid separation from the country. In the course of the century, city walls finally lose their defensive function, retaining only that of a civil and fiscal boundary. Although they confirm the long political and cultural subordination of the country to the town, they become less symbolic of a clear separation of the two. Towards the end of the century, in some towns, such as Genoa and Turin, the link with the country developed through a process of consistent urbanisation of the peasants, which increased the population of the towns but which brought in its wake new tensions arising from shortage of housing, unemployment and the high cost of living.

The towns remain at the heart of political and economic life in the Italy of the first half of the century, though there is undeniably a shift of interests, productive initiatives and political and cultural attention towards the countryside. This phenomenon becomes more noticeable in the second half of the century when there was a move to re-evaluate the role of agriculture, and new voices were heard on the problems of the peasants, crops, agricultural prices and food supplies. Sometimes, this new recognition of the central role of agriculture and the countryside encouraged a perception of the towns (particularly those with a high population) as destructively devouring and parasitical. But the town remained, or became, the place where the administrative and judicial duties of the states tended to concentrate. The inevitable consequence was the growth of the tertiary sector, the turning of political attention to the provinces and an increased monetary circulation. By appearing as political and cultural leaders, the position of the towns was strengthened by the implied possibility, in some situations, of imposing domination or at least privileges – a power which the countryside did not possess. Despite the transfer of various economic activities to the country, the towns remained the centres of sizeable groups of artisans and provided an environment which favoured the development of the first industrial concentrations. The greater part of the income from the land was deposited in the towns and here too it was spent, invested or saved. Thus the profits of ecclesiastical benefices remained within the town walls. At least until the middle of the century, spurred on by the success of those religious orders which arose with the Counter-Reformation and by the many private donations which it continued to receive, the Church continued its urban expansion, acquiring in almost all Italian towns numerous sites on which churches, convents, seminaries, hospitals and charitable institutions were built.

In the eighteenth century Italian society retains its peculiarly urban nature, characterised not only by the large number of densely populated towns (six Italian towns had more than 100,000 inhabitants, Messina, Milan, Palermo, Rome, Venice and Naples, which, with more than 200,000, was with Paris and London the most populous town in Europe at the beginning of the century), but also by numerous other smaller urban concentrations. These were particularly frequent in the central-northern plain where, both in external remains and in cultural traits, the structure of an urban civilization laid down four centuries earlier still persisted. In the South, by contrast, the towns were fewer in number and more widely spread. This arrangement had not changed appreciably since the sixteenth century, nor had the overall number of important towns, despite the total increase in Italian population. A comparison of Beloch's reconstructed list of towns of over 20,000 inhabitants around 1770 with the list for the second half of the sixteenth century reveals very little change. Only two cities drop out, with populations fallen below that figure: Siena and Mondovì; while Pavia, Leghorn, Modica and Turin appear for the first time.

The towns in central-northern Italy retained the appearance they had assumed during the period of the city-states, and show the civil traits of an ancient pride founded on a municipal autonomy and freedom which, though it had been reduced, had not been eliminated by the process of state central-isation in the sixteenth to seventeenth centuries. These cities had reached their peak of economic development in the sixteenth century, and in the eighteenth century they maintained a stability that was more apparent than real. The political weakness of the old city patriciates was becoming more evident as they diminished everywhere in number and became socially more exclusive, and more rigid in their defence of ancient political laws even though they were not unaware of the new needs and demands of the absolute State. Other towns, like Rome, presented a Renaissance and baroque appearance moulded in the years of papal glory. Where Spanish domination continued into the seventeenth century, as in Milan and Naples, it gave rise to important changes in the urban scene and to new tastes and customs. The capitals of the republics, on the other hand, retained almost unaltered an architectural appearance which dated from before the seventeenth century. Turin is unique, its streets built in a uniform and restrained baroque style as a result of dynastic control over urban development. Compared with the vitality of town life seen in previous centuries, at the beginning of the eighteenth century the towns established during the period of the communes and the seigniories seemed generally less vigorous in the civil and political spheres. The growing importance of the regional states increased the driving force of the capital cities. These, through the concentration of state powers, came to exercise new forms of control over the lesser centres, which often saw their ancient tra-ditions of autonomy weakened as a result. This phenomenon was most marked where, as in Piedmont, the ruling dynasty invested much administrative and political energy in the construction of a more centralised state.

The majority of Italian cities still show in the second half of the seventeenth century significant economic energy, strong enough to repair, in a greater or lesser period, the ravages caused to the urban fabric by the plagues of 1630 and 1656–57. All the larger cities, hard hit by the epidemic, almost entirely recovered their previous level of population, drawing in labour from the countryside to fill the vacancies in trades and service. Added to this, almost everywhere domestic industry created job opportunities of some importance. But if the northern and central towns, such as Turin, Leghorn, Genoa and Florence, required labour and used it actively while at the same time containing the problem of vagrants, the major centres of the South, Rome, Naples and Palermo, grew great on the poverty of the country. From there came seasonal or permanent influxes of population into the towns where protection and assistance for the poor were more easily obtained. During the eighteenth century, the towns which had an important administrative role, such as Naples, Palermo, Rome and Turin, and those which were centres of internal and foreign trade, like Genoa, Cagliari, Leghorn and Ancona, all generally show significant population increases. Industrial and manufacturing centres do not as a rule show similar increases.

The unique character of demographic development in Turin has already been referred to. Turin, capital of the State of Savoy from 1563 when Emanuele Filiberto moved his capital from Savoy to Piedmont, had, at that time, some 20,000 inhabitants. It was not then the main town of the State, but a place of medium size, which had grown up on the plan of the ancient Roman town and which was little marked, either architecturally or culturally, by the Renaissance. During the seventeenth century Turin was radically altered under the influence of the ruling dynasty, which imposed a consistency on the town's development, still observing systematically the ancient Roman street plan, by the use of a restrained baroque style. The two extensions of the city which took place in the seventeenth century show a town on the move, asserting itself ever more clearly as both political capital and centre of intense activity in trade and commerce. In 1707 Turin had 43,000 inhabitants and the end of the War of the Spanish Succession over 46,000.[4] During these years the feverish building of the second half of the seventeenth century which had been slowed down by the war now started up again. Turin became the capital of a kingdom and Victor Amadeus II endeavoured to fit it for its new duties. The architect Filippo Juvara of Messina was commissioned to plan a third extension of the city and this plan, carried out between 1714 and 1728, was to remain for more than 150 years the model for future enlargements. The quantitive size increased: in mid-century there were more than 58,000 inhabitants, a gradual but massive increase of more than 25 per cent slowed down only by the Wars of Polish and Austrian Succession.

Turin was on the way to becoming the centre of political and economic activity in Piedmont. As the capital grew, the other towns of Piedmont remained stable. Migration into Turin came not only from the areas which traditionally fed it, such as Savoy, Nice and Oneglia, but also from the Piedmontese provinces which formerly had gravitated towards other urban centres. The reasons for this development are numerous. One, undoubtedly, was the success of the policies of Savoy, which aimed to impose centralised institutions on all areas of the province and to attract the ruling classes to the capital to supervise their preparation for the exercise of their social duties, to fit them into the fabric of the State and to bind them more closely to the ruling dynasty. The rise in population reflects too an expanding productivity which increased the number of traders and professionals as well as that of the new incoming workers. Finally there is the social, and also physical, *rapprochement* of the Piedmontese nobility to the kings of Savoy and the rise of new classes who invested part of their financial capital in the building of houses in the capital city and employed a large domestic staff. But social mobility was much reduced, and while new groups from the country were absorbed, particularly from areas going through a period of crisis, social divisions nevertheless remained intact.

Very different is the demographic picture in Milan, where the plague of 1630 had inflicted a cruel blow, halving the population from 130,000 at the beginning of the seventeenth century to some 66,000. Despite a vigorous and rapid recovery, bringing the population up to about 126,000 around 1688, Milan in the early eighteenth century had not recovered its demographic equilibrium. It was further upset by a slight lowering in the years of the War of the Spanish Succession. The Austrians took possession of a capital which in 1715 had a population of some 120,000 people – a figure which remains constant during the first half of the eighteenth century. The urban textile industry did not recover from the depression of the seventeenth century which had hit the wool industry particularly hard and which saw the almost total disappearance of once numerous and flourishing industries. The stagnation in the manufacture of both silk and wool, despite the efforts to re-establish the latter, emphasises the lack of an impetus to expansion which particularly characterises Milanese society at this time. Thus the appearance of the city, despite the renewed activity in private and public building, remained essentially that of the Spanish seventeenth century.

Venice, the other large town of northern Italy, also slowly recovered a population decimated by the plague to a figure of 140,000 inhabitants – fewer than at the end of the sixteenth century.[5] Venice, a city-state but also a privileged city with regard to the Po Valley hinterland which it had acquired in the fifteenth century, drew a large part of its wealth from the mainland: about half of the income from land in the provinces went to the Venetian laity and to churchmen. The greater part of the administration and judiciary were concentrated in the capital, and it was also the centre of the most important industries of the Veneto. It was protected by a corporate system which gave it a monopoly of production and distribution of goods in the internal market, thereby impeding the creation of any competition on the mainland. Finally the capital's dominant position was reinforced by the presence of the port. The architectural appearance of Venice, unique in all Italy for the extraordinary beauty of its palaces, churches and squares which seem almost like backdrops for one of the many Venetian theatres, was not altered in the seventeenth century. Verona is one of the few towns of the Veneto where an urban economy was able to develop without total dependence on the capital and where an autonomous ruling patriciate arose. The plague of 1630–31 hit Verona's population more severely than in Venice, reducing it from 50,000 to less than 20,000. At the end of the seventeenth century it had climbed again to more than 30,000 and continued to increase in the following years until in 1738 it reached 42,000. Nevertheless, in the course of the eighteenth century Verona was unable to regain its sixteenth-century level.

Between the second half of the seventeenth century and the 1720s Venice lost her long supremacy in the Adriatic under the pressure of the Turkish wars, and because of the military and economic advances of competing foreign powers such as France, England and Holland. These in the course of the seventeenth century had established direct commercial links with the East, depriving Venice of the monopoly she had long enjoyed. A further reason for this decline in the Adriatic was domestic: in this same period the Venetian nobility and bourgeoisie were diverting their capital to investments in land. This weakness allowed other ports on the Adriatic to emerge as alternative commercial centres. Trieste was made an Imperial port when, in 1719, Charles VI declared it, together with Fiume, a free port. This meant that goods could be freely imported and exported without the payment of duty. In the same year in Vienna the Levant Company was set up which was to exercise a monopoly over trade with the Turkish Empire. The Viennese rulers invested considerable capital in Trieste to strengthen the port, to create a naval shipyard and to provide an arsenal for the Austrian military marine. In this way Trieste expanded by means of an economic and military operation directed by the Austrian State which encouraged the immigration of workers from other provinces of the Empire; they were to be employed both in the construction of the port and the enlargement of the town, brought about by a massive land-reclamation scheme. The success of this policy led in 1747 to the extension of exemption from customs duty to the whole of the Trieste trading area and in 1755 to the founding of the commercial stock-market.

Trieste was developed in this way in order to become the most viable competitor on the Adriatic to Venice. With the provision of a port, with the exceptional support of the Empire, and with the new patterns of exchange established between the port of Trieste and the German, Bohemian and Hungarian regions of the Empire, Trieste was indeed able to offer competition to Venice. However, Venice's primacy remained intact during the whole of the eighteenth century in so far as she maintained a high level of trading, while only after 1760 did a real expansion in the volume of trade become evident at the port of Trieste. This upward swing, late in coming given the grandiose but not altogether realistic plans of the early eighteenth century, was connected with the policies of Maria Theresa. She suppressed the resistance of the oligarchy of Trieste, which was little inclined to become involved in mercantile development, and she aided those, mostly German but also

Greek, Dalmatian and Slav, who had set up around Trieste, attracted by the favourable trading conditions there. Trieste was the experimental model of a mercantile policy financed by the State which, ignoring the opposition of the local nobility, provided a new impetus to production and trade, and transformed society by the introduction of outsiders. They changed the very appearance of the city, which now centred on the port, the shipyard and the communication routes with Austrian Lombardy and northern Europe. In the middle of the century industry expanded with factories producing candles, leather, playing cards, rope and an 'imperial' printing press. Trading links now reached as far as the western coasts of Africa.

On the Italian side of the Tyrrhenian Sea, on the other hand, the clear economic supremacy of any one port is not apparent. From the coast of central Italy up to France, two ports, Genoa and Leghorn, were rivals for trade, but for a number of reasons, the Ligurian port suffered a diminution in its volume of traffic. Genoa had reached the peak of its economic expansion between 1550 and 1650 when it had built up great financial power in Habsburg Europe.[6] The major changes in urban development also date from this period. In 1638 the town had some 75,000 inhabitants and after the devastating plague of 1656 this figure was reached again by the 1740s. At the beginning of the eighteenth century Genoa's position in Europe was seriously threatened. Political and commercial relations with Spain had weakened, other financial influences had taken the place of the Genoese in the great courts of central Europe, and the attempt by Genoese merchants from the 1650s onwards to re-establish trading links with Constantinople had failed in the face of the hostility of the French and the Ottoman governments. Local industries were slowing down production because they could no longer find markets abroad as before. Unlike the Venetian nobles who in the seventeenth century had partially redirected their investments, transferring them to the mainland which provided a secure income, the Genoese nobility had remained tied to the city both politically and economically. The territories of the Ligurian coast, part of the Genoese Republic, and Corsica, which Genoa held until 1769, were allowed a wide degree of social autonomy, and Genoa's policy in their regard never extended beyond the area of taxation.

In the last years of the seventeenth century another factor was added to the traditional competition from the French port of Marseilles to contribute to the Genoese recession – the expansion of the port of Leghorn, which had been chosen as a trading base by English and European ships. The fall in revenue at the Genoese free port (which in any case was only applied within strict fiscal limits and not for all ships that docked there), falling from 250,000 lire in 1667 to about 114,000 in 1700, was merely the confirmation of a malaise which the ruling class was unable to cure. The frequent adjustments to the free port system made in the early eighteenth century gave no appreciable results, and the fluctuation in the volume of goods landed at Genoa was more than anything else a reflection of the variations in trade at Marseilles and Leghorn.[7] After the War of the Spanish Succession Genoa had also to contend with the improved ports of Nice and Oneglia, the latter encouraged by Savoy, which further diverted trading opportunities from the Genoese Republic, even if to a lesser degree than Leghorn. Genoa's acquisition of Finale in August 1713, one of the last successes of a policy under increasing pressure from the great powers, was able to counterbalance in part the expansion of Savoy. The failure of Genoa's plans to take over the feudal domains of Lunigiana and Massa, however, put an end to the possibility of a more balanced response to competition from Leghorn. Similarly, attempts to reorganise the rules of the free port in order to offer conditions as attractive as those of Leghorn were unsuccessful. Genoese trade did not rely entirely on the port. Genoese merchants dealt directly from Tolfa, Naples and Sicily where for a long time they had placed their capital at the disposal of the Spanish monarchy; they enjoyed in return exceptionally remunerative conditions both in trading and in the management of tax collection, thereby establishing themselves as an economic power in the island. From the Tyrrhenian ports they organised trade for Spain and northern Europe. In addition they controlled the land routes which linked the port to Milan, Germany and France. The decline in Genoese commercial power started in the second half of the seventeenth century when England, France and Leghorn made their presence felt in the grain trade with the East, the most reliable commodity in the maritime trade of the Tyrrhenian.

From this time too dates the decline of the monetary and financial system which the merchant bankers of Genoa had established in the fifteenth century.[8] The theatre of their financial operations, once so large, touching Europe, America and Africa, became restricted to northern Europe. They were to some degree excluded in the traditional financial capitals of Europe – Madrid, Naples, Seville and Antwerp – from where they had for two centuries directed the monetary and financial market. In the seventeenth century new centres of European finance emerged, where the Genoese bankers were less in evidence. As for industry, the 1690s had seen a severe contraction in the production of silk and wool, unable to withstand the competition from French goods which were cheaper and more up to date.

Despite these undeniable signs of recession, Genoa remained a significant economic force which enabled it to fill the gaps in population left by the plague of 1656 by importing labour from the Ligurian territories, to be used in the various industrial and craft enterprises or in one of the many service industries demanded by the city – muleteers, coalmen, artisans, fishermen, boatmen and similar categories who lived on the outskirts of the town. It was precisely from this class of workers that in 1746 one of the few urban uprisings in eighteenth-century Italy before the French Revolution took place, the result of a long economic and political malaise which the Austrian invasion sparked into an explosion. But of this more will be said later.

At the beginning of the eighteenth century Leghorn had fewer inhabitants than Genoa, about 31,000,[9] making it the twelfth largest Italian town and second, after Florence, in Tuscany. The population explosion had started in the previous century and continued throughout the eighteenth century, reaching a high point of c. 41,000 inhabitants at the end of the century.

During the War of the Spanish Succession, Leghorn had been the only Tuscan centre to maintain its economic energy. In addition, it had also benefited from the events of the war, further increasing the volume of its sea trade. Its prosperity depended almost entirely on the port and on the particular exemptions which it enjoyed. Declared a free port in the mid-seventeenth century, Leghorn had become the centre of a flourishing maritime trade both for warehousing and for transit, supported for the most part by foreign capital. English, French, Flemish and the many Jewish merchants, who controlled almost all the trade with ports in the East, had built their fortunes on the special position that Leghorn had established for itself. With their political and economic influence, the foreign traders had always defended Leghorn's international and extraterritorial character. In fact these groups had prevented the formation inland of any industrial and commercial base which might have altered Leghorn's situation. The wealth derived from the trade by sea did not extend beyond the customs barrier and had only a slight effect on the economy of Tuscany.

The international outlook of Leghorn, Tuscany's chief port, is underlined by the absence of any adequate Tuscan merchant marine. The same demographic and economic picture extended down the Arno and into the inland provinces. The southern and central areas were, by contrast, sparsely populated and poor with little industry. The Maremma coast was almost uninhabited, and the Leghorn plain in structural, demographic and economic terms was little different. In this situation, the fortunes of Leghorn were almost entirely independent of those of the Medici State. This was clearly seen during the War of the Spanish Succession when Leghorn was the only town of the principality to have an increase in the volume of business, favoured as it was by its neutral status, and guaranteed by the great powers, who sheltered it from economic reprisals and changes in international trade. During these years, Leghorn became the port of call for ships which had formerly gone to other Tyrrhenian ports. Nor was its expansion weakened by the Tuscan law of 1683 which prohibited the merchants and financiers of Leghorn from practising their trade in foreign cities, with the aim of protecting the Tuscans who were less in evidence abroad. These protectionist measures had a negative effect on the port but did not diminish its commercial growth. Trade continued to be much more influenced by international events. In the eighteenth century, both because of the changes taking place in the Italian market which was contracting and the economic policies of the Lorraine rulers which required a greater national identity for the port, Leghorn's role as an international market became less important. In addition, Leghorn and its urban development were affected by Leopold's more general policy for an improvement in Tuscan agriculture and industry. The system of land communications was reorganised and improved, and was indicative of a plan to 'nationalise' the port of Leghorn.

Leghorn is an exception in the history of Italian towns in the eighteenth century, both for its recent emergence as a growing urban centre and for the elements which accounted for this growth and which, at least until the end of the Lorraine regency (1737–65), had little to do with political decisions and internal social processes, but were determined more by economic factors. Leghorn is an isolated case in the history of population in eighteenth-century Italy, as is, for other reasons, Turin. The latter's increase in population was largely influenced by the monarchy which brought the capital to a new position of importance in administration and politics while furthering its aim to centralise power. In Leghorn, on the other hand, international factors, increasing trade and financial dealings were of more importance.

The growth in population and economic importance of Leghorn was unique in the Tuscany of the last Medici. Other cities diminished in importance, like Florence and Siena; maintained their previous position, like Pistoia and Arezzo; or slightly increased their population, like Pisa.[10] In general the towns of Tuscany were in a static phase, though tensions and problems were mounting up unseen, that at the beginning of the eighteenth century still lay beneath the surface but which were to erupt in the years to follow. Only a partial awareness of the commercial and industrial stagnation in the Tuscan towns penetrated the consciousness of the ruling classes, and they were incapable of offering the towns, hampered by a combination of unfavourable conditions, any scheme for recovery along the lines of the mercantile policies tried in other states. Meanwhile the countryside needed capital and labourers, thereby partially draining the towns of wealth and men. In addition, though contemporaries were less aware of it, there was a political and demographic crisis within the ruling classes themselves. The families holding political power were diminishing in number but they nevertheless continued to put up a fierce defence of their institutions and customs, sanctified by time but now in increasing difficulties.

As the Medici dynasty drew to a close Tuscany was in a state of severe political decline, behind which lay the more general decline affecting, to a greater or lesser extent, all the European and Italian states with republican or seigneurial governments. This trend was reflected in the population patterns of Tuscan cities. According to Beloch's estimate, the population of Florence had increased in 100 years by 5.7 per cent, from 69,000 inhabitants in 1642 to c. 73,000 in 1744–45. Pisa and Siena had about 14,000 inhabitants at the same date, but while for the former that represented a slight increase, for the latter it was a significant drop. Siena in 1580 had more than 20,000 inhabitants while in the mid-seventeenth century it had only 16,000. This was not followed by a recovery – on the contrary, there was a further decrease in population. The physical appearance of Florence confirmed a general climate of decline in the city during the period of the last two Medici rulers. There was no overall urban development, nor was it even planned, and apart from a few buildings belonging to the great patrician families, there were no important additions to the town.[11] It was rather the clerical atmosphere which permeated civil life in Florence under Cosimo III and Gian Gastone, which took physical shape in the building of new churches and convents. In all, the architectural appearance of the city was little changed and retained its sixteenth-century character. It was only with the arrival of the Lorraine rulers and particularly during the government of Leopold II of Habsburg (1765–90) that public and private building started up again and plans for the restoration of the architectural patrimony and ideas for new urban planning were suggested and executed.

The towns in the duchies in the Po Valley, Modena, Parma, Piacenza and Mantua, were of a similar size, with populations varying from 20,000 to 26,000.[12] The plague of 1630, the wars, famines and the passage of foreign armies had affected them all similarly in the seventeenth century and during the eighteenth-century Wars of Succession. They emerged from the wars and the rearranged alliances among the great powers with various different political conditions. Modena remained the capital of the Este Duchy, Parma after various vicissitudes passed to the Bourbons, and Mantua with the War of the Austrian Succession was annexed to the State of Milan. During this period the Po Valley states underwent a progressive process of political subjugation to the great European powers.

Rome, capital of the Papal States, was in the eighteenth century the second largest city in Italy.[13] In the first half of the century its population grew from 134,000 in 1720 to *c*. 158,000 in 1750. About 10 per cent of the total population of the State lived in the capital. No other large town – Naples, Turin or Milan – had at that period such a disproportionate balance between the populations of capital and State. Rome was a town of sharp social contrasts, with a few very rich families sharing with the many cardinals the greater part of wealth and power. Below them came sizeable groups of intermediaries, administrators, lawyers, then of artisans and workers and finally the great mass of the poor and homeless. The population of Rome was subject to variations according to the seasons, as when the Abruzzese shepherds came down to the city in winter to find work. Religious feasts, particularly during the Holy Years (1725, 1750 and 1775) attracted pilgrims from all over the world. Finally, agricultural results affected population figures, a bad harvest being enough to flood the city with poor peasants seeking protection and assistance. Already at the beginning of the century the more perceptive intellectuals, such as Nuzzi, Belloni and Pascoli, were denouncing the parasitic nature of Rome's economy, revealing the city as a place of squandered wealth, of luxury enjoyed only by the few, a centre of monopoly of income, of rigid centralisation of power, with a supply of food guaranteed by the *Annona* and drawn from the most fertile areas of the Roman countryside. There is no doubt that these observers identified many aspects of the supremacy of the capital, but it should not be forgotten that Rome at the same time tied together a state fragmented to a degree unusual in Italy which found in its capital and its special international position its chief *raison d'être*.

From the architectural point of view, at the beginning of the century Rome had altered little from its appearance of two centuries earlier. The town plan and baroque style of the sixteenth century brought in by Paul III, Gregory XIII and Sixtus V had remained as they were even where unfinished. All the great palaces of the Roman aristocracy – the Colonna, Orsini, Muti, Doria, Chigi, Boncompagni, Borghese and Caetani families – had been built earlier.

Thus the numerous convents and monasteries (in the mid-eighteenth century there were at least 181 scattered all over the city) dated from between the sixteenth and seventeenth centuries. Rome was no longer growing, but to a certain extent it attempted to perpetuate a former splendour which was continually contradicted by reality. There was no upsurge of economic and civil renewal in eighteenth-century Rome as had happened in Naples, Milan and Venice even if the new voices of the European intelligentsia reached it, to be diluted by the shrewd spirit of Catholic supremacy.

The place occupied by Leghorn in the Tuscany of the Medici and House of Lorraine fell in the Papal States to Ancona, though one must bear in mind the difference in level of economy and population. Ancona had only 7,000 inhabitants at the beginning of the century.[14] At one time a cosmopolitan town of over 20,000 inhabitants with large colonies of Jewish, Ragusan, Greek, Levantine, Armenian, French, German and Flemish merchants, Ancona had paid a heavy price in terms of economy and population during the crisis of the seventeenth century. At the beginning of the eighteenth century it started to recover in a way reminiscent of Leghorn. In 1732 Clement XII exempted the port from customs duty, following the example of the free port of Trieste, to allow it to compete on an equal footing with the other Adriatic ports. This move gave positive results, at least in the early years of the free port. The volume of traffic increased, foreign dealers were attracted back and the economy of the whole State prospered.

Unlike Ancona, which was growing in wealth and population, Bologna had entered a period of depression at the end of the seventeenth century as a result of the crisis of the textile trade which had been the mainstay of the town's economy.[15] Its role as an industrial and commercial centre of primary importance weakened. Foreign competition and the loss of important markets in the early eighteenth century caused its silk and hemp manufacturing industries to lose their important position, and with them went the whole industrial structure of the town, once so robust and thriving with forms of organised production unusual in Italy at that time. Even though Bologna had defended a strong autonomy from Rome in the areas of tax, finance and excise, nevertheless the loss of the court in 1506 and close proximity to the Roman State had brought a halt to any development of influence by Bologna over the surrounding territory. Besides, the areas over which Bologna had had any influence were not large. It had been an important centre, with its university and schools of painters and music, attracting all Europe with its atmosphere of culture and sophistication, but between 1600 and 1700 these institutions diminished in importance. A combination of these factors brought about a period of total inactivity which finds confirmation in the population figures and the urban development of the town. In the first half of the eighteenth century, Bologna maintained the level of population reached in the previous decades when it had recovered from the losses caused by the plague. Until 1750 the population remained roughly at the 65,000 level, a total reached as early as 1718 and a figure including a high number (5–7 per cent) of clerics. Nor did the appearance of the town alter from that determined in the fifteenth and sixteenth centuries, while urban development was contained within the limits of the ancient walls.

The largest Italian city in the eighteenth century was still Naples, capital of the Kingdom of the Two Sicilies.[16] Naples had had its largest increase in population between the sixteenth and seventeenth centuries when it had exceeded 300,000 inhabitants which made it for a while the largest city in Europe. The anti-Spanish revolt of 1647–48 and particularly the terrible plague of 1656 had emptied the city. Other disasters – the earthquake of 1688, another less serious outbreak of plague in 1691 and recurrent food crises – caused less significant losses but kept the population at a weak and insecure level. The recovery took place in the first half of the eighteenth century: from a population of 220,000 in 1707, Naples reached one of 270,000 in 1734 and about 315,000 in 1742, to a peak of 420,000 at the end of the century, having emerged relatively unscathed from the disastrous famine of 1764. Placed in the centre of a populous basin extending over a radius of 50 or 60 km and where lived more than 40 per cent of the population of the southern provinces, Naples was the focal point. From these areas were to come the largest groups of immigrants. The growth of Naples was also due to its position as political and administrative centre which it had assumed in the southern State from the time of Spanish rule. As seat of the law courts and all the other institutions of a centralised state which here was split up into many different bureaucratic organisations in addition to the pre-existing institutions of feudal origin, Naples was in effect the bureaucratic and political centre of a state which looked to its capital for all matters of general import. The great feudal families lived in Naples, controlling the civil administration almost entirely, and spending the greater part of their income in the capital. There were also numerous ecclesiastical centres – churches, monasteries and charitable institutions – to be found in many of the streets of Naples.

Already in the seventeenth century Naples had struck visitors as a city overcrowded by an excessive population and by the constriction resulting from chaotic and unplanned growth. But the town did not live only on income from land rents; textile industries were widespread and it appears that in the mid-seventeenth century 25 per cent of the inhabitants were involved in them. In addition, the port was one of the most important in the Tyrrhenian, handling the greater part of the trade in southern Italy. The ships that called at Naples brought the capital grain, wine and other agricultural products of the Adriatic plains. But there was no flow of goods in the opposite direction. The most basic need in Naples was supplies of grain from Apulia, to supplement those produced in the areas around the capital. To ensure this supply was the task of the *Annona*, the pivot around which revolved important economic and political interests which gave the capital a monopoly of the grain trade. The port, the arsenal, the building trade, the textile industry and the many opportunities in service and artisan work did not guarantee work for all the resident population. Many Neapolitans lived by begging on the margins of society.

Apart from the occasional intervention of the political rulers, the urban development of Naples had been determined by a process of spontaneous expansion which gave the more populous districts a precarious and disordered appearance, which was intensified by the closeness of one house to another. The growth in population which occurred in the eighteenth century tended to exacerbate the living conditions in the town as it continued to expand without any supervision or planning. Attempts were made during the Austrian viceroyalty to reorganise development but they left no appreciable traces. With the rule of Charles of Bourbon (1734–59) hopes were raised for an improvement along with the new economic and civil developments. The government took a series of measures intended either to improve the inherited civil infrastructures already in existence (such as the improvement of the port and the opening of new roads to speed up the movement of trade between the port and the city or provinces) or to provide new urban solutions (the great *Albergo dei Poveri*, the cavalry barracks, the conversion of the *Palazzo degli Studi* into the Royal Bourbon Museum, the San Carlo Theatre and, outside the city, the palace and park of Capodimonte and the royal palace at Portici). The new elements in the eighteenth-century conception of the city, no longer in the late baroque style, did not, however, stamp a new style on the streets, the squares, the hill or the sea-front, but remained isolated, almost foreign to the predominating style of the sixteenth and seventeenth centuries. With the demolishing of the town walls, between 1740 and 1787, new spaces were created on which dwellings were built for the rapidly increasing population of the eighteenth century. The town was freed from its old boundaries and the overflow population established itself in the suburbs.

The other southern capital, Palermo, had over 100,000 inhabitants at the beginning of the century (some estimates give a larger figure, 145,000 inhabitants in 1714).[17] The rectangular town plan and the gardens which embellished the city went back to the time of Arab rule, but the Arabs were not the only influence. The urban appearance of Palermo had in fact been formed in the sixteenth century by an intensive building campaign, both private and public, encouraged by the Senate and the Spanish viceroys. It was then that Palermo had acquired its predominantly mannerist architecture, later overshadowed by other constructions, such as the religious buildings put up during the Counter-Reformation. A strategic port of considerable import- ance in the Mediterranean, Palermo had been endowed with a defensive system which in the early eighteenth century was still carefully maintained by the governors, as can be seen from the plan for an imposing fort designed probably by the military engineer Giuseppe Ignazio Bertola of Piedmont who worked for some time in Sicily during the period of Savoy's domination (1713–18). The fort, to be built between the town and the new harbour area, together with the plan for expanding the walls, completed the strategy of reinforcement of the military and mercantile structures of the port. These proposals gave rise to a period of prosperity for the port which was just emerging from a phase of severely diminished foreign trade; this had reached a low point during the War of the Spanish Succession when the ban on trade with England and Holland, Spain's enemies, had heavily penalised the port. In general the building work carried out in the eighteenth century, some of considerable architectural worth and taking its inspiration from the baroque, did little to change the face of the city, which had reached completion in previous centuries. However, a new trend which did have an effect on the shape of Palermo was the building of villas for the nobility outside the town in the neighbouring countryside among the plantations of olive and fruit trees which were expanding as a result of a renewed interest in agricultural production.

Society in Palermo was under the unchallenged control of the great feudal families who were protected by a system which favoured them and by the powerful guilds, whose leaders, although inferior to the nobles, enjoyed great social and political prestige. Unlike Naples, Palermo lacked a middle class of magistrates, lawyers and officials who might have offset the dominant role of the nobility and the important ecclesiastical hierarchy. In the first half of the century Palermo was one of the few Italian cities to show an increase in population greater than that in the countryside, having more than 150,000 inhabitants by 1750.

The other great Sicilian port, Messina, did not succeed in reviving its economy.[18] The unsuccessful uprising of 1674–78 had brought about economic penalties which had not been overcome by the beginning of the eighteenth century. Undeniably, the granting of free port status in 1695 had encouraged foreign trade, but the subsequent wars had cancelled out any positive results. The foreign traders, Flemish, English and French, abandoned Messina at that time, though those from Lucca and Genoa remained. The local merchants diminished in number, from forty-one in 1664 to only eight, without any resulting concentration of wealth. Goods like grain and silk, once basic to foreign trade, were exported in ever smaller quantities. It was only in about the 1740s that trade in Messina, and Palermo too, picked up. In this case the change was due more to the expansion of international trade than to the ability of the local economy to reactivate itself. However, the importance of the trading policy of Charles of Bourbon for the encouragement of production and trade should not be underestimated. An unexpected fall in population occurred in 1743 when one of the last plague epidemics in Europe struck Messina, reducing the population to little more than 40,000, but not halting the move towards economic recovery.

From this survey it can be seen that Italian civilisation remained based essentially on the role and presence of the towns. In them the ruling élites had gathered for centuries, and they reflected their social presence. In them the hierarchies of society took shape, revealing the traits of the varied origins and events which have marked Italy's history. The roads, the squares, the palaces and the churches of countless Italian cities reveal an age-old history, stratified and frozen in the townscape. It is visible in the eighteenth-century towns, planned by the official directives of the regional states or of the mercantile policies of the dominant powers (Turin, Trieste), in towns like Florence whose urban appearance was moulded in the fourteenth and fifteenth centuries and where the historical continuity of aristocratic rule is most apparent, and finally in those towns which were changed more recently, in the sixteenth and seventeenth centuries, like Naples where the arrival of the Spanish viceroys heralded a new urban structure together with a movement of classes and ideologies which were to change profoundly the society of the Mezzogiorno.

NOTES AND REFERENCES

The first scientific studies on Italian demography in the eighteenth century were made at the beginning of the twentieth century by the German historian J. Beloch. See Beloch, J. (1965) 'La popolazione d'Italia nei secoli sedicesimo, diciassettesimo, diciottesimo', in Cipolla, C. (ed.) *Storia dell'economia italiana*. Turin. For more recent and precise figures, see: Cipolla, C. (1965) 'Four centuries of Italian development', in Glass, D. V. and Eversley, D. E. C. *Population in History*. London; Bellettini, A. (1973) 'La popolazione italiana dall'inizio dell'era volgare ai giorni nostri. Valutazioni e tendenze', in *Storia d'Italia*. Einaudi, Turin, vol. 5, pt I, pp. 489–536; various authors (1980) *La popolazione italiana nel '700*. Clueb, Bologna.

1. Villani, P. (1973) *Mezzogiorno tra riforme e rivoluzioni*. Laterza, Bari; Galasso, G. (1965) *Mezzogiorno medievale e moderno*. Einaudi, Turin.
2. Aymard, M. (1971) 'In Sicilia: sviluppo demografico e sue differenzazioni geografiche', in *Quaderni storici* 17, pp. 417–46.
3. Various authors (1975) *Dalla città preindustriale alla città del capitalismo*. Il Mulino, Bologna; Sica, P. (1976) *Storia dell'urbanistica*, vol. I of *Il Settecento*. Laterza, Bari.
4. Levi, G. (1975) 'Mobilità della popolazione e immigrazione a Torino nella prima metà del Settecento', in *Demografia storica*. Il Mulino, Bologna.
5. Beltrami, D. (1954) *Storia della popolazione di Venezia dalla fine del secolo XVI alla caduta della Repubblica*. Cedam, Padua.
6. Costantini, C. (1978) *La repubblica di Genova nell'età moderna*. UTET, Turin.
7. Giacchero, G. (1972) *Origini e sviluppi del portofranco genovese – 11 agosto 1590–9 ottobre 1778*. Genoa.
8. Felloni, G. (1971) *Gli investimenti finanziari genovesi in Europa tra il Seicento e la Restaurazione*. Giuffré, Milan.
9. Bortolotti, L. (1970) *Livorno dal 1748 al 1958. Profilo storico-urbanistico*. Olschki, Florence.
10. Parenti, G. (1937) *La popolazione della Toscana sotto la Reggenza lorenese*. Le Monnier, Florence; Del Panta, L. (1974) *Una traccia di storia demografica della Toscana nei secoli XVI–XVIII*. La Nuova Italia, Florence.
11. Fanelli, G. (1980) *Le città nella storia d'Italia. Firenze*. Laterza, Bari.
12. Marini, L., Tocci, G., Mozzarelli, C. and Stella, A. (1979) *I Ducati padani, Trento e Trieste*. UTET, Turin.
13. Caravale, M. and Caracciolo, A. (1978) *Lo Stato pontificio da Martino V a Pio IX*. UTET, Turin.
14. Caracciolo, A. (1965) *Le port franc d'Ancône: croissance et impasse d'un milieu mar-*

chand au XVIIe siècle. SEVPEM, Paris.
15. Ricci, G. (1980) *Le città nella storia d'Italia. Bologna.* Laterza, Bari.
16. As well as the previously mentioned books by Villani and Galasso, see: Petrac-cone, C. (1974) *Napoli dal Cinquecento all' Ottocento. Problemi di storia demografica & sociale.* Guida, Naples;   De Seta, C. (1973) *Storia della città di Napoli dalle origini al Settecento.* Laterza, Bari;   Alisio, G (1979) *Urbanistica napoletana del '700.* Dedalo, Bari.
17. De Seta, C. and Di Mauro, L. (1980) *Le città nella storia d'Italia. Palermo.* Laterza, Bari.
18. Ioli Gigante, A. (1980) *Le città nella storia d'Italia. Messina.* Laterza, Bari.

CHAPTER TWO

The countryside: structural weaknesses and signs of revival

Allowing for differences in interpretation, historians all agree on the persistence in the first decades of the eighteenth century of the economic depression which had characterised Italian society in the seventeenth century and which continued, though becoming less severe, until the 1740s. Because of this the early eighteenth century is not seen as offering a significant break in economic history, even if it is possible to glimpse, in the depression of the first two decades, the signs of revival which, fading again in the slump of the 1730s, then reappear with new vigour around the middle of the century.

At the beginning of the century agriculture, despite attempts at revival and partial agricultural reform introduced into some areas of Italy by the more go-ahead landowners, was clearly dominated by the decline in production which had occurred during the seventeenth century. This can only be properly understood if one views the weakness of the Italian economy within the larger framework of the European system. From the seventeenth century onwards Italy began to fall behind the more developed countries of Europe, such as England, France and Holland. This was not unconnected with the peculiarities of an economic system fixed towards the end of the Middle Ages, even if up to the sixteenth century sizeable areas of the Italian economy had managed to maintain their position with other European countries. When in the 1620s conditions made for a recession, the most deeply rooted weaknesses of the Italian economy became strikingly apparent, and dragged production backwards to dependence and stagnation. Whenever, as in this case, reference is made to underlying characteristics in the Italian economy, one thinks in general of the historical analysis which places between the fourteenth and fifteenth centuries the definitive triumph of the *latifundia* system in large areas of the country, particularly the South, which were drained of men and investments as a result of this and of the move from the country to the towns. The social and economic weakness of the peasants was aggravated by the grasping usurers and by their legal and personal dependence on the great landowners – rich lay and ecclesiastical feudal lords and restricted oligarchies from the towns.

During the seventeenth century agricultural production fell compared with

22

the levels reached in the sixteenth century and vast areas of the Italian agricultural landscape showed signs of impoverishment. The recession was severe and brought Italy to a position that was economically weak and vulnerable. Given the changing patterns of Europe, it should be stressed that the recession in agricultural production occurred mainly in areas directly linked to the movement of commercial capital. In this case the slackening in production anticipated and reflected the contraction in trade and commercial areas in the Italian states. Already apparent in the 1580s, the fall in agricultural production precedes by some decades the decline in trade between Italy and the rest of Europe. In addition, the European division of labour, rearranged in the seventeenth century, tended to cast Italy in the role of exporter of primary materials (grain, oil, wine) and semi-finished goods (raw silk) and importer of finished products. Thus Italy abandoned a position which in previous centuries had seen her as an active participant in the European market, and now had to adapt herself to a subordinate role from which she was unable to emerge in the following centuries.

If one looks for signs of the recession in the internal changes of the Italian economy, first place must go to the process of decay of the agricultural landscape and the increasing move away from the land by the peasants. These and other signs of a widespread impoverishment among the workers and a massive lowering of production are related to a more or less steady movement of capital derived from commercial enterprises to the acquisition of estates, country properties and state bonds. To describe this transference of wealth from the mercantile sector to investment in land and to express the social implications of this process, historians have coined the term 'refeudalisation'. It means, in other words, the spread of economic practices that place little emphasis on the expectation of profit, and limit any tendency to invest or to intensify and rationalise methods of work. To this was preferred the immediate profit from invested income and its continuation over the years. Commercial ventures which resulted from this situation were not so much intended to create wealth for further investment as to defend social positions already attained and to stabilise income. The result of this change in the political scene was to underline the tendency towards a fragmentation of the structure of the states and a more corporate society.

Even if the term 'refeudalisation' is questioned today, nevertheless it serves to describe certain backward-looking and obstructive influences. It can be seen too how the dominance of town over country to some extent blocked the way to economic expansion. In the great families of the towns, speculation in the income from land became more apparent, since it had become easier to acquire such an income during the seventeenth century thanks to the refinement of the methods for collecting seigneurial dues, and to the strengthening of the legal institutions which rigidly upheld social and territorial institutions such as the *fidecommesso* and the *annona*. The widespread use of *fidecommesso* in all the political and economic capitals of Italy is the most persuasive proof of this tendency. The rich families of the great cities, nobility of ancient or recent origin, were concerned to protect the unity of their inheritance and their political dominance, thus the institution of *fidecommesso* was exhumed, so to speak, from ancient Roman law. At the same time, with prudent political marriages the urban aristocracies tried to secure the wealth on which rested their social position and undisputed political power, while the Church acquired more land. This process did not, however, take the same form everywhere. The most clearly marked differences can be seen in central-northern Italy with its ancient municipal tradition, where the urban aristocracy extended their ascendancy by defending citizen privileges, and in the South where a process operated which was in many respects the complete opposite. In the southern provinces it was more the feudalism of the country which caused men to move to the cities, where sumptuous palaces were built – symbols of a pride that was ostentatious because forced, while at the same time there was an increase in the number of feudal communes, on which not only the barons but also the fiscal system depended. At the start of the eighteenth century, under the rule of the Austrian viceroys, out of 1,999 'lands and hamlets' (*terre e casali*), only 59 were not enfeoffed.

The overall success of the *annone* which were mainly set up in the sixteenth century, apparent in their expansion and in their practical efficiency in fulfilling their function of providing bread for the towns and controlling its price in the urban market, is an indication of the type of processes set in motion by the crisis of the seventeenth century in the areas of the commercialisation of cereals, price-fixing and collection of agrarian revenue. The growing poverty of the peasants caused them to move into the towns, where the established manufacturing industries were failing. The result was that the urban ruling classes strengthened their defensive systems, first and foremost those concerned with the food supply. Thus they gave more precise duties and powers to the *annone*, so as to protect themselves from the risk of famine and revolt. In almost all Italian cities, the office of *annona* became an important institution with a considerable number of officials. Around it formed a network of political and economic interests, involving officials, important merchants, representatives of the town council, speculators, major producers of cereals and money-lenders. Some *annone*, such as the one in Rome, became increasingly more privileged, becoming a financial power of great influence in the town's economy.[1] As well as providing bread, they had powers to regulate prices, and to intervene in commercial dealings and the system of production through their buying and selling of grain and credit to the producers.

The most sensitive power of the *annona* was that of being able to fix the price of bread sold in the towns. Controlled prices and tariffs appeared almost everywhere, particularly from the seventeenth century on. The power to control the price of the staple food in the towns gave the officers of the *annona* a leading role in the political management of the town and in the defence of the interests of the landowners. The *annone* gave their most careful attention to the need to safeguard social peace inside the city walls against the ever-present possibility of a popular revolt. Increasingly during the century, the poorest social groups – the unemployed, the homeless, paupers, beggars and immigrants from the country – began to appear as a threat to the ruling classes who became increasingly of the opinion that the danger these people represented could only be offset by some kind of institutional control. The great buildings for the shelter or confinement of the poor which were built in the seventeenth and eighteenth centuries are evidence of the scale of this phenomenon and the decision to contain it by isolation.

The decisions of the *annone* were influenced not only by considerations of public order, but also by economic policies, in the belief that the political control of the price of bread can protect and stabilise high levels of income from the land, in the face of destabilising factors such as climatic variations, wars, fluctuations in prices and movement of capital. In the case of the *annone* in Bologna[2] and Rome, it is clear that the devices adopted to fix prices guaranteed to the landowners the best price when the grain was sold to the bakers, and allowed them to exercise a total monopoly over the market with the minimum of commercial risk. Price controls in Bologna also allowed goods to be placed on the market very rapidly, avoiding storage and speculative hoarding and thus paying back in a short time the producers' capital. All over Italy the system showed an ability to function with considerable efficiency up to the 1760s when a disastrous famine called the whole institution into question. Nevertheless, the *annone* managed almost everywhere to survive the attacks of famine and reformers and remained active right up to the Napoleonic era.

The changes which took place in the Italian economy during the long period of depression which lasted from the early seventeenth century until at least the 1740s were grafted on to the most vigorous aspects of the structure of the country and reflect their variety. Agricultural Italy at the time can be divided into three large areas: the feudal South with its *latifundia*; central Italy dominated by the *mezzadria* system; and the North where, in the flat areas at least, there were forms of management and organisation of production which were open to the changes of capitalism. This is of course to oversimplify. Differences in environmental structure, institutions, social relationships, professional attitudes and commercial dealings existed which divided the country into many smaller segments, each one with its own peculiarities. One need only think of the South and the importance of geography in production, or analyse the dichotomy between the Apennines where settlements of medieval origin had arisen and the areas on the plain which were still sparsely populated and offered little employment in relation to the resources which the area could offer.

The Tyrrhenian plain, which stretches from north of Naples to Salerno and to Nola and Avellino inland, was irrigated, easy to cultivate and very productive. On the larger Adriatic plain, which extends from the Tavoliere delle Puglie to Murge and Materano, the drier conditions were adapted to the cultivation of cereals, olives, almonds and grapes, providing goods that, because of their high commercial value, had for a long time been important on the European market. Settlements were large and concentrated. By contrast, Lucania, Calabria, some valleys in the Abruzzi, the area of Salento, marshy and malarial, had a more backward economy where poverty, hunger and harsh working conditions had blighted for centuries the lives of the peasants. Because of the inaccessible ruggedness of the land, the unpredictable rainfall and the aridity of the few areas of flat land, the geography of these areas – and particularly of Calabria and Lucania – was an obstacle to specialisation in agriculture which retained archaic forms of cereal cultivation along with an economy based on olives and seasonal grazing. So in the valleys of the Abruzzi on the less hospitable land there was a predominantly pastoral type of agriculture while in the flatter areas intensive farming was practised with mixed crops.

Grain was the chief element in the southern economy. Its cultivation was static, technically undeveloped and low in productivity, and it was typical of the great landed properties which were taken over by feudal institutions, but even so, they differed from place to place. In the fiefs in the Abruzzi rent was paid in tithes and in rights of tillage, while in other areas rent was of the baronial type and based not only on tithes but also on the right to collect taxes, and there also the control of the communes was the key to the social domination of the barons. In the cereal-producing areas of the South, the increase in grain production which took place in the seventeenth and eighteenth centuries came about as a result of the increase in land area put under cultivation. Large feudal properties once used only for grazing and only rarely for crops were turned over to grain. This change had a striking demographic, social and economic effect. It favoured, for example, the colonisation of once uninhabited areas, like inland Sicily, and the concentration of the population in a few large centres. The price of land rose causing a high increase in the cost of agricultural loans, driving the peasants still further into debt and enriching the middlemen and the creditors. In addition it hindered the development of agricultural technology, the guarantee of fixed, even if low, returns giving no incentive for experiments in new methods of farming.

Thus it was not in the purely cereal-growing area but in the areas of mixed farming that there were possibilities for expansion. It should be remembered that in the South mixed farming based on field- and tree-crops was confined to only a few areas. Here small and medium properties were common, growing grain alongside other more productive crops such as grapes, olives and citrus fruit, which yielded greater returns. These properties were, as has been said, in the minority. There is an example of one such in the Valle Caudina, described by Gérard Delille in his recent study.[3] In this area the weak economic situation of the first half of the seventeenth century brought about a restructuring of land and work contracts which led to the rise of a peasant class which, by entering into partial forms of landownership through the subdivision of the *latifundia* and the adoption of emphyteuses, was less vulnerable to poverty. These changes encouraged the establishment of a more flexible system of farming which undermined the exclusive production of cereals and diversified into vines and fruit-trees. The Valle Caudina was not, however, typical; rather it was a proof, by being exceptional, of the social, economic and technological restrictions associated with the *latifundia* system.

In the greater part of the South the *latifundia* were secure and, as Aymard has ably demonstrated, the conditions from which arose the eighteenth-century revival remained unchanged for more than a century.[4] The *latifundia* guaranteed the landowners a growing income in periods of rising agricultural prices, drawn from a vast reserve of land where peasant emphyteuses had not taken root and where it was possible to extract ever-increasing earnings without any significant investment. In the seventeenth century when the economic system was turned upside down, i.e. from 1620 on, income from land too contracted, as a result of the fall in prices. To make up the balance, the barons and great landowners turned to drawing money from legal rights, administration, collection of taxes and money changing – in other words from that great reservoir of wealth controlled more directly in the seventeenth century by the southern landowners. Between the landowners and the agricultural workers there arose different social groups which made the productive system more complex and did not encourage the setting up of intermediate businesses between the landowners and the wage-earners. This is illustrated by the way in which the great estates were frequently divided up and administered by tenants and subtenants, who formed a chain whose elasticity allowed the recipients of income to weather with ease the periods of recession, but at the same time put a brake on any attempts at the setting up of new enterprises.

Along with the grain-producing *latifundia* went the day-labourers, poor and without land, who supplemented their earnings by making use of the common land which had been their customary privilege for centuries with rights of chestnut-harvesting, hunting, wood-gathering and pasture. These traditional rights on the one hand were an obstacle to experimentation with new crops and farming cycles in the way in which they dictated the tempo and quality of peasant labour, but on the other hand were a stabilising factor in the agricultural world by allowing the possibility of compensating for fluctuations in production, absorbing losses and standardising food consumption.

In Apulia a particular type of productive unit had been widespread for a long time – the *masseria*.[5] This was a large farm which differed from the fief in that it gave work to many wage-earners, it survived entirely by commercial dealings and was geared to the intensive cultivation of grain, not for home consumption but for selling. Because of these characteristics the *masseria* absorbed greater investments than the more frequent seigneurial estates and encouraged more advanced methods of management and cultivation even if it did not develop a capitalistic system of labour.

After the disastrous plague of 1656–57, the last straw for an economy incapable of meeting the demands made on it, gradually in the South a delicate balance between production and consumption was re-established, aided by the period of low prices and the diminished pressure of population. Only after 1730 did these conditions change with the increase in population, prices, trade and revenue from land.

The case of Sicily is somewhat different in that the figure of the economic middleman appears in the areas of the *latifundia*, while he is less apparent in southern Italy. The *gabellotti*, as they were called in Sicily, have been seen by historians either as entrepreneurs, the *'fermiers* of southern Italy', when their activities as tenants and middlemen in the circulation of agrarian wealth are emphasised, or else solely as speculators when historians highlight their function as money-lenders and intermediates in agrarian contracts. In the towns they played an important role in the municipal oligarchies. From the middle of the sixteenth century a large part of the management of municipal duties fell to them and over which often they exercised a real monopoly which boosted their level of income. In periods when revenue from land was slow, the *gabellotti* were absent or less apparent in the channels of the extraction and circulation of wealth, whereas they reappear when revenues were rising. Between the second half of the seventeenth century and 1720 in southern Italy land income is a gauge, either remaining stable or falling, of the period of the crisis of production. When later this trend was reversed, particularly after 1730, the *gabellotti* came to the fore again: 'they block price rises, they control agricultural credit, they monopolise the contracts for the supply of food to the communes; thus they profit at all levels from the landowners' income, the peasants' earnings and the spending of the consumers'.[6] The presence in society between the landowners and the workers of such middlemen as the *gabellotti*, dealers, small farmers and landowners not belonging to the nobility, is coupled with the absence, going back into Italian feudalism for centuries, of some characteristics considered fundamental to other models of a feudal economy, such as, first and foremost, serfdom. This does not, however, mean that the Italian countryside was any less feudal in character, particularly in the South where feudalism weakened the factors and impulses which could have led to an intensive development of production.

Between the fifteenth and eighteenth centuries the *mezzadria* system can be seen over a vast geographical area which from central Italy, Tuscany and the Marches extended to Emilia-Romagna, including the Ferrarese and various parts of Piedmont. This system brought with it social and economic contradictions which to some extent characterise the agrarian history of this part of Italy. In the *mezzadria* system the gross product was generally divided equally between landowner and *mezzadro* (tenant). The landowner had no incentive to invest in stock or means of production because he could not reap the full benefit of the investment. Thus he preferred to increase production by demanding more work from the *mezzadro*, which is to say, by intensifying production but not productivity, which in general in such a contractual relationship was of a very low level. The peasant in turn tended to resist these demands since they brought no increase in his earnings, in order to defend the productivity of his work and to prevent it all going to benefit the landowner. Carlo Poni, in his study of the Emilian *mezzadria* system, writes that the peasant carries out

willingly the work essential to the growing of crops and vegetables to feed him and his family. But, although ignorant of Bartolo, he leaves off productive work when it starts to have any lasting beneficial effect on the land (digging, improvement of the soil, etc.), in favour of increasing his immediate return in case of cancellation

28

of the contract which was renewed annually. In general he defends more the productivity of his work and of its contributions in means of production, from an instinctive comparison between the cost of living and his marginal productivity.[7]

However, it should be said that while the *mezzadria* system may have held back the forces of production encouraging stagnation and while it may have been backward-looking, relying on mere subsistence, it is equally true that it protected, often at the lowest level, the income of the tenant families. It shielded them from fluctuations in the economy with which the *mezzadro* was better able to cope than the wage-earner, by varying his production and taking directly from the land the basic necessities for himself and his family without having recourse to the risks of the open market. It allowed him too to farm on land which he would not have been able to obtain in any other way. It should also be remembered that the *mezzadria* system was not identical everywhere. The exact terms of the contract varied from place to place, as did the position of the *mezzadro*. Maurice Aymard has listed the wide range of situations in which he could find himself:

sometimes almost a contractor on the edge of the middle classes, sometimes almost a day-labourer; groaning with debts or well-off, threatened every year with eviction or settled *de facto* for several generations on a farm ranging from a few hectares to over thirty; governed by tenancy agreements which grew ever more restrictive or which on the contrary were increasingly relaxed by a landowner who could expect from his land either an increased production of goods or just the assurance of a supply of food for his home plus a modest but regular income.[8]

It follows that the social conditions of the *mezzadro* clearly depended to a large extent on the precise contract by which he was bound and that this varied greatly from place to place, depending on area, type of farming, on the presence or otherwise in the same concern of other forms of contract such as leasing, emphyteusis or farm-managing. Between these four types of contract the most marked differences can be seen when *mezzadria* and leasing on the one hand are compared with emphyteusis or direct management on the other. The contracts of *mezzadria* and leasing entered into in central-northern Italy do have points of resemblance, such as the shorter duration of the contract, the non-participation of the peasant in investments in the build-ings on the land (the farmhouse, for example), while at the same time taking on all the costs of cultivation, even those which for years gave no yield (for example, the renewal of fruit-trees) or which involved improvements which would affect the land for a long time (for example ditches and field paths), and finally the equivalent value of the varying elements in the rents paid. The differences become even smaller where agriculture takes on a capitalistic dimension, as in the irrigated Po Valley where there were huge farms, massive investments, the use of large amounts of working capital and the maximum exploitation of productive factors.

In places where small and medium-sized properties prevailed and where the overall production was unvarying, the most clear-cut difference in contract was between *mezzadria* and emphyteusis. The latter allowed the peasant the use of the land for long periods or even in perpetuity, on the condition that he maintained and improved the land and paid annually a low rent in money or kind. In addition he could buy the contract and become the owner of the land. As can be seen, the differences are substantial: *mezzadria* maintains a permanent link between landowner and farmer; emphyteusis does away with this reciprocity and can lead to a transfer of property, while it guarantees, more than does leasing, the separation of profit and income, which was determined for long periods and not subject to annual variations as was the leasing contract. In the South, as has been seen, emphyteusis sometimes indicated an improving economic situation where the worker was acquiring more income and security. In central-northern Italy, on the other hand, it appears that the land where emphyteusis was usual was unproductive and difficult to cultivate, thus not furnishing a profit that would benefit the tenant. In central-southern Italy, mixed farming (wheat alternated with other cereals which can coexist with fruit-trees or industrial crops) seems rather to have been regulated by the tenant-farming system.

Embracing a very wide range of types of work and income, the *mezzadria* system survived unchanged for several centuries, particularly in the central belt which divided into different areas of production ranging from the land of the Agro Romano around Rome, sparsely populated and malarial, used for permanent pasture or cereals, to the rich lands of Montalto or Castro south of the Maremma and not far from Rome which the pope took from the Farnese family in the second half of the seventeenth century. Inland it is possible to draw an imaginary line of poverty, running between the northern Abruzzi and upper Sabina, Umbria and the Legation of Urbino – all areas short of grain. The provinces of the Marches and Romagna, by contrast, furnished a considerable grain surplus for export.

Along the Agro Romano in the coastal areas of Lazio there had existed for a long time a type of feudalism which, when compared with that in the South, had fewer jurisdictional privileges and a more pronounced concentration on administration and inheritance. This did not, however, prevent the feudalism of Lazio from holding back agricultural development. The presence of merchants in the countryside, a powerful and active class who acted as financial middlemen, did not introduce any progressive, capitalistic features into the economy, but rather, as in Sicily, was one particular variant in the many-shaped feudalism of Italy.

Moving to Emilia-Romagna, one sees a greater division in crops and methods of production. In the hills and low mountains where farms were scattered, crops alternated with wooded areas; in the valleys where small and medium-sized farms were most common, there were vines interspersed with trees. The *mezzadria* system was widespread in these areas which were very broken up. On the plain the landscape was entirely different, scored by irrigation channels and arranged in a way which showed a more developed organisation of work with the reclaimed land (*campi a larga*, so called because of their large size) enclosed by canals along which ran lines of poplars, growing cereals, fodder and industrial crops such as hemp and beets.

In the hilly areas of Tuscany (some 70 per cent of the region) and in Umbria, agriculture was of a different type, organised in smallholdings which spread out from a central farmhouse. The system here was of the *mezzadria* type; mixed crops of cereals interspersed with vines clinging to elms, maples and olive-trees. In Umbria industrial crops were introduced in the seventeenth century, such as tobacco and mulberry-trees, while at the same time the importance of cattle and wood was increasing. In the Tuscan mountains around Pistoia, the land could not provide the peasants, generally owners of small and medium-sized plots, with enough to live on. Thus they were forced to move with the seasons to the plains or the hills. The plains of Pescia and Florence had a more developed agriculture and better standard of living as did the Valdarno, Valdichiana, Valdinievole and Pisano.

Along the upper Tyrrhenian coast of Tuscany right through Liguria stretched a typically Mediterranean landscape, with olives and vines. In Liguria olive-growing took over large areas from the sixteenth century on, when it started its expansion, until the early nineteenth century. Mixed with other types of trees in most of Liguria, on the west coast of Italy olives were a specialised crop and one which functioned as a kind of barometer of farming, reflecting the frequent changes in agricultural conditions resulting from climate or the state of the market.

The modernity of the plain of the Po Valley was commented on by many foreign visitors in the eighteenth century, the most famous of whom, Arthur Young, described the expanse of irrigated fields and the arrangement of the agricultural cycle. (In the fourteenth and fifteenth centuries the cultivation of fodder as well as grain had been introduced, while after 1650 rice and maize plantations became widespread.) The planting of mulberry-trees along the edges of the fields and the growing of hemp and flax bear witness to an economy that was adaptable and varied, offering greater possibilities for investment and innovation. Over this proto-capitalistic economy loomed a decline in production during the seventeenth century, as a result of a saturation of the market or a fall in demand. These phenomena are linked with the standstill in population and the contraction of the European market for products from the Po Valley in particular and from Italy in general. In the Venetian plain, inhabited by one of the densest concentrations of rural population in Italy, from the second half of the seventeenth century until the 1730s, some 90,000 ha of communal land were sold, in order to meet the financial demands of the republic. Much of the wealth of the Venetian nobility was invested in this land. This redistribution of property encouraged the spread of the growth of cereals and the cut-back in land for grazing and grass, but the new owners did not introduce new farming methods, preferring to divide up their property into small plots. The landowners' 'villas', indications of a new presence which did not of itself bring more rational methods or management, grew up alongside the farmhouses in the Veneto, rich with men and vegetation, where property remained broken up into small farms and the crops mixed but concentrating on grapes, cereals and grass. In some areas of the Veneto, there was a move to more intensive farming, as in the

31

Euganian Hills, where wine production predominated, or on the shores of Lake Garda where the Mediterranean olive grew, or the flat plains around Verona and Vicenza, which during the seventeenth century were gradually turned over to rice.

In the plain of Piedmont too rice appears as a new crop full of potential, along with the more widespread cultivation of cereal. The Piedmontese countryside was largely untouched by the decline of the seventeenth century, showing rather signs of adaption and growth. One cannot, in the case of Piedmont, talk about a widespread return to feudalism; instead there occurred a legal breaking up of the great fiefs. In the Astigiano Hills the landscape was characterised by rows of vines and smaller plots of cereals and vegetables. Everywhere, mountainous regions were low in resources and the communities that lived there did so in conditions of poverty, closed, though not totally, to any type of trade. In Lombardy the same divisions as have been made for other areas with mountains, hills and plains also apply, but with two particular features. The first is that in this region in general the divisions of the landscape and economy are more related the one to the other, linked by more trade; the second is the aforementioned capitalistic evolution of the irrigated plain.

The economic scene in the Po Valley too was rich with many facets and cannot be easily labelled, even bearing in mind that the labour relations and advanced agronomy – strongly influenced by the type of environment – in the irrigated areas were opening the way to an economy capable of accumulating wealth which, more easily than in the South, was productively reinvested in the land. In addition, feudalism in the northern countryside was generally less oppressive than in the South and was already beginning to disintegrate in the seventeenth century, as can be demonstrated by the increasing lack of interest in feudal privilege shown by both the ancient and new noble families. In Lombardy the attitude of the Habsburgs to the fief was no different from that of Spain in the seventeenth century: the fief was a commercial entity, a source of tax, an instrument for marking the ascent of the new aristocracy grown up in public office. In the eighteenth century state revenue from feudal sources fell, since the State could not keep up with the changes in ownership of the fiefs nor, consequently, could it enforce the laws of transfer. The fiefs too seemed to be paying less well than in the past: duties, taxes, tithes, judicial rights and other methods of extracting feudal wealth were yielding, in general, lower rates of income than in the past while feudal jurisdiction itself met increasing obstacles from communal administration and the powers of the central State. With some slight differences this state of affairs also extends to Piedmont and the Veneto. Thus it will be seen that feudalism in northern Italy had fewer juridical privileges and a weaker social force than in the South, and that in addition it had already entered a period of decline that would reach a crisis in the eighteenth century.

NOTES AND REFERENCES

For a general outline see Aymard, M. 'La transizione dal feudalesimo al capitalismo', in *Storia d'Italia Annali* I, *Dal feudalesimo al capitalismo*. Einaudi, Turin, pp. 1131–92.

1. Revel, J. (1972) 'Le Grain de Rome et al crise de l'annone dans la seconde moitié du XVIIIe siècle', in *Mélanges de l'école française de Rome*. Rome, vol. 84, fasc. I, pp. 201–81.
2. Guenzi, A. (1977) 'Il "calmiere del formento" controllo del prezzo del pane e difesa della rendita terriera a Bologna nei secoli XVII e XVIII', in *Annali della Fondazione L. Einaudi* XI, pp. 143–201.
3. Delille, G. (1973) *Croissance d'une société rurale. Montesarchio et la vallée Caudine aux XVII et XVIII siècles*. Guida, Naples.
4. Aymard, M. 'La transizione del feudalesimo al capitalismo', in *Storia d'Italia Annali I, Dal feudalesimo al capitalismo*. Einaudi, Turin, pp. 1178 ff.
5. Lepre, A. (1963) *Contadini, borghesi ed operai nel tramonto del feudalesimo meridionale*. Feltrinelli, Milan.
6. Aymard, M., op. cit., p. 1190.
7. Poni C. (1963) *Gli aratri e l'economia agraria nel Bolognese dal XVII al XIX secolo*. Zanichelli, Bologna.
8. Aymard, M., op. cit., p. 1155.

CHAPTER THREE

Trade and manufacture. The historiographical problem of the crisis of the seventeenth century

The process of agricultural development was related to the state of European trade in which the great Italian ports played a key role. Naples was an important market for oil, grain, cloth, silk and wool. The French were among the most active in these areas, though partially replaced during the seventeenth century by English and Dutch competitors. Venice had been for several centuries a vital bridge between the Islamic East and the European nations and during the whole of the seventeenth century, even when trade declined, she remained the emporium for spices, dyes, textiles and other products bought by Europeans from the Arab market. From the Adriatic ports, Venice directed oil, salt, wool, fresh and dried fruits on to the roads of central Europe and northern Italy.[1] Building timber, leather, wool and cotton cloth were in turn taken from Germany to the Adriatic ports. The other Italian ports were less important, such as Genoa,[2] which kept up considerable commercial activities, Ancona, Palermo, Leghorn and Messina. In the seventeenth century an indication of the fall in trade between Italy and the rest of Europe was the changes in the routes of Italian ships. The journeys were shortened and confined to internal waters; there were fewer sailings to and from the ports of the East and the great commercial centres of central and northern Europe. First the Dutch and then the English took on a greater share of the European market, squeezing out the Italian companies.

Although not disastrous, the economic decline of Venice in the seventeenth century nevertheless meant that the port suffered more than most from the effects of the increased commercial aggression of the ports of northern Europe and also from the consequences of the wars of the seventeenth century and the struggles against the Turks which ended with the Peace of Passarowitz in 1718. Venetian shipping routes contracted: only the ports of Smyrna and Constantinople were still used with any frequency by the ships of *la Seren-issima*; only two or three Venetian ships a year called at Cyprus by the end of the seventeenth century; there was a similar decline in journeys to Sicily and the Tyrrhenian and those to Cadiz, Lisbon, London and Amsterdam became very infrequent and always threatened by attacks from pirates. The loss of the Morea and the establishing of the free port of Trieste by Charles

VI weakened the commercial might of Venice which had, more than in the past, to contend with competition from Fiume and Ancona.[3]

Behind this crisis of commercial development lie more general causes which relate to the changed economic hierarchies of Europe and to the move towards speculation in defence of their previously acquired wealth by those elements who had supported the development of manufacturing in Italy in the preceding centuries. With the weakening of Italian industry and agriculture came not only the loss of her important position in commercial Europe but also what we might call the 'parasitic' nature of trade carried by Italian ships, particularly those of the republics. It was not so much the size of the market which put Genoa and Venice in an increasingly inferior position *vis-à-vis* Amsterdam, as the effectiveness of their methods of dealing with the new economic situation. Inland from the Italian ports no network of trade in agricultural and industrial goods appeared which could have brought to international trade the strength of an internal framework of production. Things were similar in the case of Leghorn, a port which showed no traces of the crisis affecting other maritime cities. The intensity of port traffic in Leghorn was not directed towards the economy of its hinterland, but the resources were consumed on the spot or rerouted to other European centres. Changes which may be seen during the seventeenth century in other key international trading centres, such as Milan, Rome and Naples, increasingly involved foreign traders who supplanted the Italian merchants. It should be noted too that the move of Italian merchant wealth into European finance in a period which encouraged monetary speculation because of the national debts of the great states, as in the case of the Genoese patricians described by Felloni, brought no benefit to the country, in so far as it did not increase productive investment but was consumed in the limited demand for luxury items.

The drop in the amount of European trade controlled by Italians went together with a similar fall in the internal market. In the place of an economic network which had become national in the previous centuries of development, now the narrower horizons of the regional or local market predominated. Corn from Apulia and Sicily no longer found a ready market in the towns of the North, since they now relied on their surrounding regions to supply their needs. At the same time the industrial products of the North, linked to agricultural production, were increasingly seldom available in southern markets. The Italian economy was breaking up into smaller centres where land emerged as the main source of wealth. Landownership, as has been said, assured more than hitherto not only a more secure income, because less vulnerable to crises, but also a tangible social status.

Since the detailed research of Gino Luzzatto,[4] it has been recognised that the distinguishing feature of Italian industry, both domestic and otherwise, from the fifteenth century to at least the middle of the nineteenth century was its dependence on mercantile capital. The merchant-entrepreneur was the central figure in this system of industrial production. His profit was derived more from the marketing of the product than from the making of it.

Historians today do not entirely share the pessimistic analysis of Romano,[5] who highlighted only the regressive aspects of the seventeenth century. As well as the crises in industry they now also see its ability to maintain production. At the same time, it cannot be denied that the reorganisation of European industry and strong foreign competition ended up by casting Italy in the role of exporter of raw or semi-finished materials and importer of finished goods. Decentralisation into the countryside of the textile industry was not the only solution to problems of production. In Tuscany, according to Paolo Malanima,[6] the towns and their economy held on to the greater part of industrial production, maintaining a not insignificant strength. Similarly, Bologna had until the early eighteenth century a solid industrial base in silk and hemp. During the seventeenth century between 2,500 and 6,000 workers found jobs in the town in over 100 silk mills. In the Veneto on the other hand rural industry seems to have made up for the crisis of urban production whether in the large factory at Schio or the home-based textile industry run by merchant-entrepreneurs, which produced linen, hemp and cotton cloth in large quantities. In Modena the seventeenth-century crisis encouraged the move to the country of the preliminary stages of the processing of silk as had already happened with the wool industry in order to avoid the restraints imposed by the guilds and to lower production costs which were higher in the town than the country.

In the South too, thanks to the work of M. Aymard and M. A. Visceglia,[7] one can trace the extension after 1650 of a wide scattering of rural textile industries and the presence of some small industrial centres producing also for export. An important axis in the artisan and industrial network of the South was the 'wheat road', the central artery in southern trade, opened at the end of the sixteenth century, joining Naples and Apulia. Several communes along this road experienced a considerable flowering of craft industries, for example, Nola, Avella, Mugnano del Cardinale and Avellino. The latter was one of the most vigorous centres of the wool industry in the South. Other important industrial and commercial establishments were in the Salernitano and in the communes of Amalfi, Cava dei Tirreni, San Severino and Girfoni. In Calabria, Cosenza and Catanzaro were important centres of the silk industry.

Many more examples of this ability to adapt and improve could be cited, such as the silk-spinning industry in Piedmont where from 1708 in the town of Racconigi the 'Bolognese mill' was used, the subject of a recent study by Carlo Poni. This was an integrated mechanised system for silk spinning, forming an embryonic industrial complex. It is nevertheless true that the picture was gloomy and that industrial production from raw materials slumped in the seventeenth century, not reviving until the first decades of the eighteenth century. The wool industry was the most vulnerable. During the seventeenth century it declined more or less everywhere and showed no signs of recovery, threatened as it was by intense foreign competition and the inability to re-establish itself on the market with increased quotas. It remained on the edge of the textile trade, paralysed by its traditional role of supplying the restricted luxury market, while in the countryside it was produced almost exclusively for home use by the peasants. The silk industry was rather different, and although affected by the depression showed greater resilience and signs of a recovery of production which became more apparent in the late eighteenth century. Piedmont, with more than 100 spinning mills, according to Giuseppe Prato,[8] specialised at the beginning of the eighteenth century in the production of raw silk destined for the weaving industries of Lyons and London. About two-thirds of total Piedmontese exports came under this heading. The technological innovations that were being introduced in the early eighteenth century are a confirmation of the entrepreneurial capacities and drive existing in this area that allowed Savoy to overcome the monetary storm which broke there in the wake of the collapse of Law's finances in France (1720). In the State of Milan, the silk industry, less specialised than in Piedmont, showed in the first twenty years of the eighteenth century a rapid decline in spinning which involved mainly the big towns. Mills were set up instead in areas nearer the border and their product went to the major textile-producing areas such as Lyons, Zurich and Genoa.

Silk weaving, on the other hand, went from a period of decline between the late seventeenth century and the early eighteenth century, to one of strong recovery beginning in 1715. In this year the number of looms stood at 500 compared with some 200 at the end of the seventeenth century. Production was based on the putting-out system. In the 1730s there were signs of a new recession when industry in Lombardy, particularly silk, reached the lowest point of the century. In Genoa the slump in textiles was apparent from the 1690s. Genoese industry could not withstand the competition of French products, cheaper and more up to date, and lost a great number of its foreign markets, for luxury goods at least. Bruno Caizzi's studies show that in the Venetian Republic there was a big increase in silk production which spread in those areas where there was an increase in the cultivation of mulberry-trees and silkworms, that is in the areas between the Adda and Adige rivers in the Veronese, Bresciano and Bergamasco, in the province of Vicenza and in Friuli. In the countryside of the Veneto, as in Piedmont, not all the processes of silk production were carried out, being limited to the rearing of silkworms, the reeling of the cocoons and spinning without, however, successfully mastering the process of spinning.

Silk production was an important part of the rural economy of the Venetian mainland, where labour and raw materials from the countryside were employed. The cotton, hemp and linen industries, with a capitalistic form of management by merchant-entrepreneurs, increased a not unimportant export trade, as did too the production of paper, which was much prized abroad, the manufacture of weapons, which declined along with the military importance of Venice, wool and minerals. At the beginning of the century a nucleus of industries still existed, some of which were less prosperous than in the past. Such was the fortune of the arsenal whose production was cut down on account of the fall in mercantile and military activity. In the mid-seventeenth century, 2,239 people were employed by the arsenal, in the

1750s fewer than 1,500, while in 1711 the Venetian fleet consisted of 35 ships built in Venice and 46 built abroad. In difficulties too were the printing industry, reduced to thirty-five workshops, the glass industry which fell in quality and quantity, and the soap industry which was suffering from competition from the new factory at Trieste, while the china, tobacco and wax industries appeared stronger.

We have little or no information about industry in the rest of Italy, though the new initiatives and attempts to increase production which occurred in the first decades of the eighteenth century, often under the influence of the princes, cannot have appeared from nowhere. At the same time the difficulties they had in making headway is an indication of the unfavourable climate for the establishing of a solid basis of production.

In this brief look at the seventeenth-century crisis it should be remembered that the downward turn in the Italian economy was an integral part of a European recession; but it is also true that during this period of depression some nations with a more robust economy took steps to revive production while others, Italy among them, suffered a more widespread stagnation where conservative factors came to the fore which appeared to hold back moves towards the development of capitalism. It is precisely this question of the beginnings of capitalism, its development and ability to stimulate the economy starting from the period of the communes, which divides the various historiographical interpretations of the seventeenth-century crisis. In the case of Italy the argument revolves, today as in the 1960s, around the debate on the 'transition from feudalism to capitalism'. To understand how the analysis of the economic revival during the eighteenth century, particularly in the second half, is influenced by the attitude adopted by historians to the question of the seventeenth-century recession, we need to look at those interpretations which have, above all, taken fully into account the many recent studies in economic and social history. We will concentrate on those of Ruggero Romano, Aldo De Maddalena, various Marxist historians, and the recent work by Maurice Aymard.

Drawing together many different pieces of research in economic history, Ruggero Romano, in his two very full essays in the *Storia d'Italia* (published by Einaudi), encapsulates one historiographical position.[9] He presents a general interpretation of the Italian economy from the thirteenth to the eighteenth century, his aim being to reassess the historical stereotype, emerging during the years of positivism, that saw Italy first at the time of the communes and then of the seigniories as taking the economic lead over the rest of Europe. This consisted of the widespread appearance of capitalistic characteristics, showing a very precocious development in Italy compared with other European economies. This hypothesis reflected an economistic view of capitalism based not so much on the importance of the overall structure of society as on single and separate elements of economic history. In other words, such historians tended to see capitalism wherever there was an increase in the monetary economy, in banking, or in mercantile capital in international trade, while ignoring the complexity of social relations. Romano is prepared to agree that the anomalous development of Italy compared to the rest of Europe is to some extent 'precocious', but at the same time he denies that one can talk of evolved and dominant capitalistic forms. On the contrary, he states most explicitly that the history of the Italian economy from the fall of the Roman Empire to the eighteenth-century industrialisation is characterised by a 'feudal impasse', in that for more than fifteen centuries feudalism was the major determinant of social relations, thinking and institutions so that, in his opinion, 'between this supposed capitalism . . . and the reality of Italian economic history there lies a huge gulf'. The rapid disappearance of serfdom is not enough to exclude Italy from the feudal model, because, 'basically it is still true — and this will be very characteristic of Italian economic history — that the wage-earner finds himself hedged about by a system of laws which again and again re-establish a certain coercion reminiscent of serfdom'. By feudalism, Romano means

an economic system which is basically the appropriation of one man's work and land by another. Basic because founded essentially on principles of natural economy (notwithstanding the superficial forms of a monetary economy, however striking); basic because — notwithstanding the freedoms that may be guaranteed by civil law — it is founded on harsh servitude in private law; basic because the inspiration for every economic action is essentially founded on the notion of plunder rather than on that of ground-rent, of usury rather than profit.

This is the unvarying background against which Romano describes the phases of the Italian economy. He considers population, prices and currency. In the light of these three indicators the economic recession of the 1580s which continued until the 1740s was severe. The population, according to the estimates of Beloch and recently revised by G. M. Cipolla and A. Bellettini, suffered from a long decline: from the 13.3 million inhabitants of the early seventeenth century it decreased to 11.5 in 1650 and then slowly increased until at the beginning of the eighteenth century it was back to its early seventeenth-century level. This fall in population involved all Europe and should not, according to Romano, be automatically attributed to the plague which is usually seen as the most dramatic moment in the famine–epidemic–famine sequence. Similarly the level of prices, first and foremost of wheat, shows a trend marked by the tendency to stagnate which came to an end in the 1740s. In the monetary area, Romano points out the shortage on the Italian market of precious metals, while the monetary confusion increased, a problem to be inherited by the reform movement of the eighteenth century and which it dealt with by restructuring the whole system. If, as has been said, agriculture and commerce are analysed according to these three indicators, population, prices and currency, a rather inevitable picture appears of an economic 'crash' without precedent in intensity and size since the Middle Ages and which affected the whole century. The decline in agricultural production, according to Romano, appears to precede by at least twenty years the beginning of the crisis, since in as early as 1580 the signs of recession are clear. Italy was no longer self-sufficient in cereals, having to

39

import them from abroad, agricultural prices were not moving, land improvement was suspended.

In industry and commerce in the seventeenth century the situation was the same. The textile industry was cutting back severely in production and failing to compete with foreign products. Nor could they any longer protect themselves by concentrating on the production of luxury goods or by transferring some processes of production to the country into smaller units. Romano traces identical signs of crisis in the other important industries, such as building and shipbuilding. In the countryside the increased number of vagrants was an indication of the laying-off of labour. The merchant wealth of the cities sought a defence against recession in landownership. Romano used the term 'refeudalisation' to describe (in a single historiographical category) a many-sided financial movement apparent in many parts of Italy, from Lombardy to the Veneto, from Piedmont to central-southern Italy. The massive move of capital into land brought about a contraction in communal property and smallholdings, while at the same time the growth of the great noble and ecclesiastical estates did not result in investments with a cumulative element but ended up instead by reinforcing the feudal nature of the Italian economy. This process increased the social power of the nobility which gained might and prestige by reviving rural seigneurial rights and dues, taking on the collection of taxes and acquiring public offices and the jurisdiction that went with them. Refeudalisation in this sense comes to mean much more than a movement of capital, in that it includes a much wider process relating to social relations, institutions and attitudes. Romano speaks of 'social immobility', the 'disintegration of state power', and of the 'anaemia of the civic body'. In this analysis, Romano draws a wholly negative picture, setting aside signs of movement and emphasising what was permanent and the resistance to change.

Another picture with points of similarity but placed in a very different framework is that offered by the Marxist historians. Among the most important and representative are Emilio Sereni, and, more recently, Renato Zangheri and Giorgio Giorgetti.[10] Sereni used the term 'refeudalisation' to describe the historic sense of the seventeenth-century crisis, but with several substantial differences from Romano. First of all, the seventeenth-century recession is not seen as part of an unmoving feudalism, but of a process of transition towards capitalism in which the elements of the crisis, in particular the rise in cost of precious metals and the fall in prices and profits, are indications of a slowing down of the original financial accumulation. In this interpretation, the move of capital into landownership is, for Sereni, an absorption into the feudal system of the financial and mercantile bourgeoisie, which at the same time introduces contradictory elements into the economic structure of the country by laying the foundations for the growth of industrial production. In this case Sereni thinks that the expulsion of agricultural workers from the land, as a result of the usurpation of state-owned and common land, made available labour which could potentially be absorbed by manufacturing industries. He maintains furthermore that the situation of central-northern Italy was very different from that of the South. In the South it would be more correct to speak of the 'commercialisation' of land: into the continuity of the feudal regime, the seventeenth century introduced commercial enterprises which did not challenge feudalism but on the contrary reinforced the exploitation of the peasants. In central-northern Italy, according to Sereni, it is more accurate to speak of refeudalisation, as witnessed by the growth of mortmains and the extension of the *fidecommesso* and primogeniture. It is important, however, to appreciate how different the seventeenth-century nobility was from that of earlier times. It had a diminished military, political and administrative function and instead greater financial and trading interests.

The history of agriculture shows a different form of the same phenomenon. In the seventeenth century the agricultural landscape was generally deteriorating. Grazing land and the open field system were extended, marshy and uncultivated areas increased and cultivated land decreased. But this did not happen over the whole country. In some areas of central-northern Italy there was a revival of the system of rotating crops and fallow land, lines of trees were planted, fodder crops appeared as well as more complex forms of specialisation and crop rotation, while agricultural produce was distributed over a wide area. The most obvious dichotomy of recent Italian history, that between the North and South, was already putting down tenacious roots in the seventeenth-century crisis. For Sereni the seventeenth century is part of the longer period of preparation for the origins of capitalism and is a time full of contradictions. The same phenomenon of refeudalisation hints in some cases at the transition to capitalism of the countryside, while in others it accentuates the feudal inheritance.

It will be seen that Sereni's interpretation disagrees with that of Romano, because movement is reduced to the opposition between the painful and strongly opposed emergence of capitalistic elements and the permanence of the feudal system which surrounded them. The Marxist historian Giorgio Giorgetti returned to this interpretation, confirming the concept of transition as a slow emerging of conditions of development from within a static system.

Precisely because the process of transition, which began in some areas in the late Middle Ages, develops in the context of property relations which are still essentially feudal, if a capitalist system is not reached very rapidly, as happened in England, so the overall economic stimuli which bring about this process, as in Italy at the beginning of the modern era, cannot but be weakened or fail altogether, while the new forms which do emerge, while establishing themselves in their contractual outlines, tend necessarily to be reabsorbed by the old system and become crystallised in an essentially stagnant climate. This, then, blocks or holds back for long periods the move to a capitalist agrarian system and can even represent a step back to the past, as for example the so-called process of refeudalisation in the Italian countryside in the sixteenth and seventeenth centuries.

Renato Zangheri has used similar terms to describe the seventeenth-century crisis, comparing English industrialisation with the situation in Italy. In Italy the accumulation of resources derived from the development in agriculture from the late Middle Ages to the sixteenth century (a development without doubt more precarious and insubstantial than in sixteenth-century England), 'which in some ways lay at the base of the great expansion of urban life and Italian society and culture, were not transmitted to industry, did not give industry a jolt, a progressive push, and in the final analysis were dispersed during the crisis of the seventeenth century'.

An authoritative economic historian, Aldo De Maddalena,[11] has put forward an interpretation of the seventeenth-century crisis which criticises the findings of Marxist and other historians. He does not offer an explanation of the complex characteristics of the whole Italian economy but rather a working model for a specific geographic and economic area – that of the Po Valley. Even if this model cannot be applied to the whole country, nevertheless it provides an interesting point of view which has received much attention in historical analysis, because it is an area where the most marked tendencies for expansion in the Italian economy took place. In De Maddalena's opinion, to talk of refeudalisation, in Lombardy at least, as a way of resolving the problem of the seventeenth-century crisis, can lead to a misunderstanding of the social forces at work in the seventeenth century, starting with the rapid political growth of a new nobility, whose fortunes were largely founded on the extension of the legal and tax privileges in the different states. De Maddalena thinks that these developments in the states and the privileged position of the new nobility should be emphasised in the historiographic interpretation. In the State of Milan, and also in other parts of central and northern Italy, the centre of gravity of economic energy was moving from the towns to the country. In the former the increase in costs in the manufacturing industries, the absence of new initiatives and the élitist character of the outlets for the industrial market weakened the structure of urban industry.

In the country, by contrast, producers found better protection. The vitality of the countryside, maintains De Maddalena, is a result of the death-agony of the town, 'from which had fled the surviving and perhaps most courageous business men, going to stand alongside those who in earlier times had already made the smallholding, the farm and the village the centre of their activities. It was these landowners of recent or less recent standing, these producers, merchants, agents, bankers and financiers who breathed new life into the countryside.' This potential did not, however, provide a new productive impulse, but remained close to traditional habits, rights and rules of work. In Milan, one can see the affirmation of new social groups which were increasing in economic importance and making political headway, yet without bringing about any decisive reform in the old economic order.

Opposed to Romano's thesis, and with a more analytical and somewhat different historical character from the Marxist historians and De Maddalena, is the accomplished interpretation given recently by Maurice Aymard of the Italian economy between the end of the Middle Ages and the eighteenth century.[12] The anomaly of the transition in Italy from feudalism to capitalism compared with other model examples, particularly that of England, can be summed up for Aymard in the formula 'from a precocious defeudalisation to a delayed industrialisation'. In the place of the unchanging structure of

Romano's 1,500-year-old feudal system, Aymard offers a more active picture which does not see as mere survivals from the past all those conditions – particularly noticeable during the crisis of the seventeenth century – which acted as a break on the Italian economy and which should, rather, be looked at alongside the capitalistic conditions which had for a long time been apparent in social relations. So one should not speak of a delay in economic development so much as of a precocity in surpassing many feudal institutions. From this Italy was unable either to build a broadly capitalistic agriculture or to develop industrially. Between the sixteenth and seventeenth centuries those early and particularly capitalistic characteristics showed signs of failing – for example, 'the very early weakening of legally binding relationships of personal dependence relating to the land', 'the disappearance or early decline of the small peasant farms', 'the general weakening of communal procedures', 'the expropriation of the peasants and the increasingly large concentrations of land', the appearance of middlemen involved with mercantile capital, such as 'the tenant-farmers of Lombardy, the *gabellotti* or the big farm managers of Sicily and Apulia who had available considerable financial means and who were at the same time intermediaries and tenants'.

The weakening of these and other social phenomena of a dynamic character became more marked during the seventeenth century when the restructuring of the economic hierarchies of Europe brought Italy to a period of decline. So we are not dealing with an insuperable historical backwardness, nor with a chronic delay on the part of Italy compared with the rest of Europe, but rather with the 'failure' of a development which had preceded other European economies on the road to overcoming feudalism. It failed to call forth elements of modernity because of internal and international obstacles. In this analysis the seventeenth century and the economy of the South represent most clearly the time and place of a severe regression. At the same time, according to Aymard, even given Italy's peripheral position in the European economic system and her decline in production, most acute in the seventeenth century, the country 'shows a remarkable capacity for initiative and innovation'.

At this point all the data taken from economic history are interpreted in a way diametrically opposed to that of Romano. For example, Italian industry, which was certainly going through a period of contraction, did not, according to Aymard, suffer such a severe crisis as had been suggested by some historians who made the mistake of judging it in the light of figures for English industrial development in the early nineteenth century. Even rural industry, according to him, made up very well for the recession in urban industries and in several cases set in motion an important new dynamism, even in southern Italy. Technological innovation too, he says, took on a significant role in some areas of the country. Finally, the transfer of capital to the countryside brought about a growth in production as a result of increased investment.

And so, for Aymard, what are the causes of the seventeenth-century decline? They fall into two categories. On one side there is the changed position of Italy in the European system, where she had a smaller and inferior share of trade, emerging as a country which exported raw or semi-finished goods and imported finished industrial products. On the other side there is the contraction of the internal market and the increasing constriction of social and institutional bonds which hampered production and trade. Southern feudalism is for Aymard the proof of this phenomenon.

NOTES AND REFERENCES

For a detailed analysis of the history of Italian industry from the eighteenth century onwards see: Caizzi, B. (1965) *Storia dell'industria italiana. Dal XVIII secolo ai giorni nostri*. UTET, Turin. The problems related to the organisation of work are analysed in Dal Pane, L. (1944) *Storia del lavoro in Italia dagli inizi del XVIII secolo al 1815*. Giuffré, Milan.

1. Caizzi, B. (1965) *Industria e commercio nella Repubblica veneta nel XVIII secolo*. Banca Commerciale italiana, Milan.
2. Bulferetti, L. and Costantini, C. (1966) *Industria e commercio in Liguria nell'età del Risorgimento (1700–1861)*. Banca Commerciale italiana, Milan.
3. Romano, R. (1951) *Le commerce du Royaume de Naples avec la France et les pays de l'Adriatique au XVIIIe siècle*. SEVPEN, Paris.
4. Luzzatto, G. (1963) *Storia economica d'Italia. Medioevo*. Sansoni, Florence.
5. Romano R. (1972) 'Una tipologia economica', in *Storia d'Italia* I, *I caratteri originali*. Einaudi, Turin, pp. 231–56.
6. Malanima, P. (1982) *La decadenza di un'economia cittadina. L'industria di Firenze nei secoli XVI–XVIII*. Il Mulino, Bologna.
7. Aymard, M. (1978) 'La transizione dal feudalesimo al capitalismo', in *Storia d'Italia Annali* I, *Dal feudalesimo al capitalismo*. Einaudi, Turin; Visceglia, M. (1978) 'Lavoro a domicilio e manifatture nel XVIII e XIX secolo', in *Studi sulla società meridionale*. Guida, Naples.
8. Prato, G. (1908) *La vita economica in Piemonte a mezzo il secolo XVIII*. Società tipografica editrice nazionale, Turin.
9. Romano, R. op. cit.; idem (1973) 'La storia economica. Dal secolo XIV al Settecento', in *Storia d'Italia*. Einaudi, Turin, vol. II, pt I, pp. 1813–934.
10. Of the many works by Sereni see especially: (1966) *Capitalismo e mercato nazionale*. Editori Riuniti, Rome; 'Agricoltura e mondo rurale', in *Storia d'Italia*, vol. I, pp. 136–255. The essay by Zangheri, R. referred to is in Jones, E. C. and Woolf, S. J. (1969) *Agrarian Change and Economic Development*. Methuen, London; Giorgetti, G. (1974) *Contadini e proprietari nell'Italia moderna*. Einaudi, Turin.
11. De Maddalena, A. (1964) 'Il mondo rurale italiano nel Cinque e Seicento', in *Rivista storica italiana* LXXVI, pp. 386 ff; idem (1977) 'A Milano nei secoli XVI e XVII: da ricchezza "reale" a ricchezza "nominale"', Ibid., fasc. 4–5, pp. 539–61; idem (1982) *Dalla città al borgo. Avvio di una metamorfosi economica e sociale nella Lombardia spagnola*. Angeli, Milan.
12. Aymard, M. op. cit.

CHAPTER FOUR

The gradual recovery of the Italian economy in the eighteenth century

The differences between the South, the Centre and the North of the country (not forgetting that within these categories there were further divisions – ecological, political, linguistic, economic and legal) became more marked during the seventeenth century, and between the North and South in particular those first signs of a gap appeared which were to brand the South as the weak area of the national economy. Aymard has pinpointed these signs in the agricultural and technological developments in the North during the seventeenth century, such as the extensive cultivation of 'noble' cereals, the increase in maize and rice, the progress in the growing of fruit-trees and textile plants, the integration of the wheat crop with that of fodder crops and the improvements in working methods. We shall examine these individually.[1]

In the northern plains a considerable area of productive land was given over to the cultivation of the so-called 'noble' cereals (rye and wheat) to the detriment of the lesser cereals such as millet, sorghum and spelt, leading to the partial achievement of a cereal monoculture. In Piedmont cereal-growing seems to have been a well-run and profitable area of agriculture so that in years not affected by bad weather or wars it was possible to export large quantities of produce. In the second half of the seventeenth and the first decades of the eighteenth centuries Stuart Woolf notes a considerable expansion in this area.[2] In the neighbouring State of Milan at the end of the sixteenth century cereal-growing took up more than 70 per cent of the cultivated land and the fall in production appears to have been overcome around the 1660s. In some parts of the Milanese, for example between Pavia and Lodi, it has been observed that the economic recovery went together with an increase in the amount of land devoted to the major cereals, which set back the percentage of production of the lesser cereals. Similarly from Beltrami's work we learn that in the plain of the Veneto the cultivation of cereals predominated and during the sixteenth and seventeenth centuries went through a period of expansion.[3] We have little detailed information on the success of cereal-growing in central and southern Italy. In the Papal States, despite the bad years and military devastation, the Roman countryside was apparently still able at the beginning of the seventeenth century to supply a significant export trade, while during the seventeenth century it is apparent that there was a gradual decline which was to leave the Agro Romano, once so fertile, in that state of impoverishment which the economists and reformers of the Enlightenment were to try to remedy. Our knowledge is incomplete and uncertain about the production of cereals in southern Italy between the seventeenth and eighteenth centuries, but the importance of Campania, Apulia and Sicily as major areas of production and export is clear as is the sharp fall in harvests in the seventeenth century.

From the work of Salvatore Pugliese and Emilio Sereni it emerges that great progress was made in rice-growing in the countryside of northern Italy from the sixteenth century onwards.[4] At the beginning of the eighteenth century rice took up 7 per cent of the land area of Vercelli and 3.4 per cent in the State of Milan. The provinces of Lomellina and Vigevano, studied by Aldo De Maddalena, are indicative of the intensity of this development: between 1549 and 1723 the increase in land used for rice-growing was from 450 per cent to 1,300 per cent. In Piedmont up to the seventeenth century rice was not grown in rotation with other crops but in special rice-fields in marshy areas. In the second half of the century, production began to be concentrated in the eastern area, even in dry corn-growing areas. The 'march of rice', to use Sereni's expression, advanced to the Mantovano, the plain of the Veneto and to Emilia, despite legal prohibitions. Because of the higher returns, the technical infrastructure and the changes in contract which resulted, it is fair to describe the advent of rice as a 'decisive impulse in the development of a capitalist form of agriculture'. In the same period in the South the opposite process, a reduction in rice-growing, was taking place.

Along with rice, maize was another indication of progress in production.[5] Like rice, maize gives a considerably higher yield than wheat − 1 : 30, at most, compared with 1 : 4 or 1 : 5 − which guaranteed a higher and more consistent level of production, stabilising prices and the workings of the market. Important too were the indirect results of the extension of maize-growing. One only has to think of the better possibilities of crop rotation and the reduction of areas originally needed for wheat and the lesser cereals, which freed new land for pasture and grazing.

From the Veneto in the seventeenth century maize extended to the provinces of Lombardy, Piedmont and Emilia where it speeded up the development which was already taking place in the well-watered areas. In the Duchy of Parma it appeared at the beginning of the seventeenth century and had already by the end of the century taken over a considerable area of farmland and the urban market where it appears from the 1680s onwards. It did not catch on, however, in Tuscany or central-southern Italy. In the latter it was to appear in the eighteenth century when, in the Po Valley, it emerged decisively as the staple food.

Likewise, if we analyse the relationship between the agricultural evolution of the North and the South on the basis of the different forage crops, we generally find a similar contrast. In the irrigated areas of the Po Valley the cultivation of fodder crops was becoming increasingly widespread. It was linked to agricultural production by the close relationship between animal-rearing and crops and allowed a greater productivity than in the South where, as De Maddalena writes, bearing in mind the scarcity of recent studies, 'with the gradual improvement in the crop rotation system, the amount of grazing land increased. In other words, there was a return to the old mixed grazing and crop-growing economy, in which the production of fodder is essentially accidental and is not a predisposed link in the sequence of crops, and does not lead to any improvement on the practical level.' Almost all the agriculture in the Po Valley showed signs of a marked rationalisation which allowed a very intense exploitation of the productive capacities of the land, to which the ancient and well-tried system of crop rotation was adapted, alternating nitrogenous crops with crops which exhausted the land.[6] The spread of textile plants – hemp and flax – in the northern plains, led to the expansion of rural industry, which was widespread throughout the area and whose products were principally intended for consumption by the peasant families themselves.

Up to the eighteenth century technical improvements in farming do not seem to have been important, even if new methods of ploughing indicate that there was some development, while the agricultural landscape of central-northern Italy was more varied having vines and fruit-tree cultivation too. Among the latter, the growing of mulberry-trees boosted the silk industry which in the seventeenth century was expanding rapidly. To sum up – Italian agriculture, seen from the point of view of the relationship between production and agronomic decisions in the seventeenth-century crisis, in northern Italy defended or introduced conditions which slowed down the fall in production and which allowed a more intense and flexible use of labour and a more rational exploitation of natural resources, while in the *latifundia* areas of the South signs of a greater inflexibility of production become more apparent. The recovery of the eighteenth century was to proceed from this initial situation.

From the middle decades of the eighteenth century the Italian economy began to show signs of emerging from its century-long stagnation. Limited and incomplete, with recovery in some areas only, nevertheless they indicated the beginning of evolution and a growth in production while at the same time confining themselves to specific geographical areas and concerning sectors that were not always essential to the productive process. By this it must be understood that the Italian economy of the second half of the eighteenth century, while undergoing significant changes, was not heading towards an agrarian revolution and even less towards an industrial revolution. It is very evident that it is not possible to apply the same criteria to Italy and to a country like England: in Italy industrialisation arrived late, at the dawn of the twentieth century, and the agrarian revolution was certainly a nineteenth-century phenomenon. Nevertheless, already in the eighteenth century, even in a situation held back by a tangle of outmoded structures, in some agricultural areas developments were taking place capable of sparking off important changes. The chief catalyst was the rise in the price of cereals in Europe as well as all over Italy, from the Vercelli area where the increase in agricultural prices was as high as 70 per cent, to the entire Piedmontese countryside, the Po Valley, the Bologna region, the Papal States and as far as Sicily. Italy, the granary of Europe, was feeling the effects of an international situation characterised by the growth in demand for cereal products and she responded with greatly increased production. This does not mean, however, that these rises were accompanied by any signs of capitalistic modernisation in the countryside.

In some agricultural areas, such as Sicily, the expansion was accompanied merely by greater intensification of work and a passive extension of land under cultivation. It was no coincidence that in the island along with cereal prices there was also an increase in income from speculation, the cost of middlemen and economic parasitism.[7] More generally, in the whole of the South the movement of capital into schemes of agricultural change was rare and unimportant, while investment in long-term developments remained insignificant. It was rather the public sector which carried out considerable works of land reclamation and improvement, but this led to nothing more.

Further north in the cereal-growing areas of central Italy, the land improvements carried out under Popes Benedict XIV, Clement XIII and Pius VI, and in particular the draining of the Pontine Marshes, were immensely costly undertakings, completed at the time of the growth of cereal production. Here too, as in the South, economic policy tended to meet rapidly the exceptional increase in demand; but, all in all, to put it rather simplistically, it remained essentially within the confines of a mercantilistic attitude, which is to say, one that was concerned only with the commercial balance with other countries. In this case too, the rising production, stimulated by the upturn in the economy, did not become a lever to encourage change in contractual relations in the countryside or capitalistic rationalisation of the farms.

Similar considerations, in the light of recent studies in agrarian history, can be applied to the countryside of the Veneto, where the principal factor holding back development was not so much the large amount of property in the hands of the nobles as the particular type of overall involvement − financial, human, cultural − which the owners had over many centuries developed in relation to their land. The detachment of the owners from their land, the consequence of a way of life directed entirely towards politics, luxury and urban interests, created a situation where the land and its problems retreated into the background and did not become the focus for far-sighted and industrious entrepreneurial attitudes. The tenant-farmers or *mezzadri*, able to enjoy a relative independence within their subordinate position, aimed to extract the maximum immediate advantage and to keep up with the growing demands for money that their property made on them. The intricate complexity of leasing contracts in the Veneto (a veritable jungle of laws and privileges which both contemporaries and historians have struggled to penetrate) in fact resulted in a general stagnation, unshaken by processes such as the proletarianisation of the peasants and the great increase in demand for cereals, which could have had a modernising effect if they had sparked off changes in the cycle of crops and brought 'to the countryside that capital which was so badly needed to raise cattle, grow fodder, fertilise the land and improve the vineyards'.[8]

As has already been said, in the countryside of the Veneto, the changes in production and crop rotation had already established themselves in the second half of the seventeenth century, when triennial rotation based on the cycle of one crop of maize and two of wheat had become usual and guaranteed a substantial balance entirely directed towards self-sufficiency for the producers. The introduction of maize was a stabilising factor in that it freed the peasants of the Veneto from the old spectre of famine, even if their standard of living remained at subsistence level. Maize was the necessary staple food to support the increasing population of the eighteenth century but it was not the herald of an agrarian revolution, as has, however, often been thought. With the inexorable advance of maize, wooded and grazing land shrank, so that for its meat supply Venice had to turn to the Hungarian and Turkish markets – with grave repercussions for the balance of trade. Of little or no use were the efforts and theorising produced by the agronomic movement of the Veneto in the second half of the eighteenth century in the numerous agrarian academies which had sprung up in the 1770s in the chief agricultural centres of the Venetian Republic. The effect of the academies was restricted to small circles of noblemen and, with the rare exception of a few enlightened and enterprising landowners, found no echo in the countryside. At the same time, the economic policy of *la Serenissima* was equally ineffective, being slow to take legislative action and firm in its defence of sectoral interests. To loosen the stranglehold on an agrarian economy which showed no signs of movement towards capitalistic development there came neither a general movement of opinion nor a political initiative. Marino Berengo is right when he writes:

The work of the academies of the Veneto and the republic's agrarian legislation in the second half of the eighteenth century are an important indication of the spread and strength of ideas which were certainly new. But in the agrarian economy of the State they carried no weight at all. In order to reform agriculture it was necessary first to reform rural society. And this no government of the *ancien régime*, and Venice least of all, was prepared to do.[9]

Moving to the countryside of neighbouring Lombardy, we find a situation very different from that in the Veneto, particularly in the southern, irrigated area where an ancient and wise system of improvements, channelling of water and rational productive management of the land represented the jewel of Italian agriculture. On the basis of an agricultural system which had already for some time been evolving towards capitalism, there took shape developments which along with contemporary developments in Flanders and England, laid the foundations for the technological advances of the nineteenth century. The view that there was an agrarian revolution in eighteenth-century Lombardy has been superseded by the theory that the Lombard countryside even in the second half of the eighteenth century remained under the influence of a 'substantial stability of the landowning system, contractual relationships and cultural and productive attitudes', a stability which should not, however, disguise the correct assessment 'of the evolutionary tendencies which, most noticeably in the second half of the century, appeared in Lombardy in answer on the one hand to the changes in institutions (particularly in the taxation system) and on the other to the demands of the market'.[10] The truly new thing which was present in the Lombard countryside, of such importance that it demanded change, was the influence on society of the far-reaching economic and financial policy introduced by Maria Theresa's census, completed in 1760. This political initiative, coinciding with an already progressive situation, was the greatest impulse to agricultural change. The view that the Theresian *catasto* was an instrument for 'a more complete and more intense exploitation of the soil'[11] was already known to contemporaries, from Gian Rinaldo Carli who was a faithful official of Habsburg absolutism in Milan, to Pietro Verri the Milanese *illuminista* who was an early proponent of free trade, anticipating the analyses and views that Adam Smith was to set out so thoroughly in his *Wealth of Nations*. Their view would be taken up by later historians.

The Milanese *catasto* was to be the model for all those to follow. It provided the landowners with objective fiscal data, because it was based on the area and type of land. It was an incentive to profit-making because, as contemporaries were quick to see, it made taxation proportional to capital value, formerly considered immutable and defined for all time. At first the reactions of the big landlords to the new land register were unfavourable, but when in the 1770s the rise in prices, profits and income was not diminished by a proportional rise in taxes, their attitude changed and many came to believe that the new register would be a guarantee for the landowners since in fact as time passed it made the land-taxes lighter.

The financial policy of the government which consisted of a reduction in the rate of payment on investments in state bonds, brought about a move of capital to private enterprises. Thus released, the flow of savings went towards either productive investments or to the purchase of luxury goods. From the information we have, it is not possible to estimate how much of this private capital was reinvested. While it may be true that some noble families spent enormous sums on building sumptuous palaces and surrounding themselves with royal pomp, it is also certain that considerable sums were invested in works intended to improve agricultural productivity. These included irrigation channels, cultivation of new land, tree clearing, experimentation with new crops and the building of farmhouses. Despite all this, Lombardy should not be thought of in the often exaggerated terms of the English agronomist Arthur Young in his *Voyage en Italie pendant l'année 1789* (Paris, 1796). As Carlo Capra reminds us, Young's description is very partial, being confined to a single seigneurial estate. In other words, one should not conclude that the majority of the Lombard nobility had transferred its financial interests and civil enthusiasm from city to country, or that it was changing into a class of entrepreneurs. The lack of interest of the nobles in the land remained pronounced; and the various middlemen did not always assume a capitalistic role, but often remained as parasitical if not grasping intermediaries, standing between the income of the nobles and the exploitation of the peasants. But it is equally certain that attitudes towards the direct management of estates, the control of agrarian investments and agricultural decisions took root in the minds of some aristocratic families of Lombardy, and were the beginnings of a change of direction that would mature during the following century when investment in land and involvement in production were to become normal activities for the nobility and rich bourgeoisie.

An analysis of the changes in crops brought about by the developments in the second half of the eighteenth century in Lombardy reveals a tendency for the cultivation of mulberry-trees in the dry and hilly areas with cattle-rearing and the making of dairy products in the wetter areas. The resultant increase in silk has been estimated to be in the order of 40 per cent between 1750 and 1780. Silk, raw or spun, increased the flow of exports, constituting about half their total value. Other crops which were expanding rapidly were rice and maize. During the eighteenth century the latter became firmly established and the growth in production was in line with the growth in population, without however new and consistent quantities of maize being put on the foreign market.

In the western part of the Po Valley, that is in the area belonging to Savoy, the role of mulberry and silkworm production was even more important, the silk harvest doubling, going from 1.5 million kg to 3–4 million kg at the end of the eighteenth century. Here too the product found a market in Europe which gave excellent returns for invested capital. In Tuscany there was a similar expansion in the growing of mulberry-trees. In the South they appeared at the beginning of the century, but the grip of an archaic economic system caused possibilities for a development in the production of silk to fail. The difference between North and South becomes manifest, as Alberto Caracciolo has written, for while in the South the silk industry was in the hands of speculators who were only

concerned to resell at once to foreign buyers or to the state industry, in many provinces of Lombardy and Piedmont it was the agricultural capitalists themselves who took advantage of the industry, becoming involved in the processing of the silk on the spot and marketing it. Thus the earnings from it returned to the place of production rather than into the thousand channels of trade. . . . An ever-increasing differentiation between the different regions of Italy was becoming clear. The developments in Lombardy in the irrigated farms and the silk industry were the most progressive solutions which Italy, emerging from the eighteenth century and the subsequent revolutions, could offer by way of economic development.[12]

Tuscany is a case which seems to confirm the success of a combination of spontaneous tendencies in the economy and political intervention. According to the studies of Tuscany under Leopold made by Mirri and Giorgetti,[13] Tuscany seems to gain in importance from the economic policy adopted at the end of the 1760s when the government, in order to release public and ecclesiastical property, leased large plots of land to farmers *a livello*. This kind of contract allowed a tenancy of long duration, and in distinguishing between formal ownership and rights of working ownership assured a sort of ownership of land and free negotiation over the plots of land received. The *a livello* contract, which became common in place of *mezzadria*, established a positive balance between public property and private interests and encouraged agricultural change. In this case too we see how trends in development became part of a more general movement of change, in cases where there was a government able to develop the right economic policies and where there was a social situation in a condition to make use of favourable moments for plans for long-term development.

The recovery in central-northern Italy was assisted by the improvement in communications. The most important of the many works carried out during the eighteenth century were the making of the road joining Florence and Leghorn, the opening of the Apennine passes of Futa and Abetone in Tuscany, the access to the Adriatic coast, the improving of communications between Milan and Leghorn and Milan and Genoa, the construction of canals between the Adda and the Po and the improvements to the road to Switzerland, a vital link in relations between Italy and central Europe.

Manufacturing industries in eighteenth-century Italy showed little development and the system of production remained trapped in the old cottage-industry patterns dependent on the figure of the merchant-entrepreneur and split up into many small artisan workshops. The geography of manufacturing Italy also remained the same and continued to be strongest in the countryside. Very slowly, however, signs of movement were appearing. For example, the whole system of the guilds in the second half of the century was giving way under the attacks of measures in favour of free trade, the result of the needs of production which could no longer expand within the confines of closed and protective organisations. In the 1780s the silk industry boomed, most noticeably in the cities of Lombardy, particularly Como and Milan, and of Piedmont. At the root of this veritable leap in production lay, on one hand, a fiscal and customs policy which favoured the silk industry and, on the other, the crisis in the great industrial centre of Lyons which had an advantageous effect on the Italian industry which was called upon to reorganise and equip itself in order to put a finished product on the market. But the whole of the agricultural-manufacturing silk industry remained unstable, prone to sudden and violent crises like the one that struck the silk mills of Como in the late 1780s. Cotton was generally manufactured only for home consumption and it was not until the end of the century in the northern provinces that there was the beginning of change. The wool industry had not recovered from its old problems which could not be ignored despite the modern manufactures of Schio in the Veneto, Prato in Tuscany and Biella in Piedmont. These were isolated oases in an archaic system of production which left the users of wool dependent on English production. Plans for modern mining technology, the search for new deposits and signs of modernisation in the production of metals can be seen as the first and hesitating steps towards a development which, in this as in the preceding sectors, was to flower during the nineteenth century.

NOTES AND REFERENCES

For a general evaluation of the Italian economy in the eighteenth century see Caracciolo, A. (1973) 'La storia economica', in *Storia d'Italia*. Einaudi, Turin, vol. III, pp. 533–54.

1. Aymard, M. (1978) 'La transizione dal feudalesimo al capitalismo', in *Storia d'Italia Annali* I, *Dal feudalesimo al capitalismo*. Einaudi, Turin.
2. Woolf, S. J. (1962) 'Sviluppo economico e struttura sociale in Piemonte da Emanuele Filiberto a Carlo Emanuele III', in *Nuova rivista storica* XLVI, pp. 1–57.
3. Beltrami, D. (1961) *La penetrazione economica dei veneziani in Terraferma. Forze di lavoro e proprietà fondaria nelle campagne venete dei secoli XVII e XVIII*. Istituto per la collaborazione culturale, Venice–Rome.
4. Pugliese, S. (1908) *Due secoli di vita agricola. Produzione e valore dei terreni, contratti agrari, salari e prezzi nel Vercellese dei secoli XVIII e XIX*. Turin. For Sereni's studies see Chapter 3.
5. Messedaglia, L. (1932) 'Per una storia del mais in Italia', in idem, *Per la storia dell' agricoltura e dell'alimentazione*. Piacenza.
6. Aldo De Maddalena has recently discussed the problems of the Lombard economy in a long review to Sella, D. (1979) *Crisis and Continuity: the economics of Spanish Lombardy in the seventeenth century*. Harvard University Press, Cambridge (Mass.), London. See De Maddalena, A. (1981) 'Vespri e mattutino in una società pre-industriale', in *Rivista storica italiana*, fasc. III, pp. 559–614.
7. Cancila, O. (1980) *Impresa redditi mercato nella Sicilia moderna*. Laterza, Bari.
8. Berengo, M. (1963) *L'agricoltura veneta dalla caduta della repubblica all'Unità*. Banca Commerciale italiana, Milan, p. 7.
9. Ibid., p. 21.
10. Sella, D, and Capra, C. (1984) *Il Ducato di Milano dal 1535 al 1796*. UTET, Turin, p. 562.
11. Ibid., p. 562.
12. Carracciolo, A. 'La storia economica', in *Storia d'Italia*, Einaudi, Turin, vol. III, p. 564.
13. Mirri, M. (1955) 'Proprietari e contadini toscani nelle riforme leopoldine', in *Movimento operaio* 2, pp. 173–229; Giorgetti, G. (1966) 'Per uno studio delle allivellazioni leopoldine', in *Studi storici* 2, pp. 245–90.

CHAPTER FIVE

Classes and institutions: the hegemony of the nobility and the role of the State

Recent research into the nobility and aristocracy of some of the Italian states during the *ancien régime* has raised again historiographical problems which had seemed settled, and which have confirmed the thesis that suggests a clear hegemony of the nobility throughout the eighteenth century and even later. To sum up the various studies made of the political élites one can say that up to the eighteenth century there was no real change in the ruling class of Italy, just as there were no deep changes in the stratification of classes and their hierarchies. This does not mean that the balance established in the sixteenth and seventeenth centuries continued without any change, for Italian society was shot through with factors which anticipate a break with the social order, institutions, ideals and economic practice which had lasted for so long. In the eighteenth century new tensions between the classes, originating generally from the conflict of attitude and interests which divided the different social groups – old nobility, new nobility, sectors of the new bureaucracy, feudal enclaves, urban aristocracies, the rich bourgeoisie, professional classes – all in various ways disturbed Italy's equilibrium.

Nevertheless, the elements which made up society at whatever level remained substantially unchanged, being in Italy as in the rest of Europe much more adaptable than is generally thought. Historians have gradually come to agree that Italian history up to the end of the eighteenth century does not reveal a bourgeois strength capable of taking over the power of the old and new nobility, that the moves towards capitalism are insignificant, and that for the whole of the eighteenth century the political and economic power attained by the bourgeoisie at the expense of the nobility was generally slight. Indeed, the reverse is true: historians today generally recognise the exceptional influence of the noble classes, even if numerically very small – in northern Italy for example they were 1.1 per cent of the entire population – in the spheres of policy and economics in the eighteenth century. They concentrated in their own hands the ownership of the land with an extraordinary political resilience, unaffected by new regimes. They succeeded in fact in sharing in the leadership of the states on an equal footing with the new bureaucratic groups, even where the political power deriving from the emperor, king or grand duke attempted to rationalise the state apparatus with the aid of a personal administrative staff. More often the noble groups took up office at the highest level as officials and magistrates, handing on their offices to members of their family. Everywhere they successfully defended the autonomy of the town administrations which were often controlled by small, rich, powerful oligarchies of nobles. By means of their management of the legal and political institutions in the towns they regulated the aspirations to a higher social position of the new emerging classes. These, in order to reach the highest positions and to increase their prestige and become part of the political élite, had to accumulate wealth and qualifications sufficient to prevent sudden replacement at the top of the social ladder. This, precisely because of the hegemony of the nobility, remained static – blocked by hierarchies which were self-perpetuating or which gradually co-opted the new bourgeois groups.

Having said this, it should not be thought that we are dealing with an Italy ruled by inertia. Not at all. Tensions and conflicts, albeit within a so far unbroken framework and varying from state to state, marked the recurrent aspirations of new social groups to a more important role in policy-making. The sources of these tensions are numerous. In some cases they are to be found within the aristocracy which was not so compact or homogeneous as not to have its own differences, whether of generation, attitudes, income or culture. The small ruling nuclei were internally divided not only by differences in wealth but also by political hierarchies which in some cases sanctioned a distinction between that section of the nobility who by virtue of birth were offered the highest offices in the town, and that whose function was less important. The relationship between the highest class of nobles, or patricians, at least in the towns which could boast of a tradition of municipal autonomy, and the other social groups – the bourgeoisie of business men or officials whose importance increased along with the power of the State – was very diverse. It ranged from extreme hostility on the part of certain restricted noble élites which showed no inclination to absorb or recognise in any way the political rights of men from another class, to the opposite extreme of osmosis or gradual absorption of other classes through the granting of new noble titles. At the beginning of the eighteenth century, differences were still felt in the upper classes, particularly of the towns. These had originated two centuries earlier when a governing class of merchant origin had arisen, which isolated the ancient military nobility on the feudal estates and joined with the nobility of the robe – the judiciary – whose origins were linked to political power which they had captured through the performance of administrative and judicial duties. Italy, like Flanders and Switzerland, was rich in patricians. It was not only the republics – Genoa, Venice and Lucca – which were governed and led by a patrician class, for a political, cultural and economic leadership of patrician character can also be seen in many other smaller centres, especially in central Italy, the Po Valley and Tuscany.

The new protagonist to intervene in the social process from at least the sixteenth century was a central and centralising authority which could be a prince or a city oligarchy and which in the area of the consolidation of a state on a regional basis brought new sources of discord. In Venice for example, where there was a municipal and republican oligarchy which had taken over a territory which it assimilated into its own institutional structures, differences showed up in the clash between the old local aristocracies and the ruling class of the conquering city which excluded the nobles of the outlying areas from the political running of the State, while nevertheless ratifying their ancient identity. Where, on the other hand, the laying of the foundations of the modern State was the work of a prince, that is of an authority derived from the early Signori, from the Empire or from foreign domination, then friction arose as a result of the interference in local self-government and from the imposition of new entities which were forerunners of a bureaucracy. This was particularly true in the periods when a policy of realignment of power was being set in motion, intended to strengthen the links between the central institutions and the outlying government bodies. This is not to say that the reforming intentions of the prince, at least until the reforms carried out by Joseph II in 1786, had a clear class content, based on the opposition between nobility and the official and professional bourgeoisie; but rather that the reforming prince would try to appease the nobles, drawing the aristocracy into a public sphere not by opposition but assimilation. In cases like these the ennoblement of the upper classes of the State, the upgrading of the judiciary and the silencing of the ancient representative bodies of the feudal nobility, such as the *Parlamenti*, were all means to this end.

The response of the different élites – urban patricians and feudal lords in the country in particular – when faced with this new political State was various. In broad terms, on one side there was a jealous defence of their military and chivalrous origins and on the other an acceptance of new ideological values which required an emphasis on the cultural, civic and economic aspects of their class. An important treatise by Scipione Maffei, the *Scienza chiamata cavalleresca* (1710), was published at a moment when noble society was disturbed by contrasting tensions, feeling both a need to recover its political dignity, put in the shade during the seventeenth century, and to become more firmly identified with a public function along with other social classes. Maffei described very well the workings of an ideology which Claudio Donati had described as one 'of service to sovereign and state'.[1] For Maffei nobility (*virtù*) should no longer rely on birth and military traditions, but rather on professional expertise and administrative and juridical office in the state courts.

For the nobility of central-northern Italy whom Maffei is addressing, the problem which posed itself at the close of the seventeenth century, and which was to reappear later, was that of how to combine an appeal to civic usefulness, which Maffei carefully helped to foster, with the more historical and traditionally ingrained need to defend, without yielding, political preeminence. This implied the need to monopolise for as long as possible the posts of high office in the cities and, where possible, in the State. It seemed possible that the patricians of the Italian cities, accustomed for many centuries to considering themselves and being considered as the only ruling class, and repository of the municipal and administrative traditions of the *res publica* (even if often with entirely private means and ends), might willingly agree to share power with another authority, with another political group, and renounce the privileges on which they had built their fortune. Indeed, Claudio Donati has put forward the theory (a theory not yet entirely confirmed by facts) that the ideology of 'service' to the prince was 'perhaps more attractive to a tradition of chivalry'.[2] The example of Piedmont, as we shall see later, can partly confirm this hypothesis in so far as the alliance of the old nobility with the policy of the House of Savoy was not troubled by resistance or opposition. But Piedmont was a region where there had been no tradition of communal society and patrician domination had not developed before the gradual formation of the absolute State. Piedmont was not a land of patricians and city-states, and neither was the South, whose social system was permeated by feudal influences which, in the seventeenth century, had increased their power over southern society without, however, showing any tendency to exercise their sway, or allow it to be exercised, in the sphere of the State.

The permanence of the social and institutional systems which signified the pre-eminence of the aristocracy does not necessarily mean that there were no economic processes pointing towards an advance beyond traditional agriculture and indicative of entrepreneurial dynamism. A more active picture has emerged from recent research showing in some areas of Italy signs of the emergence of a bourgeoisie within the feudal framework, or the presence of groups among the nobility, particularly in the North, who were prepared to take considerable risks in experimenting with new types of farming, in investing large amounts of money in improvements, and in undertaking business trading which called on a considerable portion of their inherited reserves of wealth. It is true on the other hand that these nobles who did not merely live comfortably on income from land-rent but who were prepared to consider agricultural change and become involved in commercial speculation, were to be found chiefly in those areas involved in a capitalistic type of agricultural development. In other areas the nobility was, between 1600 and 1700, inactive or in decline, often not only economically but also politically and numerically.

Lombardy was distinguished for many centuries by the social make-up of its ruling classes who were connected with the city and not the land.[3] Since the age of the communes it had been the urban patricians who provided political leadership for the region, retaining this function during the seigneurial regime of the Viscontis and Sforzas, under the Spanish and then the Austrians, at least until the 1750s. Through these different regimes they successfully defended their basic political and administrative autonomy. Already in the time of the Viscontis an internal hierarchy had formed within the city nobility which, as the oligarchy of the capital, Milan, not only ran the entire administration of the city, but also had control over the provincial centres whose courts were to some extent subordinate to those of Milan.

The urban rather than feudal origins of the élite that held a large slice of political power and was beginning to participate in the State's regional government may explain, according to recent studies, why the Lombard nobility accepted the State as well as the increase in its public functions: at least until the reforms of Joseph II in the 1780s there was no cause for conflict since a broad equilibrium had been established between the different social groups – nobility, feudal landowners, upper bureaucracy, rich bourgeoisie – which survived despite changes in the historical situation. Within the ranks of the Milanese patricians a smaller group can be seen made up of some sixty of the most ancient and wealthy families, who shared between them the highest civic offices. The social importance of this nucleus of Milanese nobles did not lie only in their monopoly of the municipal administration, but also in the whole network of economic, political and personal links which united them to the Lombard aristocracy.

The influence of the feudal class on Lombard society was markedly less when compared with the power of the urban patricians. In general the feudal aristocracy came lower down on the scale of social hierarchies. This is not to say that in Lombardy feudalism was not common. On the contrary – large landed estates were given over to the feudal system which assured the land-owner of important fiscal and juridical privileges, such as tax exemptions, protection against division of the patrimony, judicial functions delegated to them by the State, which the landowner exercised through the *podestà* who was chosen from among the graduates of Pavia University, and, finally, many rights to impose agricultural and other taxes. All this, however, did not become the basis for domination; and the feudal estate remained an institution of secondary public importance precisely because of the pre-eminence of the towns, and therefore of the patricians who had attached themselves to the institutions of the State.

From various recent studies, particularly those of Domenico Sella,[4] it can be seen moreover that from the 1650s onwards an antifeudal attitude arose, not only in the city oligarchies, but in the landowning classes of the countryside. This attitude must have concealed both a desire to prevent the local feudal lord from interfering in the economic enterprises of the bourgeoisie and an ambition to increase non-feudal possession of land by taking over common land which generally under feudalism was considered to be of public utility and therefore not for sale. Unlike the local landowners, the peasants were generally more favourable to the enfeoffment of the community for it was often considered a means of legal and social protection and a defence against economic exploitation. Not only was the position of the feudal lord inferior to that of the patrician but also the whole feudal world of Lombardy was in decline in the second half of the seventeenth century, from the point of view both of its jurisdictional privileges, being deprived of office or challenged by communal and central administrations, and also of its privileges of rank – censuses, taxes, tithes – which were in general becoming fewer. It was a society guided not by the values and powers of the fief but by those of the aristocratic patricians who had concentrated in their hands the most important political and administrative offices. First the Spanish and then the Habsburgs did nothing to upset this balance, which rested on the identification between city aristocracy and state, and an original combination of private interest with the defence of public institutions. This essential agreement between state and patrician lasted until at least the middle of the eighteenth century with few conflicts.

Milan is a useful model in order to understand the relationship between the central power of the ruling State – Spain until 1707 and Austria during the rest of the eighteenth century – and the local ruling classes. The governor, representing foreign domination, never interfered in the internal life of the Milanese patricians and, though it was up to him to nominate the *decurioni*, the highest post in the capital, in fact his role was a purely formal one in that the whole mechanism for the choosing of the decurions was controlled by the patricians themselves, and they were careful to see that only families of the Milanese nobility with an influential genealogical tree and enormous wealth were appointed to these posts. It was a self-perpetuating system controlled by a very small élite. The families who monopolised the *decurionato* generally ensured the continuity of their positions of prestige by passing it on to the eldest son. In this way a closed hereditary line was maintained which prevented the dispersion and multiplication of offices, consolidating the political attributes of the *decurionato*. For younger sons instead there were other less important openings in the civil courts, the royal tribunals, the army or the Church. To become part of the Milanese patriciate it was necessary to meet conditions as strict as those required of candidates for the *decurionato*, such as residence of the family in Milan for at least a century, membership of the ancient nobility and no dealings whatsoever with trade or other professions considered to be inferior. It was thus necessary that the new members of the patriciate should be already in some degree of the same kind as it, both in social position and in ideology.

The political body which chiefly represented the aristocracy of Lombardy was the Milanese Senate,[5] which already in the sixteenth century had been taken over by the Milanese patricians who had made it their instrument for the defence and exercise of their political privileges, both as stronghold of local autonomy against the prince and as guarantor of aristocratic continuity. With regard to the prince, the Senate drew up a very detailed description of its own status in order to confirm its autonomous identity as the ruling class since this was not sanctioned by any other authority. At the same time it guarded jealously all its most important responsibilities, such as the power to interpret the laws and the nomination of the judges, thereby safeguarding patrician management of the State. In the face of those emerging from below, from the end of the sixteenth century onwards, the patricians imposed increasingly rigid conditions so as not to dilute the political and social compactness of the nobility with too many newcomers.

In such a society it is clear that the study and exercise of jurisprudence were essential to the maintaining of the existing balance and to the intro-duction of changes in the social order. Jurisprudence was the road to a social rise in society. The *nouveaux riches* who tried to become part of the nobility, having once abandoned trade or other humble employment, managed by studying law to rise to those posts as notary or small-time lawyer which were the first rungs on the ladder to social elevation. After a few generations the family was able to purge itself of its humble origins and acquire honours and prestige by the pure exercise of legal functions, so arranging things that the first-born son could clear the last hurdle and become a member of the College of Jurisconsults. At this point elevation to the nobility was assured and the most important careers, both municipal and ecclesiastical, were thrown open to him. In other words, in order to be acceptable to the patriciate, a family had to rid itself of commercial involvements, amass a significant fortune through public office, and maintain these through the years. The acquisition of a fief or office could assist this rise. For this reason it is not correct to assume that there was a rigid opposition of interests or clear social divisions between the feudal nobility and the patricians of the city. Rather, there was between the sixteenth and eighteenth centuries a *rapprochement* brought about by opportune political marriages while much economic interweaving took place, bearing in mind also that the fief still had considerable prestige which was often sought after by the patricians. This process of interweaving did not, however, wipe out the gap between the two classes, the origin of which was, as has been said, on one side the general weakening of feudal power and on the other the hegemony of the towns and their dominant groups made up of oligarchies which had arisen through the magistratures.

Unlike that in other parts of Italy, the patriciate of Lombardy does not appear to have been, at least in the eighteenth century, a closed class. On the contrary, it showed itself prepared to renew itself through periodic concessions of noble titles to well-to-do families in the capital and provinces who had reached the top of the social ladder by means of well-chosen marriages and sufficient investments in shares and property. Throughout the period we are considering this noble and patrician hegemony was not opposed by the Spanish or Habsburg sovereigns. Only after the middle of the eighteenth century and particularly with the reforms of Joseph II were there signs of policies designed to impose considerable changes in the social hierarchies through the weakening of the Milanese patriciate. For the first half of the century the social structure of Lombardy was not seriously upset either by the new census initiated by Charles VI in 1718, which set out by means of the redefinition of property to regulate the tax privileges enjoyed by the urban and feudal lords, or by the new economic measures of a mercantilist nature, such as the institution of a council to deal with illicit trading in 1715, which were able to set up types of management more directly dependent on the central power as alternatives to the traditional organisation of work and trade. Tension was building up, however, between aristocratic autonomy and the first attempts of the State to impose a framework of rational administration, but these did not break out into open conflict, partly because the reforming intentions of the State were hesitant and weak, not backed up by public machinery or social consensus.

The first signs of the clash between the State and the different social classes appeared during the reign of Maria Theresa. In 1746, shortly after she had regained control over Lombardy, Maria Theresa transferred one of the most powerful officials of the Empire, the Genoese Count Pallavicini, from military command, making him minister in charge of finance from 1746 to 1750 and then governor of Milan. Pallavicini put forward a far-reaching plan for reorganising the finances and administration of Milan, inspired by the certainty that the future health of the State implied a limitation of the traditional privileges which powerful local groups had enjoyed over the centuries. The measures he proposed to wipe out the state deficit, exacerbated by the costs of war, forced the Milanese aristocracy to contend with a new force, that of the absolute State. The moment the latter imposed and carried out important changes in the administration and political organisation of the State, it attacked social positions which were anything but weak.

The reforms of 1749 implemented by the governor Von Harrach were of great importance in that for the first time the basic principles of the bureaucratic State were formulated in a coherent and organic way. These were centralisation, hierarchical dependence, the impersonality of public offices, and the separation of the different offices. The existing institutional structure was, by contrast, based on separate autonomies, the interweaving of power between different administrative bodies, on the private management of public offices and on the absence of a hierarchical system. In other words, in 1749 there were present in embryo all the elements of the battle for reform which in Lombardy was to emerge fully from the 1760s onwards and which attempted to replace institutional fragmentation and aristocratic hegemony with strong political leadership by the State, limiting the power of the nobles and setting up in opposition to them a class of officials with different civil values and new administrative powers. Joseph II developed this policy to its furthest extent, unleashing the full force of the State against the Lombard aristocracy, but this abstract plan failed because it was not supported by a sufficiently wide consensus. The Lombard aristocracy would manage to retain its position of power, emerging unscathed but also changed from the storm and reappearing on the threshold of the nineteenth century as the dominant group also capable of great political far-sightedness.

Turning to the Mezzogiorno and an analysis of the elements of both change and permanence in society during the period between the mid-seventeenth century and 1734, when the Neapolitan viceroyalty passed to Charles of Bourbon and opened a historical phase that was in many ways new, we notice profound differences in the social fabric and the institutional system. This was the result of a particular historical development which made the South so different from the North. In the middle of this period Milan and Naples underwent an identical political experience – the change from Spanish Bourbon to Habsburg domination. The Habsburgs, while retaining almost intact the different political structures of the two regions, introduced needs and tensions which partly resembled one another. But the social and political environment was profoundly different. In the rural areas of the South, for example, the polarisation around the two opposing social groups, the peasants and the feudal landowners, was much greater, even though they were not united social classes and had many internal differences.[6] For the peasants the differences sprang from the various contractual relationships, the types of land and relations with the political authority of the place. For the feudal land-owners there were other differences, such as the amount of land owned and for how long. A large part of the southern population was in fact dominated by a very ancient feudalism which covered large areas of land and controlled many communes. It should be distinguished from the more recent fiefs, generally more numerous but less rich or powerful.

Between these two extremes of society a southern bourgeoisie that might have introduced some tensions into the social order was almost entirely lacking, for though there were certainly groups of merchants, tenant-farmers and other wealthy men, their influence remained almost entirely within the limits of the traditional feudal order. In the provinces the presence of state officials was of little importance for though their powers had certainly increased between the sixteenth and eighteenth centuries, they had not seriously dented the barons' hold over society. And yet at the same time it is true that in the countryside during the eighteenth century there was a slow loosening of the feudal grip, in which groups of local patricians, the well-to-do, and state officials played a role. This acted in varying ways within the system, but tended to erode some of its many restrictions, increasing the number of small and medium-sized farms released from the barons.[7]

In Naples, the political and cultural capital of the South, social life, while reflecting all the tensions in the provinces, developed at the same time along different lines and with institutions not found outside the city, but which nevertheless made their influence felt throughout the viceroyalty. The social composition of Naples was complex and the different classes can be identified according to different affinities – cultural, institutional, professional and hereditary – without this last element necessarily having an important place in the classification of Neapolitan society. The nobility in Naples was a complex and very heterogeneous group. There were nobles whose Spanish origin dated back to the early sixteenth century and who traditionally held the most important offices of the capital. There were also nobles of Italian or Spanish origin attached for two centuries to the service of the Spanish monarch and closely identified with him. There was a 'local' nobility, of ancient origin, which had become closely associated with the municipal administration and which drew its wealth from rent of a basically feudal type, from administrative office, from business and from the management of the national debt. Finally there was a group of nobles who did not have their own political representation in the city.

As can be seen the nuances are many and probably the most visible clash at the end of the seventeenth century was that between the represented nobles, who controlled almost all the administration of the city and who consisted of about 130 families generally enjoying a secure inherited fortune with close links with the barons in the countryside, and the 'unrepresented' nobility who, while part of the city aristocracy, had no significant institutional powers. Political representation was through the *Piazze*, which elected a governing council consisting of five nobles and one commoner. This was the mouthpiece of the viceroy and had wide powers within the town in the areas of taxation, public order and food supply. This last duty which the urban nobles shared with the representative of the people gave them enormous control over business in the capital, in that they could fix the price of grain bought from the provinces and control import and export, not only deriving immediate advantages of a speculative nature from this, but also keeping the levels of income from land, which were determined to some extent by the *Annona*, very high. The nobles in the *Piazze* were not all alike, differing in wealth and degree of nobility. In some cases they were of the richest and generally most influential aristocracy while others came from the lesser nobility. When the regime changed in 1707 from the Spanish to the Austrians the lesser nobility increased its political importance in Naples in so far as the *Piazze* consisting of the higher nobility were reduced by the exile of those who had defended the Spanish government or else by the departure for the Viennese court of the pro-Habsburg members. As in Milan, during these years the political demands of the urban aristocracy came to the fore and the change in regime encouraged this, allowing them to glimpse the possibility of greater political recognition.

The basic difference from the Milanese situation lay in the fact that in Naples the urban aristocracy was less closely identified with the state institutions. It kept up the pressure for autonomy which was countered not so much by the viceroys as by the whole edifice of the great state institutions which had multiplied and strengthened under the Spanish.[8] In Naples contemporary observers had noted the action of a middle social group between the nobility and the commoners which was often described as the *ceto civile* and which should not be confused with the bourgeoisie. It was characterised rather by its institutional and ideological affinities, and consisted of magistrates, lawyers, officials and university professors; but it also included some nobles who identified themselves with the defence of the role of the State. This sometimes meant espousing attitudes that were anti-aristocratic and, more often, anticlerical. Often the *ceto civile* came close enough to the nobility to be part of it, but at other times the opposite happened and the nobility fell in with the attitudes of the *ceto civile*, especially when it came to defending Naples from the recurrent claims of the Roman Curia.

Within the civil class the so-called *ministero* had a particular unity. This consisted of those who made up the government apparatus of the capital. This was a genuine nobility of the robe, like that in France, held together by a specific ideological identity and by all the professional attributes which enabled it to exercise an important power of intervention in socal conflicts, while being a fusion of different classes. The strength of this administrative élite came from the possession and transmission of jurisprudence, which was the real basis of its social pre-eminence.[9] Whether co-opted by the viceroys or acquiring their legal posts by their own efforts, the Neapolitan *ministri* all came from the Bar, from which came the majority of the non-noble ruling class of Naples and which constituted a place of close and daily contact between it and the people of Naples. It is not known precisely how many jurists – that is, those who were involved in various ways in the courts – there were at the beginning of the eighteenth century. An Austrian viceroy suggested 50,000, while other estimates indicate a figure of 26,000. In any case, either figure shows that they were a significant number, exercising consistent political power even if they were not members of the nobility. It must be remembered too that the Bar was one of the few routes that the bourgeoisie of town or country could take to rise in society, this being ensured not so much by the work as a lawyer as by the possibilities which opened up to a Neapolitan lawyer of entering into the service of some important figure in the political world in one of the various tribunals.

It should not be assumed that the structure of the Neapolitan tribunals, which had administrative and judicial powers according to that mixture of powers which is typical of an institutional system of the *ancien régime*, provided a basis for a bureaucratic state. It is more accurate to define the body formed by the public offices of Naples as a pre-bureaucracy, in that it retained a series of characteristics which place it in the category of institutions where there is as yet no separation of powers, no formal and absolute value of law, no separation of offices nor a hierarchical delegation of responsibilities. Even if analysed from the economic point of view, Neapolitan government was a complex web of interests, its role being to guarantee the stability and continuity of that particularly Neapolitan economy which was neither feudal, though living mainly on income from the fiefs, nor capitalist even if the port offered opportunities for a wide range of investments and speculation. It was characterised rather by the consumption of income derived from the national debt (taxes, the contracting out of taxes, offices) and which was administered by the Neapolitan tribunals.

The Neapolitan nobility lived no ivory tower existence, but was open to influences from other social groups. There were close links with the big grain merchants operating in Naples, who formed a power group which may have been small but which had strong ties with those social groups which derived their wealth from parasitic income, financial speculation and the management of the national debt. Other sectors of the merchant bourgeoisie had vast fortunes, such as the traders in clothing, wine, firewood and weapons, while at a lower level came jewellers, printers and silk manufacturers. There were many wealthy doctors, chemists, surgeons, architects and lawyers. The common people of Naples, living as hangers-on of the law-courts, working as servants in a nobleman's house, or at the port, as artisans, or traders with little stalls in the streets, or surviving by means of casual labour, public assistance and church charity, were passive protagonists in political life because only the noble or ministerial élites could give a precise orientation to their actions and reactions. It was common knowledge in the ruling classes in Naples that no discontent among the people, however threatening, could have any political consequences unless guided by the more influential social classes. Finally, the barons in the country and the nobles in the towns were linked by double ties to the Church. This permeated all aspects of southern society, whether through the religious orders or the diocesan clergy, and it had accumulated vast amounts of property and income, state bonds and *arrendamenti* (see glossary), becoming an economic force of great importance.

The years of Habsburg rule (1707–34) saw the tensions between the different social groups in Naples coming to the surface more than once, without, however, any change in the equilibrium established in the previous years, which the *ministero* maintained. Many times the nobles of the city tried to win favour with the viceroy, even showing a willingness to bow to the State and lose some of their political privileges. Instead the Austrian viceroys continued to rely on the *ministero* which held firmly on to all the powers which had been granted to it. This balance of forces prevented the implementation of the plans for reform which were being proposed on all sides, in a symbolic way in the case of those which concerned taxes, the economy and justice, whereas in the field of the jurisdictional struggle against the Church there could be a broad front. There was pressure from Vienna for a new census which would allow an updating of the allotment of the tax burden in the viceroyalty, but it was opposed particularly by those of the nobility who feared the loss of some of their privileges. Similarly, the establishment, between 1725 and 1728, of a public bank, which was to be the financial instrument for the recovery of the fiscal rights of the State which had been allowed to pass to private individuals, failed completely on account of the opposition of the nobles of town and country, the Collateral Council (the chief political body of the viceroyalty) and the Chamber of the *Sommaria* (the chief administrative and financial body). Nobles, magistrates and tax-collectors (*arrendatori*) found themselves united the moment there appeared to be a threat to that system of parasitical income on which they were dependent. The Junta too, created in 1708 to assist foreign trade, was short-lived. This was the only attempt at a modification of the political and economic structures made by the Austrians who preferred to uphold the institutional edifice inherited from the Spanish and to confirm the different social groups in their traditional positions.

After the fall of the Austrians, the monarchical government of Charles of Bourbon gave rise to many hopes of renewal and received at first general support. Attempts at reform were not lacking even in the first few years when it was proposed that the barons' excessive power be reduced and that they should pay taxes. A law of 1738 placed particularly serious judicial procedures under the control of state justice, such as murder, which no longer lay within the jurisdiction of the barons. Economic policy moved towards the gradual reacquisition of *arrendamenti* which were taken away from the great feudal lords or the Church who generally owned them. In 1740 the machinery for the new *catasto* (land register) was set in motion. But all these embryonic anti-baronial policies got no further. The law of 1738 was revoked within a few years; the buying back of the *arrendamenti* was stopped from shortage of money in the middle of the century; the *catasto*, which had already started out on the basis of unsuitable criteria, remained unfinished.

In the same period, the 1750s, when in Milan Maria Theresa was laying the basis of a renewal of the State which threatened existing social hierarchies, the reform movement in Naples became bogged down in the age-old problems. The absence in Naples of any pressure for reform independent of local forces and carrying the prestige of a great multinational state, as was the case in Milan, made itself sorely felt from the moment when, in 1746, the kingdom acquired national independence. If at first this had appeared as an occasion for new reforms, it soon became apparent that it would bring greater oppression. It was necessary to wait for the emergence of new social classes, linked with a period of economic and population growth, and the spread of ideas close to the Enlightenment, for the debate on the role of the nobility, the State and the Church in southern society to be thrown open again. Even then, in the 1760s and 1770s, when the anti-baronial controversy was to take on the tones of a well-justified and widespread denunciation, no real ability to act changed the old relationship between government and social groups – a relationship rendered immobile by the endurance of widespread feudal conditions in the rural areas. The Neapolitan bureaucracy retained during this period the socially mixed nature which it already had at the end of the sixteenth century, through the absorption of both the nobility – ancient, new, urban and provincial – and the jurists of bourgeois origin, without any one group acquiring a clear dominance in the running of the State.

Both in Milan and in Naples the apparatus of public power did not become a vehicle for the rise of new social classes except to a very small degree and with a clear subordination of the latter to the aristocratic hegemony. So too in the republican states we find the same social barriers, upheld by the exercise of political and judicial power. Indeed, in the republican states the city oligarchies were generally more exclusive and more jealous of their institutional privileges so that even partial or limited changes in the ruling groups were almost completely non-existent. In Venice the patriciate was formed of a very old nucleus of merchants enriched by maritime trade, who retained through the centuries their involvement in this business, the source of their wealth and power. It is true that in the seventeenth century some of this capital was transferred to investment in land during the massive move to acquire estates on the mainland, as discussed earlier. In this case there was a partial economic change in a class which, despite this, did not basically alter its character or the form of its control over the institutions of government. For the whole of the period under consideration, that is up to the mid-eighteenth century, the merchant oligarchy of Venice held sway over the towns of the mainland, excluding the local nobility from access to the central institutions and restricting them to narrow administrative posts. A tenacious discontent began to take root in the provinces towards the centralising aspirations of the capital.[10] The Venetian nobles and those of the mainland taken together came to about 10,000 in the mid-eighteenth century, or 0.7 per cent of the total population. In Venice the percentage of nobles was higher, about 3 per cent, but it was shrinking fast. It has been calculated that from 1550 to 1717 the number of nobles belonging by hereditary right to the *Gran Consiglio* had fallen by 62 per cent.

The political prerogatives of the Venetian nobles were not all identical, but, as we have already seen in Milan, a small section of the aristocracy tended to secure the most influential posts in the complex institutional web of the republic. Around the Senate, which had assumed the task of general running of the State, there were offices with a smaller number of members with powers over specific areas. Two bodies made up the power of the Senate: the Great Council, of which almost all the Venetian nobility were members and which was principally an elective body; and the Council of Ten, so called from the number of nobles on it, which functioned as the government of the republic. The balance of power swung in favour of the latter every time there was a move towards greater institutional inflexibility by the most powerful oligarchy, or even if there was only a tendency in that direction, while it swung in favour of the Senate when the nobles as a whole identified with the decisions of the Venetian State, or when the less privileged classes managed to contain the centralising pretensions of the richest aristocracy. There was a dividing line within the aristocratic class separating the rich nobility from those who, if not poor, were less rich. When political offices returned a financial reward which varied according to the importance of the post, then the struggle for entry into certain institutions became also a conflict between different groups of the nobility distinguishable by their wealth.

Centralisation is not, however, the most accurate word to describe the forms of the republican State, since it might lead one to think that the successive acquisition of the provinces and cities of the Veneto had done away with, or at least greatly reduced, individual local autonomy. This was not the case: Venice's expansion into the mainland did not result either in a federal state or an absolute state along the lines of those in some other European nations. Instead a middle way emerged where Venice held a privileged position *vis-à-vis* the provinces where the ruling class had been confined to office in local administration. Indeed it would have been useless for them to aspire to high office in the capital which was strictly the preserve of the Venetian aristocracy. For this reason among the cities of the mainland, as in the case of Verona studied by Giorgio Borelli,[11] we find a 'nobility of the sword' reviving the cult of the old military virtues which, even if increasingly rarely needed, gave it the only possibility of identity as a privileged class, since other developments of aristocratic ideology were closed to it and freedom for political manoeuvre or upward movement was limited. There were several cases of Veronese nobles who in the second half of the seventeenth century turned their attention to agriculture with daring investments in new techniques and crops. In this case we are seeing a progressive transformation of the local élite from patricians to landowners. And that was not all: the feudal characteristics of the estates took a back seat in favour of a new enthusiasm for investment implying a type of capitalist agriculture, discernible in places where works of rational utilisation of the hilly areas and the planting of rice in rotation were carried out. Thus the attitudes and the habits of the Veronese nobility, or at least a part of it, changed, but without a change in its political position which was based on an unchallenged control of local administration and a total exclusion from state office in Venice.

The gravitational centre of the republic, once confined to the many ports and customs points along the Adriatic coast and in the Aegean, moved from the sixteenth century towards the Veneto, but this change in boundaries was not accompanied by a realisation among the Venetian aristocracy of the need to pay more attention to the mainland which now constituted the main body of the State. Instead, institutional structures were not revised and a power balance was upheld which aroused profound dissatisfaction in the provinces. It should be remembered too that in Venice, a city-state without territory until the fifteenth century, there was no trace of feudalism among the nobility who all came from the merchant class, and that the flood of wealth in the eighteenth century was chiefly derived from the landed revenue from the mainland, and which ended up half in the hands of laymen and churchmen in Venice, and half in the hands of the noble and bourgeois oligarchies of the provinces. Thus there was a close relationship between Venice and the mainland to which that exceptional reinvestment of capital by the Venetian patricians was directed and which had led to the expansion of their properties, particularly in the province of Padua, and which had been supported by the active intervention of the State.

There was, however, no corresponding creation of a state organised on a similar regional scale. The institutional system, which can be described as one of limited autonomy and imperfect centralisation, could only partly ensure effective working and consensus. It lacked a co-ordinated relationship between central and peripheral prerogatives. At the same time the class exclusiveness both in the government bodies of Venice and in those of the other cities had tightened up. In this way the decline in number and in wealth of the nobility of the Veneto which took place in the eighteenth century, the obstacles to any change in the ruling class, the political exclusion of the new bourgeois forces which were emerging in the countryside, the absence of institutional channels to co-opt these new forces in the mechanism of government (for example, in Venice even the posts of secretary and chancellor were given only to citizens of long residence), and the precarious compromise between the nobles of Venice and of the mainland, all contributed to the weakening of the republic. Its complex structure of government might still have been an object of admiration for many on account of its balance and control of powers, but the more acute observers were aware of the reality of a system increasingly unfitted to meet the social needs taking shape in the eighteenth century.

Turning to the Republic of Genoa, we can see some traits in common with Venice in its political structure and the social attitudes of the nobility.[12] In Genoa too the aristocracy, after the great expansion of the sixteenth century which coincided with the increase on a European scale of her trading and financial activities, had entered a period marked by a contraction of their numbers and a strict social exclusiveness. The studies by Bulferetti and Grendi have provided figures which show this very marked fall in numbers: from roughly 2,500 nobles at the beginning of the seventeenth century the figure had fallen to only 1,802 in 1630 of whom a good 306 were absent from the city for various reasons. A century later, in 1725, the Genoese nobility had lost another 1,000 members and now stood at 804 of which 72 were absent. A final contraction took place in the following decades, with the nobility losing about 23 per cent of its number between the years 1700 and 1760. Grendi, with good reason, uses the expression 'diaspora' to describe one of the two factors which explain this exceptional fall in the number of Genoese nobles, that is their frequent departure from home and transfer to other European cities for military, commercial, maritime or financial reasons. This élite had a tradition of emigration; serving the Spanish monarchy, important members of the Genoese aristocracy found employment in the army, diplomatic corps and government. In the most important European market-places and in the ports of the entire Mediterranean, Genoese merchants and business men were often to be found operating. And the majority of these men came from the ranks of the nobility.

But this is not enough to explain how the Genoese nobility once composed of more than 2,000 people could have been reduced to less than 1,000 at the beginning of the eighteenth century. There is another reason for the fall in numbers, related to population. The demographic trends of the eighteenth century all led to a contraction of the class. There was a greater propensity to accept celibacy, there were increasingly few remarriages of widows and widowers, the number of children fell (from six to eight children per family at the beginning of the eighteenth century to three to five children around the middle of the century), the number of childless families increased, while the mortality rate remained unchanged. It has been observed that in these demographic changes there was a marked decline in cohesive values, which accompanied and accelerated the social crisis of this class.

The fall in numbers did not bring about any kind of legal inclusion of new bourgeois elements. The nobility remained strongly exclusive as can be seen from the fact that out of a total of 10,856 names entered in the *Liber Nobilitatis genuensis* from 1528 to 1797 about 10,000 were accepted *quomodo filii patris*, or through paternal descent. It was rather through marriage that non-noble blood crept in. In the eighteenth century, noble endogamy was not always respected and marriages between nobles and plebeians were frequent. In this way the Genoese nobility did not risk its governing role, which it defended from any possibility of infiltration from, or osmosis with, other social classes. On the other hand, in individual behaviour it showed a definite tendency to open up, giving up the respect of once widely held values. So, if it is possible to talk of a crisis of the nobility during the eighteenth century, it is one which chiefly attacked ethical values and the norms of individual behaviour which began increasingly to diverge from political attitudes.

The Florentine patricians too, at the beginning of the eighteenth century, retained all the typical characteristics of a merchant nobility which had managed to keep its dominant position through the centuries in the commercial dealings of the Medici Duchy by means of political office and position at court which had protected and extended their trade.[13] The changes which took place in this class in the sixteenth and seventeenth centuries, such as their entry into the ducal bureaucracy or the acquisition of feudal titles, did not obscure the mercantile character of the Florentine patriciate. Though there was a contraction in the amount of business which it handled, especially in the European markets which were increasingly dominated by Dutch, English and French capital, it did not yield its position as trader in Tuscan, and especially Florentine, manufactures. Within the Florentine patriciate there formed a group of big capitalists who were involved either with the running or financing of the silk industry, the banks and the chief trading companies, with a sphere of action which often extended beyond the walls of Florence and into the national and foreign market.

This trading nobility took advantage of the predominant position it held under the Medici. From the top echelons of the magistratures and state offices, the patrician families controlled the city's economy through their hold over the money supply, the management of finances and the regulation of the urban market and the manufacturing activities which depended on the guilds. This situation, with the Florentine nobility closely linked to the business world, exploiting both a preceding tradition and the positions of power which it had maintained under the Medici, can be explained in part by the characteristics of the Medici State as it had evolved from the time of the principality of Cosimo I. It was a state built on the preceding republican model, without excluding the old Florentine patriciate but merging it with the bureaucratic classes. From the formation of the Medici State and for all its duration until its end in 1737, there was no clash between the social classes but rather a more complex compromise between the ancient aristocratic families with their economic and political strengths and the new groups that were linked with the extension of state office. The period between the foundation of the principality (1532) and the end of the Medici dynasty (1737) saw the emergence of a political class created directly by the prince and not subject to the rules of the aristocratic *Comune*. It was composed of the most prominent men of the Medici bureaucracy – the new institutional organisation which overshadowed the old civic bodies – and of representatives of the aristocracy from the smaller towns of the surrounding areas. Unlike Naples where, as has been seen, there were considerable links between big landed estates and fiefs, in Tuscany landownership developed outside the feudal system. In terms of the extent of land owned, the fiefs were few and did not constitute a significant element in Tuscan society. Land increasingly attracted the Florentine capitalists as a safe investment and its ownership came to be equated with arrival at the top of the social ladder, but the income derived from land could not be compared with the much higher profits which were obtained from trade, banking or manufacture.

With the arrival of the Habsburgs in Florence, the relationship with the political authority did not continue as before, for a new element appeared which was to call in question the old structures of dominance, often with the intention of overthrowing them. While one cannot perhaps talk of an anti-aristocratic policy *tout court* and while it should be remembered that the principal objective of the new Lorraine Regency (1737–65) and the government of Leopold (1765–90) was principally the Church, at the same time it must be recognised that the policies adopted had an immediate effect on noble hegemony. For example, in 1739 the regents dismissed all the consuls of the city's major guilds, for centuries the preserve of the nobility, and substituted people designated by the government who were to carry out the new economic and fiscal policies. In this way a political channel was opened up to the rich urban bourgeoisie which was to give it more weight in Tuscan society. In the following years some of the red tape which impeded freedom of trade was abolished and the customs controls at the port of Leghorn were taken out of the hands of the Florentine tribunals.

The whole fiscal system, too, was put under the charge of a single body and a grand-ducal commission was created with the task of settling any disputes in this area. Along with these reforms the tax demands of the new regime, heavier than before, prompted a restructuring of the methods of assessing and collecting of taxes which overturned ancient privileges. The intention of the rulers was not so much to weaken the noble classes as to control them and bring them under government management. This explains both the law of 1747 which regulated the institution of *fidecommesso*, placing precise limits on its duration and application, and the law of 1750 which defined the legal status of the nobility. To qualify for it, noble families had to prove their aristocratic origins – such as citizenship, enjoyment of particular political rights – thereby greatly limiting membership; 268 families, some 2 per cent of the total population of Florence, were able to prove their ancient patrician ancestry. These achievements of the Regency's reformism paved the way for the policies to be advanced by the future Grand Duke Leopold.

In the Papal States feudalism was generally more like that of northern Italy. The elements which combined to determine the particular type of feudalism in, above all, Umbria and Lazio were two: the priority of administrative and patrimonial powers over rights of jurisdiction, and the political and military subordination of the barons to the papacy.[14] In other areas, on the other hand, an almost unlimited feudalism appeared. Active groups of the merchant class were present in the cities, connected with the more advanced agriculture of the Po Valley and close to the trade routes of northern Italy such as Bologna, Ferrara and the towns of the Ravennate. Thus in areas of greater economic progress, groups of big capitalists were active, showing a preference to invest not as private operators but from within enterprises of a public nature which dealt in the contracting out of tax collection (*appalti*) in the provinces and in Rome. In the eighteenth century the number of foreign citizens involved in these banking and commercial activities diminished and was replaced by subjects of the pope. For this merchant class it was very hard to obtain recognition of their achievements without joining the ranks of the nobility and abandoning trade, which was what was required by the dominant aristocratic order in the towns of the Papal States, even in those where, as in Bologna, there was a merchant and manufacturing tradition which continued despite the crisis in these areas in the second half of the eighteenth century. In Bologna, the weakness of the town's economy affected the landed wealth of the aristocratic groups who had since the fifteenth century controlled the institutions of local government in a stable balance with the powers of the papacy, but alternatives to aristocratic leadership did not appear before the nineteenth century. Bologna too was an example of how the patrician oligarchies were able to preserve the political institutions formed two centuries before and maintain their position of strength essentially intact during the whole of the eighteenth century. From the work of B. G. Zenobi, the same conclusions can be arrived at for the lands of the papal Marches, that is the province of Ancona.

In the Papal States a career in the Church was the usual way to social advancement. In the administrative and legal apparatus of the capital and the provinces there were inevitably churchmen of various ranks who came from noble families or who had ambitions to become noble. This link between nobility and Church lessened the importance of other routes which could have led to social promotion, such as law, medicine or the army, and allowed little room for the growth of more modern groups of the bourgeoisie of officials and financiers.

An autonomous ruling class of merchant origin and later ennobled, typical of the city-states, which managed with great success until the end of the eighteenth century to defend its political privileges against the interference of princes, was entirely lacking in Piedmontese society.[15] The State of Savoy, by contrast, had an unusual combination of ducal absolutism and feudal absolutism. Institutionally resembling very closely the French monarchy, the Savoyard state during the seventeenth century perfected the instruments by which it extended its control over society. The most immediate method for the bourgeoisie to conquer political pre-eminence alongside an ancient nobility that was increasingly being forced to accept the requirements and institutional conditions of the State in order to retain, in part, its position, was through the purchase of government offices. In this way, as well as trading, banking and manufacture which in Piedmont were developing with relative speed and were generally run by a class of wealthy local notables, taxfarming or judicial and administrative posts created a class of bureaucrats consisting of rich bourgeois and nobles trained in the law who owed their fortunes to the State and its expansion.

The nobility was confined to its feudal estates though it was not without influence. Though still clinging to its chivalrous traditions, in order to join in the government of the State it had to some extent to bow to the demands of the Savoyard dukes and coexist with the bourgeoisie of officials. The land occupied by fiefs, added to that owned by the Church, covered only 18.03

per cent of the entire country, according to Luigi Einaudi's estimate for the beginning of the eighteenth century. The income received from this was not more than 24 per cent of the total income from land for the whole of Piedmont. Thus it was a social force that was not supported by large feudal patrimonies or important political privileges, though it should be remembered that the Piedmontese nobility possessed great wealth from non-feudal sources. A decisive confirmation of this peculiarity of the State of Savoy can be had by comparing the composition of the town council (*consiglio comunale*) of Turin with that of the other towns we have looked at. It will be remembered that in Milan, Venice and Naples, to take three historically very different developments, political offices were entirely or almost entirely in the hands of the aristocratic class. In Turin, by contrast, from the second half of the sixteenth century the town council was divided exactly between noble councillors and bourgeois councillors, with two elected mayors, one for each group. Thus at the top level of administration in the capital could be found not only lawyers, engineers and bankers, but also representatives of the business or professional bourgeoisie, such as doctors, pharmacists, merchants and traders, who were less wealthy and had no academic titles.

At the beginning of the eighteenth century the social traits of Piedmont seemed already to be clearly defined. The upper nobility had been expelled from the chief government posts and from the top levels of administration, while its place had been taken by a class of bourgeois functionaries of merchant and financial origin. The dukes of Savoy kept the nobility at the court while at the same time devaluing the social worth of the feudal title. In fact, as in France, the acquisition of a fief did not always alter the social standing of the acquirer who was not thereby ennobled. On the other hand, there was an increase in titles given for political merit to those men belonging to families which had won the favour of the duke through their exercise of state office or who had through their own efforts gained power and esteem. Under Victor Amadeus II, the enterprising Duke of Savoy who became king in 1713, the most decisive effort made by an Italian state before the reforms of the 1780s was carried out to limit the power of the old nobility and to uphold instead the government of the bureaucracy. The nobles were deprived of the fiefs to which they could not claim legitimate ownership and tax exemptions were reduced. Fiefs acquired in this way by the State were re-sold to those who had amassed their fortunes under the wing of the administration and from the economic policy of the State. The new Code of 1729, which reorganised legal matters and gave secure legislative guidelines to judges and lawyers, also aimed to sanction the restrictions on feudal justice. The important reforms of Victor Amadeus II which revived and expanded a political tradition, contributed to make the Piedmontese State a military and bureaucratic organism which was not only an efficient and reliable instrument for the policies of the Savoyard kings in the following decade, but also an organism which did not shackle society in rigid anachronistic orders. It allowed, along with a relative mobility and importance for the bourgeoisie, a remarkable convergence of society and institutions, which functioned without conflict throughout the eighteenth century and which constituted the strength, but also the limitations of the history of this State.

NOTES AND REFERENCES

For an accurate description of the nobility in Europe and in Italy in the eighteenth century see Capra, C. (1978) 'Nobili, notabili, élites: dal "modello" francese al caso italiano', in *Quaderni storici*, 37, pp. 12–47. Another useful work on the relationship between class and institutions is Mozzarelli, C. (1976) 'Stato, patriziato e organizzazione della società nell'Italia moderna', in *Annali dell'Istituto storico italo-germanico in Trento*, II, pp. 421–512; See also the proceedings of the seminar held in Trent 9–10 December 1977 published under the title *Patriziati e aristocrazie nobiliari*, eds Mozzarelli, C. and Schiera, P. (1978). Libera Università degli studi, Trent.

1. Donati, C. (1978) 'Scipione Maffei e la Scienza chiamata cavalleresca. Saggio sull'ideologia nobilitare all'inizio del Settecento', in *Rivista storica italiana*, I, pp. 35–71.
2. Ibid., p. 40.
3. On the nobility of the State of Milan see: Roberts, J. R. (1953) 'Lombardy', in Goodwin, A. (ed.) *The European Nobility in the 18th century*. A. C. Black, London; Arese, F. (1975) 'Patrizi, nobili e ricchi borghesi del dipartimento di Olona secondo il fisco della I Repubblica Cisalpina', in *Archivio storico lombardo*, pp. 95–161; Pino, F. (1979) 'Patriziato e decurionato a Milano nel secolo XVIII', in *Società e storia* 5, pp. 339–78.
4. Sella, D. (1979) *Crisis and Continuity: the economics of Spanish Lombardy in the seventeenth century*. Harvard University Press, Cambridge (Mass.); London.
5. Petronio, U. (1972) *Il Senato di Milano. Istituzioni giuridiche ed esercizio del potere nel ducato di Milano da Carlo I a Giuseppe II*. Giuffré, Milan.
6. Villani, P. (1968) *Feudalità, riforme, capitalismo agrario*. Laterza, Bari; Massafra, A. (1972) 'Giurisdizionalismo feudale e rendita fondiaria nel Settecento napoletano: un contributo alla ricerca', in *Quaderni storici* 19, pp. 187–252; *Problemi di storia delle campagne meridionali in età moderna e contemporanea*, ed. Massafra, A. (1981). Dedalo, Bari.
7. Petraccone, C. (1974) *Napoli dal Cinquecento all'Ottocento. Problemi di storia demografica e sociale*. Guida, Naples.
8. Labrot, G. (1980) *Baroni in città; residenza e comportamenti dell'aristocrazia napoletana, 1503–1734*. Società editrice napoletana, Naples.
9. Ajello, R. (1976) *Arcana juris. Diritto e politica nel Settecento italiano*. Jovene, Naples.
10. On the Venetian nobility see: Berengo, M, (1975) 'Patriziato e nobiltà: il caso veronese', in *Rivista storica italiana* III, pp. 493–517; Beltrami, D. (1961) *La penetrazione economica dei veneziani in Terraferma. Forze di lavoro e proprietà fondiaria nelle campagne venete dei secoli XVII e XVIII*. Istituto per la collaborazione culturale, Venice – Rome; Davis, J. C. (1962) *The Decline of the Venetian Nobility as a Ruling Class*. J. Hopkins, Baltimore.
11. Borelli, G. (1974) *Un patriziato della terraferma veneta tra XVII e XVIII secolo*. Giuffré, Milan.
12. On the nobility of the Republic of Genoa see: Felloni, G. (1971) *Gli investimenti*

finanziari genovesi in Europa tra il '600 e la Restaurazione. Giuffré, Milan; Grendi, E. (1974) 'Capitazioni e nobiltà genovese in età moderna', in *Quaderni storici* 26, pp. 403–44.

13. On the Tuscan nobility see: Litchfield, R. B. (1969) 'Les investissements commerciaux des patriciens florentins au XVIIIe siècle', in *Annales E. S. C.* 3, pp. 685–721; Marrara D. (1976) *Riseduti e nobiltà. Profilo storico e istituzionale di un'oligarchia toscana nei secoli XVI–XVIII*. Pacini, Pisa; Baker, G. R. F.(1972) 'Nobiltà in declino: il caso di Siena sotto i Medici e gli Asburgo-Lorena', in *Rivista storica italiana*, III, pp. 584–616.

14. For the Papal States see: Zenobi, B. G. (1979) *Dai governi larghi all'assetto patriziale. Istituzione e organizzazione del potere nelle città minori della Marca dei secoli XVI–XVIII*. Argalia, Urbino; Giacomelli, A. (1980) 'La dinamica della nobiltà bolognese nel XVIII secolo', in *Famiglie senatorie e istituzioni cittadine a Bologna nel Settecento*. Istituto per la storia di Bologna, Bologna, pp. 55–112; Pescosolido, G. (1979) *Terra e nobiltà. I Borghese*. Jouvence, Rome.

15. On the Piedmontese nobility see: Woolf, S. J. (1963) 'Studi sulla nobiltà piemontese nell'epoca dell'assolutismo', in *Memorie dell'Accademia delle Scienze di Torino*, a. IV, n. 5. Accademia delle Scienze, Turin; Stumpo, E. (1979) *Finanze e stato moderno nel Piemonte del '600*. Istituto storico italiano per l'età moderna e contemporanea.

Political ideas and pressure for reform in the first half of the eighteenth century (Giuseppe Ricuperati)

CHAPTER SIX

The renewal of the dialogue between Italy and Europe: intellectuals and cultural institutions from the end of the seventeenth century to the first decades of the eighteenth century

It is possible to see, even in the years when baroque conceptions seemed to predominate, the signs of the new cultural mood which was to come to the fore in the next century. In Rome, in 1668, was published the first *Giornale de' Letterati*, which was to last for more than a decade and represented the first attempt at a learned journal aimed at Italian intellectuals. The models were clear: on one hand the French *Journal des Sçavants*, which appeared in 1665, and on the other the *Philosophical Transactions*, scientific mouthpiece of the Royal Society. The first learned Italian journal was published in Rome with the backing of men of the Curia. Notwithstanding the crisis which had become apparent particularly after the papacy of Urban VIII, Rome was still an important cultural centre with a considerable tradition of international relations and a cosmopolitan outlook which had not diminished even during the decades of the most rigid application of the ideas of the Counter-Reformation. In the mid-seventeenth century a group of the intellectuals of the Curia, including those who had gravitated towards the scholarly institutions, universities and colleges, began to see the necessity of reviving contacts with European culture rather than limiting themselves to a defensive attitude. From this desire was born the *Giornale de' Letterati*, brought about by men like Francesco Nazari, professor at the *Sapienza*, Monsignor Giusto Ciampini and various professors of the *Collegio Romano*.

The aim was to introduce to men of letters Italian and foreign books and to publish scientific experiments and cultural curiosities. The enterprise had a noteworthy success, even if not without internal dissension which came to the surface in 1675 when two editions were published, one edited by Nazari and the other by Ciampini. In this first Italian journalistic experiment, the compilers, in forging a new Italian participation in the *res publica* of letters, drew on several different elements. First of all there was the Galileian tradition as it had been revived in Rome in the *Accademia dei Lincei* and as it had manifested itself in Florence in the *Accademia del Cimento*; secondly, the search for a link with other intellectual experiments, such as that of the *Accademia degli Investiganti* in Naples; finally, the desire to offer Italian culture a forum for the discussion of method and research similar to those of the Maurists in France. The cultural plans of the *Giornale de' Letterati* were not without results, having a significant influence in Rome as can be seen from the progressive founding of new academies, relating to different subjects and disciplines, in all of which Ciampini was involved. One has only to think of the *Accademia del Concili*, which attempted to update ecclesiastical history through an interdisciplinary approach or the *Accademia dei Fisiocritici* which tried to introduce into Roman circles the new scientific developments sketched out in Florence during the brief period of the *Accademia del Cimento*.

After some years of silence, a new attempt at journalism was made in Parma and then in Modena at the end of the 1680s, in response to the urgings of Jean Mabillon who was completing his *Iter italicum*. After meeting him Benedetto Bacchini and Gaudenzio Roberti, librarian to the Duke of Parma, had lamented the absence of such a useful aid to Italian culture and felt encouraged to follow in the footsteps of the Roman periodical. Bacchini, a Benedictine of the Maurist school and soon to become one of theleaders of Italian religious culture, threw himself enthusiastically into the enterprise, counting on the help of Roberti who, as librarian of the Farnese family, was able to get hold of the materials and books needed for the journal. Meanwhile the European models had multiplied. Alongside the *Journal des Sçavants* had appeared both the Leipzig *Acta eruditorum* and Pierre Bayle's *Nouvelles de la république des lettres*. Bacchini, while keeping these examples in mind, also went back to the ideological values which had inspired Ciampini before him, that is, Galileism and Maurism. The difference was above all one of attitude to the social institutions, in the sense that the political reference point of the Parma periodical was no longer the Roman Curia with its tensions and problems, but the world of the small Italian courts – the Farnese court in Parma in whose circles the first volumes of the *Giornale de' Letterati* were published and the Este court in Modena where Bacchini moved and resumed the interrupted work. The concept of culture too, apparent from the first pages, is more complex. The writer claims the right to know and judge the world of books, following up what had been suggested by Bayle's model of criticism. Bacchini led a cultural campaign that was less general but more open-minded than that of Ciampini. In a particularly important piece of criticism, on Mabillon's *De studiis monasticis*, Bacchini outlined the rights and duties of an ecclesiastical intellectual, passionately defending the revival of religious culture and its potentiality for becoming the starting-point for a renewal of civil culture itself.

As well as through his links with the library in Parma which was to supply material on foreign books, Bacchini could count on the outstanding collaboration of an intellectual like Antonio Magliabechi. This great scholar and Florentine bibliophile, with his national and international connections, was the main, if not the only, collaborator with the tireless Benedictine. While

Bacchini was in Modena he attempted an interesting experiment in revitalising the journal, by drawing up an editorial board where the most illustrious names of the academic and university world of Modena appeared, from the doctor Benedetto Ramazzini, future author of *De morbis artificum*, an early example of the study of industrial medicine, to the geographer Jacopo Cantelli. On the board, along with the ecclesiastics, were laymen, although only a minority, and more specifically doctors of medicine and jurisprudence – in other words, the two professional cultures not absorbed by the Church. The experiment came to an end shortly before the end of the century. The discouraged Bacchini had to abandon the enterprise since foreign books were not arriving in sufficient numbers. But for a little over ten years (1686–97) his journal had been an essential reference point for Italian culture. For a moment Modena had stood at the centre of a very complex relationship between Florence and Magliabechi, Bologna and the Marsili circle, and Padua, the university town where soon Antonio Vallisnieri was to emerge as an important figure in scientific culture and journalism.

At the same time, in the south of the country, a great cultural movement was developing which was very different from that in Rome. Southern culture appeared chiefly in secular surroundings and had its roots in Renaissance naturalism, in that philosophy formulated by the great intellectuals such as Telesio, Bruno, Campanella and Giambattista della Porta, and which represented one of the cultural traditions least easily controlled by Catholicism. The *Accademia degli Investiganti*, founded in Naples in the second half of the seventeenth century, had had the courage to compare this tradition with Galileism and with scientific learning and European philosophy. The choice of name was in itself significant: the *investiganti* (investigators), from the very first, declared that the area of greatest interest was the natural sciences. The members of the academy, doctors and jurists, associated themselves with that revival of civil life and of the State which had characterised the second half of the century.[1] The most important figure was probably Tommaso Cornelio, author of the *Progymnasmata physica*, a work in which the southern tradition was reinterpreted in the light of Cartesianism, stressing its mechanistic aspects. A solution that was nearer the experimental and Baconian traditions came from another great Neapolitan physician, Leonardo di Capua, author of the famous *Parere sull'incertezza della medicina* of 1681. The work was to become famous for the radical way in which it swept away the dominant scientific traditions, revealing them as fallacious and uncertain, and proposing a reworking of the discipline, founded rather on observation and the collection of empirical facts.

Galileo, Bacon, Descartes, Gassendi and even Spinoza became familiar in the intellectual world of Naples, which was becoming increasingly aware of its own originality. A good indication of this was the *Biblioteca napoletana* by Nicola Toppi, a first attempt at a portrait of these intellectuals.[2] This work, examined and discussed by Antonio Magliabechi, was the beginning of a relationship between the great Florentine bibliophile and the intellectual world of the South, where the most important figure emerging was that of

Giuseppe Valletta.[3] A merchant and jurist, Valletta became famous mainly for his wonderful library which was to introduce Dutch philology of the sixteenth and seventeenth centuries to men like Vico and Doria. Few intellectuals at the end of the seventeenth century were so consciously part of a *res publica* of letters which knew no bounds either of state or of religion. His library was conceived as an institution of this *res publica* and was open not only to local scholars but to foreign visitors like the learned Frenchman Jean Mabillon and Gilbert Burnet, the Anglican bishop who came to Naples in the last decades of the century. The intellectual relations which Valletta kept up through books and letters reached all the most lively centres of European culture of the time: the England of the Royal Society, the Holland of De Witt and Jean Leclerc, the Geneva of tolerant Calvinism, the Germany of the great Leipzig scholars and the France of the academies and Maurist learning. Valletta's library, along with the Italian *Giornale de' Letterati* (in the Rome, Parma and Modena editions), included as well Mencken's *Acta eruditorum*, the *Journal des Sçavants*, the *Nouvelles de la République des lettres* and the Dutch *Bibliothèques*. This decision to be for Naples something similar to Magliabechi in Florence, that is, an active intermediary in that *res publica* which was being established among the scholars of Europe, was qualitatively changed at the end of the 1680s. Then the ideas of the *Investiganti* were attacked by the famous trial known as the trial of the 'atheists', which was to have widespread repercussions not only in public opinion but also in the consciousness of the times from Vico onwards.

A pettifogging Neapolitan lawyer had accused Basilio Giannelli and Giacinto de' Cristoforo, two young Neapolitan intellectuals, of propagating libertine ideas, that is, of maintaining that Jesus was nothing but an ambitious political impostor, of denying the literal reading of the Holy Scriptures, of denying the truth of miracles and the existence of hell, heaven and purgatory. Clearly the attack on the two young men was aimed higher, in so far as the whole of the *Accademia degil Investiganti* was involved in the accusation of atheism. Valletta intervened with his *Lettera in difesa della moderna filosofia e dei coltivatori di essa*,[4] written between 1691 and 1697. This letter should be seen in the context of a fierce political struggle between Church and State. The local clergy and the Roman Curia tried to use the trial to justify the intervention and organisation of the Inquisition in Naples. This was answered both by the municipality and its institutions and by the representatives of the *ceto civile* and the *ministero togato*, among whom were Amato Danio and Serafino Biscardi. The lawyers' arguments dealt more than anything else with the question of the Holy Office and they aimed to exculpate the city from any accusations which might give credibility to the terrible and sinister ecclesiastical tribunal.

Valletta too had intervened with his essay, *Intorno al procedimento ordinario e canonico nelle cause che si trattano nel tribunale del S. Ufficio nella città e nel regno di Napoli*. But he felt the need to give a broader defence of modern culture. The *Lettera* deals with some of the essential points which were to be revived and developed by the next generation: modern philosophy does not contradict the Christian religion; the Aristotelianism which opposed modern philosophy stirs up heresy; philosophy and faith should be kept separate; the freedom to philosophise is now a victory of learned and Christian Europe; modern philosophy offers an opportunity for dialogue and tolerance which in the name of Italy's ancient traditions must not be ignored. This was to be confirmed by the 1697–1704 version, known as *Istoria filosofica*, which was to lead directly to the heart of the eighteenth century.

The trial of the 'atheists' was not without consequences for the 'moderns'. The need to find a solid centre for discussion and defence made them incline to the possibility of organising an academy protected by political power – a possibility which was offered to them by the viceroy, Luis de la Cerda, duke of Medinaceli, who aimed at strengthening an intellectual and social consensus, which would allow him not only to defend the rights of the southern State, but also to deal with the inevitable uncertainty which would ensue on the death of the sovereign, Charles II of Spain. La Cerda's administration had already shown a definite antifeudal and anti-curial attitude, and the opposition to the Holy Office had to some degree united the urban nobility, the *ceto civile* and the *ministero togato*. One of the latter, Nicolò Caravita, already singled out as one of the leaders of the 'atheists' and instigators of the attack on Rome, was ready to grasp the opportunity and organise the academy which took the name of Medinaceli.[5]

There has been much discussion of the cultural and ideological content of this academy which was a complex organisation which found a unifying point in the fact that in it could be seen all those elements of the State and civil society which had lined up with the 'moderns' to resist the desire of the Roman Curia to impose the Holy Office. There is no doubt that the viceroy expected the academics to back up the government and to take an anti-French stand. There are many references to this political requirement in the proceedings of the academy. But on the cultural scene an important new element emerged: history became a central topic of discussion. This academy, born of the meeting of intellectuals and a power that felt insecure, not only investigated in depth the origins of empires, but took as a basic subject for discussion Roman history, and Imperial history in particular, almost as if to study from that model, chosen as an *exemplum*, the stages of decadence and the possible remedies.

From the scientific and epistemological point of view, it is possible to see in these events the poverty of the investigative tradition and their relative backwardness in relation to the new European models (the quotation from Newton in Agostino Ariani's lecture of 1703 is not enough to show a knowledge of the former's work). Nevertheless, the academy was significant because questions were raised which were to be important in the following decades. Foremost of these were the role of the State, its power and the right which justifies that power. Directly, or concealed under the transparent metaphor of Roman history, we also find numerous examinations of specific public offices such as the general of the army, the commander of the fortresses and the magistratures. The ordering of society was investigated and questioned – what is the nobility? What are its origins? What is its relationship to the State, to society? What are the origins of the fief? Even though contained within the ivory tower of the academy where everything tended to become rhetorically homogeneous, more than once external tensions broke in, sometimes quite dramatically. These tensions were linked to the political crisis which the imminent dissolution of the Spanish Empire made more acute, raising questions and debate on the origin of power, the role of the absolute State and the position of the aristocracy and the bureaucracy within the State. These were all matters which revealed emerging fears and disagreements in the period of transition from a Spanish regime to a new order as yet undefined.

Between the end of the seventeenth and the early eighteenth century the intellectuals did not insist on the need for national unification. Not only was it an unrealistic political aim, but there was an ever-clearer realisation of the loss of position and prestige of Italian culture compared with the rest of Europe. It was becoming obvious that now the centres of intellectual creativity were Paris, London, Amsterdam and The Hague. These cities were very different from one another: some were in powerful national and mercantile states, like Louis XIV's France, able to encourage, through magnificent academies, a cultural policy of great breadth; others had the strength of a civil society that was free and able to express itself culturally, as in England and Holland. In each case what emerged was a realisation of the inferiority of Italian intellectual life, even starting from the view that modern culture was no more than a revival of ancient Italic wisdom. This was a myth fraught with problems, capable of developing retrogressively, causing thinkers to bury themselves in the past seeking models for the modern age in the ancient world. But it had a positive function too, for it stimulated concrete proposals from the Italian intellectuals which might to some extent remedy the ills that were all too easy to see. It is in this area that once again in Rome a proposal was put forward for an organisation of intellectuals that in a limited way pointed out a need and furnished an answer. This was the *Arcadia*, an academy that was to cover the whole of Italy by means of its *colonie* and that can be seen almost as a definition of the period of transition from the Counter-Reformation to the Enlightenment.[6] One of the most recent and convincing studies of the *Arcadia* sees it rather as the instrument by which the Roman Curia was able to trap and then disarm the rationalist trends and innovations of Italian culture at the end of the seventeenth century.

This is a complicated argument which is worth examining in detail. The first fact to emerge is that the *Arcadia*, founded in 1690 under the protection of Christina of Sweden, was not at first any different from the hundreds of other academies which had sprung up in the mid-seventeenth century. What, if anything, did single it out was the fact that, having been formed in Rome, it was able on the one hand to benefit from the cultural flowering of Ciampini's time, and on the other it was able to set up links with the important and various experiments in cultural renewal in the different regions, particularly in the South and Tuscany. With the aim of defining an anti-baroque literary culture, it was now possible for many differing trends to come together, as can be seen from the fact that in the founding group of the *Arcadia* are such various figures as Ciampini, with his history as editor of the *Giornale de' Letterati* and organiser of ecclesiastical and scientific academies, or Ludovico Sergardi and Gian Maria Crescimbeni, aware of the need for the process of renewal to be firmly controlled by the Curia, or Gian Vincenzo Gravina.

The latter was then a young intellectual who had come to Rome to represent the interests of the Archbishop of Naples, Francesco Pignatelli, having had a remarkable education through the teaching of Gregorio Caloprese. He had then been in contact with the great cultural movement of the South, particularly during the years of the trial of the 'atheists'. He was drawn into this culture, as can be seen from his early anti-Jesuit work, the *Hydra mystica*, which reflects many aspects of the Neapolitan school. From the earliest formation of his thought, there emerged from Gravina's work a strong anti-institutional and anti-hierarchical message from within the Catholic world. The lay intellectual had the duty to combat the ills of the Church and to demand reform which was characterised by a rejection of all the laxistic and probabilistic elements introduced by Jesuits. But it meant too identifying in the baroque (seen right from the start as a new Middle Ages, a return to barbarism) a *Jesuiten-Stil* to be fought. Seeing links between the Jesuits' cultural hegemony and the devotional and intellectual models they offered, Gravina undertook to set up a civil and cognitive concept of poetry and literature to counter the baroque style of rhetoric: poetry is a form of knowledge and must regain all those elements which in the past had made of it a sort of natural and poetic theology.

During the fruitful years of his private and university teaching, Gravina attempted to transform the models of literary culture, to make literature into a science. Bringing reason into poetry meant necessarily clashing with not only morality but also with the Jesuits' educational establishments, since it had the strength to present a rival theory of culture. But it was not enough. The intellectual that Gravina had in mind was not so much, or only, a *letterato* as a jurist, who could bring the light of reason to the drawing up, interpretation and rational keeping of the laws. Gravina was here too starting from his experience of the ideology of the *res publica* of the Neapolitan jurists, but taking from it particularly the most reformist and positive implications. He saw in the jurist not only the ideal legislator of ancient times and the founder of civil society but also the only rational curb on the abuse of absolute power and the interpreter of a need for democracy and liberty which underlay the foundation of states. This particularly republican and constitutionalist element was to lead him to exalt the idea of the *lex regia* as a founding agreement, and to some extent still present in every legitimisation of the sovereign power. Later this was to lead him to choose as the intellectual and moral hero of one of his tragedies, *Papiniano*, the jurist who fell victim to Caracalla. This element must have been present in Gravina's thought right from the early years of his time in Rome, since Sergardi, now his enemy, in an attempt to unmask his subversive role in the *Arcadia*, sarcastically, but deliberately, called him Philodemus.

The success of the *Arcadia* was immediate: 1,163 members, half of them laymen, between 1690 and 1710, and by 1728 the number had risen to 2,619. From the first recruitment (in the Papal States, Kingdom of Naples and Grand Duchy of Tuscany) there was soon a network over the whole country, even if the group of intellectuals in the Papal States was always to be the largest (more than 35 per cent). Then came the Mezzogiorno and Sicily (almost 17 per cent), followed by Tuscany (over 16 per cent) and the Republic of Genoa (5.8 per cent). Numbers were smaller in regions like the State of Savoy (1.8 per cent), the Duchy of Parma (2.3 per cent), the Duchy of Milan (3.7 per cent) and the Duchy of Modena (4 per cent). But in 1711 Gravina left the *Arcadia*, causing a great stir, in an attempt to breathe life into a new academic experiment. It was the logical conclusion of a process of detaching himself which had begun earlier, after a period of hopes and of success in introducing into the *Arcadia* the great ideological energy of his contributions. These can be seen in the *Egloghe* and particularly the *Discorso fra Faburno e Alcone sopra le egloghe di Bione*. The fight against the baroque was not a purely formal matter, but one with ethical, philosophical and civil aspects. In practice, by rejecting the baroque and proposing his classicism in its place, Gravina was not only reattaching himself to Renaissance naturalism, but was also disputing the *Crusca's* rigid rules for the Italian language. The great authors were not only Hesiod, Homer and Virgil or, in the fourteenth century, Dante, Petrarch and Boccaccio, but also the intellectuals of the Renaissance.

The first germ of what had been called Gravina's aesthetic appeared in the *Discorso sopra le favole antiche* of 1696 where the author confirmed not only his interest in Hesiod and Homer, but also expanded on the meaning of his concept of the science of poetry by specifying that verisimilitude was the aim of the poet. The following years, particularly after 1699, when Gravina was appointed to the chair of civil law, were dedicated to teaching, to the elaboration of an ambitious plan for the reform of the curriculum and to the writing up of his great work on civil law. The publication of the *Origines iuris civilis* and the *Ragion poetica* in 1708 was to make him, in Europe as well as Italy, one of the most important figures of Italian culture. Until 1708 Gravina devoted himself to law: the *Orationes* were the link between his literary and legal activities and his central role in the revival of the university in Rome, which was to have such importance for Italian culture in the early eighteenth century, in that it directly inspired the university reforms in Piedmont. Gravina was unable to participate directly in these reforms because he died suddenly just as he was to leave Rome to take up the post of professor of canon law in Turin, but some of his most promising pupils were involved. The *Origines iuris civilis* shows very clearly the close connection between classicism and the concept of law, between the *ius sapientioris*, for example, and the function of the theological poets, from Homer, who represents the age of myth, to Lucretius. And the connection with Vico in this case clearly arises not only from their common background of southern culture (from Gregorio Messere, for example) but above all from the knowledge of several fundamental European texts (John Marsham and Daniel Huet) which they have in common.

In the *Ragion poetica* the elements already glimpsed in his *Discorso* on Guidi's *Endimione* become more developed, overcoming a certain classicising coldness which, for example, had prevented him until then from understanding Dante. Now, poetic reason becomes the science of poetry to the extent that the latter had a cognitive and pedagogical function. Taking his cue from jurisprudence, Gravina maintains that poetry is a science of things human and divine; the fight against the baroque is only one moment in his poetical theory, as he expresses his admiration for Homer, Hesiod and Lucretius and, among the vernacular authors, for Dante. The world of poets in Gravina's analysis is no longer something abstract, but is peopled with problems, political debates and history. Homer and Dante depicted the dramas of their own times. It is not liberty, but its misuse which is denounced by the poets who thus assume the role of prophets as well as interpreters of their own age. Gravina had not been converted to Machiavellism or absolutism, for in the same work he discusses the importance of popular judgement in terms which are not only aesthetic but also clearly political and which can only be understood by relating them to the general discussion of this section of the book. Between the people and the sovereign, just as in law there is the jurist, so in the moral and educative field there is the poet:

The poet should have that regard for people that the prince has and while the prince should not place all his faith in the affection and inclination of the people, for it changes with the wind, yet he should not hope to reign securely without it . . . thus the poet should not hope to sit comfortably on the throne of glory neither only with the help of the people, nor without the people . . .[7]

Consistent with the ideas of the Enlightenment, Gravina maintains that the functions of the poet, of the intellectual and of the jurist are those of freeing from the darkness of the passions and the body that divine spark which is in everyone, but which in the common man seems dim and dulled by the weight of the body. Thus poetry – and in this sense it recovers its pedagogical dimension – is an instrument of policy for the intellectual, a means of spreading culture and reason, a parallel to the law of the *sapientes*.

With a vision of this sort, it is easy to see why Gravina paid much theoretical and practical attention to tragedy, which of all the literary forms was the one ideologically best fitted to the communication of ideas to a people (*popolo*) which is no longer a confused common herd (*volgo*) waiting for orders from a sovereign, but which is not yet a 'civil society' capable of governing itself. Gravina on one side attacks regal absolutism and on the other tries to substitute for a rigid and unquestioned authority the force of law and the persuasive ability of its interpreters. This, among other things, explains why he was interested in tragedy not only from the critical but also from the creative point of view, his central theme becoming that of the opposition to tyranny. Gravina's five tragedies – *Palamede, Appio Claudio, Servio Tullio, Virginia, Seiano* – were published in 1712 after he had published both the

Ragion poetica and the *Origines*. It is clear, both from the themes dealt with and the hasty writing, that they are works intended to demonstrate political themes which had previously been treated in a more general way. The tragedies represent a less obviously optimistic side to Gravina's thought; the theoretical works describe how things should be, while the tragedies show the real world with its contradictions and misfortunes. But one should also bear in mind the time when they were written, in the last phase of the War of the Spanish Succession, in a climate of uncertainty and general instability with the inconclusive negotiations and the political as well as the general weariness of the opponents.

Gravina's work found an immediate European success in Protestant countries and especially in Holland. Johann Burckard Mencken, on publishing the first revised edition of the *Origines* in 1708, stated that from as far back as 1696 he had recognised the scholar's great talent from his *Opuscola* and he referred to his own review of the Neapolitan edition of the first volume of the *Opuscola*. Among the foreign intellectuals with whom Gravina was in touch, Baron Heinrich von Huyssen (1666–1739), memorable for his unusual personality, was his link with Mencken. Although a Calvinist, von Huyssen was not particularly interested in religious matters, drawing his friends both from the Lutheran Pietists of Halle and the enlightened Catholics of Rome. A tireless traveller, he had been tutor to the son of an influential statesman in Brandenburg, Danckelmann. In about 1703 he went to Moscow as tutor to the son of Peter the Great and as representative of European culture, taking part in the revival of the Moscow Academy. Von Huyssen was an admirer of Samuel Pufendorf and a pupil of his brother and of Thomasius. He had a deep admiration and affection for Gravina, whose theories he had introduced into Russia. Invited to Vienna in 1705 as a representative of the tsar, he had used his relationship with Gravina to try to win over the papacy to Russia's interests. In 1706, Gravina sent him the *Acta concistorialia*, also promising him, as well as the *Origines*, the seven *Orationes*. It should be remembered that the first of these, *Oratio pro romanis legibus ad Magnum Moscorum Regem*, had been written in 1697, at a time when Peter the Great was visiting Europe. (He was to have come to Rome, but was prevented from doing so by the uprising in Russia.) It fitted in with Innocent XII's policy of *rapprochement* with Russia as a defence against the Turks.

The new edition of the *Opuscola* (Traiecti ad Rhenum, 1713) bears witness once again to Gravina's rapid European fame. The editor was Giambattista Ancioni, who was among other things a member of that *Accademia dei Quirini* that was born of the split with the *Arcadia*. He was probably a friend of Gravina's who had emigrated to Vienna as court poet. Another sign of Gravina's fame in Europe is the numerous reviews of his works in the most important learned journals of Europe. Gravina represents a revival of interest in Italian culture. His fame in Germany and especially Leipzig, with the recommendation of Mencken who had compared him to Cicero, was reconfirmed by the edition of his juridical works of 1737 at Leipzig, reprinted at Venice in 1739 by Francesco Pitteri. The editor had been Gottfried Mascov, brother of the famous historian and defender of the rights of the Holy Roman Empire. In a profile of Gravina which also gives details of some of his curious physical features ('corpore fuit procero, sed macer, oculis utens obliquis et distortis'), Mascov emphasises his anti-scholastic, anti-Aristotelian, Telesian and finally Cartesian background and his sympathy for the ideas of Hobbes.

While this edition was to become a classic among juridical works, in Turin the edition of the unpublished *Istituzioni canoniche* was being prepared – through the mediation of Metastasio in Vienna.[8] The choice of Turin was deliberate, the result of a cultural policy of which, if anything, this edition, without introduction and with the objectivity of a manual, was the latest offering. In fact not only was Gravina to have taught in the chair of law in Turin, if death had not overtaken him before he set out, but the reforms themselves in the university in Piedmont had been in a sense carried out under the banner of his ideas. At almost the same time, in Naples, Carlo Antonio Sergio, lawyer and pupil of Gennaro Maiello, Nicola Capasso and Alessio Mazzocchi, friend of Giambattista Vico and Giuseppe Aurelio Di Gennaro, brought out his *Raccolta di opuscoli* and then an edition of the *Opere italiane* (1757) which was to be, for literature, what the Mascov edition was for the law. Exactly a year later, in Rome, Giovanni Andrea Serrao's *De vita et scriptis Jani Vincentii Gravinae commentarius* appeared. This accurate and precise biography, which describes perfectly Gravina's complex and in some ways ambiguous personality, however, differs from all the works so far mentioned. While in Mascov or Sergio's work we have the culture of the early eighteenth century, the judgement of contemporaries on one of the major authors of their time, the youthful work by Serrao[9] is not merely a last tribute from the Roman world of Bottari and Passionei to the Calabrese rigorist, but also a renewing of the link – even physically in the person of Serrao – between the pro-Jansenist rigorism of the early eighteenth century and the religious regalism, rigorist and Jansenist, of the second half of the century. This was to be championed in Naples by not only Serrao but also men like Domenico Forges Davanzati, Vincenzo Troisi and Francesco Conforti who became Jacobins, and seized on the most extreme implications of the debate between Rome and Naples sparked off by the young Gravina's *Hydra mystica*.

Gravina felt that the *Arcadia* failed where it should have united Italian intellectuals. If it did so it was only under the aegis of the Church, on the basis of a watered-down rationalism which tended to reject any innovatory elements. This relationship between Gravina and the academy may explain why an intellectual like Ludovico Antonio Muratori felt the need to propose a new Italian literary society, knowing full well that the *Arcadia* – despite its expansion – was unable to answer satisfactorily the real problems of culture and Italian intellectualism. The events in Italy in the last decades of the century also reflected processes which had taken place in Europe: the *Journal des Sçavants* and the *Philosophical Transactions* had not been the only examples of an intellectual communication behind which stood, on one side, the State of Louis XIV and, on the other, English civil society. Holland had joined in, still in its economic and cultural Golden Age, giving hospitality and a forum to intellectuals, journalists, editors, French Protestant refugees. It was in Holland, for example, that Bayle's *Nouvelles de la République des Lettres* first saw the light of day. In Lutheran Germany, Leibnitz's universal Christianity had inspired the foundation in Leipzig of the *Acta eruditorum*.

Sacred and secular erudition, history, law and science had become the currency of an international communication which could now easily overcome religious barriers and eventually proposed a plan for the union of the churches, as in the famous and lengthy dialogue between Bossuet and Leibnitz. This failed, but there was a longer life for the myth – which was also a reality – of a collaboration between men of culture, literati and scientists, united in a *res publica* of letters embracing the whole of Europe and having its own international law, which was even given a theoretical definition as *ius cosmopoliticum*. Academies, journals, correspondence and accounts of travels for the libraries were, for this universe of letters, the means of crossing the frontiers of nation and religion. Aristocrats doing the Grand Tour to improve themselves were joined by the scholars, such as the Anglican Gilbert Burnet, the Benedictines Mabillon and Montfaucon, the Dutch Calvinist Hendrick Brenckman and Jacques Vernet from Geneva. The latter was to create – in the name of tolerance and a universalistic religious identity that was to revive Calvinism in Geneva – that *Bibliothèque italique*[10] that was to be one of the first signs that Europe was once more becoming interested in Italian culture.

But let us not anticipate. The century opened not only with the threat of war which was shortly to involve the whole of Europe, but also with a breakdown of the old equilibrium which once again threatened the Spanish inheritance of Naples and Milan. Not only France and Austria, but also England had political, economic and commercial interests which now directly involved the states of Italy. International events had their effect on Italian culture and intellectuals. It was now that the priest from Modena, Ludovico Antonio Muratori, launched his *Primi disegni di una repubblica letteraria d'Italia*,[11] written in 1703 and issued in 1704. This was an important event in the organisation of Italian intellectuals, even if apparently destined to fail. Muratori started from a specific personal background: his education in the Jesuit college in Modena and a small provincial university, the contact with Bacchini and his views on sacred learning, the impact of the aristocratic world of the Borromeo family and his post as lector at the Ambrosiana Library in Milan, and his experiences in Bologna where the Marsili family had made a remarkable contribution to the revival of culture in the religious and scientific spheres.

Muratori's proposal for a literary republic had geographically wider aims but was in some ways more selective than the *Arcadia*, for the intention was to avoid it becoming simply a social meeting place for all those who saw themselves as cultured. It was to be a centre for research and the collation of the results that the best of Italian culture was capable of producing. Another difference from the *Arcadia* was linked to the fact that the cornerstones of this gigantic academy were to have been studies that were useful;

scholarship and science, rather than poetry. It is significant too that Muratori did not choose Piedmont, Naples and Lombardy to participate in the confederation, selecting instead five provinces (Rome, Venice, Florence, Modena and Parma) not directly involved in the war. He thought that the first *Arconte*, who for three years would be head of this republic, should necessarily be from Rome and should be chosen by the first of the great protectors, the pope. And this was not the only sign of a still ambiguous ideology. Muratori realised that in practice if it did not include Rome, the republic would be so isolated from if not actually opposed by, ecclesiastical culture that it must collapse. In fact at this time he was still strongly committed to the desire to include ecclesiastical culture in the plan for civil reform which was also to be a reform of teaching. Muratori was addressing not only the intellectuals in the Church in general, but specifically those responsible for the scholastic institutions which were then the only 'public' schools and for which he proposed a plan of reform of the curriculum. There was to be no more Aristotelianism and scholastic theology, but an inclusion of the experimental sciences, sacred and secular learning, history, modern physics, mathematics and geometry. He declared that he did not wish to replace Aristotle with Descartes, but merely to choose according to good taste and reason. This was the beginning of an intellectual adventure that was to last for more than forty years.

It is worth looking at the names of the *Arcontes* in the literary republic. They were the ones who were to have chosen the other intellectuals by a rigorous method of co-opting. In the first of the lists, forty-eight of the members, over half the total, are clerics, and with prestigious names, from Franceso Bianchini to Giusto Fontanini. After them come doctors and scientists, such as Vallisnieri, Sbaraglia, Ramazzini and Fardella, jurists like Antonio Gatti, librarians like Magliabechi and Muratori himself, and famous educators like Caloprese. There were few nobles and these were mainly patricians, such as Giangiuseppe Orsi, Filicaia and Bernardo Trevisan. (Muratori, under his Arcadian name of Lamindo Pritanio, made use of Trevisan for the publication of both his *Primi disegni* and *Riflessioni sopra il buon gusto*. Venice was intended to be the second great protector.) The list, with a few exceptions, reflected the five chosen provinces, and concentrated particularly on the universities of Bologna, Padua and Modena, as well as Rome.

The second list saw the balance tipping in favour of the laity, with a strong southern presence, among whom figure the remnants of the *Investiganti* and the new exponents of the Medinaceli Academy which had recently been dissolved. Among these were Antonio Monforte, Giacinto de Cristoforo, Costantino Grimaldi, Gian Vincenzo Gravina (who had, however, been teaching in Rome for many years), Biagio Garofalo and the merchant, philosopher and man of letters, Giuseppe Valletta. Present too were Alessandro Marchetti, Lorenzo Magalotti and Giovanni Maria Lancisi, whom Trevisan intended to follow Bianchini as *Primo Arconte*. One cannot fail to notice the presence of many intellectuals who had either been brought before the ecclesiastical tribunals or who had had fierce clashes with the Jesuits. This too is an indication of a gradual change of direction. Finally it must be said that Muratori understood Italy's inferiority as being not so much in the sphere of creativity as rather in that of organisation. His model was eventually to be the patronage of Louis XIV, in which the role of Louis was to have been advantageously played by five states or regional courts, such as the Papal States, the Republic of Venice, the Este court in Modena, that of the Farnese in Parma and the Grand Duchy of Tuscany.

In reality, many events were to change the ideological inspiration of this plan, to which Muratori wanted later to add an even stronger theoretical support with his *Riflessioni sopra il buon gusto*, published in Venice between 1708 and 1715. First there was the debate: the proposal was discussed by various men of letters and taken up by Venice, where three important intellectuals, Scipione Maffei, Antonio Vallisnieri and Apostolo Zeno founded a new periodical, the *Giornale de' letterati d'Italia* which was modelled on Leclerc's famous *Bibliothèques*, and referred explicitly to its desire to represent the men of letters of those parts of Italy mentioned by Muratori shortly before, meaning by that a public not only of intellectuals but made up of professionals, officials, politicians and nobles from the country – the latter being a social group that because of its wealth could easily devote itself to study and thereby revive Italian culture. Secondly, compared with the period when he had first conceived his plan, Muratori himself had been roused by the dramatic clash between the Este and the Habsburg court on the one side and the Holy See on the other over the possession of Comacchio (1708–9) to move from uncertain neo-Guelphism to neo-Ghibellinism and to ally himself with the supporters of the Holy Roman Empire, thus coming into contact with Leibnitz and completely altering his outlook. He moved from sacred learning of Bacchinian origin to profane, and from this to history, a subject in which he was to acquire European fame. Thirdly, the most enthusiastic response to Muratori's plan came precisely from those areas that the *Primi disegni* had excluded. In Naples, the *ceto civile*, in coming forward as a political group within the new Austrian regime, presented in practice an example of the collaboration between intellectuals and government, giving rise to a lively jurisdictional movement that inspired Giannone's *Istoria civile* (1723). In Turin the Duke of Savoy, Victor Amadeus II, who became King of Sicily after the War of the Spanish Succession, not only drew the whole of jurisdictionalist Europe into a famous debate over Papal authority in Sicily, but also initiated a series of reforms which were soon to involve the training grounds for the governing cadres–the universities and the secondary schools. Muratori's *Riflessioni sopra il buon qusto* and his works dealing with this area, became essential texts for the new Piedmontese scholastic and cultural policy, carried out between 1717 and 1729, the year of the university *Costituzioni*.

University reform had been discussed for a long time, in Naples, Rome, Bologna and Padua. Many different men had talked about it: in Naples, Giambattista Vico who had tried to introduce his proposals for the reform of the curriculum in the sensitive period between the Bourbon and the Habsburg regimes, and a jurisdictionalist like Pietro Contegna, who had defended the rights of the city; in Rome Clement XI, Gravina and Diego d'Aguirre had been involved in it; in Bologna the Marsili family; in Padua, Francesco Grimani and above all Scipione Maffei. This first period had resulted in either no progess at all or in the recognition of needs to be attended to in better times. The men who were actively involved in university reform in the early eighteenth century (and in fact up to the second half of the century) have some characteristics in common or, in many cases, close links. Whether ecclesiastics, like Celestino Galiani and Monsignor Gaspare Cerati, or laymen, like Francesco d'Aguirre, they all, regardless of geographical origin, had links with Rome which almost always implied the influence of, or friendship with, Gravina, that other figure who with Muratori was so influential in their projects of reform.

Muratori's plans for the religious schools and Italian universities dominated by clerics were carried out in Turin over a decade (1720–29) under the influence of a reforming sovereign, Victor Amadeus II, and a great organiser of culture, Francesco d'Aguirre.[12] His father, Diego, had been a university professor in canon law who had moved from Sicily to Rome and there had attempted to take part in the reforms of the *Sapienza* desired by Gravina. Francesco had been one of the first Sicilian intellectuals to place his ability as a jurist, trained in the school of his father and of Gravina, at the disposition of the Piedmontese king. His intervention in the Sicilian Interdict (the history of which he was later to write), his intellectual strength and political gifts brought him to the attention of a discerning sovereign as the man most suited to carry out a plan of university reform. His *Della fondazione e ristabilimento degli studi* (1717) was one of the most coherent and far-reaching plans for university reform in eighteenth-century Italy. The Savoyard king and his entourage did not seek advice only from d'Aguirre: they asked for opinions from Bologna, Padua, Paris and Holland. Maffei provided (using what he had already written for Padua) one of the most advanced texts, where among other things experimental sciences, history and Italian literature appear as new disciplines.

Of them all, d'Aguirre's project prevailed, inspired by jurisdictionalist and Gallican principles, with explicit reference to the anti-Jesuit polemics in Naples at the beginning of the century. But the most important aspect was the practical side, the search for intellectuals to carry out the reform. D'Aguirre looked to jurisdictionalist Naples, Gravina's Rome, Gallican France and then to Bologna, Padua and Verona to recruit intellectuals who could guarantee to co-operate in the modernisation of the cultural institutions of Piedmont. At first he aimed high – Gravina, Galiani and Morgagni – then he settled for their pupils. There were negotiations with Metastasio, then an unknown but ambitious young man. From Paris, where he frequented free-thinking circles, came Bernardo Lama, a Neapolitan who in Turin was to draw up programmes for the secondary schools and to write a history of the House of Savoy, spending his last years in Vienna as librarian of the Palatine and tutor in Latin to Maria Theresa. From Toulouse came the physicist and philosopher Father Roma, of the Order of Minims. Many were friends of

Celestino Galiani and had been influenced by his scientific ideas; others were pupils of Gravina, like Lama, Roma, Bencini, Campiani and Regolotti. D'Aguirre was able to put this group, which called itself 'the Roman colony', into closer contact with Muratori whose works they certainly knew. In this way he was able to carry out the Piedmontese reform under the banner not only of 'poetic reason' but also that of good taste and 'moderate devotion'.

At a time when this group of intellectuals appeared to be faltering after a period of remarkable creativity, crushed by local conservatism and by the Concordat with Rome of 1727, nevertheless, as a result of the clash with the Jesuits, Piedmont was to carry out one of the most important scholastic reforms of the whole of the eighteenth century. The State took over secondary education, closed the Jesuit colleges and founded the *Collegio delle Provincie* which each year awarded scholarships to 100 poor youths to allow them to study at the university. It was an institution from which the State hoped to recruit officials who were loyal and above all unconnected with the traditional ecclesiastical route to education. As a result of the reforms of 1729, the Faculty of Arts was to be not only an introductory course for the three faculties, but also a specific title allowing the holder to teach in the kingdom's secondary schools. How this was carried out in the long term has been excellently described by Marina Roggero.[13] Of particular interest was the desire to control completely both university and secondary education, removed from the hands of the Church, seeing the educating of intellectuals, professionals and administrators as the job of the State. The standard of the university and secondary education was not outstanding, but it provided the State, administration, legal system and professions with technical, political and professional recruits of considerable efficiency. Victor Amadeus's reform (held up as an example by Muratori himself in his *Della pubblica felicità* of 1749) was to be looked back to thirty years later in the 1760s and 1770s, when the expulsion of the Jesuits and then the suppression of the Society were to raise the question of re-establishing the secondary schools and universities.

Of the old 'Roman colony', which had been set up in the early eighteenth century in the Rome of Clement XI under the influence of Gravina and the ecclesiastical and scientific academies which had tried to understand Newton and his ideology and to reconcile Locke with rational Catholicism, two members were still destined to involve themselves to an important extent in university reform: Celestino Galiani and Gaspare Cerati.[14] Galiani, who had become *Cappellano maggiore* in Naples when still under Austrian rule, tried to define his task, which in practice put him in charge of education, by proposing to Vienna a remarkably advanced scheme of university reform, entirely based on the experimental disciplines. This plan, the text of which has been lost, was to be discussed, upheld and partly modified in a jurisdictionalistic direction by men like Giannone and Lama (1733). Galiani continued his task under the Bourbons too, paving the way for that eighteenth-century university in Naples where, although Vico was dead and his place taken by his unassuming son Gennaro, the chair in economics for Antonio Genovesi was to be created, almost symbolising the Enlightenment in the South, rather as the *Accademia dei Pugni* and *Il Caffè* did for Lombardy. Monsignor Cerati, also trained in the Gravina, Bencini and Galiani school, was until the 1760s director of the university of Pisa where, with his anti-Jesuitism, his moderate enlightenment, enlightened Catholicism and robust and empirical desire for reform, he created one of the most important centres for ideas on reform in the Italian eighteenth century.

NOTES AND REFERENCES

On periodicals see: Ricuperati, G. (1976) 'Giornali e società nell'Italia dell'Ancien Régime (1668–1789)'. In various authors, *La stampa italiana dal '500 all '800*, eds Castronovo, V, and Tranfaglia, N. Laterza, Bari. See especially Chapter I, 'I modelli stranieri e la loro ripresa nell'Italia della Controriforma', pp. 71–115. See also various authors (1979) *Politici ed economisti del primo Settecento*, with introduction by Ricuperati, G. Ricciardi, Milan–Naples. For a general description of the relations between Italy and Europe in the years of the 'crisis of European consciousness' see: Ajello, R. (1980) 'Cartesianismo e cultura oltremontana al tempo dell'Istoria civile', in various authors, *Pietro Giannone e il suo tempo*, ed. Ajello, R. Jovene, Naples, vol. 2, I, pp. 1–181. For the most up-to-date and original work on the subject see: Ferrone, V. (1983) *Scienza natura religione. Mondo newtoniano e cultura italiana nel primo Settecento*. Jovene, Naples.

1. Badaloni, N. (1961) *Introduzione a G. B. Vico*. Feltrinelli, Milan.
2. Mastellone, S. (1965) *Pensiero politico e vita culturale a Napoli nella seconda metà del Seicento*. D'Anna, Messina.
3. Comparato, V. I. (1970) *Giuseppe Valletta. Un intellettuale della fine del Seicento*. Istituto italiano per gli studi storici, Naples.
4. See Valletta, G. (1975) *Opere filosofiche*, ed. Rak, M. Olschki, Florence.
5. Suppa, S. (1971) *L'accademia di Medinacoeli fra tradizione investigante e nuova scienza civile*. Istituto italiano per gli studi storici, Naples. See also Ricuperati, G. (1972) 'A proposito dell'Accademia Medina Coeli', in *Rivista storica italiana*, a. LXXXIV, pp. 57–79.
6. Quondam, A. (1973) 'L'istituzione Arcadia. Sociologia e ideologia di un'accademia', in *Quaderni storici*, 23, pp. 389–438; idem (1982) 'L'Accademia', in various authors, *Letteratura italiana*, I, *Il letterato e le sue istituzioni*. Einaudi, Turin (especially pp. 866–7).
7. Quondam, A. (1968) *Cultura e ideologia di Gianvicenzo Gravina*. Lerici, Milan. See also idem (1970) *Filosofia della luce e luminosi nelle egloghe del Gravina*. Guida, Naples.
8. Ricuperati, G. (1970) 'Studi recenti sul primo Settecento italiano', in *Rivista storica italiana*; LXXXII, I.
9. Chiosi, E. (1981) *Andrea Serrao. Apologia e crisi del regalismo nel Settecento napoletano*. Jovene, Naples.
10. Crucitti Ullrich, F. B. (1974) *La 'Bibliothèque italique'. Cultura 'italianisante' e giornalismo letterario*. Ricciardi, Milan – Naples.
11. Vecchi, A. (1979) 'La nuova accademia letteraria d'Italia', in various authors, *Accademie e cultura. Aspectti storici tra Sei e Settecento*. Olschki, Florence,

pp. 39–72. See also: Burlini Calapaj, A. 'I rapporti tra Lamindo Pritanio e Bernardo Trevisan', ibid., pp. 73–94. For Bologna and the Marsili see: Bego, M. 'Cultura e accademie a Bologna per opera di A. F. Marsili e di E. Manfredi', ibid., pp. 95–116.

12. Ricuperati, G. (1975) 'Muratori e il Piemonte', in various authors, *La fortuna di L. A. Muratori*. Olschki, Florence, pp. 1–88.

13. Roggero, M. (1981) *Scuola e riforme nello stato sabaudo*. Turin.

14. See Ferrone, V. (1980) 'Celestino Galiani: un inquieto cattolico illuminato nella crisi della coscienza europea', in *Archivio storico per le province napoletane*, III series, a. XCVIII. Naples, pp. 277–381 (now included in Ferrone, V. (1983) *Scienza natura religione*. Jovene, Naples). On Cerati see: Carranza, N. (1974) *Monsignor Cerati provveditore dell'università di Pisa nel Settecento delle riforme*. Pacini, Pisa.

CHAPTER SEVEN

The *veteres* against the *moderni*: Paolo Mattia Doria (1662–1746) and Giambattista Vico (1668–1744)

In the early years of the *Giornale dei letterati d'Italia*, two books from the South had particularly attracted the attention of the Venetian journalists, normally little interested in the cultural aspects of the polemics on ecclesiastical benefices. They were Paolo Mattia Doria's *Vita civile* and Giambattista Vico's *De Antiquissima Italorum sapientia*. We have already encountered Doria as a member of the Medinaceli Academy. He was born in Genoa in 1662 of one of the most illustrious patrician families in the republic. In the late 1680s he moved to Naples where his relatives were owed large sums of money which he recovered and dissipated in a few years with conspicuous generosity. The autobiographical hints in his writing speak of his debut in Neapolitan society as a duellist, jealous of his honour and ready to fight at the least provocation. He himself places his conversion to philosophy and a profound change in his behaviour at the age of about twenty-two. He played an important part in the *Accademia di Medinaceli*, earning fame not only as a philosopher and political expert, but also as a military technician. But the work which brought him to the notice of a European public was the *Vita civile*, first published in 1709 and then in a slightly enlarged edition in 1710. The title itself indicated its humanist point of view, imitating a work of the same name by Matteo Palmieri written more than three centuries before.

What were the elements which so struck contemporaries and caused Leclerc to compare Doria's *Vita civile* with the works of Grotius and Pufendorf? First of all, a very significant feature was the reappraisal of Machiavelli, described as a 'pharmacopoeia for all needs'. Doria's attitude towards Machiavelli is complex, even, at times, contradictory. On the one hand he was the author who taught tyrants how to acquire power; on the other, notwithstanding the limitations imposed by Machiavelli's lack of a real philosophy, Doria could not help being fascinated by his complex and radical analyses. Through Machiavelli, Doria condemns all policies which are decided by 'reason of state'. Starting from Plato and particularly from his Renaissance interpreters, Doria wanted to construct an open model of politics, animated by a metaphysical system and a theory of politics as the realisation of the virtues and individual values of philosophy. Thus he had to inquire into the origins of political systems and their different manifestations. While denying that the state of nature is one of conflict, as it is according to Machiavelli and Hobbes, for Doria the origins of power lie in the need primitive families had of defending themselves, entrusting military power to a leader. The choosing of a leader, both strong and wise, is one of the first forms of government of mankind, appearing in both the Jewish and Greek worlds. In this way the founders of nations arose who made the first laws. But with the desire for peace and tranquillity, human beings tried to make more complex and comfortable structures of civil life.

If before there were mostly open spaces and countryside, now the seat of civil life was the town where among other things there arose the first necessary divisions into social orders, like that between governors and governed. According to Doria, the chief legislator and organiser of the State must in fact provide for three types of officials. The first he calls those of politics, who would deal with morals, social control and internal and external affairs. The second would run the judiciary and the third would deal with economic affairs. At the origin of the social divisions of the governed is the relationship between servant and master. Doria, obviously reflecting the views of a patrician, maintains that while those who serve are in their turn divided into the various groupings in the towns representing the mechanical arts, the civil body, which is single, and which differs from the former because it does not perform manual work, coincides with the nobility. The latter is born from ancient wealth, which frees it from having to work manually, allows it to hold important posts and to be useful to the country and the prince, cultivating a sense of honour which consists of the defending of both prince and country and of those who are weak. With this argument, Doria not only gives the nobility a precise function but also shows a clear preference for the urban patricians, 'the nobles of the republic' as he calls them.

This first division between the serving order and the civil order allows republics to survive by establishing a proper relationship between town and country. If in fact there were not such a division, the town would be forced to act as an army, plundering the country in such a way as to prevent any peaceful social equilibrium. As social life gradually becomes more complicated, others are born: the merchants, professionals and intellectuals. Doria describes the successive phases in civil life as it moves from barbarism to civilisation. Both evolution and regression are possible, he says, related to the fatal tendency of human things to change. For example, vicious luxury threatens what would be perfect, while moderate civil life can become better or regress to barbarism. The second part of the book, which describes the political, judicial and economic officials, gives a remarkable example of the importance which Doria had from the very start placed on the control of morals, behaviour and education.

In Doria we can already see to some extent, even if less clearly than in Montesquieu, the choices of a monarchy based on honour and of a republic based on virtue. It is difficult to know whether at that time Doria favoured the republic or the principality. His writing reflects the situation in the

South, even if he does not forget his Genoese origins. As a philosopher of
politics he directed his advice to both types of government with a greater
stress on monarchy since in Naples (which had recently undergone a change
of regime) the prince and officials were those whom he most directly
addressed. Furthermore, at this time he saw with remarkable acuteness the
problems faced by the republics in regard to the emerging absolute states.
Genoa, Venice and even Holland had to contend with formidable forces, like
the France of Louis XIV, Spain, the Empire and England. A bad monarchy
could always change into a good republic, while the decadence of the latter
easily opened the door to tyranny: 'The republic needs heroic virtue, while
the monarchy cannot do without honour, even if, though having less need
of the virtue of the citizens, it has less turbulence.' Recalling the models of
the Spartan and Athenian republics, he described the first as a society 'structured for preservation', and the second as a society aiming to conquer. Rome
was of this second type, as her history showed, permeated with unhappiness
and violence, despite the virtues and love of liberty which inspired it. Doria
unequivocally comes down on the side of Sparta and in this sense distances
himself from the Machiavelli both of the *Prince* and of the *Discorsi*.

On another essential problem Doria opposed Machiavelli while at the same
time remaining unwillingly fascinated by him: the role of the papacy in
preventing the political unification of Italy. Doria understood with great
clarity and perhaps even more deeply than other contemporaries the implications of Machiavelli's arguments and he responded ambiguously. On the
one hand he blamed the Italians, who had lost their heroic virtue and were
thus unable to oppose the barbarians, on the other he was inclined to deny
– anticipating neo-Guelph ideas – that the papacy had in fact opposed this
process. His book thus contained some remarkably original ideas and showed
a desire to reopen the discussion of politics and its relationship with society
at the point where the Humanists and Machiavelli had left it. Written with
great intellectual courage it was, if not a direct 'republican' apologia, certainly
at least part of that tradition of 'constitutionalism', to which Italian patrician
thinkers were to make other contributions, such as the *Consiglio politico* by
Scipione Maffei. Another significant element (which can already be seen in
Gravina) was the great importance that ideas, philosophy and philosophers
were to have in defining the values of political life. From this point of view,
Doria's work was a further contribution to the celebration of the *jus sapientioris*, even if it was less politically precise than in Gravina for whom the truly
wise were the 'cultured' jurisprudents.

It is interesting to see how Doria's ideas developed later. At almost the
same time as the *Vita civile* he wrote the *Massime* which described and delin-
eated the vicious principles used by the Spanish to govern the South. This
is the most 'reformist' phase of Doria's thought, not unconnected with the
fact that he was an adviser to a great jurist like Gennaro d'Andrea, minister
in the service of the new Habsburg government. Doria's critical analysis of
the South from the sixteenth to the eighteenth centuries is certainly one of
the most perceptive of those which appeared in the political literature of the

Mezzogiorno. He attributed the blame for the crisis of the Neapolitan regime chiefly to the Spanish, who in order to govern the country used 'divide and rule' (*divide et impera*) tactics, setting one social group against another. He is merciless with the barons, denouncing them with an intensity and polemical force which exceed anything which had emerged so far in the consciousness of the *ceto civile*. Nor was the local Church spared. On examination, Doria seems to see in the Spanish government a less negative phase, linked with the reforming viceroys, particularly the marquis del Carpio. This not surprisingly is during the periods of greatest agreement between the Spanish government and the more receptive judicial ministers. The *Massime* did not reach their addressee, Gennaro d'Andrea, who had fallen out of favour and died in 1710, and Doria preferred to keep them among his manuscripts.[1]

The European success of the *Vita civile*, clear from the reviews by Leclerc and the Menckens, was not repeated in Doria's following works. His mathematical works of 1714–22 were attacked, ignored and ridiculed. His contemporaries, starting with the mathematicians and scientists of Naples, began to become for Doria 'the opponents'. The man who had struck up a 'gentlemanly friendship' with Giambattista Vico, was on the way to becoming the most famous, talked about and pathetic of the Neapolitan *veteres*. In 1724, his *Discorsi critici e filosofici* chose Descartes as the target, criticising him for having opened the way to the materialism of Spinoza. Against both he proposed a return to Plato, heir to the ancient Italic wisdom, but a very different one from the atomist Plato of Valletta.

In 1728 Doria published his *Filosofia di Platone* which contained a harsh attack on Locke whose book he had read in the French translation by Pierre Coste. The attack was widened in the *Difesa della metafisica degli antichi* of 1732–33 to include Newton, whose work he knew through Pemberton's summary. These were not chance attacks, they included precise references to the situation in Naples where the choice of Celestino Galiani as *Cappellano maggiore* had meant an alliance among the *moderni* for a renewal of philosophic and scientific culture and an opening up of all the intellectual institutions to the new ideas. Accused by the Cartesian Spinelli, pupil of Gregorio Caloprese, of being a Spinozan, Doria became the chief mover of an *Accademia degli Oziosi* which set up in opposition, with its cult of the *veteres* and its precocious anti-Enlightenment stance, to the *Accademia delle Scienze* of Celestino Galiani and Bartolomeo Intieri.

Disillusionment with the modern world and a society based on commerce made Doria an acute and paradoxical critic of Europe. In his prolix but informed writings, that he intended to leave to future generations in the library of St Angelo al Nido, the attacks on mercantilistic states piled up. He spared no one, not Spain, nor the France of Richelieu, Mazarin, Colbert and Louis XIV, nor England, where there reigned, in his opinion, a 'vicious liberty', nor Holland whose decadence he saw as parallel, if less dramatic, to that of the Italian republics.

His thought swung between the two poles of Utopia and reaction. By now he rejected everything about the West, including the discovery of America which had favoured 'ideal' trade and mercantile development. For this reason he felt the need to rewrite the *Vita civile* from a decidedly 'republican' and Utopian point of view, calling this, his last work, *Idea di una repubblica perfetta*.[2] Doria had initiated one of the first and most important lines of argument against the Enlightenment, hitting not only at its scientific and epistemological models but also its economic theories, from Descartes to Locke, from Newton to Melon. He had immediately detected in Voltaire the great preacher and propagator of the new ideology. Doria wanted to be a good Catholic but had fiercely attacked the Jansenists and the 'tyrannical' Jesuits. Yet he left behind him for publication a work which upset both Church and State, so that in 1753, seven years after his death, not only was publication forbidden, but the book was burned. The Church found something vaguely heretical in the exaltation of Platonic philosophy, which Doria compared with Christianity and certainly preferred – as an ethical system – to the historical developments of the latter. The Bourbon State could not fail to see in it a refutation of absolutism, including enlightened absolutism, which was called 'tyrannical' and unjust. The ambiguities which had perhaps caused the success of the *Vita civile* are in this book, now lost, decisively resolved in favour of a 'republic' inspired once again by Plato – a republic not egalitarian but guided by wise magistrates and 'philosopher captains', where anti-Enlightenment Catholicism would become that 'civil' religion that Doria had described in the world of the *antiqui*.

From what has been said so far, it is possible to see the similarities, but also the deep differences, between Vico and Doria. They had both been – the poor professor of rhetoric and the rich patrician – in the Medinaceli Academy. But their friendship was to grow later, when Doria was writing his *Vita civile* and Vico was about to dedicate his *De antiquissima* to him. They had several things in common: the identification of Plato as the theorist of a wisdom which, born of Magna Graecia, was in every way the opposite of the 'modern' philosophy of Descartes, Locke and François Melon; contact with Grotius and his doctrine of natural law; the desire to base politics and society on a metaphysical system reconciled wih Catholicism, it in its turn having become a 'civil' religion. No less evident are the differences, which grew greater with time. For example, Doria consistently undervalues philology and erudition (following stereotypes drawn from Malebranche's *De iniquirenda veritate*). But above all, Vico's view of history and his desire to base a reconstruction of society on it, seeing the rhythms of an 'ideal and eternal history', were totally foreign to Doria. The two intellectuals met later in the 1730s in the *Accademia degli Oziosi*, to fight the 'moderns', but once again there was a deep gap beteeen Doria's showy and rather superficial participation and that of Vico which was muted and somewhat detached. In his late works, even when wanting to stress the similarities between his own ideas and those of Vico, in fact Doria only referred to the *De antiquissima* and remained quite outside the great questions of the *Scienza nuova*.

It is precisely the link with Doria, his militancy among the *veteres* and his membership of the *Oziosi* which enables us to look in greater depth at the problem of the relationship of Vico to his age. It is a subject that requires us to reconsider the commonly held view of the Neapolitan philosopher as a man isolated from his contemporaries, for it is a view which wants to see him more as an early Romantic. This theory, most clearly summarised by Benedetto Croce in his famous book, has had a reaction from modern historiography which stresses not only the importance of the *Orationes*, but also of the *Coniuratio* which was for a long time unpublished.[3] Vico's 'politics' are most closely related to the problems of his time in the years when the Neapolitan world was in some way pressed by external tensions: the change from Spanish to Bourbon rule and then the first ten years of Habsburg reformism. Here we find the ideas of the young Vico, proposing an alliance between the magistrature and the sovereign power, warning of possible violence from the barons and the plebeians. Then – as in Doria but with different results – two 'separating' elements were to come into play: disillusionment with Habsburg reformism and at the same time his strange choice of the *veteres* who led him away from those who looked back to Descartes and Newton. What made Vico very different from Doria was his profound theoretical knowledge which even turned to account his disconcerting decision not to read the works of contemporaries, to turn back to the past, to the philosophy of the sixteenth and seventeenth centuries rather than to the present, unlike Doria who continued to dispute and feebly oppose contemporary works.

In *De Antiquissima Italorum sapientia* we can already see the central core of the theory of knowledge that Vico was to propose in place of Cartesianism and the 'moderns': the *verum per factum*. He was able to react to the crisis of Pyrrhonism which had struck southern culture a hard blow, by starting from a text like that on the uncertainty of medicine by Leonardo di Capua and setting in motion a discussion which reconstructed a cognitive 'constant' as a solid foundation for knowledge. Rejecting the intellectualism of contemporary philosophic models like those of Descartes, Spinoza and Leibnitz, he turned to consider again the dimensions and constructions of man – society, law, poetry, religion and myth. The influence on him of the philosophy of natural law and particularly the ideas of Grotius, can be seen in his view of law as having a divine origin which does not diminish, but on the contrary confirms and strengthens the historical and human dimension in which law is realised. He sees human life as being characterised by the clash between mutually conflicting tensions. On one side are the demands of reason (*vis veri*) and individual and group emotions (*cupiditas*), while on the other is the force of authority (*auctoritas*). This latter is moral law, which is present in each man, and state law, which is outside man and regulates social relations.

Vico, who is his two works *De rebus gestis Antonii Caraphei* and *De uno universi iuris principio et fine uno* (1720) is more than usually concerned with the problems of his time, did not want only to provide a solution which would save *costantia iurisprudentis* from the clutches of Pyrrhonism, but also to provide a political solution for his contemporaries. For Vico the only force capable of preventing a clash between different classses was law, both a human and a divine reality. The interpreters of the law, the wise men (but also the *ceto civile*) were those most fitted to guarantee justice as a possible way of living together, between the oppression of the rich and the desire of the *famuli* to participate in political life. In the Garden of Eden, wisdom was the perfect balance between soul and mind. After the Fall this balance was lost: thus there is a double tension between the desire for order and the strength of the passions. Jurisprudence emerged as a possible way of healing this rift.

In 1723 Vico took part once again in a university competition for promotion to a more important chair of law, but without success. Because of this he was able to move on to the central part of his intellectual work: from 1723 until his death his time was to be devoted to the formulation of the *Scienza nuova*. He worked on the first draft from the end of 1723 until 1725. Because the expected financial support from Cardinal Lorenzo Corsini did not materialise, the *Scienza nuova in forma negativa* only circulated among a few friends and is now lost. In the space of about a month he rewrote it to reduce its length, getting rid of the negative structure and printing it in October 1725 with the comprehensive title of *Principi di una scienza nuova d'intorno alla natura delle nazioni per la quale si ritrovano i principi d'altro sistema di diritto naturale delle genti*, where for the first time the results of the preceding version are organised systematically. The study of the nature of nations is a development of his interest in natural law. But he was not happy with this *Scienza nuova prima*, which is why, when his Venetian editors suggested a reprinting, he offered them a heap of notes which he had compiled to comment on and complement the edition of 1725. The Venetians refused to print it. Vico then devoted himself to the laborious incorporation of the notes into the text and published in Naples in 1730 the *Scienza nuova seconda*. But the same process of corrections and additions was to start again for this version, which resulted in the *Scienza nuova* published posthumously in 1744.

Even a cursory comparison of these three versions will show the general development of Vico's thought. The 1725 edition is divided into five books: the first deals with the need to find a new science that would consist of a consideration 'of certain principles of the humanity of the nations from which, there is no doubt, all the sciences, disciplines and arts stem'. Here are gathered together all the different strands of his previous work: the defence of natural law and *costantia iurisprudentis* against Pyrrhonism, pointing out likewise the limits of the theories of natural law of men like John Selden, Grotius and Pufendorf. In the second book, Vico reintegrates sacred and profane history in order to find the basis of this science, revealing an eternal universal history against which to compare all the different histories of the nations. It is interesting to note that in this book Vico puts forward a concept of the 'civil' history of inventions, sciences, disciplines and arts which is much more far-reaching than Giannone's and closer to that of Bacon in *De augmentis scientiarum*. The third book deals with the origins of this science from the linguistic point of view, whereas the preceding part had dealt with ideas from which are born philosophy and law. In this inquiry, mythology and etymology are used to back up the view of humanity which Vico has already presented. He analyses the difference between poetry, which reflects heroic and primitive times, and metaphysics which is the product of a rational age, free of passions. In the fourth book (only a sketch) he establishes proofs, while the fifth contains a synthesis of the philosophy of humanity and the universal history of nations. Vico attempts to find identical beginnings in the antiquity and mythology of all peoples: the ages of the gods, of political heroes and of men.

The work was harshly criticised by Mencken in *Acta eruditorum*. Vico replied with his *Vindiciae* which rebutted this devastating attack point by point. At the same time he was preparing the draft of the 1730 version, published at his own expense. This, and the 1744 version, are still in five books, but the order is greatly changed. An explanation of the arrangement in the frontispiece, which is really a new introduction to the work, replaced a literary essay which attacked the Venetian printer and which Vico decided to cut out. In the *Scienza nuova seconda* the first book deals with the establishing of principles, the second with poetic wisdom, the third with Homer. The fourth deals with the course of nations. Starting from poetic, heroic and human nature Vico investigates how customs, duties, authority, reason, judgements and natural law correspond with these three ages. The fifth book concerns 'the recurrence of human things in the resurgence of the nations'. It is here that Vico lays the basis of his method of historical analysis, which consists of 'the latest barbaric history illuminated by the first barbaric history'. Feudalism is seen as a recurrent return of the heroic times which followed the age of the gods and which in turn paved the way for the age of man.

He began immediately to annotate this new edition while preparing material for the third. Despite some attacks on his work, his last years were undoubtedly the happiest. After the publication of the second version of the *Scienza nuova*, Vico had turned to the Emperor Charles VI with a petition, begging in the name of his own efforts that a pension or benefice be granted to his son Gennaro. In his petition Vico included a rapid but complete outline of his achievements as intellectual and teacher and reminded the sovereign with great dignity of the greatness of his book, 'a system of the natural law of the peoples different from those three systems of Hugo Grotius, John Selden and Samuel Pufendorf, authors whom Holland, England and Protestant Germany were able to flaunt in the face of France when she was most radiant with learned men . . . '.[4] His petition had been sent to Vienna with a very favourable recommendation from the Viceroy Harrach. The Council of Spain gave it a very positive reception and a pension of 400 ducats a year was awarded, but it is not known whether in fact it was paid. It was, however, a sign of a change of attitude. While not suspecting his real greatness, the authorities at least recognised his thirty years and more of irreproachable service and his dignified, if modest, role in Neapolitan culture. With the change of regime he did not delay in sending, before 5 July 1734, a petition to the new sovereign, Charles of Bourbon, asking for the post of royal historian. In this petition he recalled that he was 'the oldest of these public officials, holding his chair since the days of Charles II of glorious memory'. He was awarded the post in a despatch of 12 July 1735 with many flattering remarks and another stipend of 100 ducats a year. In addition, under the university reforms promoted by the *Cappellano maggiore*, Celestino Galiani, his salary was doubled. In 1737 his son Gennaro (1715–1806) began to assist him in his university teaching and in 1742, as soon as Vico reached retirement, he replaced his father. Thus Vico passed his last years, busy with the work of correcting the *Scienza nuova*.

When Vico died on the night of 22–23 January 1744, few in Italy and Europe were aware of his death. For his contemporaries he had been a scholar who was not without originality but whose ideas were confused and unattractive. This was in essence the opinion of Giannone who had written scathingly about the interest, negative or otherwise, in Vico aroused by the *Acta eruditorum*. Giannone had in fact praised Vico in his *Istoria civile*, but as a teacher and participant in the revival of Neapolitan cultural life. The *Consultore* of the *Cappellano maggiore* too, Filippo Caravita, writing about Naples University in 1714, recognised Vico's undeniable success as a teacher. The Piedmontese ambassador Roberto Solaro di Breglio, who had met him to talk about possible employment in Turin University, not only never even suspected his real greatness, but hastily crossed him off the list, calling him a tiresome pedant. In fact some elements of Vico's thought did survive through direct transmission. For example, Antonio Genovesi had read the *Scienza nuova* in 1737 and became his friend before he became his colleague. And Genovesi kept his lesson in mind, even when his own ideas developed in a very different direction. Vico's message got through also to men who were fighting for different points of view, like Appiano Buonafede, Ferdinando Galiani and Emanuele Duni. But the rediscovery of Vico was to come late in southern culture, with men like Francesco Antonio Grimaldi, Francesco Mario Pagano, Gaetano Filangieri and the circle of the Belfortes and the *Scelta miscellanea*, that in the 1770s were to read Vico in such a way as to bend his ideas on the philosophy of history to suit masonic circles, relating it to a philosophy of nature derived from Boulanger, Buffon and d'Holbach.

NOTES AND REFERENCES

The first person to study P. M. Doria in recent years was: Vidal, E. (1953) *Il pensiero civile di Paolo Mattia Doria negli scritti inediti. Con il testo del manoscritto Del commercio del regno di Napoli.* Giuffré, Milan. An important chapter was devoted to him in Capurso, M. (1959) *Accentramento e costituzionalismo. Il pensiero italiano del primo Settecento di fronte al problema dell'organizzazione dello stato.* Pironti, Naples. Similarities between *Vita civile* and *Esprit des lois* had already been noticed by Shackleton, R. (1955) 'Montesquieu et Doria', in *Revue de littérature comparée*, LVII, pp. 173–83. For his political ideas see: Conti, V. (1978) *P. Mattia Doria. Dalla repubblica dei togati alla repubblica dei notabili.* Olschki, Florence. For a biography and anthology edited by S. Rotta see: various authors (1979) *Politici ed economisti del primo Settecento.* Ricciardi, Milan–Naples, pp. 835–968. The appearance of Doria's unpublished

Neapolitan writings gave rise to a conference in Lecce in 1972, the proceedings of which are in course of publication. See *Manoscritti napoletani di Paolo Mattia Doria* (1981–82), I, ed. Belgioioso, G.; II, ed. Marangio, M.; III, ed. Spedicati, A.; IV, ed. Di Fabrizio, P.; V, ed. Marangio, M. Congedo Galatina. See also: various authors (1985) *Paolo Maltia Doria fra rinnovamento e tradizione.* Congedo, Galatina.

It is impossible to give here a bibliography for G. B. Vico. For bibliographical studies see: Croce, B. (1947) *Bibliografia vichiana accresciuta e rielaborata da F. Nicolini.* Ricciardi, Milan–Naples, vol. 2; Donzelli, M. (1970) *Contributo alla bibliografia vichiana (1948–1970).* Guida, Napoli. See also: various authors (1985) *Paolo Maltia Doria tra rinnovamento e tradizione.* Congedo, Galatina. As well as the work mentioned in Chapter 6 by Badaloni, Mastellone and Ferrone see: various authors (1969) *Giambattista Vico. An international symposium*, ed. Tagliacozzo, G. and White, H. V. J. Hopkins Press, Baltimore. See also: Rossi, P. (1969) *Le sterminate antichità.* Nistri Lischi, Pisa; Donzelli, M. (1970) *Natura e humanitas nel giovane Vico.* Istituto italiano per gli studi storici, Naples; Pompa, L. (1975) *Vico: a study of the 'New Science'.* Cambridge University Press, Cambridge; Berlin, I. (1976) *Vico and Herder. Two studies in the history of ideas.* Hogarth Press, London; various authors (1976) *Giambattista Vico's Science of Humanity*, ed. Tagliacozzo G. and Verene, D. P.. J. Hopkins Press, Baltimore–London; various authors (1976) 'Vico and contemporary thought', in *Social Research*, 4, Winter; Viechtbauer, H. (1977) *Transzendentale Einsicht und Theorie der Geschichte. Uberlegungen zu G. Vicos 'Liber Metaphysicus'.* Fink Verlag, Munich; Fellman, F. (1976) *Das Vico-Axiom: Der Mensch macht die Geschichte.* Freiburg–Munich; various authors (1980) *Vico e Venezia.* Olschki, Florence; Giarrizzo, G. (1981) *Vico, la politica e la storia.* Guida, Napoli. For a summary of present trends in studies of Vico see: Rossi, P. (1980) 'Gli studi vichiani', in various authors, *Immagini del Settecento in Italia.* Laterza, Bari. See also: Rossi, (1979) *I segni del tempo. Storia delle nazioni e storia della terra da Hooke a Vico.* Feltrinelli, Milan. On Vico's influence in Germany see: Becchi, P. (1986) *Vico e Filangieri in Germania.* Jovene, Naples. Recent studies are: Burke, P. (1985) *Vico.* O.U.P., Oxford; Mooney, M. (1985) *Vico in the tradition of rhetoric.* Princeton University Press, Princeton.

1. Doria, P. M. (1973) *Massime del governo spagnolo a Napoli*, introduction by Galasso, G, ed. Conti, V. Guida, Naples.
2. Zambelli, P. (1973) 'Il rogo postumo di P. M. Doria', in various authors, *Ricerche sulla cultura dell'Italia moderna.* Laterza, Bari.
3. See: Nicolini, F. (1967) 'Vicende e codici della 'Principum' neapoltetanorum coniuratio', in *Vico storico*, ed. Tessitore, F. Morano, Naples, pp.407 ff. See also: Mastellone, S. (1965) *Pensiero politico e vita culturale a Napoli nella seconda meta del Seicento.* D'Anna, Milan–Naple, pp.197 ff.
4. See: Vico, G. B. (1953) *Opere*, ed. Nicolini, F. Ricciardi, Milan–Naples, pp. 144–55.

CHAPTER EIGHT

Jurisdictionalism, deism and free thought: Pietro Giannone (1676–1748) and Alberto Radicati di Passerano (1698–1737)

Doria and Vico offered to southern culture not only the myth of the *antiquissima italorum sapientia*, but also the outlook of the *veteres* and thus an independence from, and an alternative to, the culture of the 'moderns', as represented by Descartes, Gassendi, Spinoza, Bayle, Locke and Newton. At the same time another cultural possibility, equally deeply rooted in the tradition of the *Investiganti* and similarly nourished by the problems which had been debated in the Medinaceli Academy, was emerging, which from the radical strain latent in jurisdictional thought was to lead to extreme consequences – both political, cultural and religious. This was represented by Pietro Giannone, the provincial from Ischitella who arrived in Naples in the last decade of the seventeenth century and had received his education not so much at the university, which was reduced to the task of distributing degree certificates, as at the Medinaceli Academy and with a few great teachers. Of these, two in particular are worth mentioning, Domenico Aulisio and Gaetano Argento, because they undoubtedly lie at the origin of Giannone's thought. The first was a professor of canon law but also a great scholar with an encyclopaedic knowledge covering philosophy, theology and the sciences, particularly medicine. He had made a youthful blunder by daring to criticise di Capua's work on the uncertainty of medicine, the central work of the Neapolitan 'moderns', thus bringing down on his head the attacks of a whole coterie of intellectuals and nearly becoming an outcast. He had read Descartes and Spinoza and discussed the relationship between these two systems not only in philosophy but also in the field of biblical exegesis. It is hard to say what Giannone really took from Aulisio except perhaps in the area of civil and canon law, and antiquarianism.[1] There are certainly similarities between Aulisio's posthumous book *Delle scuole sacre* and Giannone's *Triregno* written in Vienna. The most likely hypothesis is that from this champion of the *veteres*, by now isolated even if universally respected, Giannone was able to learn the theory of the history of institutions such as his master had applied to medicine – in a work now lost – and to the schools of theology.

Closer to Giannone's professional sphere and political inclinations was Gaetano Argento, in whose school Giannone was trained along with a group of jurists who were to have an important role in Naples in later years. In those private academies which developed specific philosophical ideas and likewise revealed the political growth and social importance of the *ceto civile* and particularly of the jurists, he discovered the theme of his most famous work. Behind Argento, who was to become the most important political figure in the Austrian viceroyalty, there was a whole tradition of jurists and lawyers, celebrated in Francesco d'Andrea's *Avvertimenti a' nepoti*.[2] The young Giannone, for the beginning of his *Istoria civile*, referred back to a theme, borrowed to some extent from d'Andrea, of the role and significance of the law of the barbarians compared with that of the Romans. This was another route back to the rediscovery of Machiavelli, Guicciardini and Grotius. When the Austrians arrived, Argento had written one of the chief works in the debate on church benefices, *De re beneficiaria*, which made him, along with Costantino Grimaldi and Alessandro Riccardi,[3] the main target of Roman attack. The ability of the State and its subjects to defend themselves against the unjust extortion by Rome, demanded in the name of religion, was just one aspect of a more general *libertas philosophandi* which it was necessary to defend and safeguard. The debate on benefices, with all its consequences, was certainly one of the most important elements in Giannone's thought. But though he associated himself respectfully and sympathetically with his master's career, he was closer to men like Grimaldi and Riccardi.

The problems faced then are well known: benefices, property acquired by the Church or the religious orders, the building of St Peter's, the right of sanctuary which impeded the course of justice – these are just some aspects of the more general dependence of the southern State on the Church. It hindered the defence of the State by government officials through the use of devices already denounced by Sarpi in the early seventeenth century, such as interdicts and censorship. Now the old answers of jurisdictionalism no longer sufficed. New instruments were needed, drawn from the lessons of history, natural law and above all public law, to oppose centuries-old abuses of power by the Church. On this matter one can see in Giannone, from his early years, an attitude that, though it may still place him within the *ceto civile* yet nevertheless differentiates him from the ideology of the *ministero togato*, at least in those aspects which could be seen as conservative. The jurists[4] had considered their distance from the court as an advantage. Giannone, by contrast, seemed convinced that significant development could only come about through a 'national kingdom', like that established by the Norman and Swabian kings in the twelfth and thirteenth centuries and revived by the Aragonese in the fifteenth. The jurists were for autonomy and the defence of local interests, while Giannone favoured centralisation and reform. In his thought it is possible to see the move – which was to be accelerated under the Bourbons – from a concentration on the jurist, whose sectional interests conflicted with the State, to the ideology of the *ministro togato* whose career and recognition of his own duties coincided with the aims of the State. Similar ideas can be traced in the whole group that was to associate itself with his work including Riccardi, Contegna, Nicola Fraggianni and Grimaldi.[5]

The latter was the author of an interesting essay calling for an increase in the salary of officials, enhancing the standing of these men and disassociating them from the venality and corruption of the past.

L'Istoria civile del regno di Napoli, published in 1723, was the high point of southern jurisdictionalism as it had emerged in the second half of the seventeenth and early eighteenth centuries under the influence of Habsburg models. By the means of history, Giannone showed in practice how the strangle-hold of the Church on the State had developed. Drawing on a model of history which went back to Machiavelli, Guicciardini, Sarpi, Bodin, Grotius and De Thou but which particularly derived from Bacon its desire to be 'civil' history, Giannone attempted to show the relationship and development of two institutions both evolving in time. On the one hand he described the history of the State, from the Greek origins of Naples, the crisis of the Empire, Lombard rule, the Frankish conquest which had re-established the Empire, the Norman invasion which had established the first firm centres of the southern State, the important period of Frederick II who had briefly made Naples a seat of empire, the crisis of Norman–Swabian rule and the successive rule of the Angevins, Spanish and finally the Austrian Habsburgs. In parallel with this he depicted the history of a church which, emerging as the one remaining political force after the crisis of Rome, had taken advantage of this position by acquiring ever greater wealth, establishing and strengthening a hierarchy which not only had not been envisaged in the Scriptures, but which progressively increased its power to the detriment of secular states and peoples.

It is difficult to summarise this book with its wealth of new ideas which decisively changed jurisdictionalist thinking, giving it a historical depth which it had lacked before and injecting new life with a civil and religious passion which, among his contemporaries, was perhaps only to be found in Riccardi. But the work does not fit easily into the category of simple juris-dictionalism though Giannone's adversaries did their best to make it do so, saying it was a text, written by more than one hand, to discredit the Church. In this way they avoided tackling the profound political, moral and religious coherence which permeated a work which contained within it the unique germ of Giannone's later ideas. The time when the *Istoria civile* was published was politically far from favourable to Giannone's work. Charles VI had in fact decided to avoid jurisdictionalist debate with the successor to Clement XI and he had sent as viceroy to Naples a man sympathetic to the Curia, Cardinal Althann,[6] who was to cause a good many problems for local culture and politics. Althann had indeed come with the precise intention of strengthening his own position of viceroy by opposing the autonomy of the local jurists. He also wanted to carry out a plan of economic renewal, but the policy of subordination to Rome and his persecution of the most outspoken intellectuals alienated the *ceto civile*, magistratures, men of learning and the municipality itself. The most dramatic episodes concern Giannone, who had applied to the viceroy for approval of the dedication of his book to Charles VI and had received a very chilly reception.

This turned to hostility and particularly a complete lack of intervention when the local and Roman churches unleashed their fury on the author of the *Istoria civile*. Argento said to him immediately that this work had set a crown on his head – but a crown of thorns. The Jesuits used every means to discredit the Neapolitan lawyer, asserting among other things that his defence of concubinage was not without interest since he himself sinned publicly in that way.[7] Even the blood of St Januarius was used to influence people against him.[8] At this point Giannone had no alternative but flight to Vienna, where he was favourably received and immediately awarded a pension on which he could live. For almost ten years he imagined that he would be able to return to Naples, holding such high office that he would be out of reach of the persecution of the Church, and able to carry out at least part of that policy whose dramatic history he had depicted so ably.

These were the years of European success for this work, which was reviewed in great periodicals like the *Acta eruditorum*, heir to Leibnitz's Christian universalism, and the *Bibliothèque italique* whose editorial staff included anti-dogmatic Calvinists like Jean Alphonse Turrettini and Jacques Vernet. It had a remarkable success in England too, where a translation was published between 1729 and 1732. Archibald Bower, an ex-Jesuit turned Anglican and a man with a colourful and rather dubious life history, was attempting to introduce the English public to the intellectual world of Italy and France. To this end he made a full summary of the work, defending Giannone from the initial attacks of the Jesuits in the London *Historia literaria*.[9]

Unable to participate directly in southern politics, though tirelessly begging the sovereign and his ministers, in long, reasoned and dignified petitions, to allow him to do so, Giannone nevertheless was able to get involved in some of the matters where his expertise was required. After 1730, Giannone's energies were directed towards a new project which, compared with the *Istoria civile*, involved a notable enrichment of perspective. To understand its intellectual strength in all its complexity, it should be remembered that Vienna through Prince Eugene and Baron Hohendorf with their English and Dutch contacts, had become a central focus of what the historian Margaret Candee Jacob has called the 'radical Enlightenment'.[10] The free-thinker Toland had sent the prince and the baron all his most daring works, including an incomplete version in French of the *Letters to Serena* and a version of his *Nazarenus* more daring than what was finally published. Quite apart from Toland's work, the libraries of Hohendorf and the prince represented the richest European collection of post-libertine, free-thinking culture. Hohendorf had died in 1720 and his collection was acquired by the Palatine. Italian historians friendly with Giannone were appointed to arrange and look after it until it was incorporated into the collections of Alessandro Riccardi and Prince Eugene. The important library owned by Garelli[11], one of Giannone's main friends and protectors in his double role as librarian and imperial doctor, was to form the basis for the library of the Theresianum, the future military college founded by the Empress Maria Theresa.

At that time the Habsburg capital was a confused melting-pot of ideas and philosophies all linked in some degree to the multinational make-up of the State.[12] As well as the Italians, who came from Habsburg possessions in Italy and had been employed at court, like Apostolo Zeno and Pio Nicolò Garelli (who had read medicine at Bologna as a pupil of Giambattista Sbaraglia), there were also Catalans, driven to Vienna by the ending of Habsburg rule in Barcelona. Some of them, like the ex-archbishop of Valencia, Folch de Cardona, or the Marquis Perlas di Rialp held high office. Then there were adventurers and intellectuals from all nations and cultures, connected with official diplomacy or Prince Eugene's unofficial version of it. There was no lack of men with contacts in the Ottoman Empire, and thus able to introduce into the Viennese circle curiosities and ideas from the East, like Alexandre Bonneval and Hohendorf himself who had both been mercenaries in the Turkish army. There was a profound gap between the local cultural institutions, run by the Jesuits and thus backward in both the scientific and the literary fields, and the atmosphere of international culture found at court.

It is in this context, of Italian and European books and libertine and free-thinking culture, as well as medicine, physics and the natural sciences, that we should see Giannone's *Triregno*, one of the most important expressions, if not the masterpiece, of the radical Enlightenment of the early eighteenth century. Giannone's thinking had developed within the traditions of vitalistic mechanism, jurisdictionalism and criticism of the present structure of the Church. The inspiration to write the *Triregno* came from his desire to examine these traditions in the light of the European ideas to be found in Vienna – those of the English and Dutch free-thinkers, the exiled French, with also the echoes of the post-Spinozan debate. The realisation that jurisdictionalism in its different forms and nuances was not sufficient to do more than denounce the abuses of the Church caused Giannone to go further, to return to the very origins of ecclesiastical power. Spinoza and particularly Toland had demonstrated that the idea of the immortality of the soul was unknown to the Jews and that it derived rather from the influence of Gentile peoples like the Egyptians. The kingdom promised by God to the Jews was an entirely earthly kingdom, based on the fertility of the promised land, on a system of punishments and rewards that affected human beings physically. Thus the primitive religion of the Jews was very close to natural religion, resting on a few basic ideas: that of a creator-god and of death as the end of all. The corruption of the Jews began, according to Giannone, with their contact with other races: first the Egyptians, then the Persians and the Greeks. Some of the Jews (the Sadducees) had kept the core of their primitive religion more intact, but other sects had been taken over by the idea of the immortality of the soul and thus by the expectation of a future kingdom, not earthly but celestial. In a world full of fears and torn apart by rival sects, which was gradually losing its autonomy and identity under the Roman Empire, the hope of a celestial kingdom was born, the basis of Christianity.

With an amazing perception which distances him from Protestant historiography and brings him if anything closer to Toland, Giannone described a Jesus set in the sectarian and prophetic climate of a Palestine in crisis. He saw Christianity as the attempt to revive the religious strength of Judaism by leading it back to a morality and faith which were much closer to its original primitive roots. Jesus preached a religion based on the hope of a celestial kingdom which was to take effect immediately, a morality based on charity and a rejection of riches, hierarchies and institutions. What had changed Jesus's message after his death – a message which did not contain the idea of immortality and thus of the spirituality of the soul, but rather the idea of the immediate achievement of the kingdom of God? Various and complex elements had intervened. First of all there was Paul. This Pharisee of Greek education had not only introduced the idea of the dichotomy between soul and body, but by ousting Peter he had also definitively removed Christianity from its roots in the sectarian Hebrew world. Secondly there had been the need for the first Christian community to explain the failure of the heavenly kingdom to appear. Thirdly, from the elders of the early days, who had been the leaders and teachers of the communities, had emerged the first distinctions between laymen and clerics and the first hierarchies. The Christian world, seen by Jesus as a single unit, was gradually divided between priests, who dealt with all sacred things, and laymen, who owed deference and obedience to the former. The Edict of Constantine had had two further consequences: firstly the Church, thanks to its prestige and to the donations and tithes of the faithful, had accumulated vast riches, and secondly it had modelled its geographical institutions on those of the Empire (metropolitans, primates, archbishops and bishops were an indication of how the Church conformed to the territorial subdivisions of the Empire).

The kingdom of heaven was, according to Jesus, only for the good who would rise again in the flesh. For the others hell would simply be non-resurrection. But the failure of this hope had brought about (against the writings of some of the Fathers of the Church, like Tertullian) not only the idea of the spirituality and immortality of the soul, but also a revival of the pagan, mythical idea of the underworld. Thus it was the principle of immortality, as Toland had already understood, which needed to be unmasked, in order to disarm the Church. The materialism of the free-thinkers that Giannone encountered in the books in Vienna, along with Cartesian physics, Gassendi's atomism and Spinoza's materialism, all confirmed for him that life was the result of the organisation of the body and that this, once destroyed, gave back to the earth matter and life. Thought and intelligence too were the products of a more complex arrangement of natural particles. The idea of God remained, but that of evil was attenuated to the extent that not only did hell disappear but also that other temporary resting place of souls, the Church's real masterpiece, purgatory. Starting from the idea of original sin which is common to all and of which mankind would be cleansed by Christ's sacrifice, leaving man with, however, a strong tendency to sin, the Church had increased its hold over man's soul, attributing to itself the power of intercession which enabled it to speed the progress of the soul to heaven. From this intervention was born the whole system of indulgences, another powerful means of amassing wealth, for it was enough simply to pay in order

111

to ensure a rapid arrival in heaven. This was the true nature and reality of the papal kingdom which Giannone had intended to describe right up to his own time and which remained no more than a sketch because of the dramatic events which overtook the author.

In 1734 the War of the Polish Succession removed the kingdom of Naples from Viennese rule. Those southern Italians still in the Habsburg capital lost their pensions. Giannone thought that the new sovereign of Naples, Charles of Bourbon, would be at last the one to realise his hopes. He left for Venice, immediately seeking permission to return to Naples. Well received by many of the Venetian patricians who saw in Giannone's ideas a reflection of those of Paolo Sarpi, he thought of having the new edition of the *Istoria*, now eagerly awaited by everyone, published in Venice by Francesco Pitteri. In Venice too he was able to meet Antonio Conti.[13] A Cartesian in training, but influenced also by the naturalistic and empirical undercurrents in the Veneto, Conti had delved deep in the philosophic and scientific culture of Europe seeking the answer to the problems of his country. Dissatisfied with his exchange of ideas in Paris with Malebranche, he had gone to England, where the two interpretations of Newtonian ideology met head-on. One was the spiritualistic interpretation of Boyle's lectures, the other the materialistic version of Toland and the free-thinkers, which was more in line with Conti's own ideas. In these years, when he knew Giannone, Conti was therefore a strong exponent of free thought, as his Neapolitan correspondents, particularly Doria, were to realise. This is proved not only by Giannone's autobiography but also by the accounts of the prosecution brought against Conti and his circle which by association also damaged Giannone, who was exiled from the republic, forbidden to return under pain of death.

The Venetian patricians, friends of Conti, were accused of denying the immortality of the soul, the existence of heaven, hell and purgatory, of having a materialistic view of the world, and of arguing that religion was a lie and a convenient *instrumentum regni*. The radical nature of their ideas can be seen from these accusations. Conti emerged unscathed because he was a patrician and the case was dropped. The real victim was Giannone who was forced to wander between Modena and Lombard territory, hunted by the Inquisition. He found safety at last in Geneva. This was no accidental choice, for here were men like Jean Alphonse Turrettini and Jacques Vernet who had tried to make Calvinism into a religion of tolerance and Christian universalism. This was the home of the *Bibliothèque italique* and a country which had shown an interest in Italian culture and particularly in the *Istoria civile*. All these things made Geneva an attractive place for Giannone, where among other things there had been an offer to translate his book into French. This translation was to be carried out by Louis de Bochat, a professor in Lausanne, and printed by March Michel Bosquet. In order to assist with and enlarge upon the work, Giannone remained for a time in this small republic from which he was brutally kidnapped by a Savoyard government induced by 'reason of state' to win the favour of the Church. He was arrested, made to abjure and imprisoned in Turin, then Ceva and Miolans and back to Turin until he died, still in prison in 1748. The State of Savoy did not want to hand him over to Rome. He signed the formal act of repentance required of him. Sincerity and calculation were inextricably mixed. What is important, however, is that he answered the abjuration extorted from him with his auto-biography, written in prison, which is a proud affirmation of his intellectual autonomy. In addition, when he was certain that he would never be returned to Naples, he tried to continue with the book he had been working on.

The *Discorsi sugli Annali di Tito Livio*, written in prison, is a dense and complex discussion of the role of religion in society. The interlocutors were Machiavelli and Toland, and there is a strong vein of republicanism. But it was the following works in particular, the *Apologia de' teologi scolastici* and the *Istoria di Gregorio Magno*, which can be seen as the missing parts of the unfinished *Triregno*. The return to a rational Christianity (following Pope and a spiritualistic interpretation of Newton) had revealed itself as a provisional and inadequate solution. In these last works there emerged again the tenacious desire to grasp the historical nature of the power of the Church right from its beginnings. In addition he revealed the incompatibility of primitive Catholicism and its values with social life, he reaffirmed a materialistic concept of the world and the idea of going beyond ecclesiastical history to construct a comparative history of all religions.

Only a portion of Giannone's work reached his contemporaries and those who called themselves 'Giannonians'. The Church had suppressed the *Triregno* and the State of Savoy the works written in prison. But something even of this Giannone, the enlightened radical and not only the jurisdictionalist, managed to escape the clutches of the censor. The Verri brothers were to hear of it; in a letter they mention a Dutch edition of the *Triregno*, which however was not carried out. Part of the manuscript (*Il regno celeste*) was in Naples in the 1760s and circulated among those who followed his ideas. A complete copy, which was to make publication possible, was transcribed from the text kept in the ecclesiastic tribunal. The story had it that it was a cardinal who smuggled it out of the Holy Office. Giannone's great biographer, Leonardo Panzini, not only knew about the *Regno celeste* in 1766, but summarised the whole of the *Triregno* in the 1768 edition of the *Opere postume*.

Alberto Radicati di Passerano belonged to an ancient aristocratic family and had received the typical upbringing of the Piedmontese nobility, with an aged father and a clannish family, permanently quarrelling with the surrounding peasantry. After an early private education from an ecclesiastic, at nine years old he was sent to the Savoyard court in Turin as a page. At seventeen he was married to a Piedmontese noblewoman. This marriage of convenience was to turn out very unhappily and contributed to his drastic rejection of the family as an institution. From what we know of his life, it is clear that he went through many very painful experiences. In 1716–17 he was imprisoned for nine months in the fortress at Ivrea, thanks to the intrigues of those two 'very evil' women, his wife and his mother-in-law. On his release, he suspected that his old father had been poisoned. He, in turn, was accused of the same crime when his wife died having given birth to a third daughter. Before he was able to prove his innocence, he had to make use of the right of sanctuary, fleeing to the Church of the Oratory in Turin. It was only with the protection of the king and of his confessor that he was able to leave the church 'without fear of any untoward consequences'. Society in the Savoyard kingdom in those years must have appeared to the young aristocrat of barely twenty as a world full of problems and torn by dissension. The War of the Spanish Succession had not only brought the conflict into the heart of the State, with the siege of Turin of 1706 (the traces of which the nine-year-old Radicati had seen a year later when he had gone to the capital), but it had also led to the acquisition of the title of king of Sicily by the Savoyard ruler, Victor Amadeus II, and given rise to a long conflict with Rome. This, starting from the question of the papal Legation in Sicily, had, as has been said, soon involved more general issues. The Sicilian adventure ended badly, with the exchange of Sardinia for the fertile Sicily imposed by the European powers (see Ch. 10). But the royal title remained and with it a desire for change, which affected in an almost visible way all aspects of society from the administration to the economy and the culture.

These were the years of university reform brought about by Victor Amadeus II with the help of foreign intellectuals, the Sicilian d'Aguirre, the Neapolitan Lama, the Maltese Bencini, the Romans Regolotti and Campiani and the Frenchman Roma. As a result, Counter-Reformation Piedmont, until then completely dominated by a moderate Jesuit tradition, was suddenly plunged into the uncertainty and crises of the European consciousness. The pupils of Galiani, Gravina and Muratori (the 'Roman colony') brought with them a scientific culture and modern epistemological models; but along with these they also brought intellectual and religious experiences which fitted less easily into the scheme of reform. It was not just a matter of jurisdictionalism, Jansenism or Gallicanism, but of other more subtle influences. Lama, for example, had known in Paris not only Malebranche and Montesquieu, but also unorthodox figures like Fréret and Boulainvilliers. These influences were all so many catalysts bringing about an intellectual freedom which was inevitably to cause rents in the fabric of Piedmontese society. Lama, in his letters to Galiani, not only provides an excellent description of the climate in Turin, but also bears witness to a factor essential to Radicati's development, that is the ease with which Protestant books could be obtained in Turin from Geneva.

The clash between reason and tradition, between new models and old culture, between a rational religion and one which relied on every kind of repression, between the past and the future, had a profound effect on the young Radicati. This isolated aristocrat, starting from no preconceived ideas, differed from the reforming intellectuals who were conducting the battle for change among a thousand difficulties. Radicati's attack, born of a youthful rebellion which turned on not only religion but also the family, could not be conducted in the restrained and reasonable accents of those who were writing at the time against Jesuit culture and its models. Released by Victor

114

Amadeus II's clash with the Church, Radicati's energy was soon to be unstoppable. Deliberately and at once he took a direction which was precisely the one that Victor Amadeus feared most: direct experience of Protestantism. Between 1719 and 1721 he was in France, the France of the Regency, ambiguous and full of contrasts, from which was to come the first masterpiece of the Enlightenment, Montesquieu's *Lettres Persanes*. He strengthened his links with the French Protestants from the South. After 1721, when he returned to his family estate in Piedmont, Radicati moved towards an evangelical form of religion which led him to the discovery of all the most egalitarian aspects of Christianity. In the conflict between the community of Passerano and his aristocratic relatives who controlled the castle, he sided unambiguously with the peasants, breaking loyalty to family and caste, even to the extent of giving evidence in their favour. This was also the time of his closest association with the reforms of Victor Amadeus, whose will to contain and limit the arrogance and abuse of power by the aristocracy he had made his own, while vastly magnifying it.

The break with caste and family was to widen in the following years, when he was accused of all manner of things, including having mistreated his daughter by his first wife, in order to get his hands on her property. In the administration of the large family inheritance too he showed signs of a different way of thinking, which clashed with all the systems of privilege and economic conservatism, particularly that of the *fidecommesso*. He was determined to speak out regardless and help his sovereign in the task of transforming both the State and society, which in his opinion should start with a religious reform. In the *Manifesto* there are many signs of this point of view. On his frequent trips to Turin and in the noble salons to which he had access, often, when arguing over the State–Church question, the majority of the aristocrats would declare themselves in favour of the latter against the decisions of the sovereign. Then Radicati would defend ever more openly, the Gospels in his hand, the point of view of the State. Rumours began to be spread that he was a heretic, which reached the suspicious ears of the inquisitor who at that time was the same Dominican Alfieri who was to extract an abjuration from Giannone.

The *Manifesto*[14] describes with a wealth of detail the situation which was to bring about Radicati's sudden flight: not only the increasing persecution by his relations, but also the uncomfortable situation he found himself in as a result of the negotiations of the minister Ormea with the court of Rome. Notwithstanding his faith in the sovereign he confesses in the *Manifesto*: 'I have feared the perfidy of my enemies, the deal with Rome and the resultant re-establishment of the authority of the tyrannical Inquisition.' But in the later autobiographical work, the *Factum*,[15] there emerges a more complex picture of his relationship with the sovereign as one not only of mere defence and protection but of a genuine request for a plan of reform. Whether this is original or is, rather, a later addition we cannot know. Certainly the central core of Radicati's political writings, the *Discours*, originated from his discussions with the Piedmontese king and in the precise hope that the latter

115

would carry out in its entirety the plan that Radicati had evolved from the king's reforms in the Savoyard State. This point of view leads us to look again at the text of the *Discours*. Unfortunately we do not have the copy sent to the sovereign in 1728 and which he judged harshly, saying that it was of such a nature 'qui le rend indigne de notre protection'. It is probable that this text corresponded in part at least to the *Recueil de pièces curieuses* published in 1736.

Looking back to the *Discours* from his later works reveals a fascinating and complex itinerary to which contribute his Protestant reading (particularly Calvinist), his discovery of Sarpi, from whom he took not only the more obviously jurisdictionalist and polemic elements, but also a deeper and more insistent desire for political and religious reform, the influence of Machiavelli (of the *Prince* and the *Storie*, but also of the *Discorsi*), and finally Bayle–the more disturbing Bayle of the discourses on the comet, which, by excluding prodigies from human history, raised the question of miracles, affirmed the rights of the freedom of conscience and thus of total tolerance, and proposed a republic of virtuous atheists. It is more difficult to know when he read Spinoza and the *Tractatus theologico-politicus* which may have been later, perhaps during his time in London, even though there was evidence of a knowledge of Spinoza's ideas in Turin.

The *Discours* offered to the Piedmontese sovereign consisted principally of a picture of Christianity entirely different from that of the Catholic Church – a religion based on poverty and equality, without institutions or hierarchies, implicitly 'communist'. That these elements were already present in his early ideas is demonstrated clearly by his decision to break with class ties and side with the peasants. The other element in the *Discours* was of a historical nature. How had the power of the Church shown itself during the centuries? It was a question similar to that asked by Giannone and which he would continue to pose in the *Triregno*. Giannone is strangely absent in Radicati's reading list, but his answers are very similar. This is particularly true for Discourses IV and V on the causes of the corruption of Christian morals and on the evils that the spread of ecclesiastical wealth had brought to the states. In Discourse VI Radicati examines the question of the origins of papal power, showing that none of the rights, whether spiritual or temporal, that the papacy had assumed had any justification in the Gospels. Discourse VIII deals with a subject that was to occupy Giannone too: the different means by which the papal monarchy had gained power – from the invention of purgatory to the Inquisition – and the exploitation of miracles and indulgences by the monastic orders. In the following sections, examining the incompatibility between the power of the sovereign and the power of the Church, there emerge the differences between Catholic and Protestant countries and in particular between Italy and England – a difference due not to climate but to the political and religious direction that in England had eliminated such a deeply negative power.

It was unlikely that Victor Amadeus would have appreciated the theories of Discourse X which was devoted to forms of government. Here not only did the author's sympathy for an egalitarian democracy emerge openly, but he declared also that monarchical government was the worst of all possible political systems. It might have been acceptable, even if inferior to an egalitarian democracy, were it possible to find a truly enlightened sovereign with all the qualities needed to be a true father to his people. But these conditions could not easily be met, and thus a monarchy could easily degenerate into tyranny. Radicati did reveal a certain interest in mixed forms of government, which he saw in Holland and England and which had the advantage of being more long-lasting.

But the influence of an author like Machiavelli could be felt not only here but also in the following Discourse (XI): in order to defend against the powers of the Church, the State and the prince should fight it on its own ground, taking over sacred matters and the power deriving from them, making them subordinate to the public good. Here Radicati was looking back, not only to Machiavelli but also to regalist and jurisdictionalist theories, going from a Utopia to reform and addressing the princes living in Catholic countries. How were lost jurisdictions and immunities to be recovered? The only way was to act as if moved by a profound zeal for religion and in this way avoid any dispute over dogma. This tactical scheme for human happiness was amply illustrated in the twelve points which summed up his proposals for an ecclesiastical policy for a prince: he should (i) take over, as Gallican tradition taught, all the bishoprics, abbeys, parishes and possessions of the monks in the land; (ii) fix the number of clerics in relation to the population; (iii) tax the wealth of the clergy; (iv) ban donations; (v) take secondary and university education out of the hands of the religious orders, particularly the Jesuits; (vi) make religious ceremonies and functions free; (vii) punish as rebellious and seditious those directors of conscience who used their position to speak ill of the prince; (viii) abolish the right of sanctuary; (ix) wipe out for ever the power of the Inquisition; (x) abolish the confraternities; (xi) reduce the number of religious festivals; (xii) distribute the Church's land among the different social classes, taxing it so as to be able to reduce the taxes of the population as a whole.[16]

As can be seen, he was proposing to the Catholic princes (let it not be forgotten that the protagonists in this work were in turn Victor Amadeus, Charles Emanuel III and then Charles III of Bourbon) an organic plan of action which drew its inspiration from the Gallican tradition, Sarpi's theories and eighteenth century jurisdictionalism. The result did not aim only at religion, but also society and the economy. The fact that several times Radicati states that these discourses were intended for a prince – the Savoyard sovereign – who had implemented at least five of the twelve points, was not mere rhetoric, but corresponded to the precise intention in this work of sticking closely to the reality which had initially inspired it.

There is no doubt that the section of the work that dates from 1728 inevitably bears traces of the books that Radicati had been able to read in the two years spent in London. His disillusionment with the Savoyard prince, and the change in his circumstances (from a voluntary and temporary exile who hoped to return under the protection of the sovereign, he had become a man permanently banished from his homeland and condemned for his ideas), were factors which contributed to the radicalisation of his ideas and were to bring to the surface all that which was implicit in these *Discourses*. But his relationship with Victor Amadeus II, to whom they were addressed, should not be undervalued. This can be seen from Radicati's concern over the king's abdication and the murky *ancien régime* drama played out in the Piedmontese court in the early 1730s.[17] At this stage, after a brief and fruitless attempt to gain audience with Charles Emanuel III, he had no choice but to pursue the opposite path, which was radical Utopianism. Both in the bitingly sarcastic pages on the religion of the cannibals and in the dialogues between Mahomet and Sosem (i.e. Moses) Radicati was on the way to a complete transformation into a free-thinker, who was now writing for an English and European public. Anthony Collins, Matthew Tindal, Thomas Woolston and especially John Toland are the influences underlying the unpublished discourses, where the attack on the Christian tradition, the role of the Gospels and miracles becomes fiercer. The culminating point was the *Philosophic Dissertation upon Death*,[18] which, while returning to themes of a materialist and libertine tradition, was the most far-reaching result of his ethical radicalism: if everything is material in perpetual motion, death, which is only transformation, should not be feared.

The last events are well known. The radical Enlightenment of the continent raised burning questions even about the system of English freedom. In 1736 Anglican reactions to his latest works resulted in the imprisonment of his publisher and Radicati's flight. There only remained Holland, where expectation of death reawakened in him that central core of religious ideas which he had embraced in his rebellious youth. Radicati died as a Calvinist in 1737, when Giannone had already been in Piedmontese prisons for a year. The remains of the Piedmontese aristocrat, in involuntary homage to his ideas on egalitarian democracy, were buried in an unmarked pauper's grave in Amsterdam.

NOTES AND REFERENCES

The first important post-war work on the 'Giannonian' tradition is: Marini, L. (1950) *Giannone e il giannonismo a Napoli nel '700. Lo svolgimento della coscienza politica del ceto intellettuale del regno*. Laterza, Bari.   On Giannone and his principal works see: Vigezzi, B. (1961) *Pietro Giannone riformatore e storico*. Feltrinelli, Milan.   After this date attention has moved away from the *Istoria civile* to the *Triregno*.   See: Ricuperati, G. (1970) *L'esperienza civile e religiosa di Pietro Giannone*. Ricciardi, Milan–Naples. See also Giannone P. (1971) *Opere*, ed. Bertelli, S. and Ricuperati, G.. Ricciardi, Milan–Naples.   A bibliographical study is: Bertelli, S. (1968) *Giannoniana. Autografi, manoscritti e documenti della fortuna di Pietro Giannone*. Ricciardi, Milan–Naples. A discussion of the interpretations of Bertelli (Giannone the last libertine) and Ricuperati (Giannone between deism and the free-thinkers) is: Ajello, R. (1976) *Arcana Juris. Diritto e politica nel Settecento italiano*. Jovene, Naples, pp. 227–72.   See also various authors (1980) *Pietro Giannone e il suo tempo*, ed. Ajello, R.. Jovene,

Naples, vol. 2.   For a discussion of the work of Ajello and Ricuperati see Giarrizzo, G. (1981) 'Giannone, Vico e i loro interpreti recenti', in *Bollettino del centro di studi vichiani* a. XI, pp. 173–84.   An important contribution to studies on Giannone is: Giannone, P. (1983) *Epistolario*, ed. Minervini, P. Schena Fasano di Puglia.

For Radicati di Passerano, the fundamental work is still Venturi, F. (1954) *Alberto Radicati di Passerno*. Einaudi, Turin.   See also idem (1979) 'Adalberto Radicati di Passerano', in various authors, *Politici ed economisti del primo Settecento*. Ricciardi, Milan–Naples, pp. 3–168.

1.   As well as Chapter I of Ricuperati, G. (1970) *L'esperienza civile e religiosa di Pietro Giannone*, Ricciardi, Milan–Naples, see Rovito, P. L. 'Scienza del diritto e prassi forense nelle opere giuridiche di Pietro Giannone', in various authors (1980) *Pietro Giannone e il suo tempo*, ed. Ajello. R. Jovene, Naples, 1,pp. 251–318.

2.   See D'Andrea, F. (1956) *I ricordi di un avvocato napoletano*, ed. Cortese, N. Naples.   On d'Andrea see: De Giovanni, B. (1958) *Filosofia e diritto in Francesco d'Andrea. Contributo alla storia del previchismo*. Giuffré, Milan;   Mastellone, S. (1969) *Francesco d'Andrea. L'ascesa del 'ceto civile'*. Olschki, Florence.

3.   On Grimaldi see Grimaldi, C. (1964) *Memorie di un anticurialista del Settecento*, ed. Comparato, V. I. Olschki, Florence;   Comparato, V. I. (1968) 'Ragione e fede nelle Discussioni istoriche, teologiche e filosofiche di Costantino Grimaldi', in various authors, *Saggi e ricerche sul Settecento*. Istituto italiano per gli studi storici B. Croce, Naples.   See also the monograph with anthology by Ricuperati, G. (1979) in various authors, *Politici ed economisti del primo settecento*. Ricciardi, Milan–Naples, pp. 739–838.   On Riccardi see Ajello, R. *Arcana Juris*, op. cit., pp. 147–225 and the monograph by Ricuperati, G. in *Politici ed economisti del primo Settecento*, op. cit., pp. 695–738.

4.   See Rovito, P. L. (1981) *Res publica dei togati. Giuristi e società nella Napoli del Seicento*. Jovene, Naples.

5.   On Contegna see: Ajello, R. (1980) 'Dal giurisdizionalismo all'Illuminismo nelle Sicilie: Pietro Contegna', in *Archivio storico per le province napoletane* III, a. XCVIII, pp. 383–412.

6.   See Casella, A. 'Il Consiglio Collaterale e il viceré d'Althann dall'esilio di Giannone alla rivincita del ministero togato', in various authors, *Giannone e il suo tempo*, op. cit., II. pp. 565–633

7.   See Giannone, P. 'Vita . . . scritta da lui medesimo . . .', in Giannone, P. (1971) *Opere*, ed. Bertelli, S. and Ricuperati, G. Ricciardi, Milan-Naples, p. 84. To defend himself against these accusations Giannone had written 'Dell'antico concubinato de' Romani ritenuto nell'Imperio anche doppo la conversione di Costantino Magno.' This was to form part of the *Apologia dell'Istoria civile* and was then published in the *Opere postume* (1755), Palmyra (Geneva).

8.   Ibid., p. 82 '. . . and as for the Neapolitans, there could be no slander more convenient for their perverse ends [that of the ecclesiatics] than to make them believe that I deny the miracle of the blood of St Januarius'.

9.   See Ricuperati, G. (1981) 'Universal History: storia di un progetto europeo. Impostori, storici ed editori nella Ancient part', in *Studi settecenteschi*, 2, pp. 7–90.

10.   Candee Jacob, M. (1981) *The Radical Enlightenment, Pantheists, Freemasons and Republicans*. Allen & Unwin, London.

11.   Ricuperati, G. (1973) 'Pio Nicolò Garelli predecessore del Van Swieten nella Hofbibliothek', in various authors, *Gerard Van Swieten und seine Zeit*. Vienna–Cologne–Gratz, pp. 137–54.

12. As well as Chapter VI of Ricuperati, G. *L'esperienza civile e religiosa di Pietro Giannone*, op. cit, see for 'libertinism and deism in Vienna' Gherardi, R. (1980) *Potere e costituzione a Vienna fra Sei e Settecento*. Il Mulino, Bologna.

13. See Badaloni, N. (1968) *Antonio Conti. Un abate libero pensatore tra Newton e Voltaire*. Feltrinelli, Milan;   Ricuperati, G. (1970) 'Studi recenti sul primo Settecento: Gravina e Conti', in *Rivista storica italiana*, a. LXXXII, pp. 611–44.

14. See Manifesto di Adalberto Radicati conte di Passerano e Cocconato, in *Politici ed economisti del primo Settecento*, op. cit., pp. 31–42.

15. 'Factum d'Albert, Comte de Passeran, par lequel on voit les motifs qui l'ont engagé à composer cet ouvrage', in *Politici ed economisti del primo Settecento*, op. cit., pp. 69–76.

16. See Radicati di Passerano, A. 'Receuil de pièces curieuses, Discours moraux, historiques et politiques, Discours XII et dernier', in *Politici ed economisti del primo Settecento* pp. 51–68.

17. Radicati di Passerano, A. (1734) *Histoire de l'abdication de Victor Amedée roi de Sardaigne* . . . Turin, de l'imprimerie royale (London, in fact).

18. This work was translated from the Italian (now lost) by Morgan, J. (1732) Mears, London. It can be found in *Politici ed economisti del primo Settecento*, op., cit. pp. 95–145.

CHAPTER NINE

The political proposals of enlightened Catholicism

The wave of creativity which had characterised the first two decades of the century seemed to exhaust itself in the 1730s. As well as the dramatic story of two intellectual radicals like Giannone and Radicati there were other indicative symptoms. After the Concordat between Savoy and the Church, the organiser of Turin University, Francesco d'Aguirre, had left Turin for Vienna. The Habsburg court was to use him in the Lombard census. The departure of this energetic and representative intellectual meant on the one hand problems for the group of foreign professors (after writing the history of the House of Savoy and the code for secondary schools, Lama in his turn was to flee to Vienna), and on the other the reacquisition of control over the Piedmontese cultural institutions by local forces. What is true for Piedmont also applied to Naples. The decade of the 1730s, divided by the change of regime, seems at first sight less rich in important works than the previous two decades, and yet there was movement and the beginnings of a different and more complex future. The appointment by the Habsburg government of Galiani as *Cappellano maggiore* had been significant. He had immediately launched a plan of reform for the university which had caused much talk in Naples and Vienna. The curriculum which he proposed corresponded to the type of culture of which he had been a shrewd and cautious strategist: the introduction of experimental chairs in the fields of medicine and the sciences, the introduction of ecclesiastical history and the opening up of new areas of research.

The change of regime in 1734 again brought about the failure of the reform, but Galiani kept his post, as a sign of the continuity between the most advanced aspects of Habsburg and Bourbon reformism. The 'moderns', who gathered round him, acquired new cultural models – no longer only Descartes and Malebranche, but also Newton and Locke. The Academy of Sciences, along with the university, became the centre for the research into, and diffusion of, the ideas of Locke and Newton, provoking, as has been said, the opposition of the *veteres*, the most militant of whom were Doria and Vico. A new generation of intellectuals – theologians, scholars but particularly scientists and economists – was growing up around Galiani and Bartolomeo

Intieri. The latter was a Florentine intellectual who looked after the economic interests of the Corsini in the southern kingdom and who was to be one of the major figures in the early southern Enlightenment, providing a link between Naples and Florence. If in the field of economics Carl'Antonio Broggia[1] stood more for the old than the new, the same environment also produced Ferdinando Galiani who was soon to amaze the world with the precociousness of his insights in the economic and monetary field. Antonio Genovesi too completed his education here.

The role in southern culture of a man like Galiani, who not only ran the university, the board of censors and the sale of books but also had influence even over the religious life of the country, is paralleled and complemented by that of Intieri. He had created the chair of economics for Genovesi which was to become a central focus for the southern Enlightenment. But his importance is not due only to the organisational abilities of an exceptional man. The achievements in Naples of this inquiring and open-minded enlightened Catholic were only one aspect of the strategy of a group which had come together in Rome and there developed a general desire for the reform of scientific, literary and religious culture. This Italian road to enlightened Catholicism had various and complex facets and took in on the way Descartes, Malebranche, Newton and Locke. Men of differing tendencies took part in the group, such as Gravina, Galiani and Muratori. These were the same men as were looked to for the scholastic reforms in Piedmont, Naples and Tuscany, where from 1733 a member of the 'Roman colony' (formed by Gravina and Galiani), Gaspare Cerati, became head of Pisa University, introducing a period of reform closely linked with the change of regime and the energetic policies of renewal of the Lorraine government.

Another factor to bear in mind is the development of the learned periodicals. If after a first glorious decade the *Giornale dei letterati d'Italia* appeared only intermittently for the next twenty years, finally ceasing publication in 1740, at the same time also in Rome there had been many attempts to set up rival journals of similar or varying persuasions, even taking and translating the title and form, if not the spirit, of Bayle's famous *Nouvelles de la République des Lettres*. The journals were still learned but the contents began to consist chiefly of notes and extracts. From these initiatives there emerged learned journalists like Angelo Calogiera and his famous series of the *Opuscoli*, which swung between a collection of texts and a periodical. Soon other centres were to compete with Rome and Venice on the periodical front, starting with Florence. But before examining this area any further, it would be useful to have a look at the differing and complex response to the problems of the 1730s of two men who had figured in Italian intellectual life since the early years of the century – Ludovico Antonio Muratori (1672–1750) and Scipione Maffei (1675–1755).

For Muratori, as can be seen from many references in his correspondence, the War of the Polish Succession was a disaster which would slow down, if not actually interrupt, not only his own vast work as a scholar but also that revival of Italian culture to which he had devoted all his energies. Working from Modena, which through his contact with correspondents all over Europe became a centre of intellectual ideas, Muratori tried to continue his own work, not only completing the *Rerum italicarum scriptores* but following it with the *Antiquitates Italicae Medii Aevi*.[2] This was his way of conducting the fight for the assertion of the cultural role of Italy, through scholarship and historical study. At the same time he continued to outline a form of enlightened Catholicism which was perhaps less far-reaching than that proposed by Galiani, but certainly more explicit, as can be seen in his *Filosofia morale* of 1736, which was a development of the themes of his *Carità cristiana* of 1724. It was not only the dramatic events of the war which distressed Muratori's pacifist and Christian conscience. It was in the early 1730s that he realised with some despair that the ideas of the Enlightenment were beginning to oppose Catholicism and thus to upset the plans for reform which he was doggedly attempting to construct, reconciling reason and faith. There is, above all, the famous letter to Girolamo Tartarotti where he seems to retreat, terrified, from the consequences of modern philosophy. In fact he saw in Locke not so much the theoretician of the reasonableness of Christianity as one of the many fathers of materialism and anti-religious radicalism. But nevertheless this dramatic realisation of the possible implications of modern ideas did not push him over to the camp of the *antiqui*, nor cause him in any way to join in the Church's repressive strategy of attacking – by means of the Inquisition – all those who opposed it. This included the first masonic groups and the jurisdictionalists like Riccardi and Giannone. This is clear from Muratori's cautious but definite involvement in protecting Giannone, who had fled from Venice and was being pursued on Modenese territory by agents of the Holy Office.[3]

At this same period one can see in Scipione Maffei too an almost dramatic realisation that the new era that was to come was less simple than had been hoped a few decades before. After his *Scienza cavalleresca*, which had initiated the discussion on the Italian Enlightenment, offering perhaps the most optimistic and clear version of the problems and hopes of an urban patriciate which was to move away from the feudal nobility, by the mid-1730s he had acquired fame and frustration. The crisis of the *Giornale de' letterati* had prompted him to try a 'municipal' road to learning and history which in some ways was to coincide with Muratori's Italian road. In this sense there is a link between his learned works, from *Verona illustrata* to *Arte critica*, and his selections as editor and even journalist in the *Osservazioni letterarie* which attempted at least in part to transfer to Verona some of the inheritance of the *Giornale de' letterati*.[4]

When he had finished the exhausting labour of the learned *Verona illustrata*, Maffei set out on the journey around Europe which was to keep him from home for some four years, and introduced him to Paris, Geneva, London, Holland and Vienna. The first stop was Geneva where Maffei was able to observe a form of republic totally different from that of Venice, in that (though social distinctions were not absent) there was no trace of a patriciate comparable to that of *la Serenissima*. On the intellectual front, the ideas of Turrettini and Vernet made the Calvinist city, until a few decades before the citadel of orthodoxy, one of the reference points for Christian universalism and tolerance, values for which men like Grotius and Leibnitz had long fought. This was not all. Vernet, in particular, knowledgeable about the French and Italian world of learning as can be seen from his involvement with a review of European culture like the *Bibliothèque*, was making every effort not only to understand the currents in the eighteenth-century resurgence, but also actively to bring about a peaceful co-operation between a rational Christianity and the emergent Enlightenment. This man who welcomed Maffei with an awareness of the meeting of minds was the same who four years later was to help the fugitive Giannone in every possible way, thus aiding, directly and indirectly, his participation in the French translation of the *Istoria civile* that Louis de Bochat was working on in Lausanne. He looked after Giannone's manuscripts, after the latter's arrest, and he was to contribute actively to Giannone's defence with the anthology of *Anecdotes ecclésiastiques* taken from the first books of the work. In his vocation as cultural organiser and mediator between religious rationalism and Enlightenment, he was to promote the publication in Geneva of two outstanding works: Montesquieu's *L'Esprit des Lois* and Voltaire's *Essai sur les moeurs*.

From Geneva, Maffei travelled to Paris, where he was struck not only by the wealth but also by the complexity of the French State and by its economic and political power. He saw more and more clearly how Italy was without influence and increasingly subjected to the decisions and conflicts of outsiders. But just at the time he was discovering how the policies even of Venice were largely determined by Paris and entirely subordinate to the movements of international diplomacy, he also received a remarkable stimulus which would transform his patrician municipalism into something more, into a genuine proposal for political reform that would strike at the heart of the republic's problems. The *Consiglio politico*, which he wrote in 1737 shortly after his return and which was addressed to the Venetian government but certainly circulated among the patricians inside and outside the city, remained unprinted precisely because of the delicate problems it raised. It was not rediscovered until 1797, in the year when the Peace of Campo Formio brought the Venetian Republic to an end. His revelation of Venetian weakness in the face of the other European states seemed to the patriots of the late eighteenth century truly prophetic. This text can be compared with Montesquieu, some aspects of whose work Maffei anticipates, for example in his analysis of the three powers and in his choice of an advanced political model along the lines of the English system. On the other hand, Maffei's ideas, like those of Doria, but in a less abstract way, are to be located in the constitutionalist tradition along with a few others such as Gravina and Doria.

Maffei's arrival in England was preceded by letters of introduction from Voltaire and by his own fame as a man of letters. In London he frequented strongly 'Italianising' circles like those of Lord Burlington and Lord Pembroke. He also went to Oxford (where he had to listen to a long speech in his honour in a Latin which English pronunciation made incomprehensible to him) and to Cambridge. He was impressed by the wealth of the ruling classes and by the involvement in political and intellectual life of public opinion, the result of liberty and prosperity. He was equally struck by Holland and the careful opulence of the patricians and rich bourgeoisie of Amsterdam, the port that, with over 400 ships berthed there, could not fail to remind him of the decline of the Venetian maritime trade. His direct observations gave him rather too rosy a picture of Dutch society. He failed to notice that this prosperity, even if still remarkable, was already menaced by crises and that Amsterdam was about to relinquish its place in favour of London. It is difficult to say whether in Holland Maffei encountered the treatises by the Catholics of Utrecht on usury, published in the theologian Nicola Broedersen's book *De usuris licitis* (1727), which was the first dent in the age-old opposition of the Catholic Church to usury. Maffei took up a similar position in his book *Impiego del denaro* (1744), which according to Muratori followed Broedersen's text. His stay in Holland must have made him understand with great clarity what an advantage was given to the Protestants by the rigid Catholic opposition to usury. It was not just a mere theological principle at stake, circumvented by means of the *Monti di Pietà* (official pawnshops), but the very future of society. When compared with other countries both Protestant and economically prosperous that believed in and practised without either moral or religious obstacles the speculative investment of money, it was impossible not to see that the laws against usury tended to set Catholicism against civil society.

If the *Istoria teologica*, written in Paris and published in Trent in 1742, represents his most defensive and thus traditional phase, the *Consiglio politico* and later the *Impiego del denaro* were the culmination of a coherent philosophy that formed a unified whole, rich with ideas for reform.[5] Liberty, economic wealth, political involvement and development of civil society were all aims which he would have liked not only to carry out in the Veneto but also to keep within the framework of the Church. For this reason, unlike Muratori and particularly Muratori's followers, Maffei finished up finding himself in a theological position closer to the Jesuits than the Jansenists. Perhaps it is relevant too that, as a Venetian patrician, he had never been attracted to neo-Ghibellinism, as can be seen in his acute but very critical remarks about Giannone's *Istoria civile*. Certainly he was to experience in person what he had already written in Paris: that it was easier to agree with the probabilistic and attractive rationalism of a Jesuit writer like Francesco Antonio Zaccaria than with rigid Jansenists like the Ballerini brothers, Daniele Concina or Celso Migliavacca. It can be said that Maffei's unique Catholic reformism exposed very early on certain conservative aspects which were characteristic of the ethics as well as the theology of the Jansenists but which the anti-Jesuit movement was to obscure for several decades more.

In the *Consiglio politico* Maffei discussed the whole delicate and complex system of balance in the Venetian government, revealing its decadence and proposing a very daring solution. The text is addressed to the State of which it speaks, the Venetian Republic, and from the point of view of a patrician of the mainland who had seen all the consequences of excluding the local ruling classes from direction of state policy. It was a system by which Venice was able to defend her survival and neutrality, but the price was stagnation and the renunciation of an international role in politics and economics. Maffei saw clearly the crisis, that was even physiological, of the Venetian ruling class and offered the first consistent critique of what was to be the solution adopted by the Senate – the co-opting of a number of patrician families from the mainland as officials in the city, opening up to them the possibility of a political career. This solution simply postponed the problem. In fact, according to Maffei, Venice's decadence had two related causes. One was economic and embraced all the Italian areas that were neither able to follow the French example (the mercantile State) nor the Anglo-Dutch model (the development of civil society), the other was political. Venice had evolved a system that was the opposite of that of the Roman Republic, estranging from itself and from responsibility the greater part of its subjects. Venice's precariousness, her inability to produce a convincing external policy and her retreat into a neutrality which disguised her impotence were the results of this system, which had excluded the patricians of cities like Verona, Padua, Brescia and Bergamo. There was no love of country, which would have been the only form of resistance to the growing pressures from the states of Europe. At this moment Maffei wondered how it might be possible to remedy matters, increasing Venice's strength and prestige, without expanding territorially.

The solution he proposed was the involvement of all the citizens. The most obvious example was still the Roman Republic. There, according to Maffei, there had been a transference of power from the people (the indeterminate multitude) to the Senate (the limited and chosen multitude) with the progressive involvement of the conquered populations, pacified and absorbed with full rights into the Roman system. Returning to subjects dealt with more theoretically in *Verona illustrata*, Maffei maintained that traces of the ancient Roman freedom were preserved in the province of the Veneto (with Venice he included the mainland) and that now was the time to recall that tradition. Here Maffei brought in, to set alongside the Roman model, examples of states that he considered to be 'republics', i.e. based on a non-absolute system, where the representative bodies retained some basic powers. In this category was England, which despite the monarchy had the two Houses of Parliament; so too was, particularly, Holland, where every province retained considerable autonomy and some powers of decision-making while cities, countryside and nobility were all represented in just proportion. Maffei concluded by examining as 'republican' models even the Empire with its Diets and the elective monarchy of Poland.

Returning to Venice, his proposal was not so much to give new life to the Venetian ruling class by an injection of noble families from the mainland, as to extend the privileges of the capital city to the whole country, extending representation not only to urban patricians but also to the producing classes, merchants and artisans. Socially this plan was not revolutionary. On the contrary, it reinforced the role of the nobility of patrician origin by giving it the functions – military, governmental, administrative and judicial – that had once belonged to the feudal nobility. The civil transformation of Venetian society (and, more generally that of Italy) had to start with the political, moral and intellectual reform of this patriciate. At this period Maffei had indeed written even more explicitly in letters of his view, which underlies his contribution to the 'science of chivalry', that it would be better for the exercise of literary culture to be confined to the nobility.

The 1740s too were scarred by war – the War of the Austrian Succession – during which the courts and their diplomatic services began to question the very existence of the Empire and its position as a great multinational state surrounding a centre like Vienna. These thoughts became more widespread after 1738, the year when an overhasty peace, which did not resolve the still implicit and threatening problems, was signed. It was not difficult to see the fragility of a solution like the Pragmatic Sanction, which entrusted to inter-national agreements the problem of a female successor to Charles VI who had no male heirs and who would traditionally have been bound by Salic law. Moving from a realisation of the European drama to the search for a working peace, the activities of the Italian world of intellectuals in the decade leading up to the Treaty of Aix-la-Chapelle (1748) underwent profound changes both of quality and quantity.

To start with, the whole situation of periodicals changed significantly. The *Giornale de' letterati d'Italia*, published in Venice, had continued to struggle along until its final collapse in 1740. Various other similar journals had started up, inspired by the same model or which attempted to exploit and steal its fame. Scipione Maffei himself had initiated a new periodical, the *Osservazioni letterarie*, which appeared in Verona from 1737 to 1740, but the review undoubtedly suffered – at least in terms of its success as a journal – from the presence of an editor like Maffei who perhaps lacked national links and who certainly had a rather egocentric character. Despite the quality of the contributions, for example a first assessment of the importance of Muratori's great work of scholarship, the *Rerum italicarum scriptores*, Maffei's journal degenerated into a miscellaneous collection of his writings, thereby losing a great part of the character of the literary periodical of his youth. In fact Maffei's lack of success as a journalist was perhaps partly due to the type of erudite journal that he was trying to produce. When the programme of the Florentine *Novelle letterarie* was announced, Maffei, who was very alert and always fearful lest his greatness be overlooked, immediately contacted Giov-anni Lami, applauding his enterprise and offering his collaboration, but not disguising his surprise at Lami's decision. Basically, he wrote in his letter to the Florentine journalist, to choose literary news as the main subject of a journal was to drag it down to the level of a gazette, as had already happened with disastrous results to one of the Venetian attempts to revive the title of Bayle's famous journal. According to Maffei, this was to confuse two trades.

The immediate success of the Florentine journal,[6] which was to have an important role in Italian culture for some twenty years, was a sign that, leaving aside the excellence of the Tuscan editors, something had changed in the public and their desire for cultural information. It was to take a very different form from the *Giornale de' letterati* which was made up of extracts and notes for the greater part, with an appendix of literary news. While the contents remained largely learned, the news itself was changed, no longer providing extrinsic and marginal information but becoming instead more of a review, giving a concise but useful judgement of the value of the book discussed. But the decision to review meant a considerable change in the task of the journalist. He had to abandon his neutrality and make subjective choices. Imperceptibly, not only the form but also the substance of the learned journal was changing. By means of the review, which made it clear in advance that the neutrality of the scholar was no longer operating, it was easier to stimulate public opinion and to influence not only the technical side of problems but also the religious and political ideas and then, little by little, economic thinking and ideas about social behaviour. This was the way towards the development of the critical review which already existed in England but which only really took root in Italy after 1760.

The editor of the Florentine *Novelle letterarie* was Giovanni Lami, a Tuscan intellectual of inquiring mind and quick intelligence who, after studying law, had chosen sacred and profane scholarship instead. He had been drawn to journalism after a period of editing theological and learned texts, becoming expert in classical philology and ecclesiastical history. While seeking books for the library of the Marquis Riccardi, his employer, he had been able in the 1730s to travel all over Europe, meeting the cream of the Italian and European intelligentsia. In Paris he had visited the Maurists, in Vienna he had met Giannone, in Florence he formed lasting friendships not only with antiquarians, but also with those inquiring and open-minded Catholics who had been fighting for over thirty years for the reform of religious culture like Antonio Niccolini, Gaspare Cerati and Giovanni Gaetano Bottari. This form of Catholicism had a very different theological model from that of the Jesuits, and attempted to reconcile different tendencies – Augustinian rigorism, Gallicanism, jurisdictionalism and modern scientific and philosophical thinking. According to the personalities and experiences involved, this enlightened Catholicism received different nuances, influences, contacts and echoes of the new Enlightenment. In general it was inevitably selective, attempting to absorb into the mainstream of Catholicism as much as possible of the new science and philosophy. The co-ordinating centres, besides Florence and Pisa, were, in Rome, the intellectuals of the *Circolo dell'Archetto*, led by Bottari and Cardinal Passionei, in Naples, Galiani's followers and, in Modena, Muratori. This network of open-minded Catholics, aware of the crisis of Italian culture and wishing to reconcile, at the highest level, Catholicism and enlightened philosophy, soon began to realise that the basic problem was one of ensuring control over various cultural institutions which would grow in importance and act on public opinion. Unlike the radicals, who allowed themselves to become isolated, the enlightened Catholics, having lost several important battles (for example when the *Arcadia*, after the defeat of Gravina, came firmly under the control of a Curia man like Crescimbeni), acted with a remarkable open-mindedness and lack of prejudice, taking over old institutions, like the universities which they helped to reform, and also academies and particularly periodicals.

In the universities it is possible to see a link between the attempts by Gravina and Diego d'Aguirre at reform under Pope Clement XI in Rome and the Piedmontese reforms (which not only Francesco d'Aguirre but also the 'Roman colony' inspired by Gravina, Galiani and Muratori were involved in). Galiani, having been on the point of moving with Gravina to Turin, became responsible for Naples University and was the founder of the Neapolitan Academy of Science. A group of these enlightened Catholics had gathered around Garelli, doctor and librarian to Charles VI, who until the 1740s provided a link between enlightened Catholicism and religious radicalism. The meeting point was political, in the area of jurisdictionalism and the struggle against the Jesuit influence in the Church. In Pisa, as we have said, the university reforms of 1733 were to be directed by another member of the 'Roman colony' – Monsignor Cerati.

Right from the start the *Novelle letterarie* aspired to become the means for the unification of the Tuscan world of letters and a mouthpiece of the desire for political and religious reform. The election to the papal throne of Benedict XIV in 1740 was to reinforce this intent, for he seemed to be prepared to realise all the hopes of reform of Italian Catholicism. Lami and the cultural policies of his periodical refer constantly to Benedict XIV and Muratori. Indeed, the journal's period of greatest liveliness coincided exactly with the period of greatest hopes and of initiatives by the papacy. During the whole of Benedict's pontificate (1740–58) Lami's anti-Jesuit stance differed from that of the Jansenists in that it was broader and more articulate. The death of Benedict brought an end to this experiment in enlightened Catholicism; Lami was brought back into line with the Jansenists and was to step up his attacks on the Enlightenment which was by now irreconcilable with his Catholicism.

In the early 1740s, intellectual life in Tuscany, stimulated by the Lorraine Regency, was beginning to bear fruit. Pisa tried again with a *Giornale de' letterati*, partly as a result of a split with the *Novelle*, where Lami was increasingly imposing his own journalistic personality. The new Pisan journal was rather different. It concentrated, both in the choice of collaborators and of the public which it addressed, not so much on learned men in general as intellectuals in the academic world which was now greatly revived. In Leghorn, which during the eighteenth century was to continue to expand as the main free port of the Tyrrhenian, new periodicals were emerging which reflected the international culture, particularly English and French, which was circulating among the resident foreigners. A little later, in the mid-1750s, even the little Republic of Lucca, after the remarkable publication of a French edition of the *Encyclopédie*, was to present the journalistic world with a translation of the *Journal encyclopédique*. Tuscany, with its many academies dedicated to antiquarian studies, natural sciences or agriculture, such as the *Accademia dei Georgofili* in the 1750s, offered the possibility of a high level of journalism both erudite and scientific, which aimed at academics, university professors, gentlemen of letters and government officials.

The 1740s, if measured by the output of important creative works, were still dominated by the generation of intellectuals which had formed at the time of Giannone, Vico and Muratori. The former obstinately continued to write in his Turin prison, and Vico finished in 1744 his definitive edition of the *Scienza Nuova* (the third after the Neapolitan edition of 1725 and the Venice edition of 1730). But the decade was above all still dominated by Muratori's great works. After his *Rerum* and the *Antiquitates*, he undertook the first civil history of Italy – the *Annali d'Italia*, drawing on the notes he had accumulated. Here, with all due deference to the papacy and the Church, he presented his main ideas: an admiration for the Lombards and barbarians in general (following Machiavelli and Grotius) and a quiet but firm denunciation of the interference of the Church. Along with this historical work, to which he added an Italian translation of the *Antiquitates italicae*, Muratori had continued his studies in the area of his *Riflessioni sopra il buon gusto*. His works such as the one on 'human understanding' and on 'imagination' lead in this direction. Hostile to historical Pyrrhonism, to the extent of suspecting Pierre Daniel Huet's latest work on the weakness of the human spirit of being the product of free-thinkers or freemasons, Muratori continued his attempt to define the civil and religious behaviour of an enlightened Catholicism. At this period his thinking coincided with that of another equally old but intellectually vigorous thinker, Scipione Maffei. Maffei had published in 1744, in the wake of hopes aroused by Benedict XIV, his *Dell'impiego del denaro* which had set him against all the 'traditional' forces of the Catholic world. In this book, which described the great economic development of countries like England and Holland unfettered by theological restraints such as the condemnation of usury, he examined once again both the Scriptures and the Church Fathers in an attempt to derive from them a Christianity more easily reconcilable with the development of civil society.

The attacks that were immediately unleashed on him by the Jansenist theologians, starting with the Ballerini brothers, were such that the state Inquisition intervened to stop the fiery scholar. He tried to involve not only Benedict XIV but also Muratori in his defence. In his letters to the great Modenese scholar, asking for his aid, he did not fail to point out that his theory of the charging of interest, legitimate in so far as it was a payment for the risk taken, was one of the many things that the enlightened Catholic movement would have to accept in order to win its battle against the backwardness and restrictions of a traditionalist society. At about the same time, Muratori had opened up another front with broad economic implications. He had appealed to the pope, asking him, in line with other directives he had carried out when he was Archbishop of Bologna, to reduce the number of religious feast-days, which threatened to harm not only agricultural but particularly artisan and industrial work. The *idéologie économique*, although

130

calling theology and the traditions of the Catholic world to account, yet seemed for a moment, through the arguments of these two great intellectuals, to be less hostile to Catholicism. While Doria withdrew with his own particular type of Catholicism, opposed to the Enlightenment, into the anachronistic and utopian world of Plato's republic, Maffei and Muratori, while treating apparently backward-looking topics like that of the *Impiego del denaro* or the reduction of religious feast-days, were in fact attempting to reconcile Catholicism and the values of the Enlightenment. The last great campaign undertaken by Maffei, which was to end on the threshold of the 1750s, on the relationship of magic to reason, should be seen in the same light.

The whole debate from the 1740s onwards had centred around elements which to some degree can be traced back to Maffei and particularly Muratori. Muratori had laid the cultural and religious foundations for such a debate, by studying the existence of superstitions in the Middle Ages and describing the defects of a legal system which allowed torture by means of which it convinced itself of the guilt of the accused, thereby identifying diabolical practices and witchcraft. He had also returned to the question of the conflict between reason and superstition in his two treatises of 1745 on 'the force of human understanding' and on the imagination, and in his essay of 1747 on 'regulated devotion', which offered a model of Christianity stripped of the abuses of the imagination and of superficial ceremonies, the sole purpose of which was to dazzle the popular imagination. Muratori and Maffei were an influence on Girolamo Tartarotti, author of the *Congresso notturno delle Lammie* of 1749 and also on Gian Rinaldo Carli who had assisted Tartarotti in his long and passionate collection of material on witchcraft.[7]

The debate was geographically localised among the intellectuals on the edges of central-northern Italy, in areas like Rovereto, Venice, Padua and Rome, not extending further than Rome. In 1751 a posthumous work by Costantino Grimaldi had appeared there, *Dissertazione in cui si investiga quali siano le operazioni che dependono dalla magia diabolica e quelle che derivano dalla magia naturale e artificiale*, printed by the Paglierini brothers who were to be the Roman editors of anti-Jesuitism. It was revised by Giovanni Bottari, one of those enlightened Catholics who had fought to save Montesquieu's *Esprit des Lois* from Roman censorship. It is interesting to trace the main arguments of this debate which was to continue throughout the 1750s. Tartarotti had taken the prudent decision not to tackle head-on the structure of an animistic cosmos, well aware that this decision would inevitably lead him into conflict with the basic tenets of the Christian tradition. He confined himself to removing a large part of this world from the irrational, making it if anything the result of fantasy, imagination and popular superstition. His distinction between magic and witchcraft gave him the opportunity for a lucid and intelligent attack on burning and capital punishment for confessions made under torture, such as that of the nun Maria Renata, burnt as a witch on 21 June 1749, the year that Tartarotti's work appeared. It did not, however, entirely persuade those intellectuals of scholarly and 'modern' training. Much more radical and uncompromising was the text by Gian Rinaldo Carli published as an appendix to Tartarotti's book, where all magic and diabolical manifestations were traced back to an animistic culture which was gradually being defeated by a rational view of science.

At the first howl of protest from the supporters of the devil, who not coincidentally were almost the same as those who attacked *Sull'impiego del denaro* – Ballerini, Concina and Mamachi – the ageing Maffei felt obliged to intervene with his *Arte magica dileguata* (1749), where, after a polite bow to the letter of the Holy Scriptures, he demonstrated the incompatibility of Christianity, now enlightened and rational, with the persistence of magic. He re-elaborated the theme in *Arte magica distrutta* which was published in Trent in 1750 under the colourful pseudonym of 'Antonio Furio, archpriest of Tignale and Valvestino, *vicario forense*'. In 1754, before he died, he was to sum up all the conclusions of this debate in his *Arte magica annichilata* which, while retaining its initial radicalness, answered all his critics, among whom it is possible to pick out many of his Jansenist enemies. This debate, which exploded in 1749, saw the emergence, alongside men of the same generation like Bartolomeo Melchiorre or Giuseppe Gorini Corio, of a new generation of intellectuals whose roots were to be firmly planted in the Enlightenment, like Gian Rinaldo Carli, Clemente Baroni and Father Paolo Frisi, the Barnabite who was to be a future contributor to *Il Caffè* and friend of Pietro Verri.

The 1730s were dominated by a deep uncertainty linked, as we have tried to show, to the emergence of the radical Enlightenment, which enlightened Catholics could hardly fail to regard with some anxiety, to the international situation and to the failure of those neo-Ghibelline theories which had aroused great hopes and then cast them down. Yet nevertheless the political divisions of Italy up to 1738 were to last unchanged. Despite the War of the Austrian Succession, in the 1740s there was a feeling, by now general and growing, that Europe had fairly successfully stabilised the Italian system of balances and that a long period of peaceful reform was on the way. It was Muratori, once again, who pulled all the threads together, not only closing his *Annali* for 1748 with a wish for a lasting peace for Europe and Italy, but also finishing his *Della pubblica felicità* (1749) which was a complete manual for moderate reformism. He did not write anything new or particularly daring. Even his reference point, that is, good princes, enlightened sovereigns capable of choosing as their aim the happiness of their subjects, did not incline Muratori to write about their power and the guarantees that they might offer. Instead it led him to accept unconditionally the point of view of the *ancien régime*. In reality Muratori was addressing a prince enlightened by Christian virtues and a philosophy of good taste and reason, who could not fail to try to carry out a programme of reform. In this work, Muratori distinguished between the search for personal happiness, which is a characteristic human impulse born of nature, and public happiness which instead 'has virtue for mother'. While the first, precisely because it is a sort of passion of the soul, can lead to the search for earthly goods until it becomes a vice, the second is always positive:

To desire and procure the public good is very praiseworthy in the eyes of God and of men, for it is done by honest means. And, oh, would to God that this noble desire, this generous affection would be more preached, more widely spread and would conquer the hearts of men and even more so the heart of he who governs over the people and over all those who have genius and apply themselves to literature. How much better would be the world . . . .[8]

From this passage, an introduction and justification of his research, we can see some elements which are essential to an understanding of the work. First of all there is the anti-Machiavellism. Muratori's *Della pubblica felicità*, a manual for princes, denies quietly but firmly the independence of politics from morality and religion. Another very important point is the responsibility not only of princes or their ministers but of all those who have genius and apply themselves to literature. Intellectuals have the duty to help the enlightened princes to 'dethrone' the private good, 'old master of the world', putting in its place public happiness.

The whole work is imbued with a remarkable and robust optimism. Muratori sincerely believes that not only is public happiness part of the job of princes and their ministers, but also that through reforms this is a realisable objective, without entailing violent upheavals. He brings together in a single work all the themes that he had written about and observed in more than four decades of passionate political, civil and religious activity. In a Europe which in 1748 reached an equilibrium that was by now fairly stable, it was possible to think of serious reforms, which would make society less unjust. Muratori's proposals had nothing Utopian about them – on the contrary, on inspection they appear to look more to the past than the future. In the face of the serious consequences of a world fiercely divided by the emergence of the rights of property, Muratori did not intend to propose more than minor adjustments, that would make the poverty of the urban and particularly the peasant masses less irksome. The State, and thus the prince who represented it, had an important role in this, as can be seen from the actions of sovereigns like Louis XIV, Peter the Great, Frederick II or Victor Amadeus II. Looking at France, Muratori did not consider so much its military strength or prestigious foreign policy as its economic policies, organised by Colbert, and its cultural policy. The steps towards modernisation taken by Peter the Great struck him as much more important, the sovereign having, from the most unfavourable circumstances, managed to drag Russia out of the Dark Ages. In the Piedmontese sovereign he saw the ability to unite administrative and economic reforms with a courageous cultural policy, in both the university and secondary sectors. He paid particular attention to the law. Drawing the lessons of the *Difetti della giurisprudenza*, he proposed as a rational solution the codification of the laws as Victor Amadeus II and Frederick II had chosen.

While Muratori's models for princes and policies all come from past examples of enlightened absolutism, yet he also looked to the future – for example

133

to the measures taken in Tuscany by the enterprising Regency, which were to some degree the counterpart of another great experiment in course of progress, the innovatory papacy of Benedict XIV. As for economic policy, the *Della pubblica felicità* in general revived all the expedients of late-mercantilism, influenced by the works of Melon. But there are differences too. From this *idéologie économique* Muratori took all the technical aspects and practical solutions while rejecting its more modern and radical implications, those which would have led to the separation of economics from morality. There remained implicit in Muratori's concept of 'public happiness' the constant welding together of reform and morality. Anti-Machiavellian, Muratori also opposed the defence of luxury as an end in itself, or considered as a motive force for the economy of the State. In his forceful proposal for the meeting of enlightened policies, an economy regulated for the public good and a rational form of religion, he provided a general plan which contained all the chief aims of eighteenth-century reforms.

The experiences of the past thus joined with hopes for the future. Closer attention was paid to agriculture, the productive sector *par excellence*. But trade too was being developed and supported, for example by freeing goods from excessive customs restrictions. Fiscal policy – where the ideas of Broggia were widely followed – should spread more widely to take in nobles and ecclesiastics and not press down on the peasants alone. The restrictions on the sale of land too were being removed, following the example of the Tuscan law on *fidecommessi* and mortmains. In a society which aimed to spread public happiness to the greater part of the population, the aristocracy too had the duty to find a role, rather than weighing down parasitically on other groups. As well as in politics and the defence and development of culture, the nobility were also invited to participate in economic enterprises, not only by studying ways in which the productivity of the land could be increased but also by investing in trade.

These were the first Italian reactions to the debate opened in France by abbé Coyer's famous work. Muratori, as has been said, had come down firmly on the side of a late-mercantilistic model, as it had developed in Europe from the end of the seventeenth century. But it was precisely his attempt to reconcile this with morality and enlightened religion which caused attention to fall not only on commerce or the primary industries (especially silk and wool), but also, and in a particular way, on agriculture. His ideal was a small or medium-sized property, made productive by the loving care of the farmer himself. The State had the right to intervene as Modena had done '. . . 500 years ago, by obliging the owners to sell, let out and exchange with neighbours these pieces of land with various well thought out directives, and by appointing public estimators to arrange this confused system: not to create large holdings but rather ones of modest and reasonable size which yield greater results than those which are too large'.[9] He emerges as being decidedly against restrictions on landownership, whether of a lay or ecclesiastic nature, such as the *maggiorascato* and *fidecommesso*, and he proposed to put in their place a system of long-term rental which would benefit the land and at the same time assure the tenant of a good income.

It is interesting to examine Muratori's attitude to luxury which Melon had defended in his *Essai politique sur le commerce*, which had been for at least fifteen years the essential text for the late-mercantilist reformers. Muratori only partly supported these ideas. Luxury, although deriving from possibly dubious motives, like vanity and the desire of the nobles to compete with each other, is not in itself a sin, if it supports the crafts and industries of the State, giving back to the productive classes a part of the surplus of the rich. It becomes harmful when it is nourished by goods not produced in the country, thus inevitably impoverishing the national economy. In reality, according to Muratori, it would be better if the rich invested their surplus in enterprises of public utility, linking their names with things like 'bridges, canals, banking houses, academies dedicated to the sciences, seminaries, libraries, hospices giving work to the poor, hospitals caring for the sick and invalid and other similar works for the benefit of one's town . . .'.[10]

Another important theme, because it was to stimulate many debates in the following decade, was that of taxes and money. The State could not survive without taxes, but these should be apportioned according to the wealth of the subjects. Using Broggia's *De' tributi* of 1743, Muratori attacked the idea that high taxation served 'to make people more industrious, in order to be able to sustain themselves as well as pay their taxes'. It was a revolutionary stance from all points of view, economic, political and moral: 'Listen to this absurdity: thus also were the slaves of antiquity treated. But that a free people should have to labour in this way just in order to stay alive, and that all the excess, if he by industry earns more than his bread, instead of using it to improve his condition and that of his family, it must fly into the prince's coffers: I must be forgiven if I cannot believe that his condition is so very happy. What is more, the princes do not hear the laments and curses of their subjects: but it would be good if they did.'[11]

Opposed to monopolies and a supporter of a realistic freedom of trade (excepting only salt and tobacco, traditionally controlled by the sovereign), Muratori tackled decisively a theme of great importance like the contracting out of taxes and the unrestricted increase of the national debt. While justifiable in exceptional circumstances, as for example a war, it should be the prince's job not only to eliminate this type of speculation, but also to reduce the national debt, preventing it from becoming a profit-making system for private speculators. He believed that debts contracted with other nations were particularly harmful, being determined by an unfavourable balance of payments. In the chapter on money, which deals with the problem from a late-mercantilist point of view, he demonstrates that wealth is related not to an amount of gold and silver but to the development of production, as could be seen from the negative example of Spain and, by contrast, the example of countries like Holland and England. What has become of the gold and silver that Spain and Portugal brought from the American mines and then were forced to pass on to the merchant countries of Europe, Muratori asks. He suggests with great insight that Turkey, India and above all China had absorbed the greater part of these precious metals.

On one question, that of militias, Muratori meets Machiavelli's ideas. He could not hide his Christian and pacifist repugnance for this subject, but he was realist enough to realise that war and the ambitions of princes were inevitable, even if to a great extent inimical to the very concept of public happiness. Wars are harmful not only because of the devastation which they cause directly, but also because of the more long-lasting consequences, not least of which are the debts contracted by the State. Resorting to violence benefits neither the subjects of the State, nor even those of the conquering State. Muratori makes an important distinction when speaking of citizen militias. In the republics of antiquity every citizen was a soldier, directly involved in the defence of freedom. This system had shown itself to be dangerous because the clashes between patricians and plebeians had paved the way to the crisis of the State. In the republics where 'the government is wisely placed with the nobility, it could perhaps be dangerous to make the common people warlike'. By contrast, such a danger did not exist in the monarchies. It remained to be seen whether such bodies, recruited from among the subjects, would be capable of standing up against trained veterans. In Muratori's opinion, these citizen soldiers should never have to take offensive action. The military training of the citizens could also be useful as an education for the young people, removed from idleness by military drilling. The fact remained that a sovereign (the most typical example being Louis XIV) could, by turning the peasants into soldiers, cause lasting harm to agriculture:

a possession so essential to every State that immense harm will result. It was not certainly counted among the triumphs of any monarch that he, with so many wars, had made such exorbitant demands of the people that the land remained uncultivated. The necessity of defence can excuse such excesses, but ambition and the whims of the ruler can never do so.[12]

The fame of this handbook of 'public happiness' and moderate reform was considerable. In 1750 at the court of Savoy, Sigismondo Gerdil contrasted it with Montesquieu's *Esprit des Lois*, in support of his theory that monarchical states too were capable of virtue. Muratori's work was translated into French and Spanish, having a remarkable success in Bourbon territories, but it was to be most famous in the Habsburg Empire where it was probably read by Maria Theresa.[13] It is possible too that it was the first introduction to enlightened policies for her sons Joseph and Leopold,[14] who were to enrich with other and much more far-reaching elements this first attractive proposal for the rational reform of society.

NOTES AND REFERENCES

The kind of crisis which followed the creative period of Gravina, Doria, Giannone and Vico has been described by Venturi, F. (1969–84) *Settecento riformatore*. Einaudi,

Turin, I, pp. 3–58. For the first half of the eighteenth century see: Ricuperati, G. (1979) 'Introduction', in various authors, *Politici ed economisti del primo Settecento*. Ricciardi, Milan–Naples, pp. ix–xxxviii. On 'enlightened Catholicism' in Italy see: Ferrone, V. (1983) *Scienza natura religione. Mondo newtoniano e cultura italiana nel primo Settecento*. Jovene, Naples. On Muratori see: Rosa, M. (1969) *Riformatori e ribelli nel '700 religioso italiano*. Dedalo, Bari.

1. On Broggia see Ajello, R. (1976) *Arcana Juris. Diritto e politica nel Settecento italiano*. Jovene, Naples, pp. 361–428. Also the monograph with anthology by Ajello R., in various authors, *Politici ed economisti del primo Settecento*, Ricciardi Milan–Naples, pp. 969–1155.

2. See Bertelli, S. (1960) *Erudizione e storia in L. A. Muratori*. Istituto italiano per gli studi storici B. Croce, Naples; various authors, *L. A. Muratori e la cultura contemporanea*; *La fortuna di L. A. Muratori*; Dupront, A. (1975–79) *L. A. Muratori et la société européenne des Pre-Lumières*. Olschki, Florence.

3. Marini, L. (1967) 'Documenti dell' opposizione curiale a Pietro Giannnone', in *Rivista storica italiana* a. LXXIX, pp. 696–732.

4. On Maffei see: Silvestri, G. (1954) *Un europeo del Settecento: Scipione Maffei*. Treviso; Gasperoni, G. (1955) *Scipione Maffei e Verona settecentesca*. Verona. See too, as well as Venturi, F. (1969–84) *Settecento riformatore*, Einaudi, Turin, *passim*, Donati, C. (1978) 'S. Maffei e la "Scienza cavalleresca". Saggio sull'ideologia nobiliare al principio del Settecento', in *Rivista storica italiana*, a. XC, pp. 30–71.

5. See Cipolla, C. (1919) 'S. Maffei e l'Historia di P. Giannone', in *Rendiconti della R. Accademia dei Lincei* S. V. fasc. 7, pp. 569–71.

6. As well as Rosa, M. (1969) *Riformatori e ribelli*, Dedalo, Bari, see Ricuperati, G. (1976) 'Giornali e società nell'Italia dell'Ancien Régime (1668–1789)', in various authors, *La stampa italiana dal '500 all '800*, ed. Castronovo, V. and Tranfaglia, N. Laterza, Bari, Ch. III, pp. 165ff. Also Cochrane, E. (1979) G Lami (with anthology), in *Politici ed economisti del primo Settecento*, op. cit., pp. 452–534.

7. As well as Venturi, F., op. cit., I, Ch. V, see Parinetto, M. (1974) *Magia e ragione. Una polemica sulle streghe in Italia intorno al 1750*. La Nuova Italia, Florence. Also Berengo, M. (1979) 'G. Tartarotti', in various authors, *Politici ed economisti del primo Settecento*, op. cit, pp. 315–90.

8. Muratori, L. A. (1749) *Della pubblica felicità oggetto de' buoni principi*. Lucca, p. 3.

9. Ibid., p. 192.

10. Ibid., p. 282.

11. Ibid., p. 339.

12. Ibid., p. 446.

13. See Zlabinger, E. (1970) *L. A. Muratori und Österreich*. Universität Innsbruck, Innsbruck.

14. On Joseph II see Venturi, F., op. cit., IV, pt 2, p. 633. For Leopold see Wandruszka, A. (1968) *Pietro Leopoldo. Un grande riformatore*. Vallecchi, Florence, pp. 27–9.

PART THREE

Reform in the first half of the eighteenth century (Dino Carpanetto)

CHAPTER TEN

Italy in the first half of the eighteenth century: the beginnings of reform

Italy had from the 1630s enjoyed a long period of peace. The treaties of Westphalia (1648) and of the Pyrenees (1659) had confirmed Spanish rule, which covered more than a third of the total land area: Sicily, Sardinia, the South, the Praesidios and the Duchy of Milan. This Spanish presence had created, in the South especially, strong cultural links which, through the immigration of the families of officials and nobles who sought in Italy a fortune denied them in their homeland, had passed into the manners, language, social relationships and perhaps even into the manner of religious expression – devout but superficial. But this pervasive Spanish presence could no longer disguise the fact of the economic, political and social crisis of Habsburg Spain which was evident not only to the local ruling classes but also to the courts of Europe. The crisis reached its culmination at the death in 1700 of Charles II, last of the Spanish Habsburgs, which unleashed that great European conflict, which had been building up for many years, the War of the Spanish Succession.

When the fighting ended the map of Europe looked rather different. The method by which a general peace was reached was a complex juggling of different elements, where once again the Italian territories were rather the spoils and prizes than the participants, with the possible exception of Savoy. England played an important part in supporting Savoy which received Sicily and the status of kingdom, as a counterweight to the Habsburg expansion in Italy. The political geography of Italy thus emerged after the Treaty of Utrecht (1713) greatly altered. The Habsburgs had held Lombardy since 1707 and now added the Duchy of Mantua and the whole of the South. Along with the Spanish the Gonzaga family had also disappeared, since Monferrato passed to the House of Savoy and Mantua was absorbed by the Habsburgs. Savoy, now the Kingdom of Sicily, obtained, as well as this rich but distant island, Alessandria, Valenza, Valsesia and the Lomellina. In 1718 it received Sardinia in exchange for Sicily. The Duke of Modena strengthened his links with Austria, while the Duke of Parma had to confirm his feudal vassalage to the Church.

The Treaty of Utrecht was, of course, drawn up without Austria which continued fighting for another year against France and Spain, until the exhaustion of the combatants and international pressure forced the Treaty of Rastatt (1714) between France and the Empire. However, significantly, Charles VI did not agree to renounce finally his claim to Spain. Philip V's Spain, which had emerged from the war greatly reshaped but also with a dynasty which promised a policy of internal reorganisation, had unwillingly had to submit to the loss of her Italian territories and had started, immediately after the peace treaties, to prepare to retake them. The Europe of the industrial and trading nations had sought a peace which would guarantee them economic hegemony both in the Atlantic and the Mediterranean, but in Italy it had been forced to accept the presence of Bourbon Spain and the Habsburgs.

This new picture presented both stability and fragility. For Italy, the period beginning with the Peace of Utrecht and passing through the new system of European and Italian balances dictated by the Quadruple Alliance of 1720 and ending with the War of the Polish Succession (1733) was complex and full of tensions. But it is precisely for this reason that it was also a period that was lively and creative. It is worth examining a little more closely the two types of action taken by the most vigorous states, the Habsburg Empire and Savoy. Here we see examples of reform or restraint, solidarity or opposition between social classes. The period of greatest expansion for these states was precisely in the fifteen years between the Peace of Rastatt and the War of the Polish Succession.

As was guessed by those great economic historians of the first decades of this century, Luigi Einaudi and Giuseppe Prato,[1] war, since the end of the seventeenth century, had been a very important stimulus to the transformation and modernisation of not only the fiscal but also the administrative institutions of Savoy. Its foreign policy, participation in European wars, the conversion of the duchy to a kingdom, the desire to expand into the Po Valley would all have been vain aspirations if they had not been based on a state that was sufficiently cohesive administratively. It was able to rely on the support of its subjects, was capable of controlling those forces which were more difficult to force to adapt to a process of modernisation, such as the Church and the nobility, and capable of guaranteeing a justice and protection sufficient to justify the increased load of taxation. When Victor Amadeus II took power, the entire population did not exceed 800,000, the territory being incomplete because Pinerolo belonged to France and Casale to the Gonzagas who were about to cede it to Louis XIV. The administrative differences within the State were important, as can be seen from the different Senates (those of Piedmont, Savoy and Nice) and the presence of differentiated autonomies, such as that of Aosta and, particularly, of Savoy. The local communities in their turn had administrative structures linked to very ancient statutes and to privileges which they had acquired during the centuries. The nobility and the Church controlled a part of the land which was certainly smaller than that which was possessed by these same forces in the South, but which (with feudal and non-feudal estates) came nevertheless to about 30–35 per cent of the most profitable land. An approximate calculation of the noble families at the end of the seventeenth century gives a figure of between 1,500 and 1,800, or a total of 10,000 people, while the religious orders and secular clergy were some 20,000. It can be seen from these figures that a little less than 3 per cent of the population owned 30–35 per cent of the landed wealth, enjoying also tax exemptions on at least four-fifths of this patrimony.[2]

The starting-point for the Savoy reforms was clear: to centralise the system of taxation, reducing as much as possible the dispersal of money caused by a disorganised system of contracted-out tax collection, by abuses and by the privileges of the richer classes. In this sense the reforms of Victor Amadeus II can be seen as part of a longer process, that of the isolating of the feudal aristocracy and the rise of a rich bourgeoisie which progressed from tax-farming to titles to government office. Victor Amadeus merely started this process up again, making use of a faithful administrative staff and various financial strategies which already showed signs of a pronounced desire for modernisation and centralisation: a single financial treasury and the construction of a General Farm to take the place of the disorganised, expensive and wasteful system of contracting out. By these means the sovereign had the power to subject his people to one of the harshest fiscal policies in Europe, but this allowed him to meet his military expenses even better than with the massive subsidies sent from England and Holland. Right from the start the first reforms were drawn up as an inevitable consequence of this. The only way to obtain increasing amounts of money was to tax the entire population, hitting privileges and exemptions. But in order to do this, the State had to be able to control the territory and create an apparatus which on a local level would be capable of carrying out the necessary controls. The figure of the intendant, copied from the French model, took over some of the duties of the governor and the prefect. He was the real representative *in loco* of central government and his powers extended from fiscal matters to administration, policing and control over the local communities.

The process which had led to the new taxation system or *Perequazione* had a long history of false starts and plans thoughout the seventeenth century and especially under Charles Emanuel II. The order of 1697 which is usually taken as the starting-point of the *Perequazione* did not formally differ from earlier orders of the same type. The declared object was not in fact an increase in revenue but a fairer distribution of taxation and better compilation and keeping of registers. The method employed, however, was very different. In 1697 a new, survey and valuation of the lands in the county of Nice was attempted. Directing operations was the finance minister, Groppello, who aimed to accomplish it 'without fuss', as a rehearsal to be extended the following year to Cuneo and Mondovì. Teams of surveyors were trained who were in the space of little more than thirty years to furnish an up-to-date economic and fiscal picture of the entire territory. They were not unopposed. In the Monregalese Victor Amadeus had to suppress the local resistance by force, which he did with his customary energy, hanging 49 people and exiling some 100 families. In the meantime the value of the intendant was becoming apparent. He could immediately make use of the data provided by the surveyor and prepare the new land registers. It was not chance that sent a man like Pierre Mellarède to Nice as intendant. He was to become one of the sovereign's chief collaborators and contributed much to the creation of a system of surveying. Measuring and assessing were extended between 1698 and 1711 to the greater part of the communities, being interrupted only between 1704 and 1708 because of the war on Piedmontese territory. In 1712 the State was in a position to draw some general conclusions from the summaries, at least so far as Nice, Piedmont and the Pinerolese were concerned.

At this point began the difficult and laborious phase of checking and verifying the figures established by the surveyors which was in some degree to take into account the different situations of the communities – a job assigned to the intendants. Though without yet tackling the question of new taxes, the State now at least had valuable information at its disposal, allowing it to evaluate resources, to find out the size and profitability of feudal, ecclesiastical and allodial property. It was to be the basis not only of the edict of the *Perequazione* in the provinces of Piedmont, which was brought into force on 5 May 1731 by the new king, Charles Emanuel III, but also of the policy towards the communities, the ecclesiastics and the nobles as it was to develop in the years immediately following the Peace of Rastatt.

The immediate result, so far as the provinces of Piedmont were concerned, which saw the full implementation of the *Perequazione* between 1731 and 1732, was not so much an increase in revenue (which varied from 4 to 6 per cent), as the recovery of allodial lands and the reduction of ecclesiastical and feudal immunities. As for the aristocracy, Victor Amadeus attempted – with an efficient empiricism – to force all those possessing feudal titles to prove their antiquity or lose them. In 1722, by using the 166 fiefs confiscated from the feudal aristocracy, a new batch of nobles was created, benefiting principally those officials who were organising the reforms. This inflation in honours was another useful way of reducing the power of the nobility and favouring that service nobility which identified itself with the State.

More generally the reform movement had its moment of greatest intensity in the years immediately following the end of the War of the Spanish Succession. The year 1717 saw the setting up of the Council of State, the main organ of government, and the General Council of Finance. The secretariat of State underwent an important transformation, losing its character of a personal service and acquiring the dignity of a real ministry. In practice the two corner-stones of the new administrative system became the first secretary of state and the *generale delle Finanze*. The edicts which reinforced and defined the increased powers of the intendants and the treasurers aimed at creating an efficient state presence in the provinces. One of the most important tasks of the intendants was that of controlling the privileged classes, particularly the nobility, preventing the abuse of power and violence which might harm the bourgeoisie and particularly the peasants. They also supervised the administration of the communities. This aspect began to make particular sense in the territories which had been acquired after the Treaty of Utrecht where the State did not intervene by immediately suppressing differences, but chose to extend its control through the intendants, cautiously preparing the way to making the administration of the community uniform, culminating in the law of the *pubblici* of 1775.

The economic policy of the State of Savoy under Victor Amadeus II was greatly influenced by a model of typically late-mercantilist development. Attention was paid particularly to the area of the silk industry, given that Piedmont produced a considerable quantity of raw silk which was exported to France and England. Victor Amadeus sought to encourage local manufac-turing industries, forbidding the sale of cocoons and every type of worked silk and attacking with ever heavier duties silk of foreign provenance. A similar attitude was taken towards the wool industry, which enjoyed some-thing of a boom in the areas of Biella and Nice in the first thirty years of the century, partly as a result of generous loans and privileges, and orders from the military given to entrepreneurs. Following this logic, the State of Savoy did not hesitate to deal with the ill-will and resistance of the English and French merchants. This attention to production also affected less important sectors, dye-works, tanneries and the paper and glass industries. From the point of view of the labour market, Victor Amadeus's state-imposed restrictions, reinforcing the power of the guilds and corporations, tended to impede free competition. Such a system, which at this period became more rigid, ought in theory to have protected both the quality of the product and the workers, but in practice it favoured the interests of the entrepreneurs and harmed free workers. The latter could only find jobs in the areas protected by the State, such as silk and wool, which were decentralised and where there was free employment, but which precisely for this reason were open to the risk of exploitation and unemployment.

In order to deal adequately with the problem of the poor who were either unemployed workers or peasants driven off the land, the State of Savoy organised an overall plan of assistance, showing itself unwilling to leave this job to the Church or the charity of individuals. From 1716 there was a succession of edicts which forbade not only begging but also private forms of assistance. Instead, in each city a system of hospices was organised, or failing this a confraternity which changed charity into something very different. This policy aimed to rescue able-bodied workers and put them to productive work, to save children from a life of begging and to prepare them instead to follow a trade. It fitted in with the theories of the Jesuit Andrea Guevarre, author of *La mendicità sbandita col sovvenimento de' poveri tanto nelle città che ne' borghi luoghi e terre degli stati di qua e di là da' monti e colli . . .* published in 1717 and translated into French in 1722 in order to extend the hospices into Savoy. It was an action which in the course of time was to yield modest profits, strengthening the inheritance of pious institutions and hospitals and thus in effect improving the assistance provided.

Another change which struck the imagination of contemporaries and contributed to the creation of the image and the myth of the 'reforming King of Savoy' concerned the law. Centralisation, elimination of local jurisdictions, strengthening of the magistratures by now seen as careers requiring particular skills and not mere offices to be bought and sold – these were the basic aims. But all this was not enough. The progress towards absolutism met an obstacle that was often inert but nevertheless difficult to overcome and that was the disordered accumulation of edicts which inevitably contradicted one another and made the execution not only of justice but also of power difficult. The Constitutions, issued in 1729, were intended to give the State, magistrates, lawyers and subjects an orderly and consistent body of law. Looking at them in the light of future events and the codifications of the Enlightenment, one can hardly fail to note the traditional, violent and almost always distorted view of justice which emerges. Social relations too remained fixed in the typical mould of a state of the *ancien régime*, where privileges were the norm and the basic idea of the equality of citizens in the eyes of the law was quite lacking. Punishments seemed out of all proportion to the crimes, the death sentence being mandatory even for repeated minor theft and torture a normal method of obtaining information from the accused. Thus the Constitutions aimed to go round rather than overcome ancient autonomies and privileges. For all this, the Piedmontese Constitutions were for decades an inspiration for Italian public opinion. Muratori refers to them again in the 1740s as an example of juridical rationality to be imitated.

But the area where Victor Amadeus's reforms opened up an important and general discussion was that of public education.[3] The reform of the university started from the need that the modern absolute State had of a more efficient, competent and faithful staff. It was, furthermore, a way of establishing new links between the State and the professional classes. The merit of Victor Amadeus's reform lay in the fact that it did not limit itself to setting in motion a machine for the production of degrees lacking in any important cultural traditions. Rather it extracted from this reform all the possible consequences that were compatible with a policy of absolutism. First and foremost, having had a broad and important programme, inspired by a lucid jurisdictionalism, drawn up by the Sicilian jurist Francesco d'Aguirre, he had looked with great shrewdness at the best cultural, scientific and religious traditions of Italy and France in order to insert them into his plan for Savoy. Thus Gravina's ideas of 'poetic reason' and Muratori's 'good taste' were taught in Turin and Piedmont, gradually taking the place of the Jesuits' teaching. So too was it to be for law, science, theology, medicine and philosophy. Until the Concordat of 1727, the reform of the university was closely related to jurisdictionalist pressure, firmly controlled by the State, but perceptible in the enthusiasm and energy with which the professors entered into the debates on, and in defence of, the new institution.

This same Concordat, which was to cause many to become disillusioned, including d'Aguirre, did not prevent the State of Savoy from resuming the debate on educational reform two years later, in 1729, now focussing on the secondary sector, removing it from the influence of the religious orders, confiscating any of their property connected with education and establishing a network of schools in the provinces which were to follow uniform cultural models decided by the university. And this was not all. The Faculty of Arts (*Magistero delle Arti*), which up to then had been considered an introductory faculty, became specialised in order to produce teachers for this level of instruction. Furthermore, the same 1729 Constitutions provided for the setting up of a *Collegio delle Provincie* where each year some 100 poor but gifted youths were to be recruited to come and study in Turin at the State's expense. Here too the State was providing an alternative to the Church, which for centuries had been the only road to cultural emancipation for the less wealthy. In this way the state university became the centre of an educational system that extended out to the provinces and which also controlled important professions for which a degree was not required, such as those of surveyor, architect, pharmacist and midwife. And, finally, it was responsible for censorship.

The most severe limitation of Savoyard reformism in the first half of the eighteenth century is to some degree implicit in what has been said so far. The total pragmatism, the lack of theoretical justifications, and the ruthless efficiency without debate revealed how the reforms had been carried out by state officials who had no desire to involve the rest of society. They made use of the relative cohesion of the different social classes but also of their passivity. The dramatic events surrounding the old king, Victor Amadeus II, who had abdicated in 1730 and then, unhappy with his son's performance, had tried a year later to return to power, had been arrested and confined until his death, smacked of the *ancien régime*, as well as irresistibly recalling events between him and his mother. In fact it was continuity more than change which prevailed in the change-over from Victor Amadeus to Charles Emanuel III. It was to be, rather, external conditions which dampened the dynamism of Savoy, curtailing her territorial ambitions. But some at least of Victor Amadeus's steps on the road to modernisation were destined to bear fruit: centralisation, development of the land registers, a rational and almost statistical and quantitive collection of information on production, and control over the communities on whom was imposed a uniform system of local administration. The intellectual reforms too left their trace, not only in their unassuming efficiency, but also as an instrument with which to weld together the State and the new ruling class which was being trained – learning, for example, a dignified Italian – in the schools and university of Savoy.

Similar in some ways, if more complex, were the Habsburg reforms, inspired by mercantilist models present in Vienna at the end of the seventeenth century. If one compares the behaviour of the Austrians in Lombardy, in Naples and in Sicily, one can see how they tried to apply those administrative, economical and political principles which had been refined by their theoreticians at the end of the century and which related to the strengthening of the Empire and the new policy of power compatible with a 'multinational' state. In this scheme the relationship between economic and commercial policy and administrative reform is clear. This made it possible for a state system different from that in England, from the merchant republic of Holland, from Louis XIV's France, not only to survive but also to play an internationally prestigious role. Vienna became the centre of a great political and economic area which linked northern Europe, the Orient and the Mediterranean. The 'multinational' nature of the Empire, increased by the victories over the Turks, allowed the theoreticians of Habsburg policies to absorb, in a much less violent way than that attempted by Louis XIV, at least two complex inheritances, that of Spain (from the Netherlands to the south of Italy) and that of Venice (trade to the Adriatic, the Mediterranean and the Orient). This composite political, economic and administrative situation took and adapted not only mercantilist theories developed in relation to the absolute State but also those developed from the anomalous Dutch 'mercantilism', as for example when it proposed the freedom of the Adriatic against the Venetian Republic. There were also some internal elements which had to some degree been renewed, ranging from the cameralist traditions to Imperial jurisdictionalism.

Through this encounter with Austrian policies, the different states which made up the unchanging Italy were forced to examine their particular situations, their forms of autonomy and privilege to which they had become accustomed by Spanish rule and by the still international role of the papacy. The Habsburg model appeared as a force for a gradual renewal because it represented a modernisation which could arouse new energies. But the relationship with Austria also provided the Italian territories with a model of economic policy which obliged the local forces to face up to a rather different situation from their traditional one, linked with factors like landed revenue, ecclesiastical benefices, complicity with the distant court, parasitism and the defence of local autonomies – the defence of a privilege which had grown up on the edges of aristocratic and ecclesiastical privilege.

At the same time it is difficult not to see the limitations of Habsburg reformism in practice. Not only its wishful thinking but also its inability to overcome on one side the resistance of local privileges and on the other Vienna's temptation to exploit the new territories. Fiscalism, brought about by the same policies of power that had allowed the new acquisitions, had the effect of negating those same reforms that the new rulers had intended to introduce into the Italian lands. The insertion of these areas into a much larger economic system, the consequent stimulus to the productive and commercial sectors, land-reform and the encouragement of maritime trade, a more rational and modern view of taxation which would make it possible to strengthen both the State and the economy, were all in effect cancelled out by the contradictions in such a policy, by the lack of proper mechanisms for its implementation in the centre and in the outlying areas, by the need to supply a costly and unproductive military machine and to pay for a policy of international prestige for which Austrian resources were inadequate.

In Naples, the meeting of Imperial jurisdictionalist policy with local anticurialism had the effect of creating a kind of alliance between the middle class, employed in administration and law, and the Habsburgs. This alliance squeezed out the nobility, although the latter had been the first to welcome the Austrians, but in its turn was not without serious ambiguities. A group of political and reformist intellectuals emerged whose aim it was to push Habsburg policies in the direction of an economic, social and administrative reform for the South. This group included not only Giannone, Riccardi and Grimaldi but also Contegna who played an important part in outlining the reasons for university reform and in reconciling jurisdictionalism, new economic policies and reform. He tried to direct the Banco di San Carlo[4] along these lines – an institution which, at least in original intention, was not intended to be merely an instrument for the recovery of *fiscali* but also to give a different meaning to the policy of anti-curialism. The Church would have to be forced to give up its inherited property to the State which would put it back on the market, giving in exchange a rate of interest fixed at about 4 per cent. With the money from these sales (which would revitalise the land market, enfeebled by mortmains and *fidecommessi*) the State would be able to rebuild that public patrimony which had been eroded through the granting of feudal rights, regalian rights and *fiscali*. The plan got beyond the purely theoretical stage and became a reality during the much debated viceroyship of Cardinal d'Althann, losing in the process much of its initial drive and ending up as an instrument for the buying back of *fiscali*, a process which was first to be disturbed and finally halted by the great need for money brought about by the imminent War of the Polish Succession.

It was these contradictions of Habsburg reformism and its frustrated fiscalism which not only aroused the mistrust of part of the middle and merchant classes, but which also continued to encourage the perpetuation and persistence of resistance from the local magistratures who, even when they spoke in a realistic language, still represented the old rather than the new. The clash between Althann and the local magistratures shows dramatically the limitations of both sides. The cardinal had been chosen as viceroy by the emperor who was seeking at this time to reduce the tensions with Rome. Althann, who was decidedly pro-Curia and thus instrumental in a series of concessions to the Church, from the failure to protect Giannone to the squalid affair of the suppression of Grimaldi's works, aroused so much hostility from the forces of reform that he severely compromised even the justified restrictions on the autonomy of local magistratures and the economic reforms which he did attempt. This clash ended up by wasting considerable political and economic energy and delaying or nullifying several important developments. Vienna's delay in remedying their error by leaving Althann in power until 1727 benefited not only the reformers but also the ideologues of the *ministero togato* who had been able to bring together against the cardinal at least some of the energy necessary for economic reform. The struggle was to be renewed with the succeeding viceroys, Harrach and Visconti, but by now the impending war and distorted fiscalism deprived proposals for reform of all meaning. Thus the Banco di San Carlo was closed down, the proposed census was not carried out and even the university reform that the new *Cappellano maggiore*, Galiani, had discussed in Naples and Vienna remained no more than an idea. Problems had emerged – economic policy, including a plan for a chamber of commerce, reorganization of taxation and educational reform – but Habsburg reformism had failed to solve them. They and other plans were left to Charles of Bourbon who took over the southern State in 1734.

Austrian domination in Sicily which began on 6 May 1720 after little less than two years of Spanish rule, fitted closely with the most important elements of Piedmontese reformism. This was clear not only from the fact that the best officials trained in this period (1713–18) in Sicily were to play important roles in the reforming policies of, respectively, Savoyard Piedmont (d'Aguirre and Pensabene) and Vienna (Perlongo and Marchese), but above all because a plan was drawn up which aimed clearly at breaking the monopoly of power enjoyed by ecclesiastics and barons, to replace it with a new government of officials, merchants and producers. It was a policy based on state intervention in all areas of production, from agriculture and manufacture to policies in land and maritime trade. The new model represented by the Habsburg state was to present the Sicilians with a problem very different from that posed by the Spanish government. Bourbon reformism was to return to these problems in the years 1738–41, when it seemed possible to impose on the island a model of modern absolutism armed with instruments for intervention like the Supreme Magistracy of Trade, which was intended to reform economic life and was, instead, to be defeated by baronial opposition, doing irreparable damage to the future history of the island.

If the impact of the Habsburgs in Sicily was to be but a parenthesis, albeit important, their presence in the State of Milan lasted much longer and had a much greater impact. The Habsburgs hoped for great wealth and resources from Lombardy, but they also wanted to bring it back to its former levels of production. In order to do this it was necessary to break the resistance of the clergy, which owned much tax-exempt land, and the nobility which controlled all the local magistratures starting from the Senate down. The problems were apparent from the beginning of Austrian rule and only a few years later, in the climate of peace ushered in by the Peace of Rastatt, Vienna initiated a programme for a coherent fiscal policy. The problem was not just that of how to increase the fiscal revenue, but also to deal with inequalities and immunities, fiercely defended under the banner of local autonomy, which effectively impeded the social and economic development of Lombardy. At the same time as preparations were being drawn up for the making of the census, the conflict between the governor, Colloredo, and the local representatives became very acute, particularly in the matter of the taxation of the property of ecclesiastics, with the *Congregazione* (an assembly of nobles and churchmen) attempting to prevent this and sending deputations to the Viennese court. Colloredo crushed this attempt to bypass him, punishing all those who had been involved in the unauthorised mission.

The most important evidence for the Habsburg desire for reform, however, was the creation of the Junta for the census at the end of 1718.[5] The men who made it up were all drawn from outside Lombardy: jurists from Naples, like the president, Vincenzo de Miro, and Giuseppe Cavalieri, and Catalan officials, like Michele d'Esmandia and Marco Marañon. This Junta, which had to send fortnightly reports on its work to Vienna, not only proceeded in collaboration with the governor and the local authorities but also made use of a staff which was remarkable both for the way it conducted the land-survey and for the accuracy of the maps that it made. The court mathematician, Giovanni Giacomo Marinoni, was placed at their disposal, and he perfected the plane-table which was used by the teams of surveyors. But rather than following this work, which was to come to a halt in 1733, in all its intricacies, it is interesting to see how it brought about a corresponding organisation of local forces. It was the city of Milan and its General Council of Sixty Decurions which took the initiative, creating an urban Junta, consisting of six *Cavalieri* (knights) and backed up by the *Vicario di Provvisione* as representative of the whole State, to co-ordinate in a systematic way the resistance of the local forces. Between 1721 and 1726 the basic tasks of measuring and estimating were completed, overcoming all opposition, including that of withholding necessary funds. In 1727, the rather more delicate phase began where adjustments were to be made to correct the data based on the rather different local estimates.

As well as the resistance from the municipality of Milan which tried in every way to prevent the State from getting hold of proper information, the census Junta encountered two obstacles that were not so easy to overcome. These were the immunities of the Church and the laity, expressed in practice by the opposition of the nobility and the clergy. The work had almost reached a conclusion, the choice being whether to create a special land register for ecclesiastical property, equalise the direct taxes or reorganise the boundaries of the communities, when it was suddenly interrupted by the Franco-Piedmontese invasion of 1733. The *catasto* was to remain an invaluable collection of data awaiting utilisation in the great revival of reform in the mid-eighteenth century when the task was taken up by Pompeo Neri. However, this material was kept, arranged and, to some extent, prepared for later use by Francesco d'Aguirre, the old Sicilian jurist who had ranged himself on the side of Victor Amadeus II, interpreting the king's reformist and regalistic will in the reform of Turin University and who, in 1730, had been sent from Vienna to Milan to reinforce the census Junta.

The War of the Polish Succession (1733–38), fought partly on Italian soil, with its dramatic events, from the Bourbon conquests in the South (1734) to the invasion of Lombardy by the Franco-Piedmontese allies (1733), was not only to interrupt Habsburg hegemony in Italy but also the strategy of reforms which, even with marked contradictions and faint-heartedness, we have seen emerging.

When Europe, and with it the Italian states, entered the War of the Polish Succession, there was a lull in the entire political and intellectual movement which in Italy had awakened a remarkable resurgence of civic life in the first decades of the eighteenth century. Exhaustion, confusion and backward-looking ideas crept into political life and were most noticeable in those men and those areas which had been in the forefront of the battle of ideas and the struggle for reform. The hotbed of reforming ideals and projects represented by the arrival of the Empire on the Italian political scene, seemed suddenly to cool under the pressure of international circumstances which were not favourable to the monarch of Austria. Following the weakening of the Empire in Italy there came the revival of a complex tapestry of conservative elements – a mixture of unsatisfied nostalgia for the past, reaction by the nobility, attempts by the Roman Curia at a counter-attack to the jurisdictionalism of the various states and, finally, national resentment.

In Naples the War of the Polish Succession, during which the Austrians were defeated by the army of Charles of Bourbon, the son of Elizabeth Farnese and Philip V of Spain, marked the end of the Ghibelline faction, which had been politically and intellectually important. In 1733 in Milan the most innovative work on the counting of landed properties to happen in eighteenth-century Italy was interrupted. In Turin in 1730, the anguished renunciation of the throne by Victor Amadeus II meant the end of the chief author of reform. The Grand Duchy of Tuscany was living through the death throes of the Medici dynasty, while in the Papal States the serious economic crisis, the money shortage and the many questions raised but unresolved which kept Rome apart from the Catholic states were the problems inherited by Clement XII and then Benedict XIV. And yet, within this tangle of problems and shattered ideals, around the end of the 1730s a movement towards reform took shape more or less strongly in the different Italian states, fed by a series of international events and internal political moves which encouraged the conscious growth of a civic optimism which in some social classes was well founded and active, in others less marked.

Between 1733 and 1748, year of the Treaty of Aix-la-Chapelle, the political map of Italy underwent considerable alteration, as a result of the changed balances of power between the great powers of Europe. Once again the Italian peninsula was caught in the middle between the opposing sides. The Bourbons returned to Naples in 1734 as a result of a military victory, and after the Treaty of Aix-la-Chapelle they spread northwards with the acquisition of the provinces of Parma, Piacenza and Guastalla, given to Elizabeth's second son, Philip. The Austrian Habsburgs made up for the loss of the South with the transfer of Tuscany to the House of Lorraine. Tuscany and the South, passing respectively into Imperial and Spanish hands, retained a particular, though partial, autonomy with respect to the European capitals, Vienna and Madrid. They enjoyed a form of separate sovereignty which was to act as an important stimulus to reform. Finally, Savoyard Piedmont continued to nibble away at provinces to the east, halting its expansion at the river Ticino in 1748.

These new pieces in the Italian mosaic were already seen by contemporaries as secure and capable of withstanding the test of time, as indeed was to be the case, if one considers that with the exception of the Napoleonic period, the main groupings of the political map of Italy remained unchanged until Unification (1861). The Treaty of Aix-la-Chapelle also ushered in the longest period of peace known in modern Italian history, the pressure of the great powers on Italy being reduced. Economic, financial and administrative problems of great consequence became once more the object of a renewed theoretical interest and a new civic enthusiasm. In many cases it was the wars which demonstrated the degree of decay in the states of Italy. They revealed the economic weaknesses and thus had a positive function in that, when the territorial balances and the spheres of influence in Italy of the European monarchs were re-established after 1748, the seriousness of the problems could not only be observed passively but could be tackled with schemes for improvement which owed part of their success to the climate of peace which Italy enjoyed for half a century.

It has already been described how in the 1730s in Italy, but not only in Italy – one only has to think of France – an upsurge of pride and a desire for revenge seemed to flare up among the groups of the most ancient nobility, feudal and chivalrous, who revived customs, styles of living, political principles and sectional demands which unequivocally looked back to the old society of the Counter-Reformation which during the years of the crisis of European consciousness and the first reforms of absolutism had fallen into disarray but not entirely vanished. Now, this reaction of the nobility half-way through the century was stopped in its tracks by the return to ideas of reform, by a state ideology born of *giuspubblicismo* and by the improvement in the economy. Italian society was moving towards a very different society from that desired and sought by the 'aristocratic reaction'. Between the nobility of the sword, that of the robe (the legal profession), public officials and business men of the bourgeoisie the ideological and economic barriers were falling, the boundaries becoming fainter and so too the movement from one group to another became easier. The tripartite division of society into clergy, nobility and third estate began to lose some of its social meaning, while retaining an important legal value. The *noblesse commerçante*, no longer just an expression, became a more widespread phenomenon than is sometimes thought, and not only in the republics but to some extent everywhere, especially in the economy of central-northern Italy, where the nobles took an active part in manufacturing and agricultural undertakings of some importance. This was reflected in a whole literary genre, imported from France and England, which depicts the noble who carries out agronomical changes or organises great trading enterprises; and which had a great success in Italy, confirming the existence of specifically entrepreneurial attitudes, a practical readiness to take part in schemes of production and to accept commercial risks rather than just an abstract leaning in this direction.

Alongside the nobles, subordinate or in competition, was the enriched bourgeoisie who both in the country and the town showed an increased economic strength even if as a social group they lacked the cohesion of consciousness, civic customs and political aims which would put them in the category of a class antagonistic to the nobility. In places where the absolute states were increasing their sphere of influence over society, through the reinforcing of the state apparatus, a class of bureaucrats formed, as yet a feeble skeleton but already clearly defined and often numerically strong. The so-called liberal professions, such as medicine and teaching and the many activities connected with the law, were similarly expanding and in some cases made great strides. There was a sizeable increase, for example, in the number of doctors and schoolteachers, which came about as a result of the growth in demand for medical services and education.

While the appearance of new social classes began to influence political and theoretical debate, nevertheless it was not yet very significant. One phenomenon, however, was clearly apparent; more contacts were being made between members of the ruling groups, which led to both a revival of political culture and a change, slow before the mid-century and then more rapid, in the social role of the political elite. The new training of the ruling groups included many elements: jurisdictionalism and *giuspubblicismo*, an ethical code which was less controversial and more sensitive to civil values, a philosophy which weakened the dominant scholastic and Aristotelian traditions and offered more up-to-date philosophical and theological theories, the study of ecclesiastical and social history. This cultural trend took root with some difficulty in institutions such as universities and colleges and more readily in the academies, salons and on the editorial boards of the gazettes and journals. The study of economics, suggested by many as the subject most fitted for providing politics with the tools it needed, began to be recognised in the universities, starting with Naples in 1754. The question of educational reform once again became central in the political and intellectual debate. This is a thread which runs from Muratori to Filangieri right through the eighteenth century, expressing an idea common to all the most acute thinkers – the need to intervene in the educational establishments in order to make of them instruments for civil growth, in an Italian society which was backward in comparison with the cultural developments in Europe, governed by very restricted elites who were aware of, and sensitive to, the general interest but almost entirely without a public whose opinion could act as a check or counterweight to political power.

While it was inevitable that the battle for reform would be fought in the area of political institutions, the importance of the press as a means for the interpretation and activation of new ideas was not yet fully grasped. It is, however, also true that from the 1740s the journals began to establish themselves as centres for the formation of public opinion, in that some of them rejected the printing of erudite and neutrally informative articles in favour of discussions on questions of economics, politics, science and religion. The change was to become even more apparent twenty years later in the more militant, secular attitude displayed in the clash of ideas by certain political journals – of which the best example is the Verri brothers' *Il Caffè* – which aimed at a public much broader than that reached by previous journals, a public no longer consisting of a few learned men but chiefly of men involved in business and economics, politicians, officials, administrators and middlemen of varying levels of education.[6] But behind the success of the journals lay not only the growth of a literate public receptive to the message of the journals. Beneath the surface the ethical code of the Counter-Reformation was gradually slipping, giving way to new collective values which were less religious and pessimistic. The periodicals played a decisive role in the exchange of ideas between Italy and Europe which became frequent in the middle of the century, particularly with those countries having the closest historical links with Italy – France, England, Portugal and Spain. From the first two Italian culture assimilated the theories described under the often vague, but here accurate, heading of Enlightenment. These included Newtonian physics, deism, the gnosticism arising from Locke's ideas, Condillac's sensism, Voltaire's historiographic, civil and political teaching, Montesquieu's ideas, late-mercantilistic economic theories and the doctrines of the physiocrats.

The policies of reform attempted to provide the State with a judicial, administrative and fiscal capability which had in part been lost and which it was necessary in part to create *ex novo*. The various plans for the simplification and consolidation of the law which were studied in Milan, Florence, Naples and Modena all started from one idea of social policy, that of limiting the power of the lawyers, notaries and judges, the traditional intermediaries between the State and the subjects. They saw the chief objective as that of restructuring the organisation of power, and in this they were anticipating the idea of the separation of the two functions, hitherto merged together, the administration and the judiciary. The theories of natural law, which sought a correspondence between operative law and the basic principles of reason and human society, called for a new codification which would be rigid in application and simple in content. These ideas were emerging at the same time as the reassertion of the state's power, one of the distinctive features of eighteenth-century reformism. In place of the separation, stratification, dispersion and juxtaposition of powers, typical of the *ancien régime*, there was beginning to be substituted the unification and differentiation of powers, equality and legal guarantees, a centralised system of law enforcement and the objective formalism of laws.

The social position of the nobility was not attacked, but in some states those privileges that represented the greatest obstacles to political unification were restricted. All over Italy the rural feudal structure remained intact, thus the position of the nobility in relation to the State was largely unchanged. They were still guaranteed a status of prestige through tax exemptions, their own courts, *fidecommessi*, preferential use of labour, special legal protections, guaranteed access to the chief offices of state, control of the army and greater financial weight. But in the new *catasti*, in the laws on *fidecommessi* and in the provisions for a reorganisation of the law, clauses were introduced which indicated a contraction, albeit slight, of aristocratic autonomy which aimed at bringing the rights of the nobility into line with public law. The feudal question was hotly debated in the 1770s and 1780s when the signs of crisis for the *ancien régime* were clear to see, but for the time being partial adjustments were the only possible course of action for absolutism with regard to feudalism and the nobility, since the aim was certainly not to dismantle the ancient power bases of the second estate, but rather to make use of the best elements of the aristocracy in the plans for enlightened reform.

The results achieved by the various Italian states on the question of relations with the Church were more tangible. Everywhere the functions of the Church in legal and economic matters which interfered with those parts of the State which were trying to get established were investigated. The whole matter of the immunity of the clergy, a veritable jungle of legal complexities, which gave the Church a special position in society and allowed it an almost total power of interference in the law, taxes and public order, was raised for discussion. There was an attempt to control the involvement of priests in education, the censorship of books and ideas and cultural research. The neo-jurisdictionalist reforms, which came to a peak between 1750 and 1770, were the area of greatest agreement in the whole eighteenth-century Italian reform movement, in that it was the area in which those who were calling for change found the greatest response and reaction from society.

The decade 1740–50 marked a change in the economic situation. After a long period of stagnation and frequent recessions in productivity, there were now signs of an economic recovery, reflecting the progressive trends in Europe. The various agricultural areas of the country responded in differing ways to the demands of the market. In the more advanced areas this response was accompanied by a transformation of agricultural techniques, the development of new equipment for transport, the stimulation of trade, preparation of land registers, reorganisation of the monetary system, simplification of tolls and duties and the revision of taxation. Around the middle of the century discussions arose about each of these subjects which Italian intellectuals and politicians followed attentively, in agreement, in this case, with the matters being debated in neighbouring European countries.

At this point one last consideration should be taken into account. If one looks at its ideological and cultural content, the progress of reform is animated by a generally pre-enlightened view of things, that is imbued with all those elements which bring it nearer to the civil climate fought for by Muratori and Genovesi than that anticipated by the Verri brothers. The Italian reform movement, in other words, did not call into question the basic structures of the monarchical and absolutist edifice of the *ancien régime* and did not aim at the building of a society renewed from top to bottom. It brought with it all the civil implications of that authoritarian paternalism, used to commanding without checks or controls, which was part of the political pride of the nobility and which corresponded with the tendency to absolutism of the princes. The juridical philosophy of the reformers of this period, Tanucci, Neri, Pallavicini and Bogino, was rooted in a legalistic conception of royal power, which saw the problem of power exclusively as a matter of the management of the instruments of policy and coercion, and ignored totally questions of legitimacy, consensus, freedom and social justice. Similarly, their economic ideas did not go any further than neo-mercantilism and often did not even have any solid theoretical basis, advancing on purely empirical grounds dictated by experience of government.

Within these limitations (and they are only limitations if one believes that the connections between reform and Enlightenment are, or ought to be, very close) the process of reform developed, having a period of great success in 1740–50, particularly in Tuscany, Naples and Milan. Later there was a brief slowing down in the central-northern states in the 1760s and then a revival with a partly renewed personnel, with more up-to-date theoretical means, until the dramatic impact of the problems of the famine which struck Italy between 1763 and 1767. Then, not only the hunger of the peasants and townspeople of the big southern cities, but also cultural problems, political unrest and economic needs which could no longer be contained within the cloak of aristocratic paternalism or the harsh bureaucratic grip of the states, led to new splits in Italian political life – and indeed cut short the more cautious attempts at reform, encouraging instead, in the places which allowed it (Milan and Florence in the first instance) the development of reformism towards social theories that pointed the way to the future.

NOTES AND REFERENCES

On Italy's relations with the rest of Europe in the first half of the eighteenth century see Guido Quazza's important essays, where a subject once distorted by nationalistic viewpoints of various types is treated with a proper balance: Quazza, G. (1965) *Il problema italiano e l'equilibrio europeo, 1720–1738*. Deputazione subalpina di storia patria, Turin;   idem (1965) 'L'Italia e l'Europa durante le guerre di successione (1700–1748)', in *Storia d'Italia*, ed. Valeri, N. UTET, Turin;   idem (1970) 'Italy's role in the European problems of the first half of the eighteenth century', in *Studies in Diplomatic History: essays in memory of David Bayne Horn*, ed. Hatton, R. and Anderson, M. S.. Longman, London.   General studies on the internal political situation in the first half of the century and on the beginnings of reform are the previously mentioned books by Franco Valsecchi and Franco Venturi.   On Piedmont during the reign of Victor Amadeus II see Quazza, G. (1957) *Le riforme in Piemonte nella prima metà del Settecento*. Società tipografica editrice modenese, Modena.   More recent is: Symcox, G. (1983) *Victor Amadeus II. Absolutism in the Savoyard State 1675–1730*. Thames & Hudson, London.   On Lombardy before the reforms of Maria Theresa see the general work *Storia di Milano*, vol. XII (1959) *L'età delle riforme*. Treccani, Milan. For the Habsburg monarchy see: Evans, R. J. W. (1979) *The Making of the Habsburg Monarchy, 1550–1700. An Interpretation*. Clarendon Press, Oxford.   For Naples see the essay by Ricuperati, G. (1972), in *Storia di Napoli*, vol. VII. Società editrice per la storia di Napoli, Naples;   Di Vittorio, A. (1969) and (1973) *Gli Austriaci e il Regno di Napoli (1707–1734)*, 2 vols. Giannini, Naples.

1.   Prato, G. (1908) *La vita economica in Piemonte a mezzo il secolo XVIII*. Società tipografica editrice nazionale, Turin;   Einaudi, L. (1908) *La finanza sabauda all'aprirsi del secolo XVIII e durante la guerra di successione spagnola*. Sten, Turin.
2.   Bulferetti, L. (1963) *Agricoltura, industria e commercio in Piemonte nel secolo XVIII*. Istituto per la storia del Risorgimento italiano, Turin.

3. Ricuperati, G. (1973) 'L'Università di Torino nel Settecento', in *Quaderni storici* 23, pp. 575–98;   Roggero, M. (1981) *Scuola e riforme nello stato sabaudo.* Deputazione subalpina di storia patria, Turin.
4. Ajello, R. (1969) 'Il Banco di San Carlo: organi di governo e opinione pubblica nel Regno di Napoli di fronte al problema della ricompra dei diritti fiscali', in *Rivista storica italiana* IV, pp. 812–81.
5. Zaninelli, S. (1963) *Il nuovo censo dello stato di Milano dall'editto del 1718 al 1733.* Vita e pensiero, Milan.
6. Ricuperati, G. (1976) 'Giornali e società nell'Italia dell'Ancien Régime (1668–1789)', in various authors, *La stampa italiana dal '500 all '800*, ed. Castronovo, V. and Tranfaglia, N. Laterza, Bari.

CHAPTER ELEVEN

The Habsburg-Lorraine model: the Lombardy of Maria Theresa, Tuscany under the Regency and the Duchy of Modena

The State of Milan was one of the regions least well integrated into the territories which made up the complex mosaic of the Habsburg monarchy. It had been conquered only relatively recently, it was separated geographically from the centre of the monarchy in the Austro-Bohemian region, and it had retained strong political autonomies through the transition from Spanish to Austrian rule. These factors may explain why it remained relatively unimportant to Vienna. However, it is also true that the political events which were unfolding in Milan cannot be understood if isolated from the more general Habsburg reform movement and the decisions made by the secretariats and offices of Vienna. The critical impetus came from the capital and then was adapted to the different local situations called upon to receive and interpret it. Very rarely, at least in so far as Austrian Lombardy was concerned, did the process work in reverse, with an impulse going from the periphery to the centre, from local society to the Viennese bureaucracy. Yet it would be a mistake to imagine from this a flat and passive picture of Lombard society. On the contrary, it produced men and ideas which found their place in the mainstream of Maria Theresa's reformism and often left their own not unimportant mark. Nevertheless, the direction of flow and the control of its development were always in the hands of the central bodies or, on a local level, of the officials who served the Empire.

Whether one looks at the dates of the reforms, analyses the principles which inspired them and their implementation or studies the political biographies of the authors of the Theresian reforms, it is clear that decisions taken in Vienna concerning the hereditary states on the banks of the Danube – the central axis of the Empire – were closely related to those that reached the Milanese officials. It has often been stated that Milan was late to move in comparison with other parts of the Empire and last to arrive. This is not quite accurate as it is clear that there was a basic synchronisation between the plans and their realisation in the centre, and those expressed and put into practice in the Italian territories. The machinery of reform moved, more or less, with the same rhythm in Vienna, Prague and Milan. This is confirmed

158

by the dates. It was only at the end of the War of the Austrian Succession that a reformist outlook emerged in Vienna, finding its first important political result in the Protocol of Bertenstein of 1748. This was as yet a confused plan, but one with a decisive effect on the development of the reforms. The empress and the group of high officials that she gathered around her, among whom were prominent Friedrich-Wilhelm Haugwitz for internal policies and Count Kaunitz for external policies, held together the strands of the different reforming initiatives that spread far and wide into many of the provinces of the Habsburg monarchy. In Milan the reform movement got under way at the same period, 1742–71 to be more exact, while the particular local situation determined only the internal development. This might of course be affected by international events, such as the Seven Years War.

One encounters similar links in both the general philosophy and in the technical details of Theresian policies. The initial impulse which was the starting-point for the Viennese rulers and which can be found again, identical, in the reformers active in Lombardy, was the precariousness of the financial situation, made worse by the huge cost of the war. In order to reduce this unusually large deficit and to maintain the flow of taxes sufficient to cover future expenses, the traditional administrative methods were found to be entirely unsuitable. It became increasingly clear that what was needed was new forms of taxation, more rational, efficient and broadly based, and above all more closely controlled by the public bureaucracy. On this basis the state taxation system was improved and administrative centralisation took another step forward. The result of these developments was a reduction in the autonomy of the classes and institutions of a 'national' type, even if during the entire Theresian period these privileges were substantially respected and upheld. In general, reformism in the age of Maria Theresa can be described as 'imperfect centralisation', because, while it tried to standardise and control from the centre the financial and administrative systems, yet it protected local differences and seigneurial, patrician and aristocratic powers which remained just as they had been in earlier centuries. The other main concern of the Viennese politicians in the 1740s and 1750s was military. In strengthening the army the preferred method was to delegate to the individual countries making up the monarchy the job of recruiting and maintaining 'national' forces which would be more able to reply to the offensive and defensive needs of an empire with extensive frontiers.

On the social level, the first wave of reforms did not cause any conflict with the oligarchies of the individual countries though it involved the absorption of these oligarchies into the state institutions and a partial reduction of some of their powers. The feudal question, first raised at this time, was not to become central to the political struggle until the 1780s. The economic policies were still generally influenced by mercantilism, while the role of the State in running the economy became more evident. Relations with the Church brought about a revival of jurisdictionalism, which now found new impetus in a broad range of political battles, resulting in areas once traditionally under the control of the Church being taken over by the State, as in the case of education, and age-old ecclesiastical exemptions, legal and fiscal, were curtailed.

The new rulers in Milan in the early 1740s inherited the consequences of Charles VI's policies which had already introduced some reforms, particularly the *catasto*, the land register, but had been unable to put them into action both because of internal weakness and the opposition of Milanese society. As soon as military and political conditions gave way to a period of peace and civic enthusiasm, the reformers returned to the uncompleted task of compiling the *catasto*. The initial phase of Theresian reformism in Milan was linked with Count Gian Luca Pallavicini. A typical example of a *grand commis* of the Empire, he was born in Genoa of that cosmopolitan aristocracy which in the past had given some of its best men to the Austrian monarchy. In 1743 he had been assigned by Maria Theresa the delicate job of reponsibility for military economy, which meant providing for the maintenance, transport and lodging of the armed forces in Italy. From first-hand experience of the financial and economic problems which became evident during the war, Pallavicini saw the necessity of reforming those bodies because they caused injustice, corruption and inefficiency. In 1744 he put into Maria Theresa's hands a general plan of reform which sketched out in broad lines all the reforms to be put into action in the following years. He proposed to finish the *catasto*, which though started in 1718 had become bogged down amidst the objections of the patricians, with all speed, to reorganise the financial system and to reduce the state deficit.

In 1747, after a brief eclipse of his political power at court, Pallavicini gave Maria Theresa a more detailed plan of reform which, compared to the first one, proposed a greater unification of the tax Farm and more public support and financial assistance for the manufacturing industries. Supported cautiously at first by Vienna and opposed in Milan by several groups, Pallavicini nevertheless succeeded in having his plan approved almost unchanged. In 1749 under the governorship of Friedrich von Harrach the roll of state functionaries was drawn up, the functionaries themselves being reduced in number, and two principles of great social importance were established: the forbidding of the sale of offices and the fixing of all payments for services performed by state officials. The first step had been taken towards a modern bureaucracy, towards the impersonal State.

The following year Pallavicini was made governor and from this position he could give more force to his ideas. In the reorganisation of the magistratures, one of the two cameral bodies, the *Magistrato straordinario*, was abolished and his duties were absorbed by the *Magistrato ordinario*. In this way the different duties of the cameral offices were combined and, more importantly, the base was laid for transferring to the State the management of the private and feudal patrimony of the prince, which before had been administered by the *Magistrato straordinario* and was often quite out of control. With extraordinary speed, Pallavicini imposed his programme in the space of three years, including those plans which had needed some time to put into action.

Between 1749 and 1750 he launched a general tax-Farm which was to concentrate in a single body the contracting out of the main taxes owed to the State and the collection of various indirect taxes. A group of tax-farmers from Bergamo, under the direction of the financier Antonio Greppi, was to take up the contracts for tax collection. The advantages to the State were considerable: there was the possibility of advances on the taxes from the farmers, a general increase in revenue from duties and ease in obtaining credit from the farmers. The danger was that of creating in Lombardy a financial group so strong as to be beyond any control and which might establish itself as a rival force in political and social relations. To avoid this danger delegates were appointed to the Farm from the *Magistrato camerale*, and Pallavicini maintained a careful watch, but this was of little use when the State was hungry for money which could only be provided with sufficient speed and in great enough quantities by Greppi's farmers.

The example of France was there to show how a power block could form around the Farm if the balance between creditor and debtor should tip too much in favour of the former, putting the State at the mercy of the farmers. In Milan too this situation arose very quickly: in 1757 the request to the farmers for a new loan was agreed in exchange for renewing the contract for tax collection before the old one had elapsed. But the matter of the farmers was to be reopened, as will be seen, a few years later, stimulated by a wave of reform of a new type. Complementing the General Farm, Pallavicini set up in 1753 the Bank of Santa Teresa which was to guarantee the State's creditors the payment of their interest and, as its long-term aim, the gradual repayment of the money owed to them. The financial importance of this body was to be felt in the 1780s when with its capital it was to be possible to close the Bank of Sant'Ambrogio, financial prop of the patrician supremacy.

The reform which lasted longest and left its mark not only on the financial system, but also on Lombard economy and society, was without doubt the completion of the *catasto*, entrusted to an able Florentine official, Pompeo Neri. After a period as professor of public law in Pisa University from 1726 to 1735 he had held administrative posts in the Tuscany of the dukes of Lorraine, distinguishing himself by his technical abilities and political judgement. He was invited to preside over the Junta established in 1749 whose job was to bring the *catasto*, started in 1718 and interrupted in 1733, to a conclusion. A large part of the practical work had been carried out by the preceding Junta. It was now necessary to finish it, resolve any problems remaining and crush the considerable resistance to it which had arisen and which was partly responsible for the previous suspension of work. Neri was well aware of the obstacles to be overcome in order to cut through the tangle of privileges and abuses that social groups, towns and provinces had encouraged for their own gain, thus adding recent disorder to ancient confusion in a delicate and complex system such as the census. He clarified his objectives and methods for himself and for his collaborators in his important *Relazione*[1] of 1750. Neri proposed the principles of fiscal justice and administrative rationalisation which were to be applied to the new *catasto*, which would be the objective basis of a more equal division of the tax burden. Like other European reformers and intellectuals, he was convinced that all taxes except that on the land should be abolished and that every privileged exemption should be swept away. It was not possible, however, to implement these measures which would have been judged too advanced. The tax on trade was retained and there was no new revision of the declarations made by the merchant bodies. Similarly the personal tax was kept, which harmed the peasants and which Neri wanted to fix at a low level. Exemptions which benefited the clergy were kept and confirmed with a few modifications by the Concordat of 1757.

Despite these limitations, the new fiscal law came into being on 1 January 1760 for all the Habsburg territories in Lombardy except Mantua. Above all it sanctioned a significant change in the relationship between the landowners and the State, in so far as it overturned the old system based on a tax declaration by the owner, replacing it with an official assessment and a division of land into cadastral parcels for the purpose of the sharing out of taxes. In addition it introduced the principle of an equal contribution from all social categories and for all the provinces, even if important exceptions continued to be granted to the clergy. In the judgement of the first commentators and then of historians, the Milanese *catasto* resulted in a noticeable improvement in agriculture, because it made ownership secure and fixed the tax on it. More than this, by linking the tax not to income but to the land it indirectly stimulated production since an improvement in the latter did not bring about an increase in taxation. Lastly, Maria Theresa's *catasto* took the job of distribution and collection of state taxes out of the hands of the local administrations, a situation which in the past had given rise to arbitrary and unfair decisions, not to mention control over local society by the nobles and patricians.

The introduction of the *catasto* meant the need for other changes and reforms in the State. The political map of Lombardy had to be redrawn in order to establish new provincial and district boundaries. In 1755, the Junta for the census set in motion a reform of great significance for the municipal administrations. Membership of these bodies was now to be based on an individual's property and the taxes he was assessed to pay, and no longer on titles of nobility.[2] In this way cracks began to open up in the fabric of a society defined by feudal hegemony in the country and the patriciate in the towns, allowing the political rise of a class made up of wealthy landowners, rich professionals and merchants. The old provincial representative bodies were not removed by the reform of 1755, and for the whole of the Theresian period they loudly protested at the continuous whittling away of their powers by new state institutions. Nevertheless the foundations had been laid in the modernisation of institutions which together with the effects of the census were in the following years to underpin the formation of a ruling class that was no longer open only to the aristocracy.

The year 1757 was a critical one for reform; there was a pause in the government's initiatives and very clear attempts at recovery by the conservative and oligarchical groups of Lombard society. The Concordat of 1757 was evidence of this slowing down. From the point of view of the defence of state prerogatives, the clauses dealing with the tax immunities of the Church constituted a definite step backwards from Neri's objectives, and if compared with the agreements drawn up in the previous decades between the Holy See and the other Italian states reveal all their backwardness. In the same year, following pressure from Beltrame Cristiani, who had succeeded Pallavicini in 1753 as governor of Milan and who followed a conciliatory line towards local interests, the census Junta was dissolved, releasing its president, Neri, who returned to Tuscany in the service of the House of Lorraine. From then until January 1760, i.e. the date of the introduction of the fiscal reform, those now responsible for the *catasto* liberally granted exemptions and exclusions to the thousands of applications made by individuals and organisations, in an attempt to silence their protests. Despite these concessions, which might have annulled the most innovatory elements of the reform, because of the great technical precision in its construction and the radically new principles which had inspired it, the census maintained its usefulness as a modern, functional aid to a rational taxation system, co-ordinated by the State. For it to become really effective, a political leadership was needed that would deprive the local powers of their authority and crush the resistance that had been offered in the first years by many social groups in Lombardy. On the death of Cristiani it was to be an Imperial official from Trent, Count Carlo di Firmian, who brought the governing of Milan back on to the path first traced by Pallavicini ten years before, giving at the same time a new and decisive impetus to the reform movement.

The second wave of reforms began in 1759 when Firmian arrived in Milan, having been nominated minister plenipotentiary in June. It should not be thought, however, that one man deserves all the credit for the reforms. Many aspects of the political, cultural and social situation were changing at that time, creating very different circumstances from those facing Pallavicini ten years earlier. Europe was again at war. The Seven Years War (1756–63), which spared the Italian provinces, brought contradictory pressures to bear on the Viennese rulers. On the one hand it became a matter of urgency to bring to a conclusion the fiscal changes that were being tried out, one of which was the Milanese *catasto*, because of the high cost involved; on the other hand the enormous debt that was once again building up for the monarchy made it equally urgent to reconsider the whole financial and fiscal system which was not yielding the results hoped for. The political and cultural climate was changing too, not only in Lombardy but more generally in Europe. The Enlightenment, which was rocking the very foundations of ancient certainties and introducing radically different ways of thinking about and describing the many facets of human experience, certainly played an important part in the changing of ideas and traditions, even if it did not everywhere provide a plan for political reform which could be accepted and tried out. Political reform was developed rather from current ideas that were more backward but more serviceable in an environment of enlightened absolutism. As far as Maria Theresa's reforms are concerned, there is no doubt that their general philosophy was influenced by different theoretical tendencies,

from Muratorian *Reformkatholizismus* to regalistic, Jansenist and Febronian ideas, from Wolff and Thomasius' natural law to neo-mercantilism and Austro-German cameralism which at just this time was finding a definitive expression in the works of Justi and Sonnenfels: currents of thought which had in common the exaltation of the State as supreme organiser and guardian of the public good, of the prince as father of the people, responsible for their material and spiritual well-being.[3]

Similar upheavals were taking place in Lombard society where the élite was changing in attitude and from whom emerged ideas and forces which no longer merely expressed opposition to the reforms but which were finding a *modus vivendi* or even some measure of agreement with them. At the same time, Firmian and his collaborators, unlike Pallavicini, were able to rely on a larger and better qualified political staff, which had been created in the early stages of reorganisation of the institutions of state power. Lastly, events in Lombardy were now being followed more attentively in Vienna, a sign of the increased integration of the Italian provinces into the political structure of the Empire. In the early 1760s an axis of collaboration was established between Milan and Vienna which was to prove very fruitful. The central figures of this relationship were, in Milan, Firmian; in Vienna, the powerful minister for foreign affairs, Kaunitz; and the referendary at the Italian Department, until 1766 the Venetian abbé Luigi Giusti, who played a leading role in the choice of men and direction of political affairs.

Between 1759 and 1761 Firmian was closely involved with the last phases of the *catasto* which was to come into operation as soon as the maps of the properties and the division of taxation was made. The completion of the *catasto* brought with it other opportunities for change, as had already been seen in the case of the reform of the administration of 1755, and was at the same time a kind of vast inquiry into the structure of Lombard society, revealing the size and distribution of estates. In this way a clear view was obtained of the extent of the ecclesiastical sector. While it absorbed about a third of overall wealth, it did not contribute in the same degree to taxation, being protected by ancient immunities touched little or not at all by the recent concordats. Thus it was natural that, faced with the need to find new sources of revenue – a need that was now urgent on account of the expenses of the war – Vienna asked the Italian Church to contribute to this financial effort. Clement XIII's response totally failed to satisfy Maria Theresa. The time was ripe to reopen the jurisdictional debate with the church hierarchy if the rulers wished to increase the patrimony, strengthen fiscal power, and provide the cultural and ideological guidance of society which were becoming the common objectives of both the government and substantial sections of society. There was the example of other Italian states where the reform movement was concentrating its energies in the area of relations between Church and State.

This was the beginning of a period of great struggle, when the rulers allied themselves with those important sections of the Catholic world that were becoming aware of the need to temper the more excessive aspects of the temporal power of the Church, and to absorb those elements most distant from the evangelical origins of Christianity into the Catholic doctrine and faith. In Milan the first blow in the reopening of the jurisdictional battle was struck in 1762 with an edict which required an *exequatur* for all instructions which the Roman Curia might in future send out to the dioceses of Habsburg Lombardy. In addition, responsibility in this area was taken away from the Senate and given to an Imperial representative. Henceforward, Lombardy was to be a testing ground where the Viennese rulers intended to assess the results and problems of the neo-jurisdictional policies which they wanted to introduce in all their territories where the Catholic Church was dominant. It was a gradual process, which began with cautious and limited steps and then introduced more radical measures where no element of the Catholic hegemony was spared.

In order to expedite matters, Kaunitz and Firmian established a special Junta, answerable only to central government, which was to bypass the Milanese magistratures and personally direct the anti-ecclesiastical programme. Set up in 1765, in the short space of two years, the Junta initiated a series of provisions and plans which were to strike deep at Lombard Catholicism. A series of regulations was drawn up, limiting the involvement of monks in civil and religious affairs. An impressive investigation was also started into the clergy's possessions, and an edict on mortmains was drafted, to be approved in 1767. The following year Kaunitz issued new instructions extending and more clearly defining the area covered by the Junta. The Austrian chancellor affirmed the principle of the separation of the functions of the Church, which were not to go beyond strictly spiritual limits, and those of the State to which 'all that which is not divinely instituted' was to belong.

The quarrel with Rome immediately intensified, the right to fiscal immunities and control of censorship over books being hotly contested by the Church. With the important edict of 30 December 1768, censorship was snatched from the hands of the Inquisition and the Senate of Milan and assigned to a *Giunta agli studi*, composed of specially trained people enjoying the trust of the state rulers. The members included some ecclesiastics, who were, however, to express their opinion only on books with a religious content. Clement XIII protested to Maria Theresa in vain. The introduction of secular censorship was accompanied by affirmations encouraging a greater freedom of thought and the press. In her dispatch which accompanied the aforementioned edict, Maria Theresa advised the committee not to be too severe in their examination of books on politics and economics, but rather to assure 'a measure of freedom in the discussion and writing on such topics', convinced that greater freedom would 'educate the nation and stimulate minds'.

In addition the gradual suppression of the Tribunal of the Inquisition continued. In 1769 the prisons in the religious houses were closed and religious ceremony was reformed, external pomp being prohibited and festivities associated with local saints being curtailed. These measures echoed the battle waged in the first half of the eighteenth century by Muratori for a more intimate type of worship and a Catholicism which was compatible with reason and social utility. In 1770 the right of sanctuary in churches and in general in all ecclesiastical buildings was abolished. To prevent the shameless exploitation of precocious vocations, a minimum age of twenty-four was set for the taking of religious vows. Venturi has maintained that this edict marked the end of a period where the State had remained within the bounds of its own rights, opening a new phase in which the State began to legislate on the internal discipline of the Church. The natural development of this line was to be perfected by Joseph II in the 1780s. This anti-ecclesiastical policy was related to the reform of Pavia University which began in 1767 and was well under way by 1773. Control of the university was taken away from the Milanese Senate and at the same time new subjects of study and more modern teaching criteria were introduced.

As has been seen, the ecclesiastical reforms and the *catasto* had been desired principally by the Habsburg rulers who found themselves either opposed by the Milanese ruling classes or at least deprived of their active co-operation. Reaction to the reform of censorship was more universally hostile than that to the policy on the Church which was followed closely by some sections of the Milanese patriciate. Relations between Vienna and local interests were very different when it was a question of revising the contracts with the tax-farmers. The latter had lost much of the esteem in which they had been held at court, both because of the meanness of their loans to the State and because of their oppression of the people of Lombardy. Increased tariffs, greater control and further taxation were the results of the power which the tax-farmers were building up, thanks to their strength which was not only financial but also military since they had their own armed body of men.

News of this state of affairs was reaching Vienna through the meetings of the *Magistrato camerale* in Milan which often referred to the woeful conditions in Lombardy resulting from the numerous searches carried out by the Farm's police. United against the abuses of the farmers and their financial power were the *Magistratura camerale*, the Milanese patricians being hostile to a company composed of foreigners, as was Greppi's Farm, and the Viennese chancellery which, inspired by the referendary Luigi Giusti, in 1764 delegated a commission dependent on the *Magistrato camerale* to draw up a plan for reforming the Farm. The Milanese *illuminista* Pietro Verri was invited to participate and his suggestions carried some weight, even if they were not entirely approved in the first instance. A partial revision of the tax-collection contract was prepared whereby government delegates were placed in the administration of the Farm, giving the government a share in its profits. The same commission was asked to propose a reform of the customs duties. The new rate, worked out in 1765, was a compromise which initiated developments towards free trade, as part of a general shift in the direction of economic policy. The census, the Farm and the tariffs were intermediate goals which did not upset any of the chief power centres. They did, however, set in motion important changes which were to be further developed in the 1780s.

At almost the same time as the reform of the Farm, a new magistrature, the *Supremo Consiglio di economia*, was set up in 1765 charged with managing all the economic and financial affairs of Lombardy. The Supreme Council wanted to exclude from economic, fiscal and financial policy-making those Milanese ruling classes who symbolised the ancient legalistic culture and who defended, less and less successfully, Milan's traditional autonomy. For this reason the presidency was given to a foreigner, Gian Rinaldo Carli from Istria, and among the councillors too the Milanese patricians were in a minority of two in a total of nine. The members of the council were chosen for their abilities and experience. The census, the Farm and trade regulation were the three areas which the government wished the council to study, both in so far as they were dealing with sectors which were infiltrated by a process of reform still in its infancy and because the organisational role which they had assumed now required constant attention. Besides administering these sectors, the council was to deal with other economic and financial matters where the need for full-scale changes was becoming apparent. But the powers which it had been given were inadequate to deal with the tasks it had been assigned: drawing up a plan of reform of the *annona*, drafting a commercial code, reviving the textile industry, new monetary measures and finally encouraging production-oriented research. The achievements of the Supreme Council did not measure up to the demands made upon it and when it was dissolved in 1771 many of the problems and needs which had led to its formation were still there.

The end of this period of reform is marked by the important decree of 6 July 1770 dissolving the mixed Farm. The State took sole charge of the collection of taxes and freed itself of the financial restrictions previously exercised by the powerful farmers. The decree started with a reference to the census, almost as if a link was seen between the abolition of the Farm and the long process begun in 1718 with the setting up of the first Junta for the census and which had similarly developed through a policy of the redeeming of *fiscali*. This leads us to a consideration of the relationship between state and feudal power, which was to be central in the struggle for reform in the following years, a struggle marked by the new direction which Maria Theresa's son, Joseph II, imposed on the course of political developments in Habsburg Lombardy.

In Tuscany, as in Lombardy, the development of reforms would be inconceivable without the appearance on the political and social scene of a protagonist from outside; this was the ruling group of the House of Lorraine who took over the Florentine secretariats on the death of Gian Gastone, last of the Medici. These men represented policies which could not have differed more from local customs: a strong sense of the State, a technical and administrative conception of politics and a moral intransigence in the handling of public affairs. These and other attitudes were to clash with habits which had become embedded in the Tuscany of the Medici and which, in the last years of that dynasty, had revealed their decadence. Even more than the projects and political decisions, it was this change of mentality which counted and which can explain the picture of Tuscany formed by Count de Richecourt, the most powerful man in the Lorraine Regency. It is worth recounting these impressions received by Richecourt from the very first days of his arrival in Florence and which he passed on to his duke, Francis Stephen of Lorraine, because it was on the basis of these observations that the outlines of change were drawn up and which the rulers attempted to carry out in the following twenty years. Richecourt was struck first of all by the chaos which reigned in the institutions of the State.[4] The Tuscan ruling classes struck him as concerned only with defending their own private interests, united by family connections, idle and ineffectual, even if there were some honest men. These remained, however, in the background, frightened.

Thus it was impossible to rely on local forces if things were really to be changed, and all the more so since the powerful families of the Tuscan nobility did not hide their disapproval of the new arrivals. Feelings both of nostalgia for the republican past which some had hoped to revive with the death of the last Medici, and, more realistically, of sympathy towards the Spanish, who were supported by a significant group of churchmen and nobles, were the principal obstacles that the new rulers had to contend with for several decades. The Spanish threat was all too real, since the war was going badly for the Austrians, occupied with fighting the Turks and leaving their southern border unprotected. At the beginning of 1738 it even seemed probable that there was to be an imminent Spanish invasion on the Tuscan coast. When the danger was past the pro-Spanish faction within Tuscany remained active. This had significant support, most importantly from the unity between some of the noble families of Florence and the Roman Curia, or rather, those sections of it influenced by the Medici faction which had great political power in Rome.

But to return to Richecourt's first impressions – he was unfavourably impressed by the internal divisions of the Grand Duchy, in which three distinct unities, Florence, Siena and Pisa and their territories, coexisted, and also by the privileged position enjoyed by the city of Florence. Corruption and private enrichment through the exercise of public functions were possible because, according to Richecourt, in Tuscany there were no controls or hierarchical responsibilities in the offices but each tribunal operated autonomously, even to the extent of leaving the rates of payment for services entirely to the discretion of the employees. The slowness in dealing with negotiations, the high cost of the tribunals, the corruption of justice, the enormous state debt, commercial frauds and the under-utilisation of the great church properties were other signs of the deterioration of the State which shocked the severe Richecourt, brought up with the principles of administrative efficiency and responsibility. The picture may have been painted even blacker than it really was, because of the bias of an inexpert observer, but there is no doubt that Richecourt's analysis focused on all that was wrong in the Medici State as it was when handed over to the new rulers from Lorraine.

It was a short step from a description of the ills of Tuscany to the formulation of possible remedies, and as early as October 1737 Richecourt had sent the grand duke a draft of reforms to be carried out immediately in order to deal with the areas of greatest confusion. It was the starting-point for a long and difficult road, but one which was to yield important results, so that Tuscany in the eighteenth century can be said to have been one of the regions of Europe where the reforming plans of enlightened absolutism most successfully took root. The early stages were difficult. As has been said, Tuscany was a country dismayed and disillusioned, having seen its age-old traditions disregarded by an agreement between the great powers, and which had not even been informed of its transfer to the dukes of Lorraine. An indigenous government, the last representative of a glorious past, had been taken over by a foreign dynasty linked with the Austrian Empire, for reasons which could not be questioned, and which ignored the desires of the country.

The two rulers from Lorraine, the Prince de Craon, made minister plenipotentiary, and Count de Richecourt, who was head of the Council of Finance, brought to political life in Tuscany from 1737 to 1757 their great political ability combined with a clarity of intention and decisiveness. This was particularly true of Richecourt who was the real leader of the state secretariat. The allocation of executive posts was balanced so as to allow Italians to be represented alongside the Lorrainers, though the latter possessed greater court responsibilities. It was vital for the new rulers to conquer the court, a focal point for Tuscan society and meeting place between the nobility and the political leaders, rather than the secretariats, to which they did not hesitate to promote Tuscan politicians. But in the secretariats too the change of personnel was total and allowed recently trained men to arrive at the top very rapidly. This was the case with Pompeo Neri who when only thirty-one was promoted to the rank of secretary of state, the jumping-off point for a life in politics that was to make him in Tuscany and Lombardy one of the most influential Imperial officials in the area of legal and economic reform. With him the legal and economic reforms that were being planned in Pisa and Siena in those years were transmitted to the Tuscan government.

In Pisa the source of the new ideas was the university that was re-emerging from the crisis through the efforts of Monsignor Cerati, the director from 1733, in which year his policy, aimed at scientific modernisation and didactic rigour, got under way. New vigour was infused into the legal and scientific traditions of the university as a result of European developments in natural law and the influence of Newtonian theories. In Siena the creative impulse came not from an institution but from an intellectual, Sallustio Bandini, who combined a vast culture embracing many interests – economic, political and scientific – with a clear realisation of the problems affecting his country and particularly the Maremma.

Of his ideas was born a remarkable and innovative proposal, contained in his *Discorso sopra la Maremma toscana* of 1737, not published until 1775. He suggested that it was necessary to change economic policy radically. Restrictive provisions, pressure of taxation, endless intervention by legal middlemen and useless *annona* regulations were no good. These corner-stones of state intervention should be rejected and in their place the free export of grain should be permitted which would make it profitable for producers to invest in agriculture in the lands of the Maremma, leading in turn to the reduction in the tax burden on the peasants. This plan was too far ahead of its time to be approved in its entirety by the new rulers, but in 1738 it was adopted in part when the free export of Maremma grain was established. This was a limited measure that certainly was insufficient to Bandini's demands which were suppressed until the 1760s when they were revived by the physiocrats and the reformism of Leopold.

Pisa University and the small school which gathered at Siena round Bandini demonstrate very clearly how new voices were coming from the provinces capable of expressing the ills of their areas. The ills of the capital, as we have seen, were shrewdly understood by Richecourt. Along with Pisa and Siena, Leghorn deserves to be mentioned, for it played a part in the reawakening of ideas which characterises the first years of the Lorraine Regency. The first masonic lodges to be transplanted from England took root in Leghorn, soon to acquire many members in Tuscany. From these masonic circles which were expanding during the first years of the Regency came a cosmopolitan spirit, an interest in scientific matters, English empiricism and a sense of belonging to a 'society' where class differences did not matter.

Tuscany was not governed directly by the Grand Duke Francis Stephen, who after his visit to the region entrusted government to a Regency Council, whose presidents were Craon until 1747, Richecourt until 1757 and Marshal of the Empire Botta-Adorno until 1765. From this date Leopold, second son of Maria Theresa, assumed control of the Grand Duchy of Tuscany, moving to the court in Florence where he stayed until 1790 when he became emperor on the death of his brother Joseph II. The political phases partly fit in with these dates. For the entire period dominated by Richecourt, i.e. until 1757, the reform movement was taking its first steps, helped by the support from Lorraine and by the leadership of some exceptional men, such as Neri and Giulio Rucellai, an exponent of Tuscan jurisdictionalism who was to direct the most important aspects of the fight against ecclesiastical abuses. With the departure of Richecourt there was a temporary lull which was soon to be forgotten in the political events of the 1760s.

As can be seen, the process of reform was intermittent, stopping and starting almost at the same dates as that in the State of Milan, though compared to which Tuscany enjoyed a greater autonomy which was to be strengthened after 1765. The needs which impelled its rulers to fight for change were very similar to those in Milan: the State's need for revenue, the reorganisation of the magistratures, control over the nobility and the curbing of some of the Church's powers. The means adopted and results obtained were, however, rather different. Richecourt saw at once that the most hostile force was represented by the Church, the only body capable of putting obstacles in the way of the new rulers and therefore one which needed to be attacked without faltering. Rome influenced Tuscany in too many ways and too closely, compromising its autonomy.

However, it was the Church which fired the first shot when in 1738 it increased the inquisitor's control over the press and began to persecute the Freemasons. The reaction was immediate, but in addition ambitious objectives were proposed and attained. Francis Stephen refused to accept publication in Florence of the papal bull *In eminenti* condemning Freemasonry, issued by Clement XII in June 1738. In the same year an edict restricting the bearing of arms meant in fact the disarming of the Inquisition's agents. Richecourt and Rucellai drew inspiration from the Venetian model and the policies that Paolo Sarpi had inspired against the Inquisition. Meanwhile the election of Benedict XIV to the papal throne raised hopes of an agreement, which very soon, however, turned out to be impracticable for Tuscany. Thus the possibility of reaching a partial accommodation was shelved and open hostilities began. With the law of 28 May 1743, drawn up by Rucellai, censorship of books and control over printing presses were transferred to the State, limiting ecclesiastics to dealing with works with a religious content.[5] This was an important gain for the State, the effects of which were to be felt in later years when Tuscany became one of the Italian states with the greatest freedom of the press and vigorous publishing houses. This law created the conditions for the freeing of the press from the more oppressive forms of control and was a safeguard for all expressions of intellectual activity.

The jurisdictional struggle did not confine itself to ideological problems, but took on the very foundation of ecclesiastical privilege, the question of immunities. Local immunities were very widespread in Tuscany, guaranteeing areas of non-intervention by civil law. In Florence alone, according to Richecourt's estimates, there were at least 243 religious bodies enjoying such immunities. There were also immunities which partially or totally exempted church property from taxes, thus the higher the income enjoyed by the Church the greater the loss to the State. Richecourt put it at 33 per cent of the overall income of the country, a figure which becomes more striking if one bears in mind that ecclesiastics formed only 3 per cent of the Tuscan population. Once again it was Rucellai who provided the answer which was already prepared in 1745 and made operative with the law on mortmain of 1751. This law was intended to prevent the expansion of the Church. It established that donations to the Church and pious institutions of moveable property over a certain value, and all donations of land and bonds, could only be made with the approval of the Regency Council, the chief political organ of the Grand Duchy. Thus Tuscany emerges as the leader in the many-sided attack on the Curia in Italy. Yet it is true that from 1740 it was Benedict XIV who sat on the papal throne, a very different figure from his predecessor who had still personified the Church of the Counter-Reformation.

As has been seen, some attempts to reform the relations between Church and State were sparked off by the demands of fiscal policy which in Tuscany, as in Milan, urgently needed to be reorganised as a result of the war, the uncertainties of the international situation and the difficulties of the government. It is important to stress the change in direction that happened in this area in the 1740s. In the first years of the Lorraine Regency, fiscal policy had been of a traditional type: it seemed that the easiest way of solving the most severe problem that the Lorraine dynasty had inherited from the Medici, the public debt, was to increase taxes and to sell off state-owned property. The general contribution ordered in 1738 did not spare the clergy. In the same year the property formerly belonging to the Medici began to be sold, with the exception of the lands and residences in the Kingdom of Naples, sequestrated by Charles III. But the sale of allodial land in Tuscany was slow and did not furnish the state coffers with the expected returns.

It was soon clear that it would be necessary to take more extreme measures rather than merely tinkering with the taxation system, if an adequate income was to be achieved. Therefore a reform was tried out under which the contract for the collection of taxes was given to a single company of tax-farmers. In December 1740 all Tuscan finances were contracted out to a French company, whose task it was to try to unravel the confused tangle of rules and regulations in operation in Tuscany, in order to extract as much money as possible, so as to make up the state deficit. Historians have differed in their evaluation of the effects of the new fiscal system on the Tuscan economy but it cannot be denied that from the financial point of view, the Farm did its job well, increasing revenue and lessening the burden of the public debt. It was also the only effective method that the reforms of absolutism had hit upon up to this time, since not only the political conditions but also the necessary technical skills were lacking which might have allowed a unified and general reform of taxation.

The old and chaotic edifice of the Tuscan State was not called into question during this period, in which other problems seemed more prominent and the road to institutional reform too risky, but a project for the compilation of a legal code for Tuscany was outlined. This decision was arrived at through a series of circumstances. Firstly, the new rulers were faced with a very intricate legal system, which faithfully reflected the customs of the Medici era, with a progressive accumulation of regulations, statutes and laws born of individual local or class instances. The State of Tuscany in fact embraced a complex mosaic of geographical and social differences. This situation has justly been described as administrative and legislative particularism, something which was not peculiar to Tuscany. There was no single body of law. Local law had been absorbed into grand-ducal law, while areas not covered by these two came under the rules of Roman law, canon law, feudal law and the *Consolato del Mare*. Corresponding to the fragmentary character of the legal system was the great social and political importance of the lawyers, notaries and judges, the traditional intermediaries between the political powers and society, which did not merely interpret the law but also created it.

In Tuscany, as in other parts of Italy, in the 1730s a proposal for reform was put up by those scholars of the law who in the light of ideas on natural law and research were advocating a new code which would simplify the existing system of law and restore to it the authority which in practice it had lost. Muratori's *Dei difetti della giurisprudenza*, published in 1742, showed the urgent need to bring some order to the chaotic jungle of the laws and to restore energy and civil utility to the practice of jurisprudence. He proposed simple and clear laws, judges able to apply them with discernment and rapidity and a simplification in dealing with legal disputes. Here, as in other enterprises, Muratori combined the defence of tradition and the need for reform. He looked for a model to Victor Amadeus II's reform of the legislature in the State of Savoy in 1723 and 1729, when all the laws of the State were brought together in a single code. Muratori's demands for the simplification of the law, his view of the judge and of justice as expressions of the sovereign and not separate powers, his fight for a reorganisation of the laws, not so much to introduce new principles as to give civil force to the practice of the law, had great influence on the ideas and plans for codification which emerged in many parts of Italy, but they remained theoretical, and were not acted upon. The most important results were the redrafting of the laws of Milan, undertaken in 1747 by Gabriele Verri, father of the more famous Pietro and Alessandro, and the plans drawn up at this time by Pasquale Cirillo in Naples and by Neri in Florence, which, however, were not carried out.

Another important stimulus to the reorganisation of Tuscan justice was the attitude of the Lorraine rulers who found the many different types of law and the chaos in the courts throughout the region thoroughly inconvenient. They were not prompted so much by the need to draw up new laws as by the more realistic desire, more typical of the juridical philosophy of the age, to summarise in a single code the multitude of laws operating in the country. In carrying out this work they would drop the more anachronistic regulations. Thus a consolidation of the law and partial revision of the statutes and of juridical organisation were to be the criteria inspiring this work which was entrusted in 1745 to Pompeo Neri and the Florentine senator Venturi Neri. Two years later Pompeo Neri handed the secretary of state a preliminary report on the work which attempted to reconcile the old and the new. Rejecting the idea of a complete revision of the code, Neri proposed a reorganisation of the laws then in force, which would respect, but modernise, the Tuscan, and more generally Italian, traditions of Roman and common law. Nothing came of this plan. It failed because of Richecourt's distrust of Neri's work and because of the political and theoretical uncertainties involved in the task allotted to the two Tuscans. It should be borne in mind that it was obviously impossible to carry out a new organisation of the law, in either its codification or procedure, without at the same time carrying out a general reorganisation of the structure of power in Tuscany, from the nobility to the Church, without unifying the many elements of the laws in operation, from feudal laws to citizen laws – in other words without a general institutional reform. But for this there lacked the will, the ideas and the consensus.

However, one reform of great social importance was introduced, dealing with the institution of the *fidecommesso*. The edict of 1747, modelled on the Piedmontese law published in Victor Amadeus II's Constitutions of 1729, allowed only the nobility to bequeath land by *fidecommesso*. In addition, inheritance through *fidecommesso* would only apply for four generations. This was not a law which would attack the power of the nobles. On the contrary, it reconfirmed the role of the nobility, while introducing correctives within the law of inheritance which was beginning to become an obstacle to the needs for a freer circulation of property. This edict not only raised the question of the entailment of landed property, but also that of the many links between the nobility and the religious bodies which the previous state of affairs had favoured. 'In fact, the Church, through the guarantee which it offered in the execution of *fidecommessi*, always ended up with a not inconsiderable portion of the landed property, swallowing them up in mortmains. The *fidecommessi*, even if they remained in the hands of laymen, entailed property, preventing the circulation of wealth and increasing the privileges of several social groups.'[6] Remembering the measures adopted in 1751 to restrict the area of mortmains, it can be seen how the reformism of the Regency developed in an organic and coherent way, particularly with regard to its antiecclesiastical implications.

A logical development of the policy begun in 1747 can be seen in successive laws which attempted to circumscribe those noble privileges which most obstructed the State's power. In 1749 measures were taken to curb the abuses of feudal jurisdiction and to bring it to some extent under the supervision of the state judiciary. In 1750 a law was passed requiring the verification of titles of nobility awarded in previous centuries. All those claiming to possess a noble title were obliged to have it certified, submitting proofs of its bestowing and transmission through the generations. Nobility ceased to be a moral concept, recognised by the reputation and tenor of a man's life, and became instead a legal reality of which the State was the ultimate guarantor. For many Tuscan nobles, the law of 1750 was both an insult and a threat to their tax immunity. The law aimed also to purge the nobility of all those who by committing crimes, engaging in professions held to be inferior or usurping titles were judged unworthy of a place in this new legally recognised nobility. The chief motive force of the reform of 1750 was not so much a desire to humble the Tuscan nobility as to bind the urban aristocracy to the new State. Prompted by the same spirit it also laid down that citizenship of the two main cities of Tuscany, Florence and Siena entitled a man to become a member of the lesser civic magistratures.

In 1757, Richecourt was recalled to Vienna where the grand duke, Francis Stephen of Lorraine, had become emperor. He was replaced by Marquis Antonio Botta-Adorno, the Imperial marshal who had commanded the Habsburg forces in the dark days of the insurrection in Genoa. The slowing down of reformism in Tuscany was due to the political mediocrity of the new regent, but also, and more, to the international difficulties created in Vienna by the Seven Years War which caused new uncertainties in Florence.

174

The political and military upheavals which hit particularly central-northern Italy during the Wars of the Polish and Austrian Succession had an adverse effect on the society and economy of the Duchy of Modena but did not affect the dynastic continuity of the Estes, one of the ancient Italian families from the Renaissance. Indeed, Modena remained the only example in the eighteenth century of a seigneurial state which managed not only to survive the stormy events of the first half of the century both politically and territorially intact, but which enlarged its boundaries and became stronger both internally and in foreign relations. Thanks to an opportune marriage between Ercole d'Este, son of Duke Francesco, who ruled from 1737 to 1780, and Maria Teresa Cybo, heir to the Duchy of Massa, the Este family acquired the Garfagnana, the corridor of land which ran along the edge of Tuscany, allowing the Modenese economy access to the Tyrrhenian. Modena had gone through a period of crisis from 1733 to 1736 when the duchy had fallen into the hands of the French. Then the death of Duke Rinaldo in 1736 had found his successor, Francesco III, far from home in Hungary where he was fighting the Turks under the Imperial flag. Returning home and assuming power in 1737, the new duke left the Imperial alliance to join the Bourbons with the aim of assuring the dukedom for himself and his descendants. After 1742 the Austro-Sardinian occupation upset his plans and seriously threatened the survival of the Este dynasty. The situation stabilised in 1748 with the Treaty of Aix-la-Chapelle, which recognised the Estes' traditional territories within the alliance with the Austrians. In the *rapprochement* with the Habsburgs, Francesco III saw his possessions assured and in the following years political links were strengthened to the degree that in 1755 he was appointed by Maria Theresa as governor of Milan.

With its return to the influence of the Empire and Maria Theresa, the political direction of Modena returned to the Ghibelline and pro-Habsburg path, which had at the beginning of the century allowed the Estes to embark on a heated battle with Rome over the territories of Comacchio and the Ferrarese, in which Ludovico Antonio Muratori, at the time librarian to the duke, had joined, lending his political and cultural weight to the State's jurisdictionalism. Now, on the other hand, in the second half of the century it kept the duchy out of the anti-Jesuit moves which were finding fertile ground in the states connected with the Bourbons. Thus precisely during these years of the greatest development of the attack on the Society of Jesus, with measures for their expulsion being taken in Parma and Naples, Modena became a haven for the Jesuits. Here they found in the works of some prominent intellectuals, outstanding among whom was the historian Tiraboschi, a defence that, while not entirely conservative, was not averse to attacking the secular and religious moves towards an educational and ecclesiastical reform. In Modena, Father Zaccaria, one of the most active intellectuals in the Society of Jesus in the 1760s, found the political protection which enabled him until 1768 to speak up in defence of the Jesuits. The events of 1764 show clearly that the Jesuits in Modena enjoyed prestige and favours at a time when other Italian states were strongly contesting their cultural influence. In this year the Jesuits managed to have their most direct enemies and rivals particularly in the field of education, the Scolopians, expelled from the duchy.

Despite this, the policy of the Este Duchy towards the Church was characterised by all the elements of neo-jurisdictionalism found in the many-sided reform movement in Italy which developed particularly in the 1760s. In Modena the route to reform was distinguished more by its coherence and determination than by its originality. Tuscany and Lombardy, the two states most influenced by the Habsburgs, provided Modena's rulers with the technical and political models for anti-curial reform. As in neighbouring Parma, in Modena the first criticisms of the Church arose from the problems of the excessive number of clerics and the implications deriving from this, such as the fiscal immunity of the clergy, its poor commitment to pastoral duties and its obtrusive political and cultural presence in all aspects of social life.

If the Este Duchy, like other Italian states, managed to break the strong links between Church and State, restricting the clergy's ancient freedoms and privileges in the areas of law, taxation, education and cultural influence, and was able to proceed to the more difficult job of dismantling the Church's patrimony and controlling the internal structure of the Church, all this was made possible to some extent by the earlier reforms carried out by Francesco III from the beginning of his reign and continued after the end of the Austrian occupation in 1748. Thus it should be borne in mind that the duchy maintained the old division between the area around Modena and that, smaller and less important, around Reggio. This dualism remained intact throughout the eighteenth century. The intention was to establish, within a strongly decentralised administrative organisation that was controlled by institutions that were an expression and guarantee of the power of the nobility, new bodies that would encourage the centralisation of decision-making as well as the subordination of the outlying regions to ducal power.

The duke took his inspiration from the great monarchies of Europe and at the same time introduced an institutional principle to be found in republics – for Italy in Venice – that of the periodic rotation of the chief political posts. He set up the Council of State, a small body that was to deal with all major internal and international policy, with a purely consultative role. Administration was entrusted to three secretaries of state to whom all other state responsibilities were subordinate, and whose power extended even to areas under feudal jurisdiction. The uniqueness of the state organisation tried out in Modena – only paralleled by that of France and Great Britain – consisted in the geographical nature of the division of tasks between the three secretaries. Each secretary dealt with the administration of one of the three departments into which the State had been divided. This system applied also to foreign policy. Bearing in mind that every four months the secretaries were rotated from one department to another, it is easy to see why within the secretariats a certain collaboration in the running of public affairs came into being. In the administration of justice too a new post was created, that of *uditore generale criminale*, whose job it was to establish uniform procedures throughout the duchy and to check on the judges, both civil and feudal.

Having regained its territories in 1748 after the Austro-Sardinian invasion, during which the Modenese had suffered severely from the effects of the war, the special contributions exacted, famine and the epidemics which raged during those years, Francesco III tried to end the many autonomies, both fiscal and administrative, in his duchy. These freedoms had led to inefficiency and corruption, preventing the building of a state on firm political and fiscal foundations. Between 1753 and 1755 a series of decrees subjected local bodies to tight controls and at the same time new measures were taken on the economy. A far-reaching programme of expropriation of ecclesiastical property, undertaken to relieve poverty, meant that the State acquired large areas of land, which were then sold or let out on perpetual lease (*a livello*). This kind of contract fixed the rent for a long period and so, by permitting the free subletting of land and the permanent enjoyment of the farm itself and any improvements made to it, prefigured a kind of landownership. But the sale and letting out of land formerly belonging to the religious orders took place against a background of illegalities, unfairness, wastefulness and fraud. Thus the people who benefited from this immense operation were rich tenants, nobles seeking new land and townspeople involved in financial speculation. Only poor results were obtained by those politicians like Salvatore Venturini who tried to increase agricultural production by introducing from above new techniques and new tools or by the appointment of a magistracy to settle disputes between landowners and peasants. All the same, from these beginnings arose liberal ideas which later, in the 1780s, were to be translated into important political reforms.

One of the most important events of Francesco III's reforms was the promulgation in 1771 of the *Codice di Leggi e Costituzioni*, not, as might be thought, a compilation of radically new laws and procedures, but rather a reorganisation, a social and institutional reinforcement and in some places an alteration of long-standing regulations and juridical practices. Thus the Code of 1771 stands alongside the work of consolidation of the law characteristic of the first half of the eighteenth century, rather than with the codes published in some European countries after 1750 and influenced by the philosophy of the Enlightenment. But while the Code was traditional, retaining all its jurisprudential framework inherited from the history of Roman law, yet its authors introduced some new elements, most important of which was the setting up of a Supreme Council for Justice, or a 'special body, distinct from the ordinary magistratures, directly linked with the sovereign, understood as depositary of legislative power, with the task of resolving uncertainties of interpretation of the law'.[7] It would provide guidance, if not exactly with force of law, for the judges and lawyers who referred problems to it. The other new element was that the Supreme Council was also the high court of justice, that is the supreme court of appeal for sentences pronounced in all the tribunals of the State.

The late 1760s mark the end of one phase of reform in the State of Modena, as also in Lombardy, the Habsburg State with which Modena had the closest political relations. At this time the attitudes both towards the

Church, which until now had gone through all the stages indicated by the revived jurisdictional movement in Italy, and towards fiscal and economic policies, resulting in the first case in the setting up of the mixed Farm and in the second in the introduction of neo-mercantilistic provisions, are more or less in line with the reform movement in Maria Theresa's Lombardy.

NOTES AND REFERENCES

For the period of reforms, the general works (also for the following chapters) are the aforementioned Venturi, F. (1969–84) *Settecento riformatore*, vol. I. and vol. II. Einaudi, Turin; Valsecchi, F. (1959) *L'Italia nel Settecento*, Mondadori, Milan; Carpanetto, D. (1980) *L'Italia del Settecento*, Loescher, Turin. For the history of Lombardy in the reign of Maria Theresa see: Valsecchi, F. (1932–34) *L'assolutismo illuminato in Austria e Lombardia.* Zanichelli, Bologna; Romani, M. (1957–59) 'Gianluca Pallavicini e le riforme economiche nello stato di Milano', in *Annuario dell'Università cattolica del Sacro Cuore*; Capra, C. (1979) 'Riforme finanziarie e mutamenti istituzionali nello Stato di Milano: gli anni Sessanta del XVIII secolo', in *Rivista storica italiana* II–III.

For the Lorraine Regency in Tuscany it is necessary to look to the work done in the early twentieth century, particularly: Rodolico, N. (1963) 'Emanuele di Richecourt iniziatore delle riforme lorenesi in Toscana', in *Saggi di storia medievale e moderna.* Le Monnier, Florence; *idem* (1908) *La Reggenza lorenese in Toscana.* Vestri, Prato; *idem* (1972) (first edn 1910) *Stato e chiesa in Toscana durante la Reggenza lorenese.* Le Monnier, Florence. For the Duchy of Modena see: Poni, C. (1965) *Aspetti e problemi dell'agricoltura modenese dall'età delle riforme alla fine della Restaurazione.* Stem-Mucchi, Modena; Donati, B. (1926) *La formazione del codice estense del 1771 e altre riforme nel ducato.* Facoltà di Giurisprudenza, Modena.

1. Pompeo Neri's account can be found in the anthology in *Illuministi italiani* (1958). Ricciardi, Milan–Naples, vol. III.
2. Mozzarelli, C. (1982) *Sovrano, società e amministrazione locale nella Lombardia teresiana (1749–1758).* Il Mulino, Bologna.
3. Capra, C. (1981) 'Lo sviluppo delle riforme asburgiche nello Stato di Milano', in *La dinamica statale austriaca nel XVIII e XIX secolo*, ed. Schiera, P.. Il Mulino, Bologna.
4. Richecourt's memoirs are quoted in Rodolico, N. (1963) 'Emanuele di Richecourt iniziatore delle riforme lorenesi in Toscana', in *Saggi di storia medievale e moderna.* Le Monnier, Florence.
5. Timpanaro Morelli, M. A. (1969) 'Legge sulla stampa e attività editoriale a Firenze nel secondo Settecento', in *Rassegna degli archivi di stato 3.*
6. Venturi, F. (1969–84) *Settecento riformatore*, Einaudi, Turin, vol. I, p. 324.
7. Tarello, C. (1976) *Storia della cultura giuridica moderna* vol. I, *Assolutismo e codificazione del diritto.* Il Mulino, Bologna, p. 524.

CHAPTER TWELVE

Bourbon Italy: Naples and Parma

The two most important changes to take place in the political and territorial order of the Italian peninsula in the eighteenth century were Charles of Bourbon's victory over the Austrians in 1734 and the successive establishment in the Mezzogiorno of an autonomous kingdom, not formally tied to Spain, though still united by the dynastic link. With the birth of the Kingdom of the Two Sicilies, the conditions were there for a different balance of power based on the return of the Bourbons to Naples and on the recognition of their separation from Madrid. For the great powers of Europe the chief change lay in the reconquest of the land of southern Italy by the Spanish Bourbons, crowning the plans of Elizabeth Farnese who was now seeing the realisation of most of her dynastic ambitions.

Europe's consternation at the reappearance in Naples of the Bourbon State in Europe was soon clearly evident from the difficulties encountered by the new kingdom in gaining international recognition and regular diplomatic contacts. Acceptance came gradually. Of the European powers it was France that took the first step in May 1734, though confining itself to official recognition without establishing for the moment any kind of diplomatic representative in Naples. The Papal States, which sent a nuncio in 1735, refused the investiture of Charles of Bourbon for several years, the Curia intending to use this as a weapon in the negotiations with the southern kingdom over various important church matters. The other Italian states and Vienna opposed more serious difficulties. In the Imperial capital there was considerable anxiety over Charles's claim, made more than once, to Tuscany. This obstacle was only removed after 1737 with the arrival of the House of Lorraine in the Grand Duchy when the Medici died out. Modena, Lucca, Genoa, Venice and Vienna then speedily established diplomatic representatives in Naples. Last of all to send its ambassador to Naples in 1741 was Savoyard Piedmont. In these early years the international support guaranteed by Spain was essential to the new kingdom and it was thanks to this that the mistrust and hostility, which had arisen in Europe at the moment of Charles of Bourbon's victory over the Austrians, were not more damaging. In addition, the king could also make use of the diplomatic personnel of

Parma to represent his interests in the courts of Europe, since by the marriage between Elizabeth Farnese and Philip V Parma had become part of the Spanish monarchy.

The easily won military victories which had opened the way for the Spanish troops to conquer Naples already indicated to Charles of Bourbon that it would not be difficult to be accepted by his new subjects. In fact the defeat of the Austrian army was due not only to tactical errors, though there were errors, nor to the failure to appear of reinforcements, which were vital if Charles's troops were to be beaten, but was rather a result of profound institutional and social weaknesses in the Austrian viceroyalty. The nobility and feudal lords, with few exceptions, did not rally against the Spanish; the recruitment of soldiers gave poor results; a notable lack of communication between the different political and military hierarchies added confusion and uncertainty to an army committed to defeat. In a few months the Austrians were chased out of the South. They were regretted by only a few. The satisfaction of the majority became expectation and optimism among almost all the most influential groups at the new political horizons opening up for the Mezzogiorno.

The picture of a national monarch, independent of Madrid – even if it was often revealed as more of a formality than a political reality – which Charles brought to Naples acted as a catalyst to the most varied hopes which arose around the new king. There was a widespread feeling that for the South a historic possibility for civil and economic redemption was opening up, the author of which would be the new monarchy which would no longer have to place local resources at the disposal of Madrid. Around this hope developed a climate of faith and participation, expressing the conviction of many that they could heal old and recent wounds with the strength which they believed the king to possess. The expectation was at times exaggerated if one looks at the real possibilities for reform, and the events of those first months often reflected conflicting demands. But this mobilisation of political and intellectual energy was justified and fuelled by the moves towards reform that Charles had showed a desire to develop from the moment of his arrival in Naples. In precisely this period all over Italy civil and economic life was languishing in a phase of acute crisis, of intellectual lassitude, a conservative backlash and political stagnation. By contrast, from Naples came signs of reform, showing the politicians and intellectuals, not only of the South, the way forward to an awakening of men's most positive energies, called on again to devote themselves to matters of economy, finance, relations with the Church and changes in the institutions.

Charles was accompanied by a group of politicians and technicians both Spanish and Tuscan. The Spanish, who had long-standing experience in the handling of state affairs, maintained the link with Madrid from where events in Naples were closely watched. The most prominent of the Spaniards who came to Naples with Charles were the Count of Santisteban and the Marquis of Salas Montealegre. The Tuscans who were already established in Naples or who were transferred there at the time of the Bourbon conquest, were given very specific legal and economic responsibilities. Among them there immediately came to the fore a former professor of Pisa University, Bernardo Tanucci, a cultivated man, armed with great technical and political experience, who already displayed all those qualities which were to make him one of the most important political leaders of eighteenth-century Italy. As secretary of justice, a key position in politics since all matters relating to the relations between Church and State passed through his hands, Tanucci showed great shrewdness and ability, becoming one of the most prominent protagonists in the anticurial battle which reopened in the first years of the new regime. The local ruling class had no difficulty in adapting to the new political system, retaining all its old representative bodies and existing institutions, apart from the *Consiglio del Collaterale* which was replaced by the Council of State. This was a change of only minimal importance which did not represent any substantial reform in the distribution of power. In general in this period the balance between the different orders and classes was not upset by Charles's policies which were careful not to interfere in the spheres of influence of the legal profession, the urban nobility or the country barons, to mention just the three most clearly defined groups in the complex socio-economic structure of southern Italy.

In the first decade some reforms were introduced following plans for the readjustment of a state structure which had reached the peak of its crisis at the end of the Austrian viceroyalty. Everything indicated that in 1734 the king had the means and the ability to carry out a radical reform of the State, which would put the kingdom among the most modern states of Europe. The brains behind this movement came from that group of jurists and intellectuals who were followers of the great Pietro Giannone (now an exile) and Gaetano Argento, master of a whole generation of jurisdictionalists, and who were ready to collaborate with the Bourbon monarchy. Montealegre and Tanucci formed a political partnership of great technical effectiveness. In this atmosphere it seemed that the alliance would be revived between the jurisdictionalism of southern culture and the legal profession, the latter being the only instrument capable of removing the more archaic and corrupt aspects of power and of substituting a more modern relationship between society and the State.

In order to eradicate corruption from the royal tribunals, to simplify the law so as to give it a greater civil usefulness, to make the administration more efficient, to introduce equity into the system of taxation, to curb the arrogance of the barons, to get the economy moving and to limit the power of the Church, it was necessary to introduce the ideals of 'good government' into a situation where pettifogging, feudal arrogance and clerical bigotry held sway. This was no easy task, and it was one that was opposed not so much by individuals or isolated pressure groups as by southern society in general, as it had formed during previous centuries. Certainly the few selfless individuals, the campaigning of a few intellectuals and the will of some of the ministers were not enough to bring order to that unresolved partnership between feudalism and the modern State which characterised social relationships in the South. Naples, which attracted intellectual activity and political debate, was the place where the most acute contradictions of this seriously unbalanced society came together, where the tensions typical of the *ancien régime* at this period took a dramatic turn: the poverty and servile dependence of the people alongside the ostentatious display of wealth of the rich nobility, the ambitions and frustrations of the poor nobility, the vanity of the jurists and lawyers, powerful mediators in political and economic disputes and the constructive proposals, sometimes aristocratic and abstract, sometimes conscious of and participating in social dramas, of small groups of intellectuals – politicians and nobles – who looked to Charles's 'national' monarchy as the only force capable of curing the ills of southern society.

The arrival of the Bourbon king created a climate in Naples where these same difficulties became less acute and prompted a determination for political action which bore fruit immediately in a series of programmes and acts aimed at redefining the role of the State. In the areas of economic and political relations with the Church, the institutional and social position of the nobility, the administrative and fiscal systems and the economy there was a fever of planning and reform which gave its best results between 1734 and 1742, then went through a period of retreat and defeat and then picked up speed again around 1750 when new theories, influenced by the philosophy of the Enlightenment, were to make themselves heard in the political debate. This period of reform in the South ended around 1765 when the famine which struck disastrously at the population, and other factors both internal and international which we shall look at below, introduced other problems and indicated new means and aims for the political debate.

The most consistent and also the longest-lasting confrontation was that with the Church. To understand its significance and range, one should bear in mind the situation between Naples and Rome. The Bourbons at the beginning of the process of internal and international consolidation of their rule in the South, had immediately to come to terms with the pope's refusal to recognise the act of homage that the King of Naples made every year following ancient tradition. The change in dynasty prompted the revival of a revengeful attitude from the Curia, which was eager to annul the few gains made by the jurisdictionalist movement in the preceding decades. This policy of intransigence, characteristic of the papacy of Clement XII, was opposed by the Neapolitan tradition of anti-curialism, supported by most of the local politicians and noble citizens, and also by some influential members of the new Bourbon administration. Tanucci, Contegna, Ventura, Celestino Galiani and Fraggianni, the most authoritative interpreters of the policy towards Rome, followed in the tracks of southern jurisdictionalism, worked out in the first twenty years of the century, and having its clearest theoretical definition in the works of Costantino Grimaldi and Pietro Giannone. They did not confront the ecclesiastics head-on for fear of the consequences for the political stability of the new government, nor did they fan the flames of the ideological battle, preferring to compromise, agreeing even to the expulsion of Costantino Grimaldi and refusing to allow Giannone to return to Naples. This refusal was to be fatal for the exile when he was forced to leave Vienna, which was no longer safe for him, for he ended up being caught in the trap set by the Inquisition through the King of Savoy. And it was in the prisons of Piedmont that Giannone was to spend the rest of his life.

Even if southern jurisdictionalism had lost its original ideological content, nevertheless it could open the fight with the Church, secure in the knowledge that any theory of revival of the State could not fail to see ecclesiastical privilege as the immediate enemy. Those who wanted to limit the power of the Church were chiefly outraged by her large properties exempt from tax, the free areas where civil law could not operate and her existence as a body separate from and in continual conflict with the State. The most burning issue was that of church immunities, which had already been the subject of critical scrutiny by the intellectuals who now passed to the politicians the job of reforming such an important area of clerical power, the basis of its privilege and separateness from the State. The Church benefited from three immunities, local, personal and that pertaining to real property. It was their local immunity which had attracted the most violent criticism, in that it, more than the others, placed limits on the role of civil justice. Whoever set foot in an ecclesiastical building – and almost all of these allowed the right of sanctuary, from churches to farmhouses belonging to religious orders, from cemeteries to the charitable institutions – was automatically protected and could no longer be pursued by the state's justice. In this way it had become very easy for thieves, murderers and criminals to find a safe and welcoming refuge. It is thought that there were some 20,000 of these *confugiati* (refugees) in 1740. Many churches had been transformed into veritable thieves' dens, being used as strongholds and headquarters for their forays. If a judge dared to set foot in a sacred sanctuary he risked excommunication from the bishop which would inevitably damage his reputation and his career, but which did not have the same power of dissuasion as the arquebuses that the criminals, the bishop's guards and often the very monks did not hesitate to use against the executors of the civil law.

Ecclesiastical law, on the other hand, did not intervene only in matters regarding the employees of the Church, but also asserted its right to try the évil-doers who had taken refuge in the holy places. There was a whole series of crimes, such as murder for reasons of vendetta, private violence and fraudulent bankruptcy by merchants, for which the Church did not agree to the extradition of the accused. As Paolo Mattia Doria had seen so clearly, the clergy wished to dominate the country by means of control over the law. Personal immunity meant that all ecclesiastics were outside the jurisdiction of civil law, while the immunity of property allowed church property exemption from taxes. In the course of time these privileges had been greatly extended, ending up by involving all the clergy and many laymen who merely had to obtain a licence from the Church in order to avoid the usual level of taxation or to be exempted from ordinary justice. In this way an area of privilege had grown which acquired legitimacy from the Church. In order to enjoy the same benefits as the clergy, the laity had used expedients of every kind. The most common method was that of leaving the family inheritance to a son in the Church, but at the same time specifying privately the true distribution of the property. In the South the Church had also created its own armed force to protect people and property and to enforce its acquired rights.

It can be seen even from these few indications of the relations between Church and State in the South that any attempts at curing the ills of the State must inevitably deal with church immunities which had created a network of complicity which had a very negative effect on public order, the economy and the culture of the country, with the Church setting itself up as a body apart, in competition with the civil institutions. The debate was rekindled by the dynastic change of 1734 which, far from offering the Curia the opportunity of revenge for the partial jurisdictional successes gained during the Austrian viceroyalty, only stirred up the quarrel, raising the necessity for some kind of agreement. This was reached, after various vicissitudes, on 2 June 1741 with the signing of a concordat between Naples and Rome which controlled legal, economic and fiscal controversies. This solution was arrived at partly thanks to the mediation of, on the one hand, Celestino Galiani, the able *Cappellano maggiore* of the Kingdom of Naples who skilfully conducted dealings with the Curia, and, on the other, Benedict XIV, pope from 1740, who unlike his predecessor, sought a solution to the conflicts with the Catholic states, even at the cost of losing important positions of power. Thus this was an exceptionally favourable moment with both sides taking up a conciliatory attitude. However, while the agreement covered many matters and provided a mutually satisfactory compromise, it did not deal with the root causes of the problem. On the other hand it set in motion a decision of great historical importance, taken in 1746, with the abolition of the Tribunal of the Holy Office in Naples, the ancient bulwark of the Church and an often brutal and violent instrument for crushing the basic freedom of conscience.

More problematic was the attempt to bring order to the other area from which the State was excluded, the fief, where the barons ruled unopposed, imposing their own laws and private interests on the local communities. Compared with previous centuries, the whole bias of feudal privileges had in the eighteenth century become markedly more economic, giving a market value to feudal powers and favouring the barons in the commercialisation of agricultural produce. The tax immunities associated with the fief remained one of the basic mainstays of noble privilege along with its legal power. The consequence of this situation was an endemic state of insecurity which embraced the whole of the South. Serious crimes, robberies and theft took place, while the forces of law were helpless to intervene. It was from this necessity to check the tide of crime, which had reached a high point at the time of the Bourbon conquest – partly on account of the presence of so many mercenaries – that measures were taken to restrict feudal jurisdiction. This was done first by reviving old laws fallen into disuse and then, in 1738, by establishing new regulations which placed the judicial provisions of the feudal courts relating to particularly serious crimes under the control of the state judiciary. This was an important change, for depriving the barons of their power pointed the way to the State's total control over the judiciary. Between

1734 and 1735 the new government decreed a revision of fiefs, offices and feudal revenue for taxation purposes. More important politically was the census of offices which also began in 1734, paving the way for the reform of 1735 whereby the sale of offices was banned in the legal sector.

This reform and the law of 1738 on baronial jurisdiction already mentioned, were the most explicit actions taken by the new government in the field of justice. In this case too, from the need to remedy the many irregularities committed in the latter years of the Austrian viceroys, there sprang a succession of reforms which divined the more general problems such as the damaging consequences, whether there was conflict or not, of sharply defined spheres of public power – feudal and state – but which did not yet manage to focus on them. Consequently the changes introduced remained within the framework of the traditional relationships between the legal profession and the barons. The interlacing and reciprocal solidarity between these socio-professional groups greatly exceeded any reasons for conflict. Venturi has rightly commented: 'Not that the Neapolitan jurists did not know about the negative and even horrific sides of the baronial world. But the magistrates, lawyers and men of the law in general were much more organically linked with the feudal world than that of the Church. They often profited from it and always lived within it. They more justified than judged that world.'[1]

Similar desires for reform can be seen in Charles's fiscal policies. These gave only modest results since the plans became bogged down in the various categories involved. The whole complex subject was studied carefully by the new rulers who were prompted both by the State's financial needs and by the proposals put forward in these years by various intellectuals. The most accomplished of these came from Carlantonio Broggia who published in 1743 his *Trattato dei tributi, delle monete e del governo politico della sanità*. The Neapolitan government seemed to be aiming in its economic policy at a reformism with many new aspects, which proposed to provide a more modern basis for taxation, production and trade. The policy of reacquisition of *arrendamenti*,[2] begun under the Austrians, continued, though slowly and intermittently. It meant that an instrument of great power in the civil life of the country was taken out of the hands of the feudal landowners who made up the most powerful group of *arrendatori*.

In 1739 the Supreme Magistrature for Trade was set up.[3] This was not an entirely new creation. In the eighteenth century there had already been in Naples two trade Juntas which had come about for similar reasons, that is an attempt to increase the circulation of goods within the kingdom and to support exports by removing obstacles such as the complex bureaucratic procedures, administrative difficulties and a mass of regulations covering taxation and public health. These juridical and political bodies had the task of simplifying procedures and stimulating with advice and concrete aid the expansion of trade. In comparison with these earlier attempts, Charles's undertaking was far more ambitious. To create and direct the *Magistrato del Commercio* there gathered together the most outstanding leaders, whose attitude originated in mercantilism and aimed at increasing production, such as Contegna, the creator of the *Magistrato*, Ventura who was asked to preside over it and the minister Montealegre who accomplished wonders to establish it and to defend it from its innumerable opponents. These made themselves heard immediately. Long-established magistratures which had always dealt with commercial matters, thereby deriving considerable profit, the guilds feeling supplanted by the new tribunal, the towns and baronial courts finding themselves without a voice in the capital – all reacted against this reform and tried to hinder it in every way possible.

In 1740 an edict gave permission to Jews to live and trade freely in all parts of the kingdom without suffering the old discrimination. In the same year it was announced that the revision of the *catasto* would begin, getting under way in 1741, at the same moment when the quarrel with Rome was resolved.[4] The Concordat and the *catasto* were not two separate reforms, since the clauses of the agreement with Rome which allowed the State for the first time to assess and tax ecclesiastical property required an instrument for their execution. It was becoming urgent too to revise the census of 'hearths', that is the assessment of taxation by households, which had not been carried out since 1669. Other and more modern expectations came together in the plans for the new *catasto*: the need to simplify the complex fiscal procedures, to relieve the poorest communes of too heavy a tax burden, to distribute taxation more fairly and to examine the legitimacy of the many exemptions that the southern fiefs had acquired fraudulently in the course of time. The compilation of the *catasto* was, however, a total failure, which put an end to hopes for reforms that would remedy the most glaring inequities.

As for economic policy, the first decade of Charles's government was characterised by its mercantilism which was evident in some decisions of considerable importance. There was an attempt to revive some of the manufacturing industries of Naples, particularly of textiles, by granting fiscal and commercial concessions, while sea trade with other European powers was regulated. In 1740 a treaty of peace, navigation and trade was signed with the Ottoman Empire in the hope that Naples could once more participate in trade with this section of the world market. Aid was given to the shipyards and the system of maritime insurance was reorganised with the aim of producing Neapolitan shipowners able to compete with the foreigners – English, French and Dutch – who had financial control over the international trade passing through Naples. The year 1743 was a bad one for the economy, when Messina was struck by a plague epidemic which left in its wake great losses and crises in the island, which together with the first rumblings of the European war over the Austrian succession were indications of political as well as general difficulties which began to undermine the work of the reformers. In the 1740s all the decisions taken by Charles and his ministers since 1734 were annulled. The law of 1738 on feudal jurisdiction which had allowed people to hope that the barons were about to be deprived of their judicial power was scrapped. In 1746 the *Supremo Magistrato del Commercio*, which it had been hoped would introduce efficiency and competence into this area, was disbanded. In the same year the edict concerning the Jews was revoked.

Later on in the early 1750s other signs betrayed the dead-end to which Charles's reforming spirit had come. The redemption of the *arrendamenti* and the *catasto* had failed or had given poor results. Trade and industry did not appear to be about to drag themselves out of the depression where they had been stagnating for years, while agriculture was left to its usual neglect. So too had the attempt to organise the law-code come to nothing, merely giving rise to an erudite compilation which was far from being the code which had initially been intended and on which great hopes had been placed for a new and definitive codification of law. The group of reforming ministers had in the early 1740s found themselves beset by an alliance of groups of conservatives, ecclesiastics and pro-Austrians, all united in the common objective of opposing Charles's most radical reforms. They were greatly assisted in this by the War of the Austrian Succession. The military threat plus the active interest of Austria in the Neapolitan opponents of Charles created between them, one inside and the other outside the kingdom, an alliance that was dangerous for the continuity and stability of the Bourbon government.

The Treaty of Aix-la-Chapelle (1748), which ended the War of the Austrian Succession, brought Charles new worries. It contained a clause by which it was forbidden to pass on the Kingdom of the Two Sicilies to the descendants of the Bourbon king. The kingdom was instead to pass, on Charles's accession to the throne of Spain, to his brother Philip who was to cede Parma to Austria and Piacenza to Piedmont. Patient diplomacy, begun in 1748, between Naples and Paris and Naples and Turin and undertaken by Tanucci, Domenico Caracciolo and Ferdinando Galiani attempted to annul this article of the treaty. The reopening of normal diplomatic relations with Austria, in 1752, encouraged this strategy. Meanwhile the jurisdictional problems left unsolved by the Concordat had returned to trouble national political life. They were approached from the regalistic point of view which kept up its strong tradition in southern society and institutions. The enforcement of the most controversial articles of the 1741 Concordat was the chief area of conflict with the Church in this decade but new, more ambitious objectives were also beginning to take shape, such as control over church property, which were in the following decades to be central in the political struggle between Church and State. The jurisdictional movement received new impetus in mid-century with the spread of enlightenment ideas and with the economic theories of the pre-physiocrats. Antonio Genovesi was the main promoter of this real cultural and political change. As Raffaele Ajello has written: 'Southern jurisdictionalism found in the lessons of the Enlightenment, translated into a form acceptable to the Neapolitan situation by Genovesi, the stimulus to free itself more decisively from the academic, antiquarian or formalistically juridical mould and to identify itself more fully and consciously with its civil task'.[5] The results of this renewal, as we shall see, were to make an enormous intellectual contribution to southern society, but

187

they were not matched in politics by correspondingly important civil gains.

In September 1759, Charles left Naples to ascend the throne in Madrid, entrusting a Regency with the responsibility of government during his son Ferdinand's minority. In the same year, the man who undertook to govern Naples almost like an absolute sovereign, Bernardo Tanucci, signed an important agreement with Austria – the result of long diplomatic efforts – by which Charles would leave the kingdom to his heirs in exchange for renouncing any future reunification of the crowns of Spain and Naples, ceding half the Tuscan Praesidios to Maria Theresa, and all the Medici property in the South to the emperor and to the Grand Duke of Tuscany.

A power group now formed around Tanucci which found its greatest *raison d'être* in anti-curial policies. Between 1760 and 1762 Tanucci's 'party' experienced its period of greatest success. The papal investiture in 1760 was also a success for this group of Neapolitan reformers in that the pope agreed to recognise the Bourbon kingdom. From then onwards the jurisdictionalists tried to minimise the significance and importance of the act of homage, a hangover from the feudal age. In the same year the publication of Pietro Giannone's *Istoria civile del Regno di Napoli* was permitted, a work which had almost become the symbol of Italian anti-curialism. The high point was reached in 1762 when a law was promulgated to oblige ecclesiastics holding benefices to give a third of their income to the poor. To many this seemed an unheard-of compulsion and an excess of anti-ecclesiastical zeal, and so a year later this ruling was rejected by the Regency. But new problems were waiting in the wings. Famine, a constant peril in the cities of the *ancien régime*, returned to rage in the South in 1764–65, bringing poverty, death and economic disaster. But the famine was also a watershed in political life in Naples, for it changed the perspective on old problems and encouraged new proposals and plans for reform.

On the political map of Italy the Duchy of Parma and Piacenza, which together with the Duchy of Guastalla was assigned by the Treaty of Aix-la-Chapelle to Philip of Bourbon, son of Elizabeth Farnese, occupies a special position. Its development was a result of different and contrived elements of eighteenth-century 'reason of state'. The oldest tradition was represented by the Farnese dynasty, of which the new prince was in some degree the continuation. Renaissance and Counter-Reformation, the exuberant luxury of the court, with its sumptuous patronage, and the triumph of clerical hegemony were the inheritance left by the Farnese dynasty, and although eroded and impoverished by financial crisis and by the beginnings of criticism of the Church's domination, these elements still accurately characterise the duchy. When Italy and Europe looked to Parma it was still with the memory of Paul III, the Farnese pope, and of this outstanding family which was so prominent in the Italian Renaissance. A second factor which influenced developments in the new regime was related to the balance of power in Europe after the War of the Austrian Succession. Once again Italy was the area where compensation and divisions of spheres of influence were sought, and the new duchy emerged strengthened from this agreement in which matrimonial politics also had a hand. Spain and France had guaranteed the transfer of Parma and Piacenza to Philip, son of the Spanish Bourbon king and son-in-law of the French Bourbon king, since he had married Louis XV's eldest daughter, Louise Elizabeth. More than other Italian states, the Duchy of Parma, which was very small and lacking in resources, had to rely on international consensus in its decisions on internal policies, especially when these, as was to become clear very soon, conflicted with the interests of the Roman Curia.

The two major spheres of influence, Spain and France, assured the duchy's continued existence and political vitality, while the Empire, claiming its right of reversion underlined by its occupation of the territories of Bozzolo and Sabbioneta, put pressure on Parma through the Archduchess of Austria, Maria Amalia, future wife of the next duke, Ferdinand. The internal political events, the rise and fall of ministers, the very course of reforms in Parma were modelled on events in the internal and international life of the three great European powers. Between the Treaty of Aix-la-Chapelle and the early 1770s, the duchy was to become 'the shop window of Bourbon policies in Europe', in the sense that both the attempts at reform which France, and more particularly Spain, were trying out in these years had an effect on the policies in Parma and in that new theories were tried out, especially concerning relations between Church and State, that had their *raison d'être* in the courts of Madrid and Paris. When the agreement between the Bourbon courts accentuated the clash between them and the Church then Parma too was inevitably drawn into the neo-jurisdictionalist battle. Parma came to the attention of all Europe on account both of her geographical position, on the borders of the Papal States, and of her history which is the history of a more than usually pro-Guelph state where the clergy had an exceptionally important social role.

It was the testing ground for the policy of defence of state sovereignty which all the Catholic states of Europe were trying to follow in the 1760s and 1770s. The ruling group itself, which governed in Parma under Philip of Bourbon, revealed these European and cosmopolitan connections. The Frenchman Guillaume Du Tillot, son of one of Louis XIV's officials, was put in charge of policy-making. An able man, aware of the new political and economic ideas emerging at that time under the influence of the Enlightenment, Du Tillot became the leader of a group of reformers who each contributed different experiences and ideas, anti-Jesuit, pro-Jansenist and enlightened – the last represented by those French intellectuals who had come to the court in Parma and were friends and correspondents of the *philosophes*. Keralio, Deleyre, Millot and Condillac brought enlightenment ideas to the duchy and by their presence and cultural connections brought Parma to the attention of the capitals of Europe. Condillac, tutor to the young Duke Ferdinand, became in the eyes of Voltaire and other French *philosophes* the intellectual who would realise their great aspiration – that of creating a philosopher-king, educated according to their values of tolerance, progress and civilisation.

In the Duchy of Parma and Piacenza, as in Florence, Milan and Naples, the progress of reform was closely related to the financial needs of the State, whose income was swallowed up by a particularly sumptuous court, which consumed in luxury and ostentatious ceremonies the meagre monetary resources which were collected with great difficulty. In addition, there were the expenses of the maintenance of the army and then that of the administration. The duchy was heavily in debt and was thus tied even more firmly to the courts in Paris and Madrid which provided loans and donations. This was a satellite state which, unlike others, did not serve as a financial reservoir for the European metropolises but, on the contrary, lived in part on the financial aid granted by friendly states. The clergy enjoyed the greatest wealth and fiscal privileges. The figures for the presence of ecclesiastics in the duchy and their property are astonishing, showing a social and economic strength unequalled anywhere in Italy. Venturi summarises them as follows:

In 1759, from interest and dues in the city of Parma, ecclesiastics had an overall annual income of 429,796 lire and the laity 272,992 lire (while 46,369 lire was divided between the two). Almost three-fifths therefore. The city had 91 churches and oratories, 19 confraternities, 4 lay congregations, 21 convents and 18 monasteries as well as almshouses. In Piacenza at the same date, out of 30,590 inhabitants, 815 were ecclesiastics, 647 clerics, 488 regular priests, 200 lay brothers, 478 choir nuns and 202 lay sisters. About one-tenth of the population. In the territory of Piacenza, two-fifths of the land, in that of Borgo San Donnino more than half, around Parma two-thirds were in the hands of the ecclesiastics and while these figures are rather uncertain, nevertheless they are indicative.[6]

One after the other the new rulers' two great problems — of finance and of the Church — were faced up to with resoluteness, though it must be said that they did not produce any general programme of reform, but rather a series of short-term and empirical solutions to individual problems. These may have contributed to decisions of historic importance, such as the expulsion of the Jesuits in 1768, but they were not able in themselves to produce long-lasting policies such as a *catasto* might have done.

It was Du Tillot, as has been said, who drafted the most important programmes of reform. His reformism was most in evidence in jurisdictional policy, attracting the attention of the whole of Italy and Europe, not so much through any originality in the jurisdictional methods adopted as because it was this most Guelph of all Italian states, with the greatest number of ecclesiastics, that was eradicating the ancient landed power of the Church. In fact the first reforms in this area imitated laws already in force in other Italian states. This was the case with the important edict of mortmains of 1764 which adapted the Genoese law of 1762 to the conditions of Parma. Similarly, the edict on the equal distribution of public offices (1765) and the setting up of a civil tribunal which was to have the tasks and power of the ecclesiastical courts, as well as the job of supervising religious bodies, were not new weapons in the anti-curial battle. But Parma, like Naples, went further: in response to the fierce opposition of the Curia and some of the local clergy, Du Tillot intensified the restrictions on ecclesiastical power, putting vetoes and controls on the Inquisition and keeping the State's watchful eye wherever possible. Behind him stood France and Spain, ready to protect him from Rome's reprisals which were in any case becoming increasingly ineffective. On 3 February 1758, following Spain's example, the Jesuits were expelled. At the same time a plan of reform for education was put forward, drafted by the Theatine Paciaudi, an energetic Jansenist who had an equally intransigent dislike for the Fathers of the Society of Jesus as for the Parisian *philosophes*. The *Costituzione per i nuovi regi studi*, published in 1768, represented one of the first attempts to create a complete system of public schooling, from elementary to university levels.

It was to prove difficult to create a school system which differed from the Jesuit ones but which would be equally prestigious, given that in Parma the Society had had in the *Collegio dei Nobili* one of the institutions that had most influenced the education of the ruling classes of central-north Italy. In the university, Paciaudi managed a complete renewal in the area of legal studies, creating a centre which influenced reformist jurists of the whole of Italy. After the expulsion of the Jesuits, other provisions which aimed to consolidate civil power followed between 1768 and 1771. The papal bull *In Coena Domini*, symbolic of a Church which had judged and restricted the political power of princes, was suppressed. On 3 May 1769, the tribunal of the Inquisition was closed down and its duties as watch-dog of orthodoxy and religious censor were taken over by the bishops, assisted by the secular powers, since they did not have their own means of enforcement. In the area of charitable aid too, rapid steps were taken to remedy the acknowledged inability of the ecclesiastical institutions to supply material and spiritual aid to the poor, the sick, abandoned girls and poor parish priests. The reform of public charity, of February 1769, transferred these tasks to the State. Financial resources were to be obtained from the property belonging to those monasteries which were about to be closed as unnecessary and to those confraternities or lay associations dedicated to the veneration of the saints and the religious ceremonies connected with it. Thus another branch of Counter-Reformation *pietas* was lopped off. This consistent and forward-moving line of jurisdictional reform marked the whole policy of the duchy until the departure of Du Tillot in 1771, under the combined pressure of different events – the hostility of Duke Ferdinand and the bishops, and the loss of French support after the fall from power of the minister Choiseul in 1770. The Church was able to take its revenge by imposing on Parma a reactionary plan which in other Italian and European states, more robust and less dependent on Rome, it was unable for the present to introduce. Parma stepped out of the limelight. A period of political regression was beginning for the little duchy which had been an inspiration for the Italian and European Enlightenment. But not all Du Tillot's work was swept away by the reaction, for many of the reforms had taken firm root.

NOTES AND REFERENCES

For the history of Naples under Charles of Bourbon see: Ajello, R. (1972) 'La vita politica napoletana sotto Carlo di Borbone', in *Storia di Napoli*. Società editrice per la storia di Napoli, Naples, vol. VII, pp. 459–718. For juridical and institutional matters see: Ajello, R. (1964) *Il preilluminismo giuridico. Il problema della riforma giudiziaria e legislativa del Regno di Napoli durante la prima metà del secolo XVIII*. Jovene, Naples. For a general history of the Duchy of Parma see: Tocci, G. (1979) 'Il ducato di Parma e Piacenza', in Marini, L., Tocci G., Mozzarelli, C. and Stella, A., *I ducati padani, Trento e Trieste*. UTET, Turin. On Du Tillot see the old but still useful: Benassi, U. (1915) *Guglielmo Du Tillot. Un ministro riformatore del secolo XVIII*. Deputazione di storia patria, Parma. A recent work on Condillac deals with the political situation in Parma: Guerci, L. (1978) *Condillac storico*. Ricciardi, Milan–Naples, Ch. II.

1. Venturi, F. (1969–84) *Settecento riformatore*. Einaudi, Turin, vol. I, p. 38.
2. *Arrendamenti* may be translated as a number of different state rights, such as customs, gabelles, dues paid on goods in store, monopoly of production and exchange as well as various public offices. See De Rosa, L. (1958) *Studi sugli arrendamenti nel Regno di Nopoli*. L'Arte Tipografica, Naples.
3. For the commercial problems of the Kingdom of Naples see: Romano, R. (1951) *Le commerce de Naples avec la France et les pays de L'Adriatique au XVIIIe siècle*. SEVPEN, Paris.
4. Villani, P. (1973) *Mezzogiorno tra riforme e rivoluzione*. Laterza, Bari.
5. Ajello, R. (1972) 'La vita politica napoletana sotto Carlo di Borbone', in *Storia di Napoli*. Società editrice per la storia di Napoli, Naples, p 537.
6. Venturi, F. *op. cit.*, vol. II, p. 214.

Reforms without Enlightenment: the Papal States, the republics and Charles Emanuel III's Piedmont

The death of Benedict XIII (1730) marked the end of a reign which had been one of the last expressions, though decadent and corrupt, of the Renaissance Church. The two succeeding popes, Clement XII (1730–40) and Benedict XIV (1740–58), brought about through their ideas and actions a change of considerable importance in the history of the Church. The nepotistic, aristocratic and military traditions of the Papal States and Catholicism in Rome were over. With the end of the last vestiges of military power and the increasing shakiness of political power, the true state of affairs was revealed in the harsh light of day; a country full of contradictions and anomalies, artificial and anachronistic and quite lacking in the kind of structure which other European states had had for a long time. The pope's domains had their own kind of political structure, and one that was unique in all Italy. The State was certainly a theocratic monarchy, but unlike all other European monarchies it did not depend on the principle of dynastic continuity which guaranteed social cohesion and considerable unity and continuity in political approach. Here, on the other hand, the changes in pope could mean a change each time in basic policies, a shuffling of ruling groups and an alteration in international alliances. Precisely for this reason the great European powers brought their influence to bear during the conclaves in order that their candidate should be elected to the papal throne. At the same time, the confusion of spiritual and temporal power began to be considered by many Catholics as an obstacle to a more persuasive development both of civil government and of the Church's spiritual mission. Economic growth and a freer intellectual climate encouraged social progress, but brought to the surface latent problems which derived from the fact that different social groups coexisted within a single state yet were not integrated with one another.

The resistance of the different provinces to Roman interference had never been entirely suppressed and from the 1730s it burst out again. On to the old civil traditions were now grafted municipalistic tendencies while economic and cultural links were forged which were increasingly independent of the capital. One such case is that of Bologna and its surrounding territory where the proposals for republican secession which were raised explicitly at the beginning of the century by influential members of the local aristocracy, could only be appeased by the granting of more political and financial autonomy, first by Clement XII and then by Benedict XIV. In the Duchy of Urbino, in the province of Fano and in Romagna power was very fragmented. Autonomies of seigneurial origin and vast feudal territories, which had mostly belonged to the Florentine Medici family and had then in 1737 passed to the House of Lorraine, formed whole areas which were almost extraterritorial and which broke up the unity of the State, undermining the pope's laws and rights and encouraging smuggling and aristocratic banditry which was by now endemic. The pressures caused by these provinces on Rome were the opposite to those from Bologna. The ruling classes in Romagna and the Marches required more direct state intervention in their economy, justice and finance because these provinces, consisting of small towns and many fiefs, could only get from Rome the institutional and military help which they needed for civil government.

Internationally, the Papal States watched helplessly as their influence declined in the courts and countries of Europe. In Paris the Jansenists and the Gallican movement from the time of the Sun King were two thorns in the flesh of the Roman Curia. Even in ultra-Catholic Spain it seemed impossible to halt the decline in Rome's political influence. In Italy, in addition to the difficulties caused by the Jansenists, Gallicans and reformists, a new element came to trouble Roman politics, in the form of the new territorial and dynastic situation. The Habsburg Empire now saw the area of its direct and indirect rule considerably increased to the detriment of the Bourbons. It was with the latter that the recent popes had forged close links. Coming to terms in Italy with the Habsburgs meant for the Curia having to face up to new jurisdictionalist pressure coming from Austrian policies and from Ghibelline tradition. Needless to say, in the non-Catholic states of Europe Rome had no influence at all.

In the face of these and other attacks on the most authoritarian powers of a Church that was heir to the Counter-Reformation, the traditional answers failed. The popes during this period had to admit, even if unwillingly, that the old methods of control were becoming useless. Prayers and excommunication were not enough to stop the States from introducing ecclesiastical reform or to dissuade rulers from taking over church benefices, controlling the powers and nomination of bishops, removing education, health and charity from the charge of the clergy, or taxing the great ecclesiastical properties. The pope was powerless to stop the Austrian, Spanish and Piedmontese armies from several times intruding into papal territory, slaughtering and laying waste and forcing the people to contribute labour and money. The military operations which took place in the papal territories at the time of the Wars of Polish and Austrian Succession had disastrous consequences for finance and the local economy, just as the fiscal demands imposed by the invaders further impoverished the population.

The crisis-ridden background against which the events of the middle decades of the eighteenth century were played out had many facets. The Papal

States were generally lacking in resources, divided internally into historically different units with their own autonomies, troubled in the north and central areas by the presence of the Habsburgs and supporting at the heart the capital, Rome, which swallowed up the wealth of the country, having to maintain the great noble families, the cardinals, the numerous church dignitaries and the Curia. It was only possible to do this thanks to the financial power it could still exercise over the Catholic world.

Clement XII and Benedict XIV, though different, both defended the most open expressions of Catholic culture. Clement XII belonged to the rich and powerful Florentine family of the Corsini, which still appeared to be capable of influencing the political and economic life of Italy and placing one of their own on the throne of Peter. As Venturi writes: 'As in Parma and Florence, so too in the Vatican a last wave of the Renaissance lapped at the edges of our modern age and then spent itself in resigned weakness and incurable impotence'.[1] Great hopes were pinned on Clement XII, as if for the Church the Golden Age were come again, and a positive civil energy developed which yielded important practical results. Provisions were introduced which aimed at solving long-standing economic problems, paying particular attention to transport, defence and trade. Bolognese land reclamation and the construction of canals for navigation in the River Po – two problems which crop up throughout the modern history of the Po Valley – received a notable boost from the funds allotted to them by Clement XII. Similarly, the commercial trade treaty made with the Empire and the establishment of the free port of Ancona (1732) were the result of a more active intervention by the State in the economy, even if the immediate results were far from those hoped for, since they ended up by increasing the subordination of the Papal States to the more enterprising foreign economic centres. The first plans were drawn up for making the Tiber navigable following the model provided by the economist Lione Pascoli, and major works on roads, ports and canals were begun, even in a period characterised by wars and financial crisis.

Clement XII allowed local social classes greater independence by not vetoing the proposals for further political development which came from the provinces. In this way, in situations such as that of Bologna where the concepts of liberty and self-government were most deeply rooted and where cultural and economic life revealed European influences, the provinces were able to benefit from a papacy which introduced moral rigour, reforms and cultural progress in the Roman Church. The War of the Polish Succession interrupted this climate which could have led to a more far-reaching reform of the State. Tensions mounted with the presence of foreign armies which oppressed the population with extortionate taxes, looting and enforced recruitment into the army. In March 1736, serious rioting broke out as a result of forced recruitment by the Spanish army. In the same year the precarious relationships established with some of the courts of Europe were upset by new causes of friction, so that Rome had to close three of her main nunciatures, in Naples, Madrid and Lisbon. As has already been seen in the discussion of the Kingdom of Naples and the Grand Duchy of Tuscany, the changes in dynasty of these years created new problems for the Papacy which did not yet have an appropriate political reaction to events but which was suspicious and hostile. Naples and Tuscany put forward energetic jurisdictional claims, which Rome was in no state to resist and yet which she did not intend to compromise over.

In the same period the economic situation was becoming desperate: a fall in population, shortage of money, scarce even during peacetime and now used up by war and by the drying up of contributions from ecclesiastical benefices in Spain, Portugal, Naples and Tuscany, difficulties in agricultural production which caused severe problems of food supply to the capital and other provinces, such as the Marches where in 1735 there was a famine. These were the clearest signs of a crisis which was not only economic and for which Clement XII had no solutions. Cardinal Prospero Lambertini, elected after a troubled conclave lasting for over six months, and who took the name of Benedict XIV, inherited these problems.

The view of Catholicism which Benedict brought to the leadership of the Church was very close to that of Muratori. Like Muratori, he was humanitarian and cautiously tolerant, prepared to listen to both the reasoning of the states that were beginning to put forward precise demands for the limiting of the power of the clergy in matters of taxation and justice, and to the demands for civil and cultural development which came from society. He was the interpreter of a middle road of Catholicism, neither Jansenist nor Jesuit, intellectually cultivated and morally sympathetic towards humanity. During his pontificate, important concordats were signed with Naples, Spain and Piedmont which, despite the opposition in the Curia, in each case favoured the State in question. Thus the obstructive hostility of the Roman hierarchies towards the demands for reform indicated by the jurisdictionalist movement was gradually overcome. Benedict broke the Church's official silence on some important matters, such as usury and religious festivals which gave rise to a lively debate among Italian Catholics where problems in the economy began to be defined. He supported the new scientific learning, introduced into Roman circles by Celestino Galiani and Giovanni Bottari. During his pontificate there were indecisions and severities of which the most explicit was the condemnation of Montesquieu's masterpiece *De L'Esprit des Lois*, but on balance, Benedict's policies opened new channels of communication between Catholicism and secular philosophy while in the area of relations with the political powers in the Catholic states it was the beginning of a rapport between Church and enlightened absolutism, often based on weak and ambiguous foundations but nevertheless capable of encouraging the grafting of civil values into Catholic institutions.

In the administration of the Papal States too, Benedict's papacy introduced many reforms which, if they lacked the resonance which accompanied such reforms in other Italian countries, nevertheless were an indication of a clear political and economic direction. Particular attention was paid to the capital, provisions for urban and administrative reorganisation were brought in and an energetic cultural policy was developed. As for state administration, measures were taken for the unification and simplification of the office of the treasury, taxation and accounts. The proposals of some economists, most important of whom was Girolamo Belloni, who fought to have the State face up to the problems of agrarian production, the grain trade, finance and money supply, found a hearing with the Lambertini pope which had been lacking in previous papacies. Under Benedict XIV, in years of good harvest, a free trade in grain was tried out. In matters of defence too and in the recovery for production of vast regions of the State – the Agro Romano, Agro Pontino and the Reno and Po valleys, marshy areas which suffered from periodic flooding – there was an indication of a readiness to depart from the old path, which had failed to bring about any real improvement, and to enter upon practical action financed by a combination of private capital and public funding. Planned during the papacy of Benedict XIV, these works were put into action by Pius VI.

When Benedict died, Ferdinando Galiani and Giovanni Lami wrote of him in the funeral oration that he was the pope who had wanted peace in Italy, had protected men of letters, poets and scientists, had come to an agreement with the states over law and taxation, had dared to consider and have discussed both the reduction of religious festivities and usury. His death marked the end of those glimmerings of interest in the Roman Church for enlightened thought which in just these years was reaching its highest expression. His successors re-established, or rather, tried to re-establish, a more restrictive and backward-looking political attitude, though even so there was no shortage of ideas and provisions of considerable importance within the administration of the Papal States.

Republican forms of government, heritage of a past rich in history rather than a vital impulse for the present, still survived in the states of Venice, Genoa and in smaller, politically insignificant states like Lucca and San Marino. These eighteenth-century Italian republics had one thing in common – the speed at which they were being eclipsed on the political scene. This can be explained by several factors. Firstly, the rigidity imposed by the republican aristocracies on their institutions through the centuries, in the face of a Europe where an important reorganisation of power aimed at the formation of bureaucratic and national states was going on, was eventually to weaken the republics, precisely because it was always there as a reference point, unprogressive and conservative, on which to rely in times of difficulty. In the eighteenth century, pressure from neighbouring states – Piedmont, Austria and Tuscany – apparent chiefly in the economic sphere, but not concealing in certain cases territorial aspirations, weakened the international image and even the internal unity of the republics, even if it never reached the point where their political survival was threatened. It was not so much these external pressures as the internal crisis which indicated the decline of the republics. It was caused by the social weakness of the institutions, the political divisions among the ruling classes and their remoteness from the rest of society. During the eighteenth century the authority of the ruling class of patricians in the Italian republics faced an insuperable crisis. They no longer had the vitality necessary to renew their link with the rest of society and to justify their continuing primacy.

The history of the republics in the eighteenth century is marked by a slow political decline, even if there was no lack of intense and energetic attempts to slow or halt this process – attempts which came to nothing on account of the prevailing stagnation which showed itself in neutrality and isolation vis-à-vis other European powers. This situation was the political price which the republics were forced to pay in order to continue to exist. In any confrontation with neighbouring states, the republics were the losers. In Italian and European markets they found themselves excluded by new competitors with great financial resources, political support and civil industriousness at their disposal. These assets, though not entirely absent in the Italian republics, were nevertheless of an insufficiently high level. Often the stimulus for entrepreneurial activity was provided by the international economic situation which mobilised the resources of a once productive society, rather than the consequence of conscious political and economic decisions. Similarly, a comparison of the reforms carried out by the enlightened sovereigns with those of the republican oligarchies, reveals clearly that while the former bear the mark of an incipiently modern view of the State and its functions, the latter reforms are rather the feeble attempt to patch up an institutional structure that was falling apart. Reformism in the republics was modest and old-fashioned. It operated in traditional areas and trod only known ground. It did not attack problems at their roots, nor did it propose any radical change of the laws. As Marino Berengo has written of Venice, though it can be said of all the Italian republics: 'In the Veneto, they talked of reforms but did not carry them out. The confused longing for a new state, widespread among the educated classes, was not to come to fruition in political consciousness: rather it dissipated itself in an endemic discontent and was expressed as disillusionment with the past and a distrust of direct involvement in a difficult future'.[2]

Among the republics Venice best retained her position of importance, which was also recognised outside Italy. She continued to have considerable economic weight which, while in decline compared with the heights reached in the fifteenth and sixteenth centuries, guaranteed her a position of strength in the sea trade of the Adriatic, the silk industry and the two-way trade between the Orient and continental Europe. She was still looked to with admiration and interest, for the wisdom of her government and the stability of her institutions which had survived the difficulties of her long history without important changes to their underlying constitutional principles. So too endured, albeit rather tarnished, the image of a state which had adopted, more than any other Italian state, those values of religious tolerance, coherent jurisdictionalism and republican liberty which Venice had taken on in the sixteenth and seventeenth centuries when she had represented the only opposition to the triumph of the Counter-Reformation in Italy.

The history of Venice in the eighteenth century emerges as a constant swinging between myth and reality, the myth being not only a nostalgia for the past but something which unleashed an important wave of idealism. Part of this myth was the image of economic splendour and political strength, of an outpost of European civilisation in the Islamic world and bulwark of the freedom of religion and thought which Venice spread about herself throughout Europe in previous centuries and to which her ruling class still appealed in order to preserve without change this extraordinary heritage. But political reality was undercutting this heritage. Venice was an internationally weak state, forced into a neutrality which appeared inevitable since the republic was unable to compete equally with the absolute states but with which she had to coexist by finding herself a position on the sidelines, outside any dispute. The Habsburg Empire was the most immediate and threatening presence that Venice had to come to terms with, since she could no longer compete politically and economically in the Adriatic and central Europe where once her patrician merchants had been dominant. There was too a marked weakness in her internal government that the more observant – including the great Scipione Maffei – had already warned against in the 1730s, attributing the causes to the unfair relationship established between Venice and the towns of the mainland, whose exclusion from the process of government was to become the source of recurrent friction. This became more acute as the provinces of the Veneto increased their levels of agricultural production and became linked economically with the important centres of the Po Valley, Milan and, to a lesser extent, Bologna and Modena.

Another element contributed to the political decline of the Republic of St Mark, the crisis of the patriciate. As its numbers continued to fall, it attempted to defend its hegemony and ended up by dragging down with it the republican institutions. The State was structured in such a way as to prevent the flexible assimilation of new social groups and to discourage the carrying out of plans for institutional reform. Thus, while other Italian states as a result of various pressures were forming a bureaucratic network which provided a temporary solution at least to the problems raised by the gradual falling apart of the old order, Venice, and the other republics too, was unable to create for itself a state structure capable of dealing with its needs. Quite the reverse, she proudly and unbendingly defended a system whose splendid façade of republicanism concealed administrative inefficiency, an inability to make decisions and political confusion. Gradually deprived of any *raison d'être* except mere survival and unable to plan the future, the ruling patrician class turned more and more inwards to its past history and the certainty, as tenacious as it was unfounded, of the invincibility of the republic. Venice did not, however, lack men ready to take note of this decline. Andrea Tron, Marco Foscarini, Angelo Querini, Carlo Lodoli and Andrea Memmo, to mention the most outstanding intellectuals and politicians of the Venetian eighteenth century, did not hesitate at times to stir up the still waters of the political debate, now appealing to the jurisdictionalist tradition and now proposing constitutional alterations, economic reforms and political changes. But their efforts, when not defeated, did not step over the bounds defined by the system of power which Venice had built up during the preceding centuries and from which, now that it could no longer guarantee the future of the republic, it was unable to free itself.

A confirmation of this incapacity to reach any general plans for reorganisation of the State, can be seen from the economic policy adopted by the republic in the early 1740s. The most striking thing about it is that when examined as a whole and compared with other states of central-northern Italy, where the same situation in production and trade prevailed, compared with the intense cultural response to the most advanced European thinking, Venice's policies were notable for their extreme caution but also for a rhapsodic reformism which attracted all sectors of society where the urgent need for change was evident, but went no further than provisions which were often incoherent and extremely timid. Such was the case of the new *catasto* of 1740 which was to update the previous measurement of land halted in 1667. It was carried out with greater objectivity and more up-to-date methods, but was very much less accurate than Maria Theresa's *catasto* of the same period. It should be said that, while in Lombardy the *catasto* was being carried out in a time of great progress where the recovery of production went hand in hand with important technical changes, in the Veneto plain the relations of production remained static, fixed by ancient traditions, and thus agricultural productivity too was impeded. The new *catasto* at least regularised the tax paid to the State and put an end to some of the nobility's tax privileges.

The measures adopted in 1735 also aimed at these objectives, foreshadowing the unification of the various contracts for levying the indirect taxes, a consequent reduction in the cost of running the fiscal machine, and thus an increase in the income of the republic. This was one of the first projects for the simplification and unification of the tax collection system carried out in the eighteenth century, but it did not develop, during the following decades, towards a direct management of taxation by the State which as we have seen happened in other Italian states in the 1760s and 1770s. Even the customs policy adopted by Venice, with important provisions such as that of 1754 which granted the free export of grain, was marked by uncertainties and indecision. Thus the edict of 1754 which seemed to be ushering in a system of free trade much earlier than other similar Italian provisions, turned out to be a prelude which did not lead anywhere, since it was not backed by a coherent economic policy, both because the new law did not abolish the other protectionist institutions, such as the public *annone*, and because it was several times suspended because of the competition from foreign grain.

New policies had also been tried for the manufacturing industries in the first half of the eighteenth century, giving results of considerable importance, first and foremost being the building up of the silk-weaving factory at Schio which provided employment for more than 2,500 workers. But these were isolated episodes and they provided only a weak impetus to the republic's trade. Even the most far-sighted intellectuals who considered the problem of how to halt the decline in production, such as Antonio Zanon, Francesco Griselini and Gianmaria Ortes, were unable to provide convincing methods for remedying the weaknesses of the economic system and changing economic policy. They preferred to fight to change men's way of thinking rather than change the legal rules or the financial methods, and this plan did yield results: in the provinces numerous agrarian academies were opened, which were supported and controlled by the Venetian Senate. Here the subject of the instruction of agricultural workers and modern agronomic education for the landowning classes was widely debated and some steps in these directions were taken by the state administration. But the political impasse remained, and so too the uncertainty of the aristocracy caught between the alternatives of the sea and the mainland, between the call of trade, now increasingly compromised by the contraction in the markets controlled by Venice, and the call of the land, where to reap profit it would be necessary to go beyond the almost colonial form of expansion by the Venetian patricians in the inland provinces.

Still strong in the eighteenth century though not so vigorous as earlier, the guild system rigidly controlled all sectors of artisan and manufacturing production and gave the patricians of the capital a leading role in society. Now it began to be questioned, on account of its cost, its paralysing effects and its cumbersome bureaucracy. From 1719 the Senate had affirmed the principle of free commercial and manufacturing activity and had undertaken to make the guilds more open and adaptable, but no steps were taken in the next half century to further this aim. The first provisions for a partial liberalisation of the labour market were made in 1752 and others followed in the next thirty years.[3] No laws of a general nature were introduced, rather the individual guilds were examined case by case and measures specific to the problems of each sector were proposed. Thus it was a cautious policy of libertarianism, careful to protect national production from foreign competition, but which if compared with the reforms in this area introduced by other Italian states, was more positive than negative.

Venice played her part in the jurisdictionalist battles of the second half of the century. The revival of jurisdictionalism had its historical justification in the rereading, from an enlightened point of view, of Paolo Sarpi by Francesco Griselini in a book published in 1760 which was the starting-point for an intense battle, lining up the defenders of the Jesuits against the ranks of the anti-Jesuits.[4] Along with books, the periodicals were the weapons in this struggle which having started from a traditional ethical and legal jurisdictionalism was gaining strength through its contact with the French Enlightenment, Spanish regalism and German Febronianism. There were few other cities in Italy where the debate reached such radical and liberal heights as it did in Venice. The disastrous consequences for the republic of the excessive number of monks and nuns, their wealth and their behaviour were particularly fiercely attacked. Someone even went so far as to propose the abolition of celibacy for priests. But this was an isolated voice and the majority fought to reduce the religious orders, to close the religious houses that were not needed for pastoral duties, to prevent the forced taking of religious vows for family convenience, to bring the monks back to a life of poverty and to reduce their influence by control of their schools and their means of propaganda. As always, the government placed one restriction on the free circulation of ideas – that the internal and international policies of Venice were never questioned.

These voices in society and the political work of Andrea Tron, the most convinced and aggressive jurisdictionalist in the Senate, led to the creation of a new magistrature, *ad pias causas* (1766), which was to look after the republic's interests vis-à-vis the Church. It was in some ways an exceptional body, different from the other branches of political power, if only because it was not subject to the periodic rotation of duties. It provided the theoretical guidelines for the jurisdictionalistic policies followed between 1767 and 1774 which led to a cut in the number of convents, mortmains and people taking vows, the forbidding of the publication of the bull *In Coena Domini*, and introduced moves to reform the schools and Padua University. This did not represent a decisive clash between jurisdictionalists and curialists, but rather a series of skirmishes, an expression of individual actions rather than a single movement. The dominant conservatism of the patricians and their close links with the Church impeded and destroyed this chance for reform too, which the patricians might have been inclined to support given their republican traditions.

The problems facing the Republic of Genoa during the eighteenth century were even more serious than those of the Venetian aristocracy, and they were apparent above all in international relations. The neutrality which the republic had been forced to adopt, except for a brief interruption during her marginal involvement in the War of the Austrian Succession in the alliance against Piedmont and Austria, was the result of an international isolation which implied at the same time dependence on the protection of the European powers, particularly France. During the uprising in Corsica the Genoese experienced the true meaning of this subjection: the future of their colony was to be principally decided by the great European states. The economy of the region too felt these restrictions as was clear in 1757 when Spain, in retaliation for Genoa's attitude during the Seven Years War, suspended commercial relations with the republic, bringing several manufacturing industries to their knees when they were suddenly deprived of a commercial outlet which took the greater part of what they produced. But in the final analysis the difficulties in her international relations also derived from the crisis of the republican State. Unlike Venice which to some extent had organised an institutional framework, albeit unfair and with a one-way relationship between provinces and capital, Genoa's rule had remained unchanged in the old form of city-state, which though it allowed a broad financial autonomy to the communes of Liguria, nevertheless on the economic front subordinated them to the capital, the monopolistic centre of all the State's activities.

The capital, where the greater part of the wealth and economic activities of the country were concentrated and which was run by its own communal magistratures, was faced with a heterogeneous domain, a collection of communities and lands with autonomous administration, annexed at various periods and each linked to the central authority by different ties and conventions. Genoa had not managed to establish herself as a natural centre for the co-ordination and balancing of the region, nor as a viable trading centre, partly because of her geographical position and the extreme difficulty of communications by land.[5]

In the capital too political relations between the population and the ruling class took a definite turn for the worse. In the eyes of many, the patriciate as a power group was too remote from the country's problems and incapable of performing the duties which they had assumed. These tensions became acute in the first half of the eighteenth century. In 1729 the Corsicans rose up against Genoa. In the same period in the Ligurian provinces a state of endemic discontent with the capital erupted into several attempts at rebellion, in the course of which the idea of political separation from Genoa was put forward. Lastly, in 1746, there was the episode of the rebellion of the Genoese people against the Austrian army of occupation, when the political impotence of the patricians was revealed to all.

In December 1746 the spark that set off the Genoese insurrection was not only hostility to the invaders but also fury at the concessions and betrayals of the aristocracy which had been incapable of putting up any resistance to the occupiers' claims. During those days of fighting between the people and the Austrian soldiers in the streets of Genoa, until the latter were driven out, the patricians remained absent, either taking refuge behind the barred windows of their *palazzi* or fleeing with all haste to the country. But there were others who took part in these events – the poor nobility and the more alert sections of the political and cultural circles in Genoa who warned that behind these events lay the possibly irreversible weakening of a centuries-old leadership. When the Austrians were driven out, there was a return to normality. The patricians, in the absence of any viable alternatives to their rule, found it easy to resume their control of the situation and bring social life back to its usual paths. The voices that had been raised pointing out the need for a reform of the State, so clearly revealed by the events of December 1746, were silenced or ignored. The most influential of these had been those of Pier Paolo Celesia and Gualberto De Soria who were working on plans for a reform of the constitution which aimed at the establishment of a united regional state, where the capital and provinces would participate equally in government. This was the clearest condemnation of the collapse of the city-state and also an affirmation of the need to create a new centralised, uniform body based on a bureaucratic structure.

Although these plans came to nothing, something was moving beneath the surface of patrician conservatism. In 1751 the law establishing Genoa as a free port answered at least in part the hopes of the more modern elements of the Genoese patriciate. It released the trading system from the more absurd protectionist restrictions and introduced partial liberalising measures. Thus competition with Leghorn could be contemplated with more flexible weapons. In the early 1760s some political reform seemed possible. During the Doge-ship of Agostino Lomellini (1760–62), a subtle politician and intellectual linked with the French Enlightenment, there was an attempt to pacify the Corsican people. In this period the Corsican rebellion had come to the attention of all Italy, taking on the almost symbolic meaning of a struggle between the *ancien régime* and constitutional freedoms. Lomellini proposed to the Senate that the Corsicans be granted autonomy, but his ideas came to nothing, partly because by now people were becoming convinced that the republic should rid itself of this rebellious island.

Only in the area of jurisdictionalism did the Genoese ruling class find unity and courage. In 1762, the *Minor Consiglio* voted in a provision to limit ecclesiastical mortmain which introduced numerous restrictive clauses in endowments to the Church. The Genoese patricians were spurred on to a confrontation with the Church not so much by clear ideals as by urgent financial necessity most recently exacerbated by the events of 1746 when the republic had fallen deeply into debt. They were influenced too by the examples of Spain and Portugal whose jurisdictionalist policies acted as models for states that were, like Genoa, concerned particularly about the financial and legal aspects of the matter. What the patrician policy lacked was continuity, coherence and the courage to carry on the ensuing civil battle. These and other attempts at reform remained confined within a small area and did not alter the political attitudes of the various republican institutions. After the short-lived events of 1762, which had attracted the attention of Campomanes and other European reformers, Genoa returned abruptly to the shadows and cultural isolation, which was broken only by a few belated voices in favour of physiocratic ideas, often permeated with conservative attitudes and in any case without any influence on policy.

The same fate awaited the little Republic of Lucca, which experienced a similar decline of patrician power as had the larger Republics of Genoa and Venice. The economic situation after 1750, as a result of international events, was very grave. For example, the Lisbon earthquake of 1755 had serious consequences for merchants from Lucca who had been very active in Portugal, and a few years later the Seven Years War deprived them of commercial outlets in the German territories. The decline of manufacturing and artisan industries, political stagnation, institutional crises and financial difficulties were all signs of the almost inevitable end of the republic. And tiny San Marino, the only republic to survive as an autonomous state in the next century, already possessed a merely symbolic value, more suitable for the creation of historiographical myths than for making history.

Piedmontese society remained on the sidelines of the reform movement during the long reign of Charles Emanuel III (1730–73), successor to the great Victor Amadeus II. In contrast to the reforms carried out or planned by his father, Charles Emanuel confined himself to straightforward management, so that his was a policy of consolidation of all that had been accomplished in the previous period. The edict of *Perequazione* of 1731, issued by the new king, merely put the definitive seal on the fiscal reforms carried out by Victor Amadeus from 1699 onwards. In this way the last acts of a long and coherent operation of reorganisation of the registration of property, were legally sanctioned, thereby clarifying two important objectives, one of an economic and administrative nature, the other social. The first was the redistribution of the land tax by means of a new survey of landed property as well as the definition of their precise value and the income yielded by them, and the effecting of a fair division among the contributors of taxes. The social objective was to try to limit the power of the nobles which had increased considerably during the second half of the seventeenth century and to gain for the crown the loyalty of those officials who had consolidated their position in the years of the War of the Spanish Succession. The reorganisation of the *catasto* was only partly successful, however, since there remained considerable disparities between one province and another, while the technical work was not carried out with that precision and sureness which characterised the cadastral reform in Lombardy of the same period.

The tradition of reformist regalism too was losing its more original content, becoming established as a rule of conduct for the ruling class, but no longer a force capable of idealistic energy. Looking closely, it becomes apparent that already in Victor Amadeus II's reformism these signs of bureaucratism, authoritarianism and tactical caution were present, becoming more open when the author of the reforms left the scene. Piedmont lacked the active involvement of civil society. There was no free political debate, and culture survived in closely supervised areas where dissent was forbidden or at least tightly controlled. The ruling class, increasingly made up of men drawn from the bureaucracy, did not distinguish itself for strategic acumen but devoted all its energies to faithful service to the monarchy and to scrupulous and meticulous administrative care. A dull and pious court, which gathered the élite tightly round the throne, influenced the climate of society, while other institutions, such as the university, faithfully carried out their institutional tasks without becoming the centres for new ideas. Just how successfully Piedmont had been developed into a socially compact state where a solid relationship had grown up between society and the Crown, can be seen by events during the Wars of Succession, particularly that of the Austrian Succession, when the House of Savoy put together the only Italian army capable of equalling the great European powers, and when hundreds of peasant volunteers, who were not regular troops, defended their lands and families in support of the king's armed forces.

But in the area of political debate and the circulation of ideas, one is struck by the flatness of the situation. None of the desire for change, so pronounced in other parts of Italy, was felt in Piedmont, where the politicians seemed only interested in technical and administrative problems. Of the many questions which animated the political debate between 1740 and 1760, all that filtered through to the Kingdom of Savoy were the ideas on monetary reform, military reorganisation and science. One of the ministers, Giovan Battista Bogino, was the most important instigator of reforms in these areas. Bogino's enthusiasm for the tradition of jurisdictionalism was revived as a result of his contact with Sardinia. This island had come under Piedmontese rule in 1718, and successive governors had tried to introduce the institutions and culture of Savoyard Piedmont. In the ensuing clash with the local Church and a particularly primitive feudalism, Bogino acted harshly, attempting to root out traditions which did not adapt well to the ideals of the absolute State. In this struggle Bogino, sometimes without wishing to, set in motion hopes and ideas derived from the philosophy of the Enlightenment. The tribunals and administration of the island were reformed with the aim of integrating Sardinia into the kingdom's state apparatus. Various feudal jurisdictions were suppressed and measures were taken to control the religious orders. Universities were set up in Cagliari and Sassari with statutes which resembled those of Turin University and which were visualised as educating a class of officials to run the local administration. During the years of famine (1764–65), the Grain Banks (*Monti frumentari*) were set up to relieve the peasants from the financial difficulties caused by the payment of interest on loans. When Bogino was dismissed in 1773, this marked the end of the economic and institutional reformism in the island which, while it had lasted, had collected a considerable intellectual movement around it.

In the second half of the eighteenth century, the Valle d'Aosta and Savoy experienced governors who were determined to introduce the rules of the absolute State into these areas and were quite prepared to engage in a decisive clash with the lacal autonomies of feudal origin. In the Valle d'Aosta the advance of the centralising State was marked by the edicts of 1757 and 1758 which transferred duties and powers from the *Conseil des Commis*, the old representative of the Assembly of the Three Estates which constituted the body of local self-government, to royal delegates. The most important events in this extension into the Aosta Valley of the system of the absolute State were, firstly, the abolition of the *Coûtumier*, in other words, of the main source of local law, and its substitution by the new law, the *Costituzioni reali*, already in use in Piedmont. Secondly, obligatory taxes were introduced which replaced the *donativo*, thus depriving the Assembly of the Three Estates of any meaning. Finally, the office of intendant was introduced, to implement the decisions adopted by central government and as a direct expression of royal power. The same tendencies could be seen at work in the government of Savoy, where between 1771 and 1792 the seigneurial regime was brought to an end with the freeing of the serfs. With an extraordinarily daring law, which was to be taken as a model by revolutionary France twenty years later, the Turin government in 1771 began to dismantle the feudal system in Savoy. This task, which had been in preparation for a long time, was brought to a conclusion after overcoming difficulties and resistance of every kind. It was an example of a kind of reformism that although not inspired by enlightened ideas, was able to carry out a plan of enormous historical significance within the context of the *ancien régime*. Thus even a state far removed from the spirit of enlightened reform, as was the Kingdom of Savoy under Charles Emanuel III and Victor Amadeus III, participated in the events of the eighteenth century with important actions which cannot be dismissed as merely the formal fulfilment of Victor Amadeus II's policies or as delayed expressions of an absolutism closer to the ideas of Louis XIV than of Joseph II.

NOTES AND REFERENCES

For a general history of the Papal States see: Caravale, M. and Caracciolo, A. (1978) *Lo stato pontificio da Martino V a Pio IX*. UTET, Turin. On the reforms see: Venturi, F. (1963) 'Elementi e tentativi di riforma nello Stato Pontificio del Settecento', in *Rivista storica italiana* IV, pp. 778–817. For Benedict XIV see the biographical monograph by Rosa, M. (1969) *Riformatori e ribelli nel '700 religioso italiano*. Dedalo, Bari. On the relations between Bologna and the Papal States see: Giacomelli, A. 1979) 'Carlo Grassi e le riforme bolognesi del Settecento', in *Quaderni culturali bolognesi*, 10–11.

For the conflict between Church and State in the eighteenth century see: Venturi, F. (1969–84) *Settecento riformatore*. Einaudi, Turin, vol. II. A summary can be found in: Venturi, F. (1976) 'Church and reform in the Enlightenment in Italy', in *The Journal of Modern History*, 2.

For the Republic of Venice see: Georgelin J. (1978) *Venise au siècle des lumières*. Mouton, Paris–The Hague; Berengo, M. (1956) *La società veneta alla fine del Settecento*. Sansoni, Florence; Torcellan, G. (1969) *Settecento veneto e altri scritti*. Giappichelli, Turin.

On the development of enlightened ideas in Genoa in the eighteenth century see: Rotta, S. (1961) 'Idee di riforma nella Genova settecentesca e la diffusione del pensiero di Montesquieu', in *Movimento operaio e socialista*, 3–4. For a general summary see: Costantini, C. (1978) *La Repubblica di Genova*. UTET, Turin.

There is no up-to-date work on the history of Piedmont in the second half of the eighteenth century. See instead the pages devoted to the intellectuals of Piedmont edited by Venturi, F. (1958) *Illuministi italiani*. Ricciardi, Milan–Naples, vol. III. An important work on Savoy is: Nicolas, J. (1978) *La Savoie au 18e siècle*. Maloine, Paris.

1. Venturi, F. (1969–84) *Settecento riformatore*, Einaudi, Turin, vol. I, p. 7.
2. Berengo, M. (1960) *La civiltà veneziana nel Settecento*. Sansoni, Florence, p. 94.
3. Dal Pane, L. (1944) *Storia del lavoro in Italia dagli inizi del XVIII secolo al 1815*. Giuffré, Milan.
4. Venturi, F., op. cit., vol. II, Ch. VI.
5. Assereto, G. (1975) *La repubblica ligure. Lotte politiche e problemi finanziari*. Fondazione Luigi Einaudi, Turin, pp. 11–12.

Italy from the reforms of enlightened absolutism to the crisis of the *ancien régime* (Dino Carpanetto)

CHAPTER FOURTEEN

Tuscany in the age of Leopold

The historiographical term 'enlightened absolutism' can justifiably be used to describe the political and cultural conditions in Tuscany during the rule of Leopold (1765–90). Here was a sovereign more 'philosopher' than despot, of shrewd intelligence and unusual intellectual perceptiveness, assisted by a group of able, experienced political leaders, and behind him a civil service that had adopted the new spirit of service in the public interest which the Lorraine governors had introduced into the region from 1737. A cultural movement also existed which, while embracing a wide range of different and sometimes contradictory theories, contributed much to the support of Leopoldine reforms. Thus a political programme for the transformation of economic law, public institutions, judicial structures and relations between Church and State took shape as significant and long-lasting reforms. In addition, one of the characteristics of Italian intellectuals in the eighteenth century – that of becoming closely involved with the problems of political government – was in Tuscany particularly pronounced. Exerting a pressure that was more technical than ideological, almost all the Tuscan intellectuals participated in various ways in the drawing up and sometimes in the execution of the reforms, without undertaking any far-reaching theoretical elaborations but inclining more to immediate and empirical solutions to problems.

That is not to say that the European Enlightenment, particularly that of France, did not have an influence on local culture: Montesquieu had had great success since the 1750s while Voltaire and Rousseau were known and discussed. But if one seeks, among the works published in Tuscany, for a book inspired by themes of moral and intellectual reform of a clearly *philosophique* type, all that emerges is *La Chiesa e la repubblica dentro i loro limiti* by Cosimo Amidei, an anti-curial treatise published in 1768, where the ideas of Rousseau and Helvétius are used to support a proposal, anticipating the future, based on the principle of the separation of Church and State. Excepting this book and a few scientific works, one can say that the influence of the *lumières* was slight and superficial, in the face of a prevalently practical and empirical attitude, of gradualistic and moderate nature, incapable of understanding the radical implications of many books which were arriving from outside and unwilling to abandon its experimental and pragmatic tradition.

There is no doubt that administrative duties, which absorbed considerable intellectual energy, helped to curb the creative independence of the Tuscan intellectuals who were far removed from those heights of philosophy reached by the *illuministi* of Lombardy and Naples. But unlike them, they were able to find a less frustrating, more positive role in the political debate. Even physiocratic theories, which had numerous supporters in Tuscany, did not stimulate an original change in ideas nor did they provide the basis for new intellectual circles. Instead they became the basic culture of a whole ruling group who were seeking realistic solutions within the framework of a positive relationship to the Grand Duke Leopold. Physiocracy was not adhered to dogmatically. Some of the protagonists in the Leopoldine reforms, such as Angelo Tavanti, Giovan Francesco Pagnini and Ferdinando Paoletti, drew on the French economists for ideas, plans and projects which they adapted to the Tuscan situation, convinced that the technical and political content of physiocratic ideas – economic freedom, the theory of legal despotism and the natural order – offered a convincing justification for their political system, within enlightened absolutism, and for their decisions which favoured a reformism which would not harm the interests of the great landowners nor question the social structure of the countryside.

On the other hand, it was these same political and economic decisions, effected in the 1760s and 1770s, which made it possible for the principles of the physiocratic school to be adopted by some Tuscan intellectuals not piecemeal but in their entirety, as postulates of a more general economic and political system. Thus they did not only uphold the idea of a free grain trade, but were also committed to the cultural and technical education of farmers. They affirmed the rights of freedom of ownership as complementary to the rights of freedom of trade, defended an absolutism tempered by the authority of the law as the optimum form of government and accepted a natural order that was moved by its own needs, just and rationally perfect. These were the most important elements that physiocratic ideas in their widest sense contributed to Tuscan culture, creating the conditions for an amicable relationship between those in power and the intellectuals.

The Grand Duke Leopold, second son of Maria Theresa, was the chief advocate of a policy of reform, and it was he who gave it a coherence and continuity that were lacking in other Italian experiments. Brought up with those values of contemporary thought known as 'enlightened Catholicism' and convinced of the importance of scientific and economic knowledge to the running of the country, Leopold thoroughly understood Tuscan society which he approached with a humanitarian and paternalistic attitude, succeeding in building between the more influential classes a basis of consensus for his reforms. His arrival in Florence in 1765 brought the Lorraine Regency to a close and paved the way for the independence of the Grand Duchy of Tuscany. In the course of the years Leopold strengthened this independence from Vienna, stressing the national values of the State which was no longer fiscally and diplomatically subject to the Habsburg capital, even if the family link meant that it still had a privileged relationship with it.

From the very start, Leopold showed his respect for the local political situation. His choice of closest collaborators reaffirmed the position of the Tuscan group that had already given proof of its political qualities in the preceding years. Thus Pompeo Neri, Giulio Rucellai, Angelo Tavanti, Francesco Maria Gianni, Giovan Francesco Pagnini and Stefano Bertolini, all men trained in the Regency, had their loyalty reconfirmed by the new prince. The only one to be replaced was the old Marshal Antonio Botta-Adorno, unpopular with the Tuscans, in whose place Leopold put his trusted Count de Rosenberg. Neri and Rucellai were kept in top jobs and for more than a decade were Leopold's chief advisers; the first on economic matters and the second on relations with the Church. The political rise of Tavanti, minister of finance in 1766 and successor to Neri after the latter's death in 1775, and the appointment as *grand commis* of Gianni promoted two most able and active officials to the heights of power. These two men were, however, divided by many differences.

The press at this period was one of the most important means of communication between society and the political rulers.[1] The Florentine *Novelle letterarie* faithfully mirrors the characteristics of Tuscan reformist thought, in both its extent and its limits. If under Lami the journal had been a forum for the discussion of religious, historical and scientific problems in general, seen through rigidly Muratorian eyes, under the management of Giuseppe Pelli Bencivenni and Marco Lastri (the latter running it on his own from 1779 to 1791) economics, demography and agriculture came to the forefront.[2] The physiocratic tendency of the journal now became more pronounced and it addressed itself to landowners, tenant farmers and parish priests, seeing them as those who could bring about the changes that the reform movement was trying to effect in the Tuscan countryside.

The development of the gazette was another sign of vitality. This long-standing form of communication, at one time simply a record of news without comment or judgement, was developing into a politically oriented journalism. The number of copies printed too, now over 2,000, was an indication of a greater public maturity. It was above all foreign policy which now took up an increasingly large space. There was a qualitative leap in this direction at the time of the American Revolution which was closely followed by the Tuscan gazettes. The *Gazzetta universale toscana*, in reporting events in America, revealed an official political line, much influenced by English sources, while the Florentine *Notizie del mondo*, thanks partly to the contributions of Filippo Mazzei, reflected the point of view of the colonies and underlined the political and constitutional problems of the new American society.

This new intellectual current reached the provinces of Tuscany too. In Pisa, the university reformed by Gaspare Cerati and now directed by the *illuminista* Angelo Fabbroni had revived and transformed the model of the *Giornale de' letterati*, turning it into a voice linking the university, the academies and the professional classes. In Siena cultural life centred around the Physiocratic Academy. Leghorn, partly as a result of its status as a free port, its growth in population and international character, had turned into a famous centre for the publishing of enlightened texts. Giuseppe Aubert published Rousseau, Beccaria and Verri. In 1770 he prepared a new edition of the *Encyclopédie*, enriching the Paris text with annotations which reflected the most advanced thinking in the Italian Enlightenment, starting with the *école de Milan*. Finally, the Florentine *Accademia dei Georgofili* held together the threads of a network of contacts with Tuscany and the rest of Italy, producing plans and making suggestions which were not without influence on Leopold's economic policy, particularly in the matters of ownership, *mezzadria*, agrarian education, agronomic revival and public hygiene.

Leopold stamped his mark on economic policy from the very first years of his government with the provisions made for the Tuscan Maremma. Already, in the last years of Medici rule, Sallustio Bandini had investigated the social and institutional causes of the depopulation of that unhealthy region, suggesting remedies which went beyond the merely technical. His analysis was looked at again in the early 1760s and confirmed on the theoretical side by the physiocratic ideas that were being taken up by various Lorraine and Tuscan officials. It was Neri who revived the proposals put forward forty years before by Bandini and who fought for the liberation of the Maremma from the Sienese administration which exploited its resources without investing in the necessary public works. By a provision of 1765, the Maremma was removed from the province of Siena and placed under direct government administration. Two years later a commission was appointed under Neri to present plans for the improvement of the area. The plans for reclamation and commercial development were beginning to seem quite inadequate to deal with the problem. It had increasingly been realised that in order to repopulate and develop the Maremma a more coherent economic policy was needed that would support the improvements in production with the introduction of a free grain trade, incentives and rewards for producers and the transfer of ownership to the share-croppers (*mezzadri*) of the lands belonging to the State or the Church. Thus the problem of the Maremma was solved by Leopold's overall economic policy and became one chapter in the struggle for free trade and a redistribution of the land.

The disastrous effects of famine prompted many sections of the Tuscan ruling classes to look for new solutions to old ills. It began in Tuscany in 1763 and, though less severe, lasted longer than the Naples famine, reaching its peak in 1766. As in Naples, the *annona* and the officials were blamed, but in Florence the revelation of the inherent distortions of a restrictive system was followed by consistent and speedy liberalising measures. Once again it was Neri who directed operations. Already in the first years of the famine, limited and partial liberalising measures were tried out which were then extended and ratified by the law of 18 September 1767.[3] Drafted by Neri, the law established a free grain trade for the whole of Tuscany, without any taxes except communal excise duties. Import and export were also to be allowed, the only restriction being a general government control. The system of *tratte*, or specific and limited concessions, was abolished altogether and in its place was put a system based solely on price levels.

The law of 1767 was historically of great importance. It was the first coherent provision for the freeing of the internal grain trade to come from an Italian state, and one of the first in Europe. In Italy only Tuscany responded to the scourge of famine with a clear change in the traditional provisioning policy, abolishing the mediating role of the State and relying instead on market forces. The law of 1767 did not result in the upheavals which many had feared, and it was possible in the following years to continue with a gradual extension of this liberalising legislation through the edicts of 1771 and 1775. This last extended free trade in corn to the foreign market. While it is possible to see in this case a link between physiocratic theories and the liberalising policies, it should be emphasised that the latter preceded the spread of the ideas of the physiocrats. Only after 1770 did state officials initiate the theoretical debate which introduced economic ideas of French and English origin, and which in the following decades became directly involved with the conduct of government policy.

The abolition of the private tax Farm (1767), the assumption by the State of the management of taxes (1768), the beginning of the release of land on *a livello* contracts (1766) and the abolition of the *Annona* were the other measures which made the first decade of Leopold's government a period of intense economic reform. Jurisdictionalistic policy too, often connected with economic reforms, developed in its own particular way, rather different from other types of reformism in Italy and elsewhere. After the first ten years the attention of the grand duke and his collaborators was turned to the reform of the State and judiciary, while ecclesiastical policy became involved with Tuscan Jansenism. One aspect of economic policy which we will examine in greater depth is that of *allivellazione*, carried out between 1766 and 1784, when the lands belonging to state-run religious bodies and to the grand-ducal patrimony were let out *a livello*, giving priority to the share croppers already working on them.[4] It is clear that one of the things which prompted Leopold's *allivellazioni* was the clash with the Church. The technical model for his policy was derived from the law on mortmain in 1769, brought about by that champion of Tuscan jurisdictionalism, Rucellai, whereby the State would control the transfer of property to the Church by private individuals. With the new policy Gianni, the principal organiser, and the grand duke intended, on the one hand, to offer the already widespread number of small and medium peasant properties a greater productive stability and, on the other, to enable the *mezzadri* and *coloni* (emphyteutical tenants) to acquire possession of the land. The *a livello* contract envisaged a long period of rental, as well as the freedom to sublet the land, with permanent enjoyment of the benefit from the ownership and improvements made there. In the decade 1770–80 the *allivellazioni* mainly involved state land and not so much that of the Church.

Gianni's aim, not shared by other Tuscan officials, of establishing an alternative form of peasant landownership to the *mezzadria* system, was largely unsuccessful because of the opposition of many officials, administrators of various bodies, and because of the greater contractual strength of the land-owners who easily managed to acquire the lands put up for auction. The agrarian economy, now in a cycle of expansion, confirmed this gap between landowners and *mezzadri*, with the financial resources of the former on the increase. Whether they acquired land *a livello* or by outright purchase, either way they were an obstacle to the acquisition of land by the peasants.

In the Tuscan ruling class the clash between these two opposed views of economic policy was identified with, on one side, Gianni, who favoured a pro-peasant policy, and, on the other, Tavanti, who opposed *allivellazione*. Tavanti followed on the path pointed by Neri who saw the *catasto* as the principal objective of agrarian reform, adding to this other proposals advocating agro-nomic improvements and the agrarian education called for by the *Georgofili*. Gianni's policy of *allivellazione* implied antifeudal proposals, since it presup-posed the suppression of the ancient common rights of the peasants (of pasture, firewood and the collection of chestnuts on common land) and of the collective servitude by which they were bound. This was one of the contra-dictions where Gianni's hypothesis fell down, in the face of worsening living conditions of the most defenceless section of the agricultural workers who were subjected to an increased exploitation and weakened by the rise in prices taking place in Tuscany, as in almost all of Europe, in the last decades of the century. It was rather the bourgeois aspects of this policy which came to the fore, in so far as the *allivellazioni* served to consolidate 'a limited nucleus of wealthier peasants and a merchant class involved as middlemen and dealing in agricultural produce'.[5] The Tuscan countryside retained all the characteristics of an area of widespread *mezzadria*, with the additional, and important, peculiarity of a nobility that concerned itself to a remarkable degree with technical and commercial advances and was prepared to invest large amounts of capital in the land.

With the *allivellazioni* and the sale of state and church properties, there was a social objective too: that of encouraging the creation in the country of a widespread class of small and middle-sized landowners who would be the basis of economic and civil development as well as those at whom the new reforms were aimed. This explains the link between the redistribution of land and the reform of the administration of the communes, which began in 1771 and was completed by 1786. The existing municipal institutions were abolished and in their place new councils were established assisted by government magistrates. Through this municipal reform, Leopold and his collaborators aimed to redistribute some of the basic powers of the State, delegating important duties to local government institutions, first and foremost that of tax collection. The local communities, planned to be thirty-nine in number, took over the administration of communal property, the collection of the communal taxes, the upkeep of the roads, the selection of the district doctors and the management of the grain warehouses. The composition of the councils was based on income since only those inhabitants of the commune paying a certain level of tax could participate. In this way a broader participation in the management of local affairs was ensured. There was no lack of opposition to these measures, starting with that of the central organs of state and then of the state officials present in the provinces (the *giusdicenti*).

The municipal reform showed up the peculiarities of Leopold's absolutism. Its originality becomes apparent when it is compared with the measures being taken by his brother Joseph in the Empire. While Joseph concentrated on a centralising reform of the State which increased the power at the top and linked centre and outlying areas in a hierarchy, Leopold instead followed an opposite course, trying to establish side by side a bureaucratic state, as it developed with a genuine decentralisation of powers, increased liberty and political rights. Leopold's goal was the creation of a constitution, which he began to work on in 1778. It was edited in its last version in 1782 by Gianni, but never came into force.[6] It is still an extraordinarily interesting document, revealing Leopold's awareness of the need to think of a transfer of sovereignty from the prince to society, so as to provide a solution to the problem which was beginning to raise its head in all the absolute states of Europe – that of the crisis of an institutional system. This was the only example in Europe of a sovereign who himself suggested an alternative which not only would have sanctioned a new pact between prince and people, but also an increase of political powers down the social ladder.

It will suffice to list briefly the contents of the planned constitution to see its revolutionary implications: the creation of an elected national assembly; the separation of political from judicial power; the partial delegation of legislative power to the national assembly; the establishment of a whole series of restrictions on the authority of the sovereign, who would not be allowed on his own to alter the state boundaries, declare war or change the judicial and municipal regulations; the separation of the sovereign's income from the State's finances; the inalienability of the property of the Crown.

The idea of giving Tuscany 'a primitive and fundamental law, investing the sovereign with legitimate authority and limiting its use and exercise',[7] as the preface to the 1782 text says, was supported personally by Leopold in the face of the hostility of jurists and politicians and the incomprehension of his closest collaborator, Gianni. Whether it was the influence of the French physiocrats or the development of European ideas on natural law up to Locke, or rather the example of the Netherlands and the demands of the American colonists which determined the evolution of a constitutional theory is a matter not yet agreed on by historians. That Leopold's plan was never put into action is due to a series of reasons, of which two are more persuasive than the others. Firstly, as has been said, the plan met a barrage of objections, resistance and incomprehension from the political and intellectual world of Tuscany which for the most part failed to see its institutional importance. If any interest was shown it was confused and critical in the face of an initiative which seemed ill-suited to Tuscany. Furio Diaz, in his book on Gianni, has revealed clearly on this occasion, as on others and perhaps even more so, the gap between Leopold's approach and that of his closest collaborators. Leopold's 'trusting appeal to the general principles of human social life, to the idea of fundamental laws for society and government, based on a contract which moving beyond previous ideas derived from natural law and Locke, seemed to be tending more towards a Rousseauian conception of popular sovereignty'[8] did not fit in with the ideas of his collaborators, such as Gianni, which were narrower and more provincial, revealing a lack of faith in the ability and the will of the Tuscans to participate in political life through the exercise of power in more or less direct forms.

Fears that 'a minority' of the people might cause a redistribution of power as envisaged by the planned constitution to degenerate into anarchy were expressed not only by Gianni, but also by intellectuals who were more open to enlightened and Rousseauian ideas, such as Pelli and Amidei, who used the presumed immaturity of the people and its political inexperience to support their opposition to the proposed constitution. In fact it should be stressed that Gianni, the diligent official and intelligent executor of Leopold's desires, came gradually, between 1779 and 1782, to assimilate his sovereign's constitutional ideas. That this was not merely opportunism or something dictated by the obligations which he could hardly fail to feel towards his prince, can be seen both from the extraordinary pains taken by Gianni to convert Leopold's proposals into legislation and from the way they continued to inspire the later development of his ideas. If one compares Gianni's efforts and the grand duke's actions on the one hand, with the ideas of the progressive intellectuals on the other, one can see an important divergence of views. The first seem much more open-minded and advanced, to the extent that it is easy to agree with Diaz when he says that 'the intellectual élite had appeared unready to accept and elaborate the great ideas of the Enlightenment, which only Leopold's initiative, with a narrow circle of collaborators, including Gianni, had managed in part to transplant and render operative in the political reality of Tuscany'.[9]

In relation to the Church too, Leopold's policy differed somewhat, even though the struggle was the same, from the other great examples of neo-jurisdictionalism in those years in both Habsburg and Bourbon-dominated states. The difference lay not so much in the content of the anti-curial reforms carried out by Leopold, which were very similar to others being carried out at roughly the same time in Milan, Parma, Modena and Naples, as in the overall tone, the nature of the enterprise and in its philosophical background. The defence of the rights of the State in Tuscany developed into a coherent and gradual series of reforms, without the hasty and traumatic changes that occurred, for example, in Lombardy under Joseph II. But this is not to say that it was not firm in its resolve to assert the authority of civil power in all areas: education, justice, economy and politics. In Tuscany, perhaps more than elsewhere, the anti-curial measures brought about the conditions which favoured the success of the new jurisdictionalism, which no longer confined itself to dealing with the Church on all the controversies raised but which also gave the State the authority to impose its own orders on bishops and priests who were to be considered in the same way as all other subjects. The alliance between the grand duke and the Tuscan Jansenists did not exploit and coerce the latter as much as in Lombardy. This alliance produced results in the early 1780s in the area of internal church reform, but it also resulted in disunity and friction because a separation was maintained between the political reformers, who did not make use of the Jansenist clerics passively to carry out their projects or interfere in theological matters, and the religious reformers who approached the question through a more general relationship with the thought of Jansenist Europe.

Leopold's anti-curial policy could rely on the results already obtained during the Regency, particularly the important laws on the press and on mortmains. Rucellai, secretary of the *Regio Diritto* from 1753 to 1770, provided the continuity between these two periods and played a central role in the fight to assert the rights of the State against the Church. The new Leopoldine government revived the anti-curial struggle which had come to a halt in the last years of the Regency. It was necessary now to resume the interrupted task and to perfect and consolidate previous gains. Thus in the first years the policy continued on the same jurisdictional path taken by other Italian states. In 1766 the inquisitor of Pisa was deprived of the power to censor books; in 1769 and 1777 the strict conditions of the *Regio Exequatur* for acts concerning the public interest issued by the Church were reaffirmed; in 1769 the earlier legislation on mortmains was revised, now set in a more general framework of economic policy, based on *allivellazioni* and on the sale of large ecclesiastical properties; the right of sanctuary was abolished. Two years later, in 1771, there began a gradual process of reform of the judicial powers of the Church. They were restricted to areas strictly appertaining to religion while all matters of general import were transferred to civil justice. In this way civil and criminal cases concerning the temporal life of Tuscan society were handed over to the state magistratures while the bishops' courts dealt exclusively with crimes of a canonical nature and those concerning the internal discipline of the Church.

In matters of the reform of the clergy too Leopold and his collaborators acted with prudence and continuity, without ever taking over-sudden measures, but nevertheless clinging firmly to their objective, common to the reforming spirit of the age, of bringing down the Church's temporal power, weeding out all those clerics not serving a socially useful function, controlling to some extent the training and work of the priests, bringing them into line with the aspirations of a civil society which was beginning to free itself from the inheritance of the Counter-Reformation.

Throughout Leopold's reign, religious houses belonging to those religious orders deemed to be of no benefit to society were closed. The more powerful and influential orders were not spared, as in the case of the Dominicans whose houses in Prato and Pistoia were closed. For the secular clergy, Rucellai and the Tuscan jurisdictionalists proposed a regime of rigorous moral discipline while at the same time reducing the often considerable differences in income received by the priests. Here too can be seen the difference in attitude between the reformers of Tuscany and those in Lombardy. While the latter were basically aiming to determine the training and activities of the parish priests, the Tuscans did not try to step over the boundaries of the two powers, religious and civil, but tried merely to define the external conditions of religious service. Until the end of the 1770s the reform movement in Tuscany remained strongly influenced by jurisdictionalism and the ideas of Muratori, but this did not exclude contact with other expressions of Catholic criticism of the predominance of the Curia and of counter-reformation ideas. Only after this date were there signs of a *rapprochement*, albeit from often opposing positions and with many ambiguities, between Leopold's reformism and the Jansenist movement in Tuscany. The leader of this was Scipione de' Ricci, Bishop of Pistoia and Prato. Leopold looked closely at the liturgical, pastoral and doctrinal reform being introduced by the bishop in his diocese and resolved to encourage its adoption all over Tuscany, particularly because in it he saw an important lead in the move to distance the Tuscan Church from Rome. This was the result that Leopold hoped to achieve by supporting the Jansenists.

The culmination of this *rapprochement*, and also the beginning of its end, was marked by the publication, by the grand Duke, of the 'fifty-seven ecclesiastical points'. This document was presented to the bishops in 1786 as a basis for an internal reform of the Tuscan Church. It contained only Jansenist ideas (such as the central role of the bishop and parish priests in the organisation of the Church, as opposed to the 'usurpations of the Court of Rome', the need to bring the education of priests into line with the doctrine of St Augustine, the elimination of the more ostentatious displays in worship and the return to an austere and internalised form of religion) and those of traditional regalism. The 'ecclesiastical points' gave rise to an animated battle within the ranks of the Tuscan clergy, and divisions emerged with, on one side, the majority of the bishops opposed to Leopold and Ricci's proposals through obedience to Rome and, on the other, a very isolated minority who were eager to take a path leading away from Rome, following the Dutch Church of Utrecht.

The Synod of Pistoia, called in September 1786 by Ricci, marked the moment of collision between a Jansenism which looked beyond the boundaries of the State, finding support from Jansenist groups in Italy and Europe, and the orthodoxy of the Roman Church which had powerful allies among the religious orders and the common people, who feared to lose long-standing religious traditions in which they found identity and cohesion. In Prato in May 1787 there was popular rioting against Ricci's innovations. These and other signs, such as the collapse of the episcopal assembly in Florence, led Leopold to withdraw his support from the Jansenist movement and return to safer jurisdictionalist ground. In the 1780s two historically important provisions were made: in 1782 the Tribunal of the Inquisition was closed down; in 1786 the nunciature in Florence, once the corner-stone of the Church's juridical influence in Tuscan society, was abolished. From then on the papal nuncio became purely an ambassador of Rome, without powers over the bishops and clergy.

The problem of the reform of the judicial system was prominent in Tuscany throughout the 1770s and 1780s. It was discussed in the columns of the journals, in the academies and in political circles. The major stimulus to this debate still came from political initiatives, since from 1771 and all through the decade a stream of provisions was forthcoming, particularly in the area of civil justice which was reformed both in its mechanisms and in its basic principles. The main changes brought about were: the abolition of the *Magistrati delle Arti*, that is of a specific and separate judiciary dealing with disputes in work and trade; the creation of career judges, putting an end to the elective and corporate nature of the post; the publication of judgments and the precise establishment of tariffs and procedures for the discussion of cases and for the awarding of sentences. But the most far-reaching changes were those introduced in the field of penal law. The inspiration for reform came not so much from the jurisprudential ideas very much in evidence at Pisa University, and which did not offer any programme for institutional reform, but rather from Beccaria's *Dei delitti e delle pene*, a book which in Pisa had been received with a certain embarrassment. From the circulation of this book in Tuscany and the discussion which developed around it, bringing to light the newly acquired ideas of the Enlightenment and of Rousseau among some intellectuals, it was apparent that Beccaria's work had fallen on fertile ground. The humanitarian inspiration, suggestions for reform and appeal for the protection of civil rights to be found in this book were to leave a lasting mark on the intellectual and political world of Tuscany. Cosimo Amidei, whom we have already mentioned as author of *Lo stato e la chiesa dentro i loro limiti*, was one of the active mediators between Beccaria and Tuscan culture.[10] His *Discorso sopra la carcere de' debitori* (1770) proposed the abolition of prison sentences for debtors, thus giving rise to an important debate involving several figures of the Italian Enlightenment.

In Tuscany in 1776, the proposal to abolish prison sentences for bankrupts became law. Leopold, like other European sovereigns before him from Gustav of Sweden to Catherine of Russia, and his collaborators found ideas and suggestions in Beccaria's book just at the time that they were beginning the restructuring of the codes. With the enactment of Leopold's Code (30 November 1786), the old penal laws, punishments and court procedures were completely demolished.[11] The reform was not, however, a mere technical operation and its authors did not propose merely to replace archaic, mistaken or anachronistic laws with other clearer and better planned legislation while maintaining intact the principles on which the legal system had been based for centuries. On the contrary, this was a genuine political reform since it aimed to overthrow the previous legal system in order to establish a new philosophy concerning punishments, the. judge and the accused. With its formal simplicity, reduction of crimes, moderate punishments, recognition of the accused's right of defence, publication of sentences and the abolition of the death sentence, of torture and of the confiscation of possessions the Code showed clearly its intention to abandon the old penal system which was based on inquisitorial procedures, secrecy and the threatening character of the judge and the punishment. Moderation in justice would be reached, according to the legislator, through the application of those utilitarian criteria based on the relationship between social needs and the coercive means of the State, in the conviction that the humanisation of justice would open the way to a more orderly and peaceful society. For these reasons it would not be exaggerated to say that Leopold's code represents one of the peaks of Italian and European reformism and one of the creations which has lasted, both in its internal workings and even more in its general principles, for the longest time.

The active and fruitful course of Leopoldine reformism suffered less than other contemporary reform movements from the worsening state of social conditions and the political situation which occurred all over Italy in the 1780s, but for all that it was not immune from the upheavals and disputes which arose both as a result of pressure from elements attacked by the new reforms, particularly the Church, and because of the economic crisis of the late eighteenth century. But these and other obstacles did not halt the development of an enlightened policy capable of carrying out major reforms in the machinery of the State. This progress came to a halt for external reasons: in 1790 Leopold's brother Joseph died and the grand duke was recalled to Vienna. He left behind him in Tuscany the demonstration of a reformism which more than any other had changed the rules and institutions of a society of the *ancien régime*, without having had recourse to authoritarian solutions but uniting absolutism and liberty in new and original forms. Leopold's famous letter of 1790 to his sister Maria Christina, ruler of Belgium, sums up in his own words the political significance of this series of major reforms in the course of which he had evolved a contractual and democratic view of power which marks a turning-point in the history of Europe between the end of the *ancien régime* and the French Revolution:

Je crois qu'un souverain, même héréditaire, n'est qu'un délégué et employé du peuple pour lequel il est fait, qu'il lui doit tous ses soins, peines, veilles . . . qu'à chaque pays il faut une loi fondamentale, un contract entre le peuple et le souverain, qui limite l'autorité et le pouvoir de ce dernier; que quand le souverain ne la tient pas, il renonce par le fait à sa place, qui ne lui est donnée qu'à cette condition et qu'on n'est plus obligé de lui obéir; que le pouvoir exécutif est dans le souverain, mais le législatif dans le peuple et ses représentants; que celui-ci à chaque changement de souverain peut y ajouter de nouvelles conditions à son autorité.[12]

NOTES AND REFERENCES

The history of Tuscany during the period of Leopold has been described from many points of view. The following works are among the best. For a history of the politics and culture of Leopold's Tuscany see Cochrane, E. W. (1973) *Florence in the Forgotten Centuries, 1527–1800. A History of Florence and the Florentines in the Age of the Grand Dukes*. University of Chicago Press, Chicago–London. A general biography of the grand duke is: Wandruszka, A. (1963–64) *Leopold II*. Druck-Verlagsgesellchaft,

Vienna.   On the reforms through a biography of their chief architect see: Diaz, F. (1966) *Francesco Maria Gianni. Dalla burocrazia alla politica sotto Pietro Leopoldo di Toscana.* Ricciardi, Milan–Naples.

1. Ricuperati, G. (1976) *La stampa italiana dal '500 all '800,* eds Castronovo, V. and Tranfaglia, N. Laterza, Bari.
2. Paoli, M. P. and Graglia, R. (1978) 'Marco Lastri: Aritmetica politica e statistica demografica nella Toscana del '700', in *Annali della fondazione Einaudi.* Turin, vol. XII, pp. 117–215
3. For the collection of Tuscan laws see: Cantini, L. (1806) *Legislazione toscana.* Florence.
4. On the policy of *allivellazione* see Mirri, M. (1955) 'Proprietari e contadini toscani nelle riforme leopoldine', in *Movimento operaio,* 2, pp. 173–229;   Giorgetti, G. (1966) 'Per uno studio delle allivellasioni leopoldine', in *Studi storici,* 2 pp. 245–90.
5. Giorgetti, G. (1977) *Capitalismo e agricoltura in Italia.* Editori Riuniti, Rome, p. 506.
6. On the Constitution see: Diaz, F. (1966) *Francesco Maria Gianni. 'Dalla burocrazia alla politica sotto Pietro Leopoldo di Toscana.* Ricciardi, Milan-Naples,
7. The text is in: Mori, G. (1951) *Le riforme leopoldine nel pensiero degli economisti toscani del '700.* Sansoni, Florence.
8. Diaz, F. op. cit., p. 311.
9. Ibid.
10. Amidei, C. (1980) *Opere,* ed. Rotondo, A. Giappichelli, Turin.
11. The text of Leopold's code is printed in: Beccaria, C. (1965) *Dei delitti e delle pene,* ed. Venturi, F. Einaudi, Turin, pp. 258–99.
12. Cuccia, S. (1981) *La Lombardia alla fine dell'ancien régime.* La Nuova Italia, Florence, p. 15.

CHAPTER FIFTEEN

The Duchy of Milan under Maria Theresa and Joseph II

At the end of the Seven Years War, the complex machinery of the Habsburg monarchy was showing signs of an institutional and social crisis which the policies of Maria Theresa and Joseph II, co-ruler and emperor from 1765, tried to solve by a series of reforms, which for intensity of planning and execution has few equals in other states governed by enlightened absolutism in Europe. These thirty years were of great importance for the history of the Habsburg territories when the work of uniting the different groups of peoples, languages, traditions and states was carried on. The current of reform begun in the previous centuries, developed both vertically, along lines of nationality, and horizontally along lines linking classes and ideologies. Beneath the mantle of the impersonal and bureaucratic State and of social values based on service and merit, a unity was building up between the different countries, states, classes and orders of the Habsburg mosaic, made up of political institutions, laws, social behaviour and ideological principles, whose origins lay in the sixteenth and seventeenth centuries. These links assured the duration of the State for another century until the explosion of nineteenth-century nationalism and the development of the class struggle undermined its foundations. Maria Theresa, Joseph II and their ministers brought the consolidation of the multinational framework to an advanced stage of development by means of a policy of major reforms, which brought profound changes to the organisation of the State, the educational system, the Church and civil life.

More than any other European state, the Habsburg monarchy under Maria Theresa and even more so under Joseph II, saw a radical overthrow of the structures of the *ancien régime*, replaced by a completely new legal and state organisation which anticipated the institutions of the nineteenth century. Such a policy has been aptly defined as 'revolution from above', since the changes brought about by the reforms, which aimed at the affirmation of an institutional and economic system capable of placing the monarchy in a leading position in the competition between the great European powers, did not seek any social consensus but were imposed by the central organs on to provinces and classes that were often indifferent if not actually hostile to the change. The great and important work of reform, more ambitious than any other in Europe before 1789, resulted initially in a success whose objective implications it would be wrong to dismiss (as many scholars have done).'[1] But the vertical nature of this process ended up by fomenting opposition from many social groups who defended themselves by reviving traditions and political-religious claims that, whether conservative or revolutionary, weakened the cohesion of the monarchy. Thus, briefly, runs the conclusion to the excellent reconstruction of Habsburg history from the sixteenth to the seventeenth century, recently published by Robert J. W. Evans, and it is quoted because it describes very well the history of Lombardy in the second half of the eighteenth century. Lombardy too was involved in the reforms of Maria Theresa and Joseph which were to represent one of the most coherent and far-reaching reform movements in Italy in the century of the Enlightenment.

Lombard reformism in the 1770s and 1780s was grafted on to the successes of the previous policies, though making a qualitative leap in terms of objectives and methods. The years 1770–71 marked a turning-point, when the Viennese ministers decided to adopt their plan of rationalisation of public administration to the Italian territories. This had already been carried out in other provinces of the monarchy and provided for the abolition of the old magistratures, replacing them with new bodies based on the principle of the separation of powers and the creation of a hierarchical system. From this date there was a rapid succession of changes and an escalation in proposals for reform, which culminated in 1786 with the abolition of all the chief political and juridical bodies of the Lombard aristocracy and their replacement by a modern institutional structure, divided into departments and dependent on the minister plenipotentiary. This wave of reform affected all sectors of society: it attacked the corporative structures, undermined the power of the old patrician ruling classes, broke up the network of municipal and local privileges, overturned the system of taxation and drastically reduced the economic and juridical strength of the Church. Joseph was the main organiser of these reforms, and the policies of these two decades can reasonably be called 'Josephism', extending the term beyond the area of ecclesiastical reform to embrace the whole reform movement.

Despite this radical restructuring of the state, Josephism in Lombardy did not have long-lasting cultural or social results. It was sometimes accepted passively, and more often gave rise to passive resistance where eventually old aristocratic prejudices and new enlightened tendencies found common ground, both rising up in defence of a heritage of civilisation which they feared would be crushed by the authoritarian rationalisation imposed by Joseph. The institutions which had kept the monopoly of political and cultural leadership in the hands of a narrow circle of aristocratic families were indeed threatened by Joseph's subversive spirit. Having said this however, we should also consider the consequences of Habsburg policy at the end of the eighteenth and the beginning of the nineteenth centuries. Most importantly it damaged the relationship of trust, albeit partial and conditional, which had survived during the Theresian period between the Habsburg officials and Viennese government on one side and the officials, politicians and intellectuals of

Lombardy on the other. Collaboration had never been easy or immediate; suspicions, tensions and rivalries punctuated the course of political events even in the period before 1770, but in general Maria Theresa's reforms found considerable support in many Milanese circles.

As time passed and the course of Joseph's reform speeded up, the suspicions increased and the opposition, although not able to block provisions it believed to be mistaken, became stronger and found its voice among those intellectuals who had not abdicated their role by taking on mainly bureaucratic tasks, but who had retained their critical independence vis-à-vis the government. It is significant that they did not establish any direct collaboration with Vienna – on the contrary, they received coldly Vienna's proposals for the organisation and support of cultural research. An example is the lack of success of the Patriotic Society, set up in Milan in 1776 and supported only cautiously by the Milanese intellectuals who feared its bureaucratic character and did not believe that it was a forum for the free expression of thought. More important than the opposition from the intellectuals was that from those classes most severely affected by the reforms of 1770–86, particularly the patriciate who saw the destruction of the state edifice which for three centuries had been the expression of its social pre-eminence. With the nobles, the local administrators, feudal landowners, magistrates and clergy formed an opposition to Josephism which, while it never erupted into organised demonstrations, nevertheless weakened the new structure set up by the reforms.

This was the chief limitation of Joseph's policy, which lacked the social and cultural backing necessary for the changes imposed on Lombard society: it was grandiose, but abstract, since the country it was to be applied to did not know how to receive it. The men and the ideas necessary to support Joseph's reforms were not there. This weakness became evident immediately after Joseph's death when all the forces that he had thought to have repressed or destroyed regained their political authority. The clash between plans and reality, between reform and resistance was apparent too in the religious field where it had seemed that the defences of traditional Catholicism were less strong. Here too the threat of the reforms, based on an alliance between episcopal Jansenism and the Habsburg monarchy, was felt at a moment when the Church in Rome was able to stir up popular religious feeling which had not been crushed by the austere teaching of those priests, state officials of the cloth, favoured by Joseph. Italian Catholicism, though little inclined to deeply felt and personal forms of piety, was closely involved in the political affairs of Rome and its legal and educational structures. Thus Lombardy, although perhaps less dramatically than Tuscany, was able to express its undefeated spirit, which Josephism had failed to vanquish, even if, and this should be emphasised, some aspects of Jansenism put down strong roots which were to emerge at a later date in the religious history of Italy.

These problems appear in a very different light when seen from the point of view of Vienna. Despite the extent and effect of Habsburg reform in Lombardy in these years, Italy was peripheral to the political concerns of the Viennese rulers who were taken up with more pressing matters such as the war with Prussia, the diplomatic clash with the great European powers, the institutional and social upheavals which were troubling some sensitive areas of the Empire (such as the peasant revolts in Bohemia), the revolution in the Netherlands and the continued opposition of the Magyar nobles. The absence of acute conflicts made Lombardy a peaceful province which existed somewhat detached from the events of the 1770s to 1790s, being far from the centres of tension and uninvolved in disputes which represented particular threats to the Viennese government. Civil life in Lombard society was unshaken by the partially organised opposition of the nobles, peasant disturbances or the serious economic problems. These decades were characterized not only by this relative social peace but also by the lessening of cultural exchange between Milan and Vienna. As Victor L. Tapié[2] has stressed, it is clear that in the second half of the eighteenth century the political and cultural contributions that Austria drew from Lombardy dried up along with the more general decline in Italian influence in the intellectual life of the Habsburg monarchy, now increasingly influenced by men educated in Germany, Austria, Bohemia and Holland. Policies on religion, education and institutions were influenced by men such as the Dutch doctor Van Swieten or the German Joseph von Sonnenfels who was the inspiration for the great legal reforms carried out by Joseph II. Around these men was an impressive group of intellectuals and politicians which contained no Lombard or Italian figures.

The Italian presence in the upper ranks of the Viennese secretariats also diminished as the Austro-Bohemian regions became the centre for the main recruitment of the administrative staff of the monarchy. But it was not just a matter of men – Italian culture too in the later eighteenth century did not find a receptive audience in Vienna. Indeed, it can be said that after Muratori (whose ideas more than those of any other eighteenth-century intellectual appealed to many Austrian readers in their method of interpreting the problems of politics and religion), the contributions of Lombard and Italian thought meeting with any success in educated circles in Vienna and the other cultural capitals of the monarchy were few and intermittent. Pietro Verri was perhaps known more for his proposals for fiscal reform and a review of the budget and for his political battle against the tax farmers than for his ideas on political economy or for his research into the origins of pleasure and pain, although these were the subjects to which Verri devoted most time and effort. The influence of Beccaria's work was, of course, different, but here we have a book, *Dei delitti e delle pene*, which came to the attention of the whole of western culture for its clear statement of the moral and political principles of justice rather than for the originality or rigorousness of its analysis. The Lombard *illuministi* themselves failed to seek out intellectual contacts with the Habsburg monarchy. They looked elsewhere, to Paris, London, the free American colonies and to Pasquale Paoli's Corsica where political events and ideology revealed more immediately the possibility of a new social order no longer based on the despotism of princes.

It should not be forgotten that the *Caffè* group which had emerged in the early 1760s as a compact circle of intellectuals ready to present a common front in the battle for a change in the mentality and rules of social life, had, ten years later, entirely fallen apart. Some members had returned to their original places in society, others had taken administrative posts and others, such as Pietro Verri, had attempted to reconcile intellectual independence with involvement in the State's political problems. Thus, in the face of Joseph's energetic reform movement which, both on account of the measures adopted and for the way in which it developed, aroused in every case strong reactions either for or against, Lombardy failed to provide a united and organised pressure group which might interpret the voice of public opinion. The varying reactions were individual but linked by a common denominator on which men with very different outlooks were able to agree: the need to protect the areas of autonomy in Lombard society which, until the mid-century at least, had been left almost untouched by a Vienna that was far away and respectful of local self-government. But already in the first plans for fiscal reform it had been apparent that there was to be a change. The significance of this policy lay partly in its centralising content which increased during the reign of Maria Theresa, reaching a high point with Joseph who carried the process of erosion of the political powers of local bodies much further. Before this series of centralising and, in some cases at least, authoritarian reforms was fully implemented several Lombard intellectuals, those closest to the ideals of the Enlightenment, withdrew their support for Habsburg reformism, which they judged to be destructive and despotic.

Writing about the period of Joseph II, Pietro Verri said:

Joseph II understood that the system was bad, but he did not understand that a simultaneous and universal destruction of the laws and practices of a country is a remedy which is worse than the ill. He paid no attention to opinion, though opinion rules the world, and he made men feel the full weight of the unlimited power of a monarch who knows no other norm than his own will.[3]

For Verri, to abandon his belief in enlightened absolutism meant developing the idea of a society governed by civil and political liberty, the exact opposite of that 'unmasked despotism' that Joseph had revealed to Lombardy. It is likely that it was precisely this realisation of the harm being caused in Lombardy by despotic reformism that unified the constitutionalistic and democratic tendencies which, born in the climate of the Enlightenment, were handed on to the generation of democrats of the late eighteenth and early nineteenth centuries. It should be said, however, that in the 1780s these aspirations often coincided with the demands of the most conservative groups of Lombard society, since, in the face of Joseph's absolutism, they sought to protect local autonomies through the restoration and increase of the political powers of the magistratures and local bodies. Verri admitted that, to the despotism of the monarch and the Habsburg bureauracy he preferred the previous despotism of those intermediary bodies which he himself ten years before had helped to topple. Now, at the height of Josephism, civil liberty was to become for him the most important thing, to be protected in every way from the attacks of the reforming zeal of ministers and officials, which was killing the political culture and the civil spirit of Lombard society, sacrificed in the name of an abstract rationalism.

If it is generally true that in the 1770s and 1780s the Viennese rulers were occupied with many grave problems, compared to which the problems of Lombardy seemed little more than normal administration, it is equally true that in these two decades moves to change the structures of the State, the rules of trade and production, the forms of justice and education and the content and organisation of religious worship which had been started twenty years before by the Viennese ministers, continued to have an impact on ancient institutions and established customs. The clash between Habsburg reformism and the resistance of Lombard society became ever more apparent. Some historians have seen a clear break between the reform policy of Maria Theresa and that of Joseph, but as Grete Klingenstein has recently written, 'the greater part of the projects undertaken at this time by Joseph with the greatest, and indeed unscrupulous energy, had already been discussed in the time of his mother. Some had already been started, as for example the regulation of parishes, the new division of dioceses, the establishing of general seminaries for the training of priests, the suppression of religious houses and the new emphasis on cultural institutions in general.'[4] These remarks which Klingenstein applies to the monarchy in general are very relevant to the province of Lombardy. The differences between Maria Theresa's regime and that of her son are to be found elsewhere: in the stepping up of government efforts in several key areas – education, Church and State – in order to maintain control over a social situation which was becoming more difficult and to meet the need for a greater state presence in society. This need arose both from the force of events and the ideology of important sectors of public opinion. The latter was to have a complete change of attitude once it was realised that Habsburg reformism was attacking the institutions of the nobility.

Of all the reforms carried out in the 1770s and 1780s, those which had the greatest impact on Lombard society were the ones concerning the Church, not only because they followed a coherent and progressive course, but especially because in a relatively brief period of time they demanded a profound change in attitudes, ideological values and collective behaviour which shook the material and spiritual foundations of the post-Tridentine Church. The political and cultural conditions which gave rise to Joseph's ecclesiastical reform were not, however, any different from those which had prompted Maria Theresa's actions. The idea of the State as an entity capable of interpreting unaided the general interests of the people better than could a series of individual bodies (of which the Church was one) and as a dispenser of happiness to its subjects had originated in the theories of *giuspubblico* (public law). It passed into the ideas of the Enlightenment and remained unchanged in the transition from Maria Theresa to Joseph. The continuity of this idea was assured by the Imperial ministers – the outstanding figure of Kaunitz being the best example – and by a whole system of ideological influence created by the State of which school and university were the chief supports.

Thus, in the area of Catholicism, late-Jansenism and ideas derived from

Febronianism still provided a breath of idealism for those who wanted to bring religion back to a moral and doctrinal purity which they saw as corrupted by too much contact with power. In the universities the greater openness to the ideas of natural law, the history of the Church, the Gallican interpretation of ecclesiastical law and the ideas of contemporary philosophers and economists which can be seen in almost all the centres of the Empire after 1750, meant that ecclesiastical matters were increasingly discussed by ever wider social groups. This encouraged the development of administrative cadres who supported the ideological theories of Viennese anti-curialism. Thus, although the ideology was already formulated and the practical political proposals made before the ascent of Joseph to the throne, now, with the worsening of relations with the Holy See and the increasing urgency of all aspects of the church problem, ecclesiastical reform came into the foreground. Joseph's response was to speed up and intensify state intervention, and it is from this point that the reforms can properly be called 'Josephism'.

The turning-point can be dated from 1770, when the *Giunta economale* of Milan, set up earlier with the aim of overseeing the anti-curial policy, abolished local immunity (sanctuary) and established a minimum age, twenty-four, for the taking of religious vows. In this way the State was no longer confining itself to the realm of legal and economic matters, but was legislating directly in the area of ecclesiastical discipline. Thus was set in motion a vast programme of church reform, with the aim of creating a 'national' ecclesiastical structure, bound and subordinate to the Habsburg monarchy and infused with ideas deriving from Jansenism and an enlightened philosophy which owed much to Joseph. The main points of this policy were the affirmation of religious tolerance, direct state supervision over religious activity, pastoral care and the training of the clergy. Far-reaching decisions concerning religious tolerance were taken in 1781. Jews were given the right to work, to trade and to hold government appointments. On 23 October in the same year the edict of tolerance was published in all the states of the Empire.

This was a political act of the greatest importance, because it recognised the existence of religions other than Catholicism within the Empire, granted them a measure of freedom of worship and outlawed all forms of religious discrimination in public appointments. Thus the principles of tolerance, religious freedom and the plurality of faiths were codified and made the basis of coexistence between men. Even if in Lombardy the act of tolerance did not have a direct significance, since there were few adherents of non-Catholic religions, nevertheless its ideological value – the affirmation of the secular nature of State and education – was a true expression of progressive public opinion.

In the attempt to free the local churches as much as possible from the authority of the pope and Roman centralism, to organise them in secular hierarchies and to give a more important role to the bishops and parish priests, Joseph took firm measures. He cut dramatically the number of ecclesiastics, he confiscated vast properties belonging to the religious orders, he suppressed the confraternities and made the secular organisation of the Church part of a national system which stressed the educational and civil duties of the clergy and sought to reduce the material and cultural discrepancies between the different levels of the Catholic hierarchies. The efficacy of this policy can be seen by the following figures: in Lombardy in 1768 there were 290 religious houses with an income valued by the *Giunta economale* at over 5 million lire; in 1781 there were only 145, with an income of less than 2 million lire.[5] The reform of the clergy was completed between 1786 and 1787 with the suppression of the ecclesiastical courts and the requirement that future parish priests should study at the general seminary of Pavia which had been reorganised and placed under the direction of pro-Jansenist prelates.

Joseph's ecclesiastical policy reveals a commitment to the changing of the traditional conditions of social life, introducing in the place of the values of the Counter-Reformation new principles based on reason and new forms of worship freed of its superstitious or irrational heritage. But this policy outraged the religious sensibilites of the country people who feared that they were being robbed of a patrimony to which they clung more fiercely than the Viennese politicians or even the Jansenist priests had realised. It was here in the rural areas with their traditional Counter-Reformation Catholicism that the opposition to Josephism took shape, becoming more substantial after 1784 and spreading to many parts of the Empire. Opposition to Joseph's policies also arose, paradoxically, from those very religious institutions set up by the emperor, such as the general seminaries, which became centres for a clergy who, in the radical climate of the 1780s, were developing ideas opposed to the absolute State. The Jansenism of many priests who, after the French Revolution, were to move towards Jacobinism, illustrates how reformist absolutism had essentially created its own future enemies.

The crux of the conflict between Church and State was the problem of scholastic organisation, a sector where the opposition was confronted by more general questions of an economic, moral and cultural nature. Reforms in this area arrived late in Lombardy compared with other parts of the Empire. After twenty years of preparation, the reform of Pavia University was started in 1771. This Lombard university was once famous throughout Europe for its school of law but was now deep in a period of decline from which there had already been one attempt, in the 1740s, to raise it. A plan prepared by the Milanese Senate was blocked by Maria Theresa, who preferred to entrust the job of preparing a reform to her own men. It was a clear signal from Vienna to the Senatorial aristocracy, who along with other bodies were to be deprived of power. Under the direct control of Kaunitz and Firmian, the drafting of an all-embracing plan for the reorganisation of university education was completed in a few years. The secondary sector (universities and secondary schools) was completely redesigned between 1771 and 1773. In 1773 the Jesuit Order was dissolved by a papal bull.

This changed the situation for the State. New and more up-to-date aspects of the subjects of science, medicine, law, literature and history were introduced, while the professional training aimed at creating a ruling group sympathetic to the ideals of the State was redesigned to provide these professionals with the technical skills to enter the bureaucracy, law and political and economic administration. Tensions and conflicts also emerged from university reform. On one hand, the Viennese government wanted to produce zealous and capable officials, while on the other the cultural reform ended up by accustoming the educated sections of society to ideas of liberty and self-government, to attitudes which could not be expressed under the increasingly oppressive guardianship of Joseph's despotism.

Immediately after the reform of secondary education, Vienna announced that the situation in the elementary schools would be examined. Here too was the moment to translate into action those plans which had been current for more than ten years among the more advanced sections of the public, which had become convinced that popular education was essential for the improvement of the material and moral condition of the common people.[6] The first attempts to create a basic network of schools were based on the results of an important inquiry carried out by the abbé Bovara, a Lombard reformer who had already been involved with the reform of secondary education. These attempts foundered on financial difficulties and the opposition of the country clergy. Neither Maria Theresa's caution nor her empiricism were enough to launch the reform. In this area too it was necessary to continue more determinedly, confiscating the wealth of those religious orders deemed to be of no social value. A part of these funds was set aside to cover the cost of education. In 1786 the Board of Studies of Lombardy, the new government body appointed to deal with education, was able to draw up a general plan for popular education – a plan which represents one of the first attempts to set up a system to bring basic literacy to peasant society and to prepare, in the larger cities, a system of public schools at the secondary level. At the same time thought was given to the training of teachers and teacher-training colleges were set up in the capital cities of the province. The ideology and organisation of the state school system are here in embryo, and it was an inspiration, not so much in the eighteenth century since there were few states which followed the Habsburg example but in the nineteenth century for educational policy in Italy.

Closely connected with the jurisdictional reforms and with the same objective of unifying Lombard society by placing the State at its centre as the chief reference point of social relationships, the policy towards the institutions and the different social classes in the years 1770–90 was determined by Vienna. Public opinion in Lombardy and the intervention of local politicians were reduced to a marginal and subordinate role. The aims of the reforms of these two decades were very clear: to restrict the political privileges of the patrician class, to limit their ancient autonomies and to install the institutional forms of the Habsburg monarchy. In this area the innovations were far-reaching and their impact was far more radical than in the previous decades. The reason for this is that from the initial and general need to increase revenue by tinkering with the existing institutions, there had developed a new concept of the State which in the early 1770s began to be carried out through the actions of Kaunitz and Firmian. The decisive years were 1770–71 when the 'general revolution of the system' which Kaunitz spoke of in his correspondence was applied to Lombardy.[7] A scheme to rationalise the public administration which had already been imposed on other provinces of the monarchy was now introduced in Lombardy, with the abolition of the old magistratures and the carrying out of the principle of the separation of powers. The Senate became the Supreme Tribunal of Justice and was divided into three chambers, criminal, civil and *camerale*. The *Magistrato camerale* covered all the economic and financial aspects of the State, both central and peripheral. Lastly, the *Camera dei Conti* (exchequer) was to deal with the auditing of the accounts and supervision of the management of finances and property. All these operations were to be simplified by merging all the state accounts into a single whole.

In assessing the overall results of the reform we need to compare the new situation with the previous system. The most important and powerful of the local magistratures, the Senate, continued to function, and indeed had its duties increased by the extension of its jurisdiction to cases concerned with taxation. The erosion of its prestige was more insidious. The Senate was, as Ugo Petronio has said,

confined in a context of broad duties, but ones which were limited by a clear barrier, unable to step at will into other spheres, divided into several specialised sections and tied to rules which just then were being clarified and made more linear. It had lost the majesty which in its own eyes and those of public opinion it had possessed, and which was due also to the reverential fear which it inspired with its boundless and undefined powers.[8]

The *Magistrato camerale*, even if it retained the name of the financial body which had preceded it, bore the marks of the new bureaucratic State. Carlo Capra lists the distinguishing features of the bureaucratic and centralised State: the assumption of the duties which had been carried out by the tax Farm, the application of methods of work which would ensure objectivity and efficiency, the branching out of the offices of state into the provinces, and the hierarchical structure of government appointments.[9] The patricians were unable to oppose this speedily enacted design and had to conform, more or less, passively. On the other hand, they were offered attractive compensations for the renunciation of their previously undisputed exercise of political, judicial and fiscal power: they received numerous favours at the court of the governor, Archduke Ferdinand, as well as an increase in wealth as a result of the fiscal policy and the economic events of this period.

It is symptomatic that this vast operation of institutional reform, from which the patriciate emerged essentially defeated, was put into action immediately after the approval of regulations concerning the nobility, intended to break down the over-rigorous barriers which protected the ranks of the nobility from sudden intrusion by new families. In this sense the policy of liberalisation of the patriciate pursued by Maria Theresa from 1768 bore fruit, in that between that date and the end of the century the Milanese patriciate underwent a considerable change with the entry of many new families. With the setting up of the Tribunal of Heraldry, which operated according to regulations dictated by Vienna, the Habsburg State asserted its right to control the mechanisms of the social definition of the nobility. The economic rewards, the shattering of the unity of the patrician class and the drawing of some leading members of the aristocracy into the new magistratures were all factors which assisted Maria Theresa in the early 1770s in bringing to a successful conclusion the institutional reforms which had been carried out gradually, combining caution with firmness and clarity.

The picture changes when we move to the ten years of Joseph's rule when 'it was not so much the direction which changed as the rhythm and style of the interventions arousing in observers a general impression of arbitrariness and instability'.[10] Under the government of Joseph the State of Milan became to all intents and purposes a province of the Habsburg monarchy, since it lost completely and definitively its political independence which had been guaranteeed until then by those bodies which Maria Theresa had already removed from absolute noble hegemony. Even the particular forms of separate representation that Milan had enjoyed in Vienna and its form of local government were weakened while direct hierarchical dependence on the sovereign increased. In the bureaucratic transformation of relations between Vienna and Milan carried out by Joseph, both the *ministro plenipotenziario* and the governor, the archduke, who represented the monarch in Milan, were removed from power, while the Department of Italy and the chancellor in Vienna who looked after the administrative and political affairs of Lombardy were abolished. In addition, in 1786 all the bodies which were expressions of the social pre-eminence of the nobility were abolished – the Senate, the *Magistrato camerale*, the *Congregazione* of the State and all the old civic bodies. In their place a new institutional system was approved, with the *Consiglio di governo* at the top, arranged in departments which dealt with the various state functions, with the exception of those concerning law. The territory of Lombardy was divided into eight provincial areas, each one governed by an intendant who controlled the *catasto*, the finances of the communes, the magistrature and the local police. The Royal Provincial Political Intendancies, as they were called, completed the structure of the provinces of the State as it had been mapped out by Maria Theresa in 1755 and then perfected through the creation in the provinces and the communes of a network of officials to represent the central power and control local administration.

To these original tasks of chiefly financial surveillance over the communes, Joseph added tasks of a more political nature, making the intendant the essential link between central government, in the hands of the *Consiglio di governo*, and local government, entrusted to the *Congregazioni municipali*. The latter, with exclusively administrative powers and controlled by prefects (*prefetti*) nominated by the government, were to co-ordinate the administration of the communes. It was intended that all social classes would be represented at these levels of the social apparatus. The restructuring and unification of the judiciary, the issuing of a new regulation for civil procedure in 1783, which was to be the first step in a codification which remained unfinished at Joseph's death, and the suppression of the old Constitutions were stages marking, in

Capra's words, 'the end of an era characterised by the plurality of the sources of law and the latitude allowed to jurisprudential intervention'.[11]

The economic policies of Joseph's period brought to completion those attempts to introduce free trade which had met with much opposition in Maria Theresa's time. The most important of these were the abolition of some of the guilds, the extension of free trade, the reform of the *annona* system and the unification of the customs and excise – reforms, which compared to events in Tuscany, seem cautious and slow in the adopting of liberalising measures.

The year of the greatest upheaval for the *ancien régime*, 1786, was also the year when Joseph's reforms had to mark time because of opposition and criticism from the authorities, fiefs, magistratures, clergy and intellectuals of his authoritarian actions and his destructive radicalism, which they feared would kill the traditions and culture of Lombard society. Because of this and because of the difficulties in the working of the new state machine, theoretically perfect but in practice defective, it became necessary to think of adjustments and partial retreats without undermining the principles of the reforms themselves. When in 1790 Leopold succeeded his brother he found himself confronted with a broad front of hostility which his own personal dislike of autocratic leadership and the new upheavals caused all over Europe by the French Revolution helped to confirm. The boundaries of the political battle now underwent a radical change, even if the central problem underlying Joseph's reforms, which saw the modernisation of the State as the answer for a society of the *ancien régime* collapsing beneath economic and cultural pressures, did not disappear and was shortly to re-emerge in all its complexity.

NOTES AND REFERENCES

The reforms in Lombardy in the time of Maria Theresa and Joseph II cannot be separated from the history of the Habsburg monarchy. See the bibliography in: Sella, D. and Capra, C. (1984) *Il Ducato di Milano dal 1535 al 1796*. UTET, Turin. This work is also recommended as a useful general introduction to the subject. See also the proceedings of a conference on Maria Theresa held in 1980: *Economia, istituzioni, cultura in Lombardia nell'età di Maria Teresa* (1983), 3 vols. Il Mulino, Bologna. The essential work for the less well known period of Joseph II is: Cuccia, S. (1981) *La Lombardia alla fine dell'ancien régime*. La Nuova Italia, Florence.

1. Evans, R. J. W. (1979) *The Making of the Habsburg Monarchy. 1550–1700. An Interpretation*. Clarendon Press, Oxford.
2. Tapié, V. L. (1972) (Italian edition) *Monarchia e popoli del Danubio*. SEI, Turin.
3. Ottolini, A. (1921) *Pietro Verri e i suoi tempi*. Sandron, Milan.
4. Klingenstein, G. (1981) 'Riforma e crisi: la monarchia asburgica sotto Maria Teresa e Giuseppe II: Tentativo di un'interpretazione', in *La dinamica statale austriaca nel XVIII e XIX secolo*, ed. Schiera, P. Il Mulino, Bologna, p. 117.
5. Valsecchi, F. (1959) *L'Italia del Settecento. Dal 1714 al 1788*. Mondadori, Milan.

6. Balani, D, and Roggero, M. (1976) *La scuola in Italia dalla Controriforma al secolo dei lumi*. Loescher, Turin.
7. Grab, A. (1977) 'Le riforme dei tribunali civici milanesi dal 1771 al 1845', in *Archivio storico lombardo* CIII, p 296–332.
8. Petronio, U. (1972) *Il Senato di Milano. Istituzioni giuridiche ed esercizio del potere nel ducato di Milano da Carlo I a Giuseppe II*. Giuffré, Milan, p. 390.
9. Capra, C. (1981) 'Lo sviluppo delle riforme asburgiche nello stato di Milano', in *La dinamica statale austriaca*, see n. 4.
10. Ibid., p. 183.
11. Ibid., p. 185.

CHAPTER SIXTEEN

Enlightenment and reform in Naples and Sicily

In 1764 Naples was hit by a disastrous famine which left many dead. The old spectre of hunger made its dramatic reappearance in the capital of the Bourbon kingdom accompanied by an epidemic which accounted for many thousands of victims, especially among those living in the alley-ways of the poorest areas of that overcrowded city. A weak economic system was thrown suddenly into crisis by a poor harvest, an uncertain international situation, the inefficiency of the *annona*, the slowness in bringing in emergency provisions from at home and abroad. The Neapolitan famine was the last and most terrible example of death from hunger suffered by a European city. For this reason 1764 is one of the most important dates in the history of the *ancien régime* in Italy. Venturi has written: 'The tragedy was so great that the whole of the eighteenth century remembered this moment with anger and pain.'[1] It was a clear signal of the malfunctioning of a backward and shaky economy, incapable of responding adequately to such an emergency. It awakened the consciousness of those who were more aware of the ills of southern society, and with this knowledge came the will to undertake new efforts for reform in order to avoid a future repetition of such a catastrophe. It inspired the intellectuals of the Mezzogiorno to denounce with a new energy the many frauds, injustices and malfunctions great and small which ate away like a canker at the foundations of the State and further weakened an already weak civil society. Thus the famine was also a powerful political catalyst which changed the terms of the debate, bringing once again to the fore the question of the barons, the Church and the many privileges enjoyed by various authorities, classes, cities and institutions which formed a network of private interests, into which any proposal giving authority to the State or imposing political and economic leadership, however rational and fair, became enmeshed.

The famine was clear evidence of the fact, long maintained by the intellectual elite, that there was a profound gap between the Mezzogiorno and other areas of Italy and Europe, revealing the backwardness of the South. Almost all of Europe suffered in the years 1763–64 from the difficult economic situation which led to food scarcity and a large increase in prices, but it was only in the weakest areas that it was impossible to hold back the consequences and prevent the deaths of thousands. But so it was in the Mezzogiorno, where the famine was fuelled by both the unproductive economic structures and the trading network which was incapable of protecting the population, and particularly that of the towns, from the threat of hunger. The capital, with its *annona* which had to feed 330,000 mouths, was the heart of this system which was inefficient in normal times and quite useless in times of crisis, as the southern *illuminista* Galiani observed.[2] The famine and the epidemic which followed were the most deadly of all the scourges which struck the South in the eighteenth century. After it had passed it is calculated that in Naples 40,000 people had died, while in the kingdom as a whole recent estimates talk of some 200,000 deaths from hunger and disease.

The basic outlines of the social and economic relations of southern society at this time had changed little in the eighteenth century from the situation inherited from past centuries. A still dominant feudal system, with its human and juridical relations, existed in almost all the provinces of the South. And, as has already been said, this was not a matter of institutions, mentality and customs belonging to the past and now decayed and deprived of effective meaning by the emergence of newer elements – quite the reverse. Feudalism still meant the social pre-eminence of the landowning nobility, who still administered seigneurial justice, manipulated the money flow at will, exercised an absolute authority over the peasants, ran almost all of the municipal administrations and maintained close links with the church hierarchies. But things were changing. Within this framework, which looks back more than it anticipates the future, there began to take shape a non-aristocratic social class consisting of wealthy locals, enriched tenant farmers and financial middlemen who infused new dynamism into the southern provinces by bringing in new developments and modernisations. These at times coexisted with the world of the barons and at others set up a radical alternative to it. But the situation was not clear-cut and it was possible to find in the countryside *latifondisti* barons involved in agricultural improvements or demanding the abandonment of old customs in order to encourage an unfettered development of production and trade.

Moving from the country to the capital, the political centre of the kingdom and the heart of all the tensions and disturbance of the South, it becomes apparent that something had changed in the intricate balance of powers. Firstly the *ministero togato* was in decline. This professional group linked to the great tribunals of Naples, which in the days of Giannone and the Austrian viceroys was a political force of great importance and the mainstay of the government, had in the following decades lost its cohesion and was no longer the support for ideas of reform. Political life was becoming more complex, since there was developing a great divergence of ideas. Above all, the Bourbon monarchy, which even after Charles had returned to Madrid, leaving behind him a Regency led by that great figure of absolutism, Bernardo Tanucci, kept the kingdom under a form of guardianship that it was to continue to exercise even after Ferdinand IV of Bourbon came to the throne in 1767.

The Regency which governed from 1755 to 1767 sought to appear like an independent centre of power rather than as the long hand of the Spanish monarchy. Royal absolutism, of which Tanucci considered himself the interpreter and custodian, was translated in practice into a political leadership held back by the many opposing interests which hampered the ministers' ability to make decisions. Their policies were even more uncertain and fragmentary because of the intervention of the judicial and administrative bodies which represented the traditions of local self-government. If power was transferred from the latter to the state secretariats and thence to the court, it was not the result of any clear political determination or of a deliberate institutional rearrangement, but rather the consequence of spontaneous changes brought about by the new and old problems which faced the Neapolitan ruling class. For example, important stimuli to the development of groups able to make decisions and voicing a genuine policy of general interest were: the need to establish trading relations with foreign countries involved in the economy of the Mediterranean, chief of which was Russia; the urgent need to define more precise administrative and economic policies for the kingdom which derived from the developments in the battle against the Jesuits and ecclesiastical mortmains; the appearance in the political debate of questions of great social importance, such as that of the fiefs. Often it was more of an illusion than a reality, since the move of political power towards those bodies which were an expression of monarchical absolutism, to the detriment of the indigenous institutions of the Neapolitan government, did not always mean the elaboration of a coherent policy of major reforms comparable to those taking shape in Milan and Florence.

Together with the secretariats of state, the court in the mid-1770s became a centre of great power, thanks not so much to the merits of the king, Ferdinand IV, a weak figure and little interested in governing, as to the efforts of his resourceful wife, Maria Carolina, daughter of Maria Theresa. She organised a strongly pro-Habsburg faction in Naples which disputed the political leadership with the Spanish faction. Tanucci, who was the leading light of the latter and was forced to resign in 1776, had taken Bourbon reformism in Naples to its furthest possible limits but had obtained in general much less successful results than he had expected. Thus, with his fall from power, a period of hope seemed to open up in Naples fuelled both by the change of political leaders and by the return to a lively debate in which the major figures of the southern Enlightenment participated. But no important upheavals shook the barons, the jurists or the nobility of Naples, nor yet the internal arrangement of powers in the second half of the eighteenth century. In order to find sure signs of a change in southern culture and society, it is necessary to look at the relationship between the capital and the provinces.

In these years the pre-eminence of Naples declined and her central political role was put in doubt. Attention was now turned towards the problems and demands of the outlying areas of the kingdom. From Calabria, Apulia, the Molise and Sicily came political events which brought the problems of the provinces to the fore while the enlightened movement analysed mercilessly

238

the distortions and ills which were afflicting the rural areas. There was not yet outright conflict between capital and provinces but the first indications can be seen of a clash which was to reach a peak in the first half of the nineteenth century. Federalist ideas did not appear at this time, nor did suggestions for a greater provincial autonomy, but there were the first rumblings in an attack on the capital which developed further in later years and gave rise to new hopes. The awareness that the problems were preventing the realisation of the great human and productive potential of the outlying parts of the country gave men the strength to propose suitable and much needed reforms. The southern Enlightenment of Genovesi, Filangieri, Longano and Galanti cannot be understood unless it is seen in the context of this tension.

Without the contribution of the intellectual energy of the provinces and without the spread of an intense interest in the politics, history and economics of the most far-flung areas of the country, the southern Enlightenment would certainly never have acquired its desire to expose and change, or its passionate and direct civil *engagement*, which were so typical of the Italian *illuministi* and which can be seen exemplified in the intellectual development of one of Genovesi's pupils, Francesco Longano. Born in the Molise, he was educated in the capital but then in later years returned to his place of origin to try to understand and to explain to others its situation and character and the state of its agriculture, industry and trade. His main purpose was to contrast the human and natural resources of the Molise with the oppressive social situation of peasant poverty and baronial power. But the work which more than any other bears witness to the attention paid to the problems of the provinces is Giuseppe Maria Galanti's *Nuova descrizione storica e geografica delle Sicilie* which began to appear in 1787. It contains a detailed inquiry into the problems of the Mezzogiorno, revealing an extraordinary historical and geographical knowledge of the South. He refers constantly to the relationship between Naples and the provinces and makes a remarkable contribution to the debate on the feudal question – valuable because based on a detailed investigation into the practical effects of the legal, fiscal and economic powers of the barons.

Political trends, too, in proposing and seeking to carry out reforms, were turning away from the capital to the provinces and looking more at forms of landownership, the administration of the communes and the functioning of justice than at the central institutions of the State. The objectives of the reforms moved from the head, Naples, to the body of southern society where the most anachronistic survivals of the *ancien régime* were to be found, such as tithes, seigneurial rights, the feudal ownership of the communes, baronial courts and all the other customs and ways of life which seemed to hold southern society in their bonds. At the same time in the provinces of the kingdom there were emerging new classes which demanded those legal and economic changes which could give them the support and incentive for an increase in agricultural production. And in two remote regions, Calabria and Sicily, the largest programme conceived anywhere in eighteenth-century Italy for the division and sale of ecclesiastical land was being carried out.

If the provinces became more important in the political events of the last

239

decades of the eighteenth century, it was due partly to the shortages, the delays and the uncertainties which made the central government of the Bourbon State so confused. The new impulse from the provinces took on particular significance in the face of the paralysing inefficiency of the administrative bodies in the capital. In Naples no pressure group formed, nor any nucleus of power with the strength to work out a social plan. Those with the ideas, like Genovesi and, particularly, Filangieri, could find no political body which could carry them out. Those with the political power, like Tanucci until 1776, were unable to find the right road for reform, capable of withstanding the clash with one of the most difficult social situations in Italy. On the other hand, it must be recognised that even in Naples after the 1760s an institutional and economic reform was appearing, its origins in the first years of the Bourbon government and its ideals looking to the jurisdictionalist ideas deriving from Giannone. But it was a reformism which as soon as it is compared with the real problems appears all too soon to be limited and short-sighted. So much so that the great historian of the Mezzogiorno in the eighteenth century, Pasquale Villani, does not exaggerate when he says:

The limitations of the reforms were insurmountable. Bourbon government was characterised by uncertainty, hesitation and contradiction. The lack of a central direction, a unified criterion and efficient co-ordination was clear. It operated from hand to mouth, with a political empiricism which some may have described as a sense of history and practicality but which to us seems the consequence of the failure to understand the problems and of the slow development of the social forces.[3]

Against the background of a political situation which impeded the development of a mature reformism, in addition to the reasons linked to the slow development of the bourgeoisie and the failure of the rulers to understand the existing problems, there are other causes too which relate to international affairs. In Italy the reforms of this period find their highest point in places where they were carried out under Habsburg direction: they owe their success to Vienna and to the pressure coming from it. From the Bourbons, on the other hand, came no general and coherent plan, a great part of the action that was taken being confined to the area of the anti-ecclesiastical battle – an area certainly ripe for modernisation but not one involving an overall revision of juridical and economic relations or a general reform of the State. This is one, and in our opinion important, reason for the inadequacies of Neapolitan reformism. The problems of political revival, the overcoming of mercantilist ideas in economic policy and the recognition of the social value of utilitarianism, tolerance and pluralism were all matters which in Naples, as more generally in Bourbon territory, remained in the background, hidden as they were by the traditional absolutist culture.

There was a profound gulf between the ideas of the enlightened intellectuals who were re-elaborating the great themes of Montesquieu, Rousseau and Helvétius, on the one hand, and the culture of the politicians on the other. Tanucci, the undisputed leader of Bourbon absolutism, seemed at times like a man outside his age, lacking as he did the sensitivity and the intellectual

240

powers to direct the forces of reform which were present in southern society.[4] His theoretical knowledge stopped at the *giuspubblicismo* and ideas on natural law dating from the 1730s and 1740s. His actions did not look towards the broader horizons of enlightened despotism, he was deaf to the ferment of new ideas and only rarely added a cultural dimension to his style of government. But Tanucci was not oblivious to the ills which tormented the country. One only has to read his correspondence to see his awareness of the poverty of a people oppressed by the corruption of public employees, the ignorance of the patricians, the arrogance of the barons and the many inefficiencies of the administration. It was rather that he lacked the necessary cultural stature needed to direct his actions to those objectives that he saw so clearly. The fact that Tanucci was untouched by, if not hostile to, the ideas of the Enlightenment and opposed to physiocracy, though briefly coming near to ideas of free trade during the famine, is not in itself a reason which can explain the delays and empiricism of his work as a reformer. It was limited more by his old-fashioned anti-curialism than by his failure to assimilate the more advanced ideas of European thought. Tanucci was not the *grand commis* of enlightened absolutism, firstly because he lacked the intellectual understanding and secondly because there was no clear way to reform out of the complex and paralysing mess of Neapolitan political life.

The relationship between the intellectuals and political power, too, tended to one or other of these two poles. On the one hand, the absence of a central power capable of imposing from above those reforms thought by many to be indispensable for curing the ills of the Mezzogiorno, and on the other the historic weakness of civil society meant that the great and original energies of the intellectuals, in evidence from the time of Genovesi until the dramatic experiment of the Parthenopean Republic in 1799, remained unutilised. In Naples the *illuministi* did not take state office, nor did they organise an independent pressure group to turn the rulers' policies in the direction of reform. Attempts to set up journals came late and were lacking in vigour. Not a single academy was set up that was a centre for the discussion of agriculture, economics or politics. Venturi is quite correct when he says: 'In Naples the intellectuals were more independent, lively, active and also more detached and remote from power.'[5] But it is also true that they lacked a basis in civil society or, if there was such a basis, it was so frail that it could not support the building of a bridge between government and the ideas of the intellectuals. Their isolation can be measured not only by their relationship to power, but also by the social utility of their theories. It cannot be denied that many of the ideas to emerge from the southern Enlightenment failed to find someone who could take them up and use them as a lever for political reform. They did not find him in Tanucci, for the reasons already mentioned, and nor did they find him in Domenico Caracciolo, although he was a man brought up with enlightened ideas who arrived in Naples too late to be able to continue the courageous reforms which he had introduced in Sicily between 1782 and 1786, and nor did they find him in Luigi Medici, the last hope of enlightened absolutism in Naples.

Nevertheless, the southern Enlightenment of Genovesi, Galiani, Longano, Serrao, the Grimaldi brothers and the following generation of Filangieri, Pagano, Russo and Delfico encouraged an atmosphere of reform inspired by European influences and raised new questions without ever succumbing to the temptation of Utopianism or a return to conservative paradoxes. From Genovesi's ideas on education and cultural organisation, the path of the Enlightenment moved to an analysis of the feudal question which in the 1780s was to become the central point of the attack and the innovatory proposals. In Naples the intellectuals confronted the crisis of the *ancien régime* with a greater awareness than in any other Italian city. They were to some extent prepared to find new institutional formulae which they were to use in the last decade of the eighteenth century in order to lay the juridical foundations of the social pact.

The different phases of the Enlightenment in Naples also show unusual features. Firstly it seemed to arrive early, as early as the mid-1750s. Since Venturi's studies, Genovesi's conversion from the study of theology to that of economics is usually taken as symbolic of a general turn in ways of thinking, and it is decisive too because of the quality of Genovesi's teaching in his university courses on political economy. Secondly, the southern Enlightenment reached its high point in the 1780s when in the rest of the country the *philosophes* were silent or uninvolved in politics and economics. One only has to think of Filangieri and his *Scienza della legislazione*, one of the most important Italian contributions to the European Enlightenment, which began to appear in 1780; or of Galanti for his already mentioned work on the southern kingdom; or Pagano's *Saggi politici* which first appeared in 1783. In addition, between 1780 and 1789 the most important works of Domenico Grimaldi, Delfico and Palmieri were published.

Too little is known as yet of the history of Freemasonry in the South to be able to answer the many questions raised. It is hard to know how much weight Freemasonry had in the civil life of the Mezzogiorno. It is easier to identify some general characteristics which give some overall indications. It should be said first of all that Freemasonry made possible the forging of a profound intellectual bond between educated men, sensitive to the need for a political and moral regeneration, regardless of their social or professional position. Its arcane world provided fertile ground, in the capital and perhaps even more in the provinces, for the spread of cosmopolitanism, of a secular and scientific form of religion of deistic origin and of the eudemonic and reforming tendencies which represent the general ideal of eighteenth-century Europe. Greatly disliked by Tanucci, who considered it, with reason, the heart of Habsburg opposition to his government and who was eventually to bring about his own downfall by his attempts to wipe it out, Neapolitan Freemasonry then underwent a profound change: 'the old traditional English Freemasonry, to which Filangieri seems to have remained mainly faithful, was undermined from within by the arrival of more recent tendencies originating in France and Germany and deriving from the mystics of Lyons and the enlightened thinkers of Bavaria'.[6] Thus it became the vehicle for more radical

242

ideas which pointed to the final break of the southern intellectuals with enlightened absolutism and opened the ways to the Jacobinism of the 1790s even if, throughout the 1780s, Freemasonry did not set itself against the monarchy but continued to believe in the possibility of directing the political system towards reformist solutions.

As has been said, there was no long series of coherent reforms in Naples, but rather a number of individual moves, often unconnected with one another, proposals which were not carried out and wishful and sporadic attempts at legislative change. These made up a partial reformism which had no effect on the most serious problems of southern society. During Tanucci's time regalistic thinking was revived by the anti-Jesuit struggle. In Naples anti-Jesuitism had distant precedents in the polemics of the early eighteenth century launched by Gravina, Doria and Giannone against probabilistic morality and the cultural hegemony of the Society of Jesus. Against this background there emerged a new generation of regalist and pro-Jansenist ecclesiastics who collaborated with Tanucci and the anti-curial ministers of the neo-jurisdictionalist reforms of the 1760s and 1770s.[7]

The event which had the greatest impact was the decree dissolving the Jesuit order, issued shortly after the similar edict by Charles III in Spain. Naples joined the rest of Bourbon Europe in banishing the Society of Jesus against whom for some time fierce attacks had been launched by the Jansenists, regalists and even, though for different reasons, the *illuministi*. The expulsion of the Jesuits created considerable problems for the Neapolitan rulers while at the same time offering a chance to try out plans for reform. New schools had to be set up in the place of those run by the Jesuits, and 661 teachers had to be replaced. It was also necessary to replace the curriculum which had existed until then in the Jesuit colleges and was defined by the *Ratio studiorum*. There was finally the problem of how best to use the properties owned by the Society in the Kingdom of Naples. Genovesi, who proposed a plan for the schools, seized the opportunity and came up with a general reform for advanced education which aimed both to create a co-ordinated system of schools from elementary to university and to alter the old cultural bias, introducing new technical and scientific disciplines and insisting that all teaching should be in the Italian language. His proposals went unheeded and the government chose a plan of reform which was little different from the preceding Jesuit model, or, if anything, inferior to it, since the experience and teaching abilities of the new teachers were far less than those of the Jesuits.

Only ten years later, after the fall of Tanucci, the government resurrected Genovesi's plan and opened up new disciplines in the College of San Salvatore in Naples. The textbooks which were to replace the Jesuit catechisms appeared at this time, published by the Royal Press. Thus there appeared in the schools texts such as the Port Royal *Grammar*, Genovesi's *Logica* and Galileo's *Dialoghi*, while the teaching of the catechism was retained, based on a cultural compromise which tried to protect traditional Roman theology without renouncing the Gallican viewpoint. The Neapolitan government followed a policy in the area of education which was quite lacking in a general framework of reference, being more concerned with getting the schools, in this new situation, to work. After 1777, with the definitive confiscation of the property of the Society and the taking over of the College of San Salvatore, the circumstances, including financial, were more favourable for the reconsideration of a reform of education and Genovesi's campaign for popular education and a new cultural basis in schools centred round history, economics and science was revived.

Particular attention was paid to Naples University which, in the previous decades, had been through a bad period, in order to restore it to its former pre-eminence. A new site was found, modern subjects were introduced, an academy of painting, sculpture and architecture was opened and a botanical garden and chemistry laboratory were set up. At the same time there was an attempt to rationalise secondary education, merging the provincial schools with the College of San Salvatore in Naples which had become the centre for post-Jesuit scholastic learning. The communes were instructed to open elementary schools, teaching the rudiments of the Italian language, Latin and the catechism. These first tentative steps towards a state school system made use of teachers who were almost all ecclesiastics, but who had to follow the educational plans of the government. The fight to dissolve the Jesuits united all the various sectors of Neapolitan anti-curialism, including agnostics like Galiani and Caracciolo, reformist Catholics influenced by Jansenism or the ideas of Giannone, anti-curial regalists, like Tanucci himself and those closest to him who were basically uninvolved in theological and pastoral matters and very respectful of the Catholic tradition, and lastly enlightened reformers, as Filangieri was to be, whose religious values were influenced by deism.

In Sicily the Jesuits owned more land than on the mainland and it included the best cultivated and most profitable areas of the island. With a courageous social policy inspired by Genovesi, who had fought for a division of ecclesiastical land which would favour the peasants, Tanucci divided up the Jesuit properties and put them up for auction, making sure that a portion of them went to the peasants. It was an impressive operation for the time, if one realises that some 45,000 ha of agricultural land were transferred, chiefly by emphyteusis. More than 3,000 poor peasants received portions of land. In the long term, however, the results were modest, both because the island's administration obstructed the most important elements of the reform and because many peasants lacked the financial support necessary to develop the land and suffered from the agricultural crisis of 1768–70. With Tanucci's successor, the Marquis della Sambuca, there was a return to a pro-baronial position and many properties reverted to the State and thence to the great landowners.

Apart from the contradictory results of this redistribution of the Jesuit mortmains, Neapolitan regalism made no important political conquests. In addition to the provisions on mortmain, laws were recommended for reducing the number of religious houses and abolishing ecclesiastical prisons, ending feudal homage to Rome (the *Chinea*) and closing down the Sicilian Inquisition. No reform that might change the social content of Catholism from within was carried out in Naples. Thus there was no leap forward, as in Milan under Joseph or in Florence with the Jansenist reforms of the Tuscan Church resulting from the jurisdictionalist tradition. Hence ecclesiastical mortmain remained very widespread.

Similar considerations apply when evaluating Tanucci's economic and social policies. The brief but traumatic period of the famine is very revealing in an analysis of his innovations and the many barriers imposed by a system which resisted any kind of change, however small. During this period of famine, Tanucci identified clearly the enemies of Naples. They were the middlemen of the capital, the tribunals and the *Piazze* and the *Annona*, a clumsy administrative body which did not show a return in terms of efficiency on the high cost of running it. Tanucci did not hesitate to denounce this state of affairs either in public or in private. However, the *Annona* was one of the most influential centres of power in the capital. It influenced the food market, controlled the city and enjoyed an economic power which gave much scope for speculative activities. It was understandable that the nobility *di piazza*, the noble families who controlled the city administration from which they derived prestige and wealth, did all in its power to bring about the failure of Tanucci's proposals, which often lacked conviction, to reform the whole provisioning system in Naples. A compromise was reached that did not undermine the existing system, confining itself merely to an undertaking to eliminate corruption and exercise state control. For the rest, Tanucci in 1764 followed the old methods of economic policy: forced contributions of grain necessary for the capital and the purchase of grain on the European market. These weak and tardy measures were only partially effective in the short term and offered no prospects for the reorganisation of the internal and international market. In all the eighteenth century no political stimulus to a renewal of the economic and commercial system was forthcoming from Naples. If there were advances, they were due only to the spontaneous developments of new social forces and were in no way supported by a forward-looking political leadership.

To deal with the Neapolitan nobility's monopoly of administrative posts, Tanucci tried another tack. In 1765 he reformed the Communal Council, adding to the fifteen noble decurions, fifteen belonging to the *ceto civile* (merchants, doctors, lawyers and judges) and fifteen of the 'third estate of the people', or the artisans and small tradesmen. In the same way he tried to oppose the authority of the State to the centripetal pressures of the feudal nobility. In this case too he looked back to the policy pursued by Charles of Bourbon in the first years of his reign, without following any organised plan. Rather than undermine feudal institutions, Tanucci wanted to reduce the amount of juridical independence enjoyed by the barons and restrict their fiscal exemptions. The measures taken were limited and sporadic and quite inadequate to deal with the barons' power, so well rooted in southern society and in no way weakened by Tanucci's policies.

The anti-baronial struggle in Sicily during the viceroyship of Caracciolo

(1781–85) was quite another matter.[8] The island had gone through a difficult ten years, the peak of the crisis being marked by the revolt in Palermo of 1773 and the overthrow of the viceroy, Fogliani. Caracciolo, member of a powerful aristocratic family, arrived in Sicily having already had an active diplomatic career which had taken him abroad for over thirty years, to Paris in 1753, Turin in 1754, London from 1764 and then again to Paris in 1771 where his enlightened ideas developed as the result of contact with the great Parisian intellectuals. The situation he met in Sicily was very different and such a man, accustomed to the courts and salons of the capitals of Europe, could not fail to find it backward, bigoted, obscurantist and violent. There were only two possibilities open to him: either to come to terms with the situation in Sicily and reach a compromise between the arrogance of a nobility used to unimpeded command and the desire of the government to set up elementary rules for the working of the public institutions or, alternatively, to attack head-on the baronial interests that dominated the island. Temperament and education led him to choose the second course and for the first time in its history the Sicilian baronage found itself facing a fierce opponent brought up on reformist and enlightened ideals, who did his utmost to force the barons to bow to the laws of the State, to pay taxes and to recognise the authority of the local administrations.

Few and weak were the means of enforcement at Caracciolo's disposal. Public opinion did not favour reform, the *ministero togato* was bound to the barons and thus unable to range itself on the side of the viceroy, there was no autonomous institutional structure and, finally, the clergy was linked socially with the nobility. Caracciolo could count on very few trusted assistants, very few coercive means and very little support in either Sicily or Naples. He was armed with little more than his lucid, if often schematic, vision of Sicilian society and the authority of his political position. The lack of support from Naples was clearly demonstrated in 1783 after the terrible earthquake that destroyed among others the cities of Reggio Calabria and Messina. Energetic measures were taken in Calabria to get rid of the most oppressive forms of feudalism and to set up small peasant properties. The area of jurisdiction of the *Cassa Sacra*, an organisation set up to assist reconstruction after the earthquake and given wide powers of intervention in matters of agricultural ownership, feudal oppression and ecclesiastical benefices, was limited only to Calabria and not extended to Sicily. An opportunity was thus lost to link up the groups and ideas of reform of the island and the mainland while the separateness of the island from the problems of southern society was underlined.

Caracciolo's government had few concrete results to show for all the efforts and ideas which inspired them. In the ecclesiastical field he abolished the Holy Office in 1782, an action which sent ripples all round Europe because it was abolishing the cruellest and most tyrannical institution of the Church. In reality it was more a symbolic act than anything else since latterly the activity of the tribunal had become reduced to dealing with a few cases of witchcraft. The other measures taken, in collaboration with a few enlightened

Sicilian prelates and intellectuals, such as Rosario Gregoria and Giovanni Agostino de' Cosmi, followed a southern jurisdictionalist line. In the area of social policy, Caracciolo instituted the freedom of work for the peasants, in an attempt to emancipate them from their age-old vassalage to the great feudal lords. He also strengthened the local councils in order to restrict feudal jurisdictions and continued the policy of confiscating church lands, particularly those belonging formerly to the Jesuits, of abolishing rights to use and lease out common land, in order to create a small and middle-sized landowning peasantry. There was little or nothing that he could do to bring Sicily's feudalism under the authority of public law. He failed, for example, to get the Sicilian *Parlamento* (the ancient institution representing the Sicilian aristocracy) to approve a *catasto* modelled on those of Piedmont and Tuscany and on which Caracciolo had pinned many of his hopes for reform, being convinced that in a socially backward situation where, however, there were important economic interests directed at the European markets in cereal and agricultural products, it was useless to follow a consistently physiocratic line which would benefit no one but the barons. What was needed was policies such as those followed in France by Necker in order to cure the economic ills of the State and get rid of fiscal immunities.

From the ethical and political point of view, Caracciolo's contribution lay in his questioning the whole system of feudalism in the island. He pointed out the objective and sometimes also a method of attacking the most tenacious enemy of modernisation and social development. When in 1786 he was called to Naples to govern the kingdom, not only his energy, but also that of absolutist reformism, were almost spent. A new, more dramatic and vital period of political struggle had already begun in the Mezzogiorno, as in the rest of Italy and Europe.

NOTES AND REFERENCES

There are many excellent recent studies of the economic and social history of southern Italy, starting with: Villani, P. (1973) *Mezzogiorno tra riforme e rivoluzioni*. Laterza, Bari. A Marxist point of view is given in: Villari, R. (1978) *Ribelli e riformatori*. Editori Riuniti, Rome. Most recent are: Placanica, A. (1978) *Alle origini dell'egemonia borghese in Calabria. La privatizzazione delle terre ecclesiastiche (1784–1815)*. Società editrice meridionale, Naples; Macry, P. (1974) *Mercato e società nel Regno di Napoli. Commercio del grano e politica economica nel Settecento*. Guida, Naples; Renda, F. (1974) *Baroni e riformatori in Sicilia sotto il ministro Caracciolo*. La Libra, Messina. See also Venturi, F. (1973) 1764: Napoli nell'anno della fame, in *Rivista storica italiana* II, pp. 394 ff. On Sicily see: Giarrizzo, G. (1978) in *Storia della Sicilia*, vol. VI, ed. Romeo, R. Società editrice per la storia di Napoli, del Mezzogiorno continentale e della Sicilia, Naples.

1. Venturi, F. '1764: Napoli nell' anno della fame', in *Rivista storica italiana* II, p. 394.

2. See Galiani's letters in: Galiani, F. (1975) *Opere*, eds Diaz, F. and Guerci, L. Ricciardi, Milan–Naples.
3. Villani, P. *Mezzogiorno*, op. cit., p. 285.
4. For Tanucci see: Mincuzzi, R. (1967) *Bernardo Tanucci ministro di Ferdinando di Borbone. 1759–1776*. Dedalo, Bari.
5. Venturi, F. 1764: op. cit., p. 451.
6. *Illuministi italiani* (1962) vol. V. Ricciardi, Milan–Naples.
7. On the Church see De Maio, R. (1972) *Società e vita religiosa a Napoli nell'età moderna*. Edizioni Scientifiche italiane; Chiosi, E. (ed.) (1981) *Andrea Serrao. Apologia e crisi del regalismo nel Settecento napoletano*. Jovene, Naples.
8. See the section on Caracciolo by Giarrizzo, G. (1965), in *Illuministi italiani*, vol. VII. Ricciardi, Milan–Naples.

The political and economic debates of the period of the Enlightenment and reform (Giuseppe Ricuperati)

CHAPTER SEVENTEEN

The Enlightenment in Naples. The school of Bartolomeo Intieri: Ferdinando Galiani (1728–87) and Antonio Genovesi (1712–69)

In 1751, in Naples, *Della moneta* was published anonymously. The author, Ferdinando Galiani, was a young man of little over twenty-one who had preferred not to sign his work, given its daring nature, for fear of stirring up controversy which might be permanently compromising. Comparing this work with the passages on finance written by Muratori in *Della pubblica felicità* (which followed Broggia), it is at once apparent that the debate begun by Scipione Maffei in the *Impiego del denaro* had come a long way, to have produced this work, a work so entirely of the Enlightenment. Ferdinando Galiani's roots were firmly planted in that southern culture which had been rekindled by the work of Locke and Newton. One of Galiani's first intellectual undertakings had been the translation of Locke's essays on financial problems, which he dropped when he heard that in Florence another version was being produced, edited by Francesco Pagnini and Angelo Tavanti.[1] Equally important were the relations between Galiani and Bartolomeo Intieri, who was one of the most significant figures in the early Neapolitan Enlightenment.[2]

Galiani's work represents a contribution to the discussion on money which swept Italy and Europe from the mid-1740s. Besides Broggia's treatise *Dei tributi* (1743) and Troiano Spinelli's *Riflessioni politiche sopra alcuni punti della scienza della moneta* (1749–50), which Galiani knew, there was also the collection *De monetis Italiae* published in Milan between 1750 and 1752 by Filippo Argelati, the well-known collaborator of Ludovico Antonio Muratori. Galiani starts out by listing his sources in the preface – Locke, Melon, Broggia and Troiano Spinelli. He refers to Muratori's *Della pubblica felicità*, but only to say that the section on money was very limited. Disagreeing with Locke, Melon, Broggia and even Montesquieu, who had all maintained the representative and symbolic value of money, Galiani states that value 'is an idea of proportion between the possession of one thing and that of another, in one man's opinion'. Thus it is a variable depending on utility and rarity. In defining the first, Galiani embarks on one of the recurring themes of the European Enlightenment, pleasure and pain. Utility is for him the capacity a thing has 'to procure our happiness'. Man is made up of passions and their satisfaction is pleasure. The acquisition of pleasure is happiness. The need to assert oneself and the desire to distinguish oneself from others are among the most important passions of man: 'such are rank, titles, honours, ennoblement, command'. A populationist, as were almost all the great eighteenth-century economists, Galiani seems, at least partly, to go beyond mercantilistic theories. He is convinced that wealth is born of the relationship between the productivity of the land and man. Though the exchange of merchandise for money may on the one hand impoverish a country, on the other it enriches it with the goods it did not have. More serious is the loss of men. When they leave a place, 'the buildings collapse and the land returns to the wild'. A state gets rich when it manages to attract foreigners prepared to settle permanently. It becomes poor when it is forced to allow its wealth to flow towards a foreign country.

Book II deals with the value of money and the differences between gold, silver and copper. Galiani discusses *alzamento*, the operation carried out by a state when it introduces a new coinage reducing the amount of silver and gold that was present in the old coins and thereby giving it a value greater than that represented by the precious metal contained in it. Galiani is critical of the prejudices surrounding this procedure, demonstrating that in fact the prince's income does not increase, nor do his subjects become richer. In reality the *alzamento* benefits the State in that the state debt is reduced, as happens for example when pensions are paid out which in fact are worth less. The person receiving the usual sum of money does not immediately realise its loss of value, because he can still buy the same things. It is rather on the international trading scene that the difference is apparent and a new relationship has to be created with this 'lighter' money. The price of foreign goods rises and thus slowly the situation is reflected in the buying power of the new money. Galiani asserts that not only is the *alzamento* not harmful, but that it should not be judged in moral terms. It is a policy, almost always dictated by necessity, which can be useful for the country's economy. Even the secondary effect of the increased price of home and foreign goods is not in itself bad. This can be worth pursuing for three reasons: to lower the public debt, reduce expenses and pay the debts contracted by the State.

Book III deals with the flow of money. Using Locke and Petty, Galiani tries to calculate the amount of money in the Kingdom of Naples, arriving at a figure of a little under 18 million ducats or about an eighth of the total value of the goods consumed within the State. Shortage of money is the real mother of usury but this is not remedied by simply increasing the money supply. Galiani suggests some methods of avoiding stagnation in the flow of money: the encouragement of small and frequent payments, the development of fairs and markets, the strengthening of verbal contracts and the rationalisation of taxes. Thus for Galiani the role of the sovereign is of fundamental importance, his function being as 'a principal motive force to the stabilising of the flow of money'. This raises what may be called the debate of the century – the meaning of luxury.[3]

Here too Galiani shows his open-mindedness, sweeping away all the moralising that clung to the subject. Nevertheless, although he understands with great clarity the origin of luxury, the result of improvements in manufacturing which make it possible to create good using less labour and time, and hence move the displaced workers to less necessary activities, Galiani starts from a different viewpoint from that of an apologist such as Melon. For the Neapolitan, luxury is the effect, not the cause, of good government and can also sow the seeds of decadence. But the prince can, at least in part, remedy this by favouring national goods rather than foreign ones. Here Galiani discusses one of the mercantilistic principles that Muratori had established in his *Della pubblica felicità*, that it is the duty of the State and the prince to prevent the flow of money out of the country, while attracting as much of it as possible from outside. Galiani criticises this principle which equates wealth with money, maintaining that the true basis of wealth is population. The task of good government should be to ensure enough food rather than gold.

In Book IV Galiani examines the role of the banks and trading companies in the economy of Europe. As a populationist, he rejects an obsession with trade, saying that it is pointless to complain that the volume of Neapolitan trade is much smaller than that of other countries, including Holland which was so much smaller in area than the Kingdom of Naples. In Galiani's opinion the correct means to commercial development still lay, for the Mezzogiorno at least, in the strengthening of agriculture. Book V deals with usury, a theme which less than ten years before, in the wake of Scipione Maffei's book, had exercised intellectuals and theologists. Resuming the discussion, Galiani refers to Benedict XIV's Bull which had been reinterpreted as a justification for the charging of interest in cases of direct damage or loss. It accepts in substance that interest is the necessary price for the risk taken. In this case too the principle of the independence of politics from morality and religion applies. The task of the State is not so much to trust in the fear of eternal damnation as to prevent the usurers lending money with *grossa usura* (exorbitant interest).

Later events in Galiani's life were to confirm much that emerged from *Della moneta*. An acute intelligence and ruthless realism, which were to earn him the nickname 'Machiavellino', also made him a marked sceptic and a man who remained outside the more advanced aspects of the Enlightenment. Sent by Tanucci to Paris, he was to be for a decade the interpreter of Neapolitan policy at the Bourbon court. At the same time he became established as one of the major figures in Parisian intellectual life, in the salons where he met men like d'Holbach, Diderot and Helvétius.[4] He found the return to Naples in 1769 traumatic and there is more than a hint of this in his correspondence.[5] But it was at precisely this moment that he emerged as one of the figures of intellectual Europe. The new *Dialogues sur le commerce des bleds*, left in Paris to Diderot and published in 1770, became the essential text of the antiphysiocrat camp. Once again, Galiani, who had seen from his privileged position in Paris the effects of the freeing of the grain trade, was able to counter physiocratic dogma with his flexible realism. In the following decades, Galiani was to be wholly occupied as minister for foreign affairs, performing his task with his accustomed intelligence as can be seen from his proposal for an international law, *De'doveri de' principi neutrali*. But nevertheless the impression remains that this former active member of d'Holbach's *côterie* referred to by Galiani as the *boulangerie* was, despite his lively and intelligent mind, becoming increasingly remote from the values of the Enlightenment, returning to erudite or purely literary themes, seeing culture as an escape, a temptation which had in any case always been present in him since the mocking collection of pieces in honour of the executioner Iannaccone which had appeared a year before *Della moneta*.

The intellectual itinerary of Antonio Genovesi was rather different and of greater significance. This young man from the provinces arrived in Naples in the mid-1740s full of hopes, ambitions and a desire to succeed. Coming from a modest family in the province of Salerno, in order to receive an education Genovesi had to enter the Church, for which he showed little disposition. After a few years, under the protection of Celestino Galiani, the possibility of a university career presented itself. For a long time he had dreamed of becoming the chief theologian of the new national State. The road that was to lead him from metaphysics to economics was a tortuous one. Recent studies have stressed the influence on him in the early years of the members of the *Accademia degli Oziosi*, particularly Vico and Doria. Thus Genovesi was more closely linked to the *veteres* than the *moderni*. But his view of metaphysics was somewhat unusual, drawing on the different currents of religious rationalism and on authors like Jean Leclerc, Samuel Clarke, Locke and Muratori.

The edition of the *Elementa metaphysicae* of 1743 stirred up the first opposition. Having obtained the approval of the royal proof-reader, his friend and a teacher of experimental physics, Giuseppe Orlandi, Genovesi had proceeded to bring out his book without bothering about ecclesiastical authorisation. Archbishop Spinelli, who had great influence at court, having been the mediator between the Curia and the Bourbons, intervened, telling Charles III that Genovesi's book was 'dangerous'. The following year was a very fruitful one for the young and ambitious intellectual, with the publication of both the *Elementorum artis logico-criticae libri quinque* and Musschembroek's *Elementa physicae* in collaboration with Orlandi. In addition he had been appointed to the chair in ethics. A few years later, in 1748, Genovesi decided to compete for the vacant chair of theology. Despite support from Galiani, he was immediately opposed by the local Curia and the nuncio. The Church clearly feared this theologian suspected not only of heterodoxy but particularly of jurisdictionalism. Genovesi was unsuccessful. Even if the Jesuit theologian appointed by the court to examine Genovesi's works had not found any unorthodox opinions, nevertheless the chair was awarded to someone who had not figured among the contestants. In addition, Genovesi was prohibited from teaching theology, although he retained permission to print his works.

These events increased his disgust with theological intrigue and his horror of a discipline so 'turbulent and bloody'. His meeting with Bartolomeo Intieri was decisive, bringing about a clear change of direction in Genovesi's thought. In this circle, in which he was to be a leading figure, he was forced to contend with profoundly differing interests: 'the majority of the discussions in the small but brilliant group at Sig. Intieri's was on the progress of human reason, the arts, trade, state economy, mechanics and physics, since Sig. Intieri was an enemy both of useless abstractions and of the pedantic study of words from which men can derive no real benefit'.[6] From this environment was born the plan to create a chair 'of trade and mechanics, to be taught in the Italian language' at the University of Naples. It soon became clear that Intieri had Genovesi in mind for this post. Before his death he sent a petition to Charles III who approved the plan. Intieri endowed the chair with a salary of 300 ducats a year and the use of his library.[7] The first incumbent was to be Genovesi, after which the chair would be appointed by competition. Only laymen and secular clergy would be able to hold it. Intieri's correspondence reveals clearly the passion which the old Florentine brought to this plan and the hopes that he had of the young intellectual who was in the process of evolving from a metaphysician to an economist.

It is significant that the first work which Genovesi wrote in 1753, *Discorso sopra il vero fine delle arti e delle scienze* was an introduction to Ubaldo Montelatici's *Ragionamento sopra i mezzi più necessari per far rifiorire l'agricoltura*. The latter had first appeared in 1752. Montelatici, after a long career as a teacher in the monasteries of his order, had returned to Florence in 1747 and enthusiastically devoted himself to agriculture. The *Ragionamento* was to be the inspiration for the *Accademia dei Georgofili* which was founded in 1753. Intieri's links with Florence explain this development in Naples. Genovesi's introduction added a great deal to the Tuscan agronomist's proposals. It has indeed been seen as a manifesto of the southern Enlightenment and a work, making allowances for scale, comparable to d'Alembert's preface to the *Encyclopédie*, with which it has much in common – the references to Bacon, the criticism of abstract scholarship with the exaltation of the technical and political value of culture and the constant appeal to reason and experience. His programme for the general good of the State was one with his theoretical premisses: the need to increase the active population, to prevent the clergy from living idle lives, to improve the standard of living and working conditions of those doing manual jobs, to develop among young people an awareness of economics and technology, to encourage the setting up of an agrarian academy whose branches would reach out to the provinces introducing and spreading new ideas and to improve customs through more rational forms of education.

This book also saw the beginning of those ideas on trade which he was to develop in the following decades in his university teaching. Like the others of Intieri's group, Genovesi looked not only to Muratori and Montesquieu, but also to Uztariz and Ulloa, whom he read in French translation. These last two were writers who had revived mercantilism and had provided Philip V of Spain with a broad programme of reform. François Véron de Forbonnais had translated Uztariz, dedicating the work to Machault, the controller of finances who had prepared a reform of taxation. Ulloa had been introduced to the French by Plumard de Dangeul, a collaborator with Forbonnais, and himself author of *Remarques sur les avantages et les désavantages de la France et de la Grande-Bretagne par rapport au commerce et aux autres sources de la puissance des états*. If the Spanish and French economists were describing a situation not unlike that in the Mezzogiorno, Genovesi was also considerably influenced by the ideas of English economists whom again he read in French translation. Thus he encountered Joshua Gee's *Considérations sur le commerce et la navigation de la Grande Bretagne* (Geneva, 1750) and the essays of David Hume. His interest and reading in this field led him to translate into Italian the *Essai sur l'état du commerce d'Angleterre*, written by John Cary but with considerable additions by Butel-Dumont and, probably, Vincent de Gournay.

As well as this work, published in Naples in 1756 under the title of *Storia del commercio della Gran Bretagna*, it was Genovesi's lectures given up to 1754 which provided the core of his book *Delle lezioni di commercio o sia di economia civile*, published in two volumes in 1765 and 1767. It is difficult to summarise this work which from a neo-mercantilistic inspiration moves ever more decisively towards free trade. Particularly striking, along with the multitude of references to European writers, including Mandeville, Hume, Rousseau and Morelly, is its optimism. In dealing with what can be seen as the crux of the eighteenth-century economic debate, the problem of luxury and its relationship with civil life, Genovesi favours moderate luxury. Although not agreeing entirely with Mandeville's view that private vices can be public virtues, Genovesi recognises that a degree of luxury can be not only useful but also necessary in society. In analysing luxury, he proposes two possible points of view – ethical and political. According to the first, the fundamental question is: are men happier for possessing it? In the second case it is: will the State increase in size and wealth because of it? He provides possible answers to both points of view. In the ethical field he is firmly against any egalitarian Utopia. He attacks particularly Rousseau and Morelly, creators of myths rather than men capable of a concrete social and economic analysis of reality. Equality is not something natural which can be aroused in society just because it is desirable. Nevertheless, it is worth while to attempt to make less unjust and destructive those inequalities that history has wrought in civil society. Here Genovesi's move towards reformism becomes apparent.

Returing to the theme of the relationship between barbarism and civilisation, Genovesi asserts that it is easier to civilise a barbarous society than to restore a corrupt and degenerate civilisation. He passionately disputes Rousseau's idea that savages are better than civilised men and demolishes the myths about the greater physical and moral integrity of those closest to nature. Although opposed to an egalitarian Utopia, he was, however, convinced that the State should attempt to correct the most glaring inequalities corrective to absolutism and re-establishes a link with Coyer's reformism and the idea of a *noblesse commerçante*. The aristocracy would still have a place if it could justify its existence by making itself useful in the areas of political administration, the army or the economy.

Genovesi was attacking social parasitism from the standpoint of an activist ethic and the view that the basic duty of man is to work for himself and for the public good. He conceived a society based on a numerous and active population, with intensive agriculture organised in such a way as to provide not only food for the population, but also the raw materials for trade and industry. Such a society would not have large disparities of wealth but a middle level of well-being, related to a fair valuation of work. Most importantly, he imagined a society without irrational privileges such as those of a feudal, exploitative and idle nobility. Here we see Genovesi's attitude to the fief, which he opposed because it usurped the jurisdiction of the State but which he accepted as a marketable property, a form of ownership, held back by archaic institutions such as *fidecommesso* and the right of primogeniture.

Genovesi's optimism can also be seen in his treatment of the subject of luxury. Convinced that civilisation is superior in every way to barbarism, Genovesi considered luxury as being almost always a progressive force benefiting society. The wealth of a state lies not in the overall amount of money owned but in the ability of its productive system to respond satisfactorily not only to internal demand but also to foreign trade. From this it is clear what should be the State's role with regard to the economy. Although influenced by the more developed countries, particularly England, and the work of Locke and Hume, Genovesi was inspired initially by the late-mercantilism of Melon, Uztariz and Ulloa. They had proposed reforms based on the reality of the situation in France and particularly Spain, where the processes of change and especially of industrialisation were unthinkable without a centralised organisation. But it is significant that in the course of his teaching Genovesi inclined increasingly towards economic liberalisation and, bearing in mind events in France and particularly the decrees freeing the grain trade, was advocating free trade. His solution was thus to some extent the opposite of the realistic but conservative response of Galiani to the physiocrats.

The famine in Naples of 1764 had made Genovesi realise the inadequacy of traditional provisioning policy which was unable to support the population in times of crisis and was at any time damaging to farming and trade. He thought that a better solution might be found in the natural cycle and in improved commercial relationships. In the first place it would be difficult for a famine to affect a whole country if that country was sufficiently large and regionally divided. In the event of a famine being so extensive that national solutions were insufficient, then a free international market could easily provide what was necessary. In any case, the momentary discomfort of a famine dealt with by emergency measures was preferable to a permanent *annona* which strangled trade and contradicted the natural laws of economics. Therefore the State should seek to improve agriculture, industry and trade, opposing parasitism of every kind and guaranteeing the security of trade and economic activity. Rather than a role as entrepreneur, *à la* Colbert, Genovesi was inclined to give the State more delicate and complex tasks – for example that of opposing the mechanisms of traditional privileges. Genovesi's dislike of the feudal aristocracy has been mentioned. He was to be the inspiration of that generation who put new life into the fight against feudal 'abuses'. But this was not the only type of anachronistic privilege holding back the economy. There was also the Church, with its vast holdings of land, the religious orders that were idle and thus parasites, and its jurisdictions and right of sanctuary which prevented the rational enforcement of public justice.

During his years at Naples University, Genovesi emphasised (in line with an Italian and European climate of opinion which led first to the banishment and then abolition of the Jesuits) his link with Giannonian jurisdictionalism.[8] His policy on education is thus of great interest. Above all he reveals, compared with other great intellectuals of the century, for example Voltaire or La Chalotais, a remarkable optimism on the subject of universal elementary education. He had no fear that it might arouse inappropriate ambitions, taking people away from manual labour. He was convinced (partly as a result of the influence of Muratori's Catholicism)[9] that popular education would contribute to an improvement in the quality of craftsmanship, as it had done in England. As for secondary and university education, Genovesi was firmly opposed to the monopoly of the clergy and Jesuits, favouring lay teachers, provided, or at least controlled, by the State. In the university, following the example of Galiani, he would have liked to stress professional and experimental studies, reducing the amount of abstractly theoretical or entirely traditional disciplines.

An energetic reformism then, linked to the most advanced aspects of the Bourbon model and Tanucci's policies, but which went further. His *Lezioni di commercio* greatly influenced the generation of intellectuals which emerged in the following decades. He had pointed the way to a more thorough knowledge of the south's territory and this task was taken up by men like the Grimaldi brothers, Francesco Longano and Giuseppe Maria Galanti. The antifeudalism of Filangieri, Dragonetti, Winspeare and Galanti was affected, directly or indirectly, by the works of Genovesi[10] and his ideas on education and religion influenced the old regalist Francesco Andrea Serrao, who was to become a 'martyr' of Jacobinism.[11] One cannot of course attribute the whole of southern culture after 1769, the year of his death, to the influence of Genovesi. Men like the Grimaldi brothers, Filangieri, Pagano and Russo had their own ideas and tackled problems in different ways. The real heir to Genovesi can be seen in Giuseppe Maria Galanti who developed, with less theory but perhaps greater social acuteness, Genovesi's ideas on the need to get to know better the Mezzogiorno and its enormous problems.

NOTES AND REFERENCES

The chief work of reference for this chapter is Venturi, F. (1969–84) *Settecento riformatore*, I, 'Il dibattito sulle monete', pp. 443–525 and 'La Napoli di Antonio Genovesi' pp. 523–644. Einaudi, Turin. For Galiani see: Galiani, F. (1975) *Opere*,

ed. Diaz, F, and Guerci, L. Ricciardi, Milan–Naples.   For Antonio Genovesi see:
Venturi, F. (1962) *Illuministi italiani*, vol. V, 'Riformatori napoletani.' Ricciardi,
Milan–Naples, pp. 3–332;   Zambelli, P. (1972) *La formazione filosofica di Antonio
Genovesi*. Morano, Naples;   Arata, F. (1978) *Antonio Genovesi. Una proposta di morale
illuminista*. Marsilio, Padua;   Pii, E. (1984) *Antonio Genovesi dalla politica economica
alla 'politica civile'*. Olschki, Florence.

1.   See: *Ragionamento sopra la moneta, l'interesse del denaro, le finanze e il commercio, scritti
e pubblicati in diverse occasioni dal signor Giovanni Locke, tradotti per la prima volta
dall'inglese con varie annotazioni* (1751). Bonducci, Florence.
2.   Venturi, F. (1959) 'Alle origini dell'Illuminismo napoletano: dal carteggio di
Bartolomeo Intieri', in *Rivista storica italiana*, a. LXXI, n. 2, pp. 416–56.
3.   See: Borghero, C. (ed.) (1974) *La polemica sul lusso nel Settecento francese*. Einaudi,
Turin.
4.   Later, when Galiani was recalled to Naples contact continued through letters.
See *Correspondance inédite de l'abbé Ferdinand Galiani, Conseiller du Roi de Naples
avec Madame d'Epinay, le Baron d'Holbach, le Baron Grimm, et autres personnages
célèbres du XVIIIe siècle*, par le Feu Ginguené, avec des notes de M. Salfi (1818).
Treuttel-Wöurtz, Paris.
5.   See: Guerci, L. (1972) 'Aspetti e problemi dell'epistolario di Ferdinando Galiani',
in *Rivista storica italiana*, a. LXXXIV, pp. 80–110.
6.   See Venturi, F. (ed.) (1962) *Illuministi italiani. Riformatori napoletani*. Ricciardi,
Milan-Naples, p. 23.
7.   Ibid., pp. 73–6.
8.   For the 'Giannonian' influence on Genovesi see: Villari, L. (1959) *Il pensiero economico di A. Genovesi*. Le Monnier, Florence.   See also: Zambelli, P. (1972) *La
formazione filosofica di A. Genovesi*. Morano, Naples, pp. 521–4; Chiosi, E. (1980)
'La tradizione giannoniana', in various authors, *Pietro Giannone e il suo tempo*, ed.
Ajello, R. Jovene, Naples, II, pp. 780ff.
9.   See: Galasso, G. (1970) 'Il pensiero religioso di Antonio Genovesi', in *Rivista
storica italiana* a. LXXXII.   See also: Ferrone, V. (1983) *Scienza natura religione*.
Jovene, Naples, pp 609ff.
10.   See (Galanti, G. M.) (1772) *Elogio storico del signor abate Genovesi*. Naples.
11.   Chiosi, E, (1981) *Andrea Serrao. Apologia e crisi del regalismo nel Settecento napoletano*. Jovene, Naples.

CHAPTER EIGHTEEN

The Enlightenment in Lombardy: Pietro Verri (1728–97), Cesare Beccaria (1735–94), *Il Caffè*

In Lombardy the new Habsburg regime had upset the old equilibrium, based on the recognition of considerable independence for local institutions, the Church and the aristocracy. Even though the bodies which represented the latter, such as the Senate, had remained substantially intact, there were moves which clearly indicated a desire for change on the part of Vienna and which, for the best of reasons, bypassed these bodies and local institutions which were seen as obstacles to a policy of development. A good example is that of the *catasto* which was also ideologically significant. Vienna had placed no trust at all in the Lombard administrators and since 1718 had delegated the task of carrying out the *catasto* to an external Junta, consisting of men not connected with the Lombard nobility. The Church and the nobility, including the Senate, had resisted and the work had foundered during the War of the Polish Succession which had resulted in Lombard territory being controlled for a few years by Charles Emanuel III. But Francesco d'Aguirre, the Sicilian who had reformed Turin University and who in 1727 had entered the service of the Austrians, had not only saved the data accumulated in the archives but had also continued the calculations. On the basis of this material, Pompeo Neri, the Tuscan economist, had been able in the few years 1750–58 to carry out the census and defend its political and economic implications in an important essay.[1] The result was not only to alarm the Lombard ruling class but also to create a reference point for new generations.

Here a comparison of the generational and political differences between Gabriele Verri and his sons is illustrative. The Verri family was of relatively recent nobility, strengthened by astute marriages. Gabriele, a man not without intelligence and literary culture, and a member of that Senate which had been disturbed to see the centralising tendencies of Vienna, was a typical champion of the conservative resistance which disputed every attempt at reform by the Habsburgs. Pietro, the eldest son, already showed himself to be very different in his school-days and his discontent increased when he was required to take a degree in law. There was a brief interval when he fought in the Seven Years War but then he returned to align himself with that power that his father, as senator, was attempting to oppose. Pietro's ideas could not fail to take account of the census and to realise not only that it had been a positive thing but that it had only been made possible by the external power of the Empire. The facts spoke for themselves: Lombardy was potentially a much richer country than appeared from the levels of agricultural and industrial production. The crises in these two sectors had seriously affected trade. But the Spanish and their greed and bad administration did not deserve all the blame. The truth was that a series of obstacles had contributed to the decline and still prevented a recovery. Though the Habsburgs had played a positive role in the matter of the *catasto*, there remained the system of the Farms, or the contracting out of tax collection, which not only resulted in the waste of a large amount of public money, but also helped to turn capital towards a parasitical form of investment, severely damaging the public economy. In fact Pietro Verri's early ideas for reform seem merely to anticipate the centralisation and rationalisation that the Habsburgs were beginning to plan for their territories, albeit prompted by military necessity.

This attitude was already bringing Pietro into conflict with his father. But he did not stop at a plan for centralisation – he tried to use it as a departure point for reform. Thus right from the beginning there was a profound difference between the pragmatic nature of Habsburg policy, supported by the officials to whom Pietro Verri looked from time to time, and the strategy for reform that he was beginning to formulate. His ideas for reform, which brought him into conflict more with the Habsburgs than the local ruling class, were accompanied, and to some extent overshadowed, by a broader aim. Reform was not possible if confined to political and economic matters. It was necessary to change the attitudes of the ruling class, make contact with the *philosophes* and open up a new view of the world. This was central to his not merely psychological differences with his father, with the *Accademia dei Trasformati* and even with one of its former members, Giuseppe Parini, and the latter's decorous and moderate enlightened views which he had expressed especially after about 1762. Verri firmly maintained the relationship between political life and culture. The intellectual, for him, was one who would use the machinery of power to carry out economic, institutional, cultural and moral reforms. In his *Discorso sulla felicità* of 1763, Verri outlined a secular and open-minded moral philosophy for himself and his group of young *illuministi* who were energetically and creatively questioning Lombard society.

There is much that is striking in this essay by the young intellectual, above all the acceptance of his own privileged status but at the same time the desire and almost the sense of obligation to use it for the public good. There is a fascinating calculation of pleasure and pain and a view of existence which is implicitly, but decidedly, materialistic not religious. There is an analysis of the passions, including ambition, 'the most deadly and at the same time most worthy'. With a moderation very different from the impression we have of him from the famous correspondence, we see Verri's desire for achievement, which is by no means narrow or banal. Here he envisages not so much an immediate success as that which results from intellectual achievement, more difficult but more lasting. The task of the intellectual is to ensure the good of all, but he must decide between the three rules of religion, honour and civil law; these may well conflict, in which case the only way to choose between them is their relative utility and value for the common good. As a basis for political action Verri puts forward an ethical system of responsibility born of utilitarianism. His realism thus prevents him from completely accepting Rousseau's egalitarian democracy; he maintains that it is better to start from the ideal of Utopia as a basis for reform. The correct course is to develop the civil laws thereby rendering unnecessary the laws of honour, which still have an application in advanced society, thus paving the way to their gradual disappearance.

Verri's theory of pleasure and pain, applied to the individual and to society, leads him to evolve a moral and political code quite unconnected with religion and reminiscent of Machiavelli. But it is not a mere mechanical system of decisions and choices, since Verri sees in man two basic emotional instincts, sympathy and the need for friendship. Man has to find a balance between reason and these two emotions. The book concludes with an excursus on human history seen as progress, a progress constantly interrupted by disasters or set-backs, but capable of benefiting and growing from these experiences. It is a history dominated by Western civilisation, Greece, Rome, the barbarians, the Middle Ages, the Crusades, the great national monarchies and geographical discoveries. Human needs are themselves a challenge and a stimulus to progress. There has been a similar progress in the forms and role of culture. If at first the republic of letters consisted only of scholars and amateurs, today's new intellectuals are scientists, engineers, surveyors and economists. 'It is agriculture, finance, trade and the art of government which now occupy scholars. The press and the mail which carry new discoveries to the furthest limits of Europe give a real existence to this diverse body of thinkers. . . .'[2] The spread of ideas, which Verri frequently describes in metaphors of light, is the real motive force of developments 'in Europe in this century, and the scholar has good reason to believe that civil liberty must spread to all nations'. No country and no sovereign can avoid it. There is no place for Machiavelli's tyrant, but only for the enlightened prince dedicated to a programme of reform.

Verri's critical and realistic optimism contrasts sharply with the view of civilisation as a state of discomfort, misery and alienation from primitive innocence. He opts uncompromisingly for civilisation against primitivism. For him, Rousseau's assertion that the savage was happier than civilised man was abstract, more an ingenious paradox than the truth. Modern man has no other choice than that of improving himself and aiming at the greatest possible degree of civilisation. Following Machiavelli and Montesquieu Verri discussed the relationship between climate and political systems, distinguishing between the West where ideas of liberty and progress had taken root in the course of history and the East where power was expressed in unchanging despotism.

If Genovesi's *Discorso sul vero fine delle arti e delle scienze* was the manifesto of the southern Enlightenment, Verri's *Meditazioni* were the manifesto of the *Academia dei Pugni*. The group which formed around Pietro Verri included his brother Alessandro, Cesare Beccaria, Alfonso Longo, Giuseppe Visconti, Luigi Lambertenghi and Gian Battista Biffi. Two other members were subsequently involved in the academy and in the publication of the famous and militant journal *Il Caffè*, which was, along with Beccaria's *Dei delitti e delle pene*, its most famous and combative product: they were Gian Rinaldo Carli[3] and the Barnabite Paolo Frisi. These two were to be very important both for their intellectual backgrounds and for their different contributions to the *école de Milan*. Carli, who was a few years older than Pietro, had received his literary education in that area of the Veneto still influenced by Maffei, Muratori and Tartarotti. His interest in economic and monetary matters had brought him to Milan from a professorship at Padua University. Compared with the other members of the academy, he harked back to the scholarly tradition of the early eighteenth century although out of this he was able to forge his own path in economics. Frisi entered the group as a result of his serious interest in science, not merely that of a dilettante, his long association in Paris with the *philosophes* and a close friendship with d'Alembert.

Although Verri's book seems today the most important and influential programme of the *Accademia dei Pugni* and *Il Caffè* group, at the time Europe was beginning first to take notice of the *école de Milan* because of Beccaria's *Dei delitti e delle pene* rather than of the journal. This work, published in 1764, transformed a young aristocrat, recognised as intelligent, though somewhat lazy, exceptionally versatile, but without as yet any clearly defined philosophy, into one of the most important figures of the European Enlightenment. This aroused the jealousy of Pietro Verri who felt that he should have most of the credit both because he had suggested the subject and because he had discussed and developed it. The question of Verri's possible joint authorship is not really significant. There is no doubt that Beccaria succeeded brilliantly in summarising in one specific topic (that of laws and the right to punish) all the elements of the Milanese philosophy.

It is easy to see with hindsight the originality and individuality of the work, and a comparison with the *Meditazioni* reveals clearly the differences between Verri and Beccaria. Beccaria looks, inevitably, to Montesquieu, Rousseau and Helvétius, but more than any other member of the *Pugni*, in the relation between liberty and democracy, he emphasises the latter. This can be seen in his treatment of the theme of honour. While Verri borrows from Montesquieu, Beccaria, though starting from almost the same premises, refuses in practice to justify the existence of privileges and differentiated forms of the administration of the law. He stands midway between realism and Utopianism. For Verri social distinctions have a meaning until the time when civil laws will prevail, but equality seems an impossibly distant ideal. For Beccaria, on the other hand, it is to be established at once as the basis of law. Here the influence of Rousseau is much more evident.

In Beccaria's work the *école de Milan* offered the most effective combination of Utopianism and reform to emerge from enlightened Europe.[4] Examining the Western system of justice with a rationalistic and utilitarian eye, Beccaria revealed its backwardness and violence, not only in allowing capital punishment and torture, but also because it left to the subjective opinion of the judge the power to evaluate the crime and mete out the punishment. He was not the first to deal with this subject. There is a whole history of the discussion of the legal system in the early eighteenth century both in Italy and the rest of Europe. As can be seen from Bourbon policy and Victor Amadeus II's constitutions, the ruling classes and governments were aware of the need to bring order to the chaos of a legal system which on one side was based on Roman law and on the other relied on a confused inheritance of customs and precedents. On a theoretical level the problem had been tackled by Muratori, starting with his *De codice Carolino* of 1726 and going on to the *Difetti della giurisprudenza* in 1742 and the *Della pubblica felicità* of 1749. Thus it is easy to find precedents for the discussions of torture, the stand against capital punishment, against the judicial repression of free thought – especially in the area of religion – against ecclesiastical tribunals and the rights of sanctuary.

What distinguishes Beccaria's work is that it puts forward a theory of justice and society that was to be central in the debate in enlightened Europe. Looking at Beccaria's work today one cannot but be amazed by the quantity and quality of original ideas it contains. The influences are many – some nearer and more apparent (Verri, Helvétius, Montesquieu, Rousseau and Voltaire) while others are more distant and concealed (Machiavelli, Sarpi, Giannone and Muratori) – but the sum of the parts is an original whole. Its conciseness and clarity also contributed to making it one of the most effective weapons for an attack on the institutions and society of the *ancien régime*. Beccaria's immediate target was the irrationality of the law, the disproportion between crimes and punishments, the barbarity of torture and the inhumanity of capital punishment. In their place he proposed a rational justice where the emphasis was not on the extracting of revenge from the guilty but on rehabilitation, reparation and social utility.

But his more indirect attack, already clearly apparent, struck more deeply at the heart of the *ancien régime*, for (assuming that torture and capital punishment were unnecessary and inhuman) what stood accused was the social system itself and its profound inequality. The discussion of the nobility, honour, duelling and aristocratic justice was just one side of the argument. On the other was the strong awareness that crime was born of the unequal distribution of wealth. Poverty which went hand in hand with ignorance was a breeding ground for crime. Therefore it was futile to use the machinery of justice to contain a malaise that went much deeper and was created by the system itself. Thus all purely repressive systems were not only unjust but also ineffective. Beccaria suggested two types of action: one, inherent in the law, that all aspects of violence, revenge and exemplary punishment be eliminated; secondly, and more importantly, that the conditions which gave rise to crime be changed. Between the lines of a renewed discussion of the right to punish one begins to read a discussion of property, of crimes against property and of the fact that the inequality of wealth, far from being natural and justifiable by natural law, was as unjust as theft. Beccaria's solution was still optimistic. Economic reform and education were the two answers that civil society and a state without despotism could provide to counter the social malaise and the consequent repression.

Dei delitti e delle pene had an immediate success in Italy and Europe.[5] It was published, thanks to Pietro Verri's cautious efforts, in Leghorn by Giuseppe Aubert,[6] who had already published the *Meditazioni sulla felicità* and who a few years later was to risk bringing out the Leghorn edition of the *Encyclopédie* (1770). Verri's caution was justified, for not only was Beccaria's book immediately condemned by the Venetian Inquisition but also in several pamphlets. One, by the monk Ferdinando Facchinei who had been quick to see the most important implications of Beccaria's argument, denounces him as a dangerous subverter of the throne and the Church, the Italian Rousseau: 'Almost all that our author puts forward rests only on two false and absurd principles – that all men are born free and are naturally equal, and that laws are no more, nor should be, than the voluntary pacts between such men.'[7] In this attack on Beccaria, Facchinei also coined the terms *socialista* and *socialismo* to describe this subversion of traditional society.

In Lombardy too the book's success was not uncontested. There was a significant reaction from Gian Rinaldo Carli who, writing about it on 1 January 1765 to Paolo Frisi and admiring the 'power, talent and courage of its brilliant author' and praising its practical utility as a tool for reform, objected to several of Beccaria's principles. 'It is a great mistake to believe all men to be the same in inclination, instinct and will, and all capable of virtue, moderation and reasonableness, when in appearance, facial features, voice and body there is so much variety and difference. And yet all the conclusions drawn by Rousseau and Beccaria derive from this principle. . . .'[8] The book was greeted enthusiastically in Tuscany, both in Florence and the academic world in Pisa. But to crown its success, news reached Milan from Paris that it was being discussed and reviewed with a translation planned by Morellet and that it had received the approval (via Paolo Frisi) of no less a person than d'Alembert. From Paris it became known all over Europe. Meanwhile the *école de Milan* had found another way to place itself at the centre of debate and public opinion in Italy. This was *Il Caffè*, a periodical published in Brescia and which, with its lively and intelligent political debate, was to mark an important turning-point in the history of Italian journalism.[9]

The success of *Il Caffè* came at a time of crisis for the scholarly periodical, whether of the classic style of the *Giornale dei letterati* (which consisted of extracts from books, scientific notes and literary news), or of the style made so successful by Lami with his *Novelle letterarie* and its reviews and news. The critical review influenced by the great English examples (particularly Addison and Steele's *Spectator*) was now beginning to appear, with publications such as Gozzi's *Gazzetta veneta*, Giuseppe Baretti's *Frusta letteraria* or Carlo Denina's *Parlamento ottaviano*, the latter being something between the *Lettres persanes* and the *Spectator*. But *Il Caffè* also looked to the *Encyclopédie* and it differed greatly from its Italian predecessors. Gozzi adapted his own pleasing literary skills to a public that liked to find, enhanced by good writing, their own ideas and values. Baretti concealed beneath a remarkable and glittering aggressiveness, a hostility directed almost always at the basic values of the Enlightenment. Denina, a pupil and disciple of Sigismondo Gerdil, used the critical review as a platform for his own Catholic reformism which still lacked any enlightened ideas.

With *Il Caffè* there was no pandering to the public, which instead was presented with all the most aggressive arguments on reform to emerge from the *Accademia dei Pugni*. Law, economy, agriculture, medicine and natural science were discussed in a peremptory and emphatic manner as being the most important subjects in the *Encylopédie*, *Il Caffè*'s most frequent source of inspiration. Many of the subjects dealt with by Verri and Beccaria were to find a broader form and link with the public in *Il Caffè*. Along with Verri, Beccaria, Frisi and Carli, other young men collaborated who in the following decades were regularly to be found in the Habsburg administration and in the *Società Patriottica*, such as Alfonso Longo, Gian Battista Biffi, Giuseppe Visconti, Pietro Secchi and Luigi Lambertenghi. They held differing points of view. Pietro Verri was certainly the person most inclined politically to use the journal for a policy of reform. In many of his contributions (on luxury, trade, etc.) we can already see the arguments that were to lead to his *Meditazioni sull'economia politica*. His brother Alessandro was more interested in law and literature while Beccaria, author of the remarkable introduction – on the nature of periodicals – to volume II, brought to the periodical not only his interest in social mathematics but also in aesthetics and the pleasures of the imagination which was to lead him to examine questions of literary style.

Il Caffè was a brilliant and lively reflection of a general programme for reform, which was critical not only of the economy, the law and the institutions, but also the arts, literature and language. Particularly important here was their anti-purist and anti-*Crusca* stance, their language being more open to foreign neologisms and generally closer to reality and common usage. Carli's essay *Della patria degli italiani* was particularly famous (partly because it was later seen as an anticipation of the Risorgimento). Following in the footsteps of Muratori, whose influence in the second half of the eighteenth century was, however, declining, Carli saw the deep sense of cultural unity among Italians who, despite their being subjects of different states, formed a single body in the sciences and arts. This was a time of optimism, when the words 'patriot', 'cosmopolitan' and '*philosophe*' were, for Verri, one and the same.

But the periodical lasted barely two years. In 1766 a brief announcement explained the reasons: 'The small society of friends that wrote these pages has been dissolved. Some are away travelling, others are occupied with other work. Necessity demands the end of an enterprise that it was not the authors' intention to close so soon, and at a time when the favourable reception of the public more than ever encouraged its continuation. . . .'[10] The travel alluded to was that of Beccaria and Alessandro Verri who were to be the ambassadors of the *école de Milan* to the capital of the *philosophes*. All went well at first, with d'Alembert, Diderot, Morellet and d'Holbach. In the home of the latter they heard the first version of the *Système de la Nature*. But then the problems began. Beccaria rebelled against Pietro's imperious insistence on directing the journey and returned to Milan. The break, fuelled by resentment and jealousy, was inevitable. Beccaria devoted himself to teaching economics and then to a career as a civil servant. Alessandro went to London and then instead of returning to Milan and publishing his *Storia d'Italia*, which Pietro was hoping would bring fame to his brother, and pursuing the path of a reforming jurist, he chose Rome, literature, love and freedom. He remained, nevertheless, a distant but constant audience for the problems, ambitions, expectations and frustrations of his brother who was now attempting, as a government employee and with others of his group, to make theoretical reform a reality.

These attempts were not without disappointments and Pietro often regretted having dissolved *Il Caffè* too soon. He tried to remedy this through a new periodical, printed from 1762 in Berne and then at Yverdon through Bartolomeo Fortunato De Felice. This former friar and professor at Naples University had fled from Italy for love and had found in Berne and later Yverdon his true vocation, as journalist, editor and cultural mediator. It was in this way that he had encountered the works of Verri and Beccaria. Later, from 1770, he was to undertake a new version of the *Encylopédie*. The *Estratto della letteratura europea*, which was in a short time to gain some fame among the periodicals of the time, was edited by Galeazzi in Milan. Besides Verri, other collaborators were intellectuals who had gathered round the *école de Milan*, like Isidoro Bianchi, who was to be Verri's first biographer, and Giambattista Vasco, who in his turn was to be one of the greatest economists and reforming intellectuals of Piedmont.

The break with Beccaria could not be healed, since Verri continued to insist, in the following years, on his role as head and inspiration of the *Accademia dei Pugni*, taking credit for all that had emerged from it. Thus it was that when Beccaria was teaching political economy in the Palatine Schools (until 1771, and which led to the *Elementi di economia politica*, not published until 1804), Verri was able to write on 10 October 1770 to his brother that the best revenge to take on the professor of political economy would be to give him a lesson in it – his way of announcing his *Meditazioni sulla economia politica*, published in Leghorn in 1771 and his most famous work, running to seven Italian editions by 1774 and immediately translated into French, German and Dutch. This work, which was in part inspired by conversations with his friend Henry Lloyd,[11] a Scottish soldier travelling in Italy who had come several times to Milan in 1768, was a clear and concise summary of the state of economic thinking in Europe before Adam Smith's *Wealth of Nations* (1776).

Here too the philosophic assumptions link up – though perhaps with more pessimism – with the *Meditazioni sulla felicità* and the theory of pleasure and pain which particularly concerned the Lombard school. From it there emerges a theory of progress which, in so far as it is a response to needs, is linked with pain, 'the spur with which nature pricks man and awakens him from that indolent state of vegetation where there is no doubt he would otherwise remain'. The savage nations, which have fewer needs and very limited ideas, know nothing of trade. Only a natural catastrophe can push them into inter-course with their neighbours. Thus the book immediately establishes its relationship with, but also its divergence from, Rousseau. Trade is the starting-point for economic development and money is the means for increasing it.

In Verri's view, money is not so much the equivalent of the value of things as a universal commodity, which makes the idea of the value of things uniform and facilitates trading, thus creating new ideas and demands. In this initial statement Verri stressed his criticism of the physiocrats, agreeing with their theory of the different stages of progress, production (or reproduction, as the French economists called it) and consumption, but not with their definition of traders and producers as members of the unproductive classes. Anticipating a society where agricultural and industrial production resulting from needs and trade would produce a larger quantity of goods than needed for consumption and thus would ensure a favourable commercial balance, Verri emphasises that such a society could not be achieved either through an egalitarian democracy nor in a situation where there was 'too great an inequality of fortunes'. The task of legislation is to guarantee a middle way between these two extremes, without using drastic and direct means such as limiting the right to property on which, for Verri, the foundations of justice in every civil society are built. To reach this optimal state for productive development it would be sufficient to dismantle the system of privileges of the *ancien régime*, abolishing *maggiorascati*, *fidecommessi* and mortmains, freeing all property from entails and abolishing or at least restricting the special rights of the nobility. Such conditions are not guaranteed by one form of government more than another. Each nation must choose its own and adapt it according to its own 'civil constitution'. Laws governing the economy cannot be abstractly prescriptive on the pretext of ordering and shaping the 'spontaneous movement of society'. The economy comes before policy because reality and its development can be understood and analysed but not compelled by aprioristic schemes.

Thus Verri was opposed to all those provisions which, even on the pretext of ensuring a better service to the public, restricted trade and production, such as the guilds, the restrictions on the export of certain goods, particularly corn, the monopolies and the laws against luxury. These latter laws are dangerous because they affect the relationship between the sellers and the buyers, artificially lowering the number of the latter. The result, however, is a fall in the number of the sellers and thus a fall in production. As for money, the universal commodity, Verri maintained that the only acceptable increase, which would not harm the economy, was that brought about by the growth of industry or trade, while that derived from rich mines or external payments had a fatal tendency to upset the economy of a country. Here Verri takes up a position which goes decidedly further than the physiocrats and their view of a society where the entire production is linked to the land. Not only would the development of trade and industry lower the price of goods and reduce the profits made on the sale of single products, but it would also encourage the development of technology and machines. Where money is concerned too, Verri maintains that the State will not benefit society by fixing a precise level of interest. It must always endeavour to intervene indirectly, maintaining confidence in the treasury and assessing, according to circumstances, the desirability or otherwise of setting up public banks.

In Verri's scheme of things, by now quite close to the ideas which Smith was to formulate a few years later, the wealth of a nation was not linked to accumulation but to production and circulation. Only this could ensure a lowering of prices and thus the possibility of participating not only as a producer but also as a consumer (thereby satisfying one's own needs) in ever more layers of society. Here it is interesting to see how Verri adapts the populationist theories of the eighteenth century. For him, an increase in population is not the way to increase wealth, but it is an indication that production has increased. It is not merely a matter of increasing the population as a labour force, but of improving the quality of the same. Thus the ideal of political economy can be summed up as the art of obtaining the maximum annual production with the minimum possible work. Both the computation and classification of the population and social analysis must bear the economy in mind. Instead of the traditional division of the social orders of the *ancien régime* or the over-simplistic system of the physiocrats, Verri postulates three classes, producers, intermediaries and consumers, attacking the moralising (or Utopian) tendency which insists that in the state there should be no idle men who are merely consumers. For Verri these men, the landowners, with their needs, had an important role since they supported industry and commerce. The rich consumers described by Verri were in the main none other than the existing ruling class.

Verri lastly examines the matter of taxes, once again reacting against the physiocrats' theory of basing everything on the land and taxing only landowners. He saw with great clarity the limitations and harm which could come from this. A tax on raw materials exported from the State was, for example, a useful expedient which, without restricting the freedom of trade, encouraged home industry. He proposed that taxes should be reduced to two types: a property tax and customs tolls at the borders. This was a significant conclusion, for he did not only outline a new policy on taxation, but also the methods of carrying it out, which concerned both a plan for involving public opinion and the preparation, education and decisions of the ministers dealing with finance and economy. The method of implementation would have to take various forms, precisely because the matters concerned needed different types of law, directly prescriptive in the first case, indirect and supportive in the second.

Verri's proposal does not merely criticise the limitations of physiocratic ideas and expose their dogmatism with the merciless realism of a Galiani. He was well aware that physiocracy had depicted a cycle of production (and hence a model of an economic system) that needed only to be extended to trade and industry. For Genovesi Great Britain (despite the translation of Cary's book) was far away, and a more concrete reference point was the reformism and physiocratic ideas of Spain and France, while the myth of the merchants of Holland was still widespread. For Verri, on the other hand, Britain, with its commercial, agricultural and industrial development, was something more. It already seemed, even from the political and social point of view, to show a possible future for Europe, with its constitutional monarchy and parliamentary institutions where the aristocrats were able to participate and where the balance between landowners, merchants and manufacturers had been developed to an advanced degree.

A comparison of Verri's book with other texts from the *école*, starting from Beccaria's *Elementi di economia pubblica*, not published until 1804, reveals, not surprisingly, many features in common.[12] An example is the treatment of the theme of luxury, seen as part of that search for happiness which comes from the calculation of pain and pleasure and which cannot be denied. There is a similarity in many of their proposals for reform which imply the end of the *ancien régime* and seek to encourage the different sectors of the economy. But there were also important differences between these texts, and not only of style, which were to influence future developments. Beccaria's relationship with Rousseau had been something more than just an encounter with a great man whose ideas were comparable with his own. It had taught him, if not how to solve the problem of inequality, at least to keep it in the forefront of all proposals for reform. For Verri (whose attitude as a rich, enlightened landowner remained unaffected), the poverty of the lower classes was a problem to be resolved only within the more general framework of the development of the economy. Greater productivity would benefit labourers and artisans, by preventing them from falling into the passive role of beggars and by involving them as consumers and giving them some purchasing power. For Beccaria social inequality and the sufferings of the poor were a responsibility and a scandal which should prick the conscience of a servant of an enlightened government. Verri (who in 1777 returned to Beccaria's theme with the unpublished *Osservazioni sulla tortura*) was to move away from the ideas of the Enlightenment to a liberal constitutionalism after the disillusionment of Joseph II's despotism and the dramatic events of the Revolution. Beccaria continued to draw on the problems posed by Rousseau to construct a programme of economic, social and intellectual reform. This on the one hand related to examples present in the most advanced commercial developments in the Habsburg Empire and on the other anticipated a return to economic *dirigisme* which was to become more frequent in the face of the final

269

and by now imminent crisis of the *ancien régime*.

In 1771 Beccaria left his teaching post to take up a career as a state official as Verri had done earlier. The decree of 1786 establishing obligatory schooling in the Lombard states, in line with the decisions taken in Austria in 1774, bears Beccaria's signature. His chair at the Palatine Schools in Milan was occupied first by one of Genovesi's pupils, Traiano Odazzi, then by Alfonso Longo, an old contributor to *Il Caffè*, writing among other things an essay on *fidecommesso*, and who was to be, with Paolo Frisi, one of the first state-appointed censors in Lombardy. In his lectures in Milan between 1773 and 1780 on political and economic institutions Longo was to reveal, compared to Verri, a greater desire to reconcile his position as a state official, sharing the regalistic policies of Joseph II, with that of the physiocrats whom he had championed in Italy, publishing, with a commentary, the Marquis de Mirabeau's *Devoirs* in 1780.

Verri's relations with Carli after the period of *Il Caffè* were strained. He had never forgiven Carli for obtaining, with the help of Kaunitz, the presidency of the Supreme Economic Council to which he himself had aspired. In fact their differences were more profound and could be detected both in their actions as state officials, Carli showing himself to be an intelligent and sceptical defender of an only marginally altered status quo, and in their ideas, as can be seen in Carli's *Note alle "Meditazioni sull' economia pubblica"* (Lucca, 1774). As has been seen, Carli had greeted Beccaria's *Dei delitti e delle pene* with favour but also with specific reservations. There is much in his early correspondence discussing this work to indicate what were to be Carli's later cultural and political ideas. He had approved Beccaria's proposal but not the more radical aspects of it inspired by utilitarianism and Rousseau. He considered only its more technical aspects and those immediately applicable to criminal reform.

Already Carli appeared to have formulated that picture of an anti-egalitarian society which can be found in *L'Uomo libero* published in 1778. The ideology underlying even his actions as a state official is clearly exposed in this text. Men are condemned by nature to a state of permanent inequality, physical, moral and economic. It is not an accident that society is divided into two classes, rich and poor. Unlike Verri, for whom economic development had in itself the power to improve the conditions of the poorer classes by allowing them to participate in consumption, and unlike Beccaria who continued to see inequality as the chief problem to be solved, Carli was convinced that development would increase not only inequality but also class conflict. The only remedy was the power of the sovereign, of a monarch who could guard against despotism but at the same time defend civil society against anarchy. He touches in this work on what was to be the theme of his *Lettere americane*: the myth of a power that, by limiting ownership and liberty, ensured – through strong centralisation – the safety and happiness of his subjects. The only example of secure happiness on this earth was that of the Incas of Peru. Without ownership and the freedom of contracts, with a wonderful discipline backed up by opinion and based on religion, those ancient kings were successful in making all their subjects happy and satisfied.'[13]

This man who felt himself to be the heir to Pompeo Neri, who had praised his census as a beginning for the development of agriculture in Lombardy, who shared all Galiani's reservations about physiocracy and a free grain trade, this great and acclaimed architect of Lombard finances, was, in his *Lettere americane*, to describe and extol an absolute and paternalistic regime so complete as to seem almost a caricature of Joseph II's system. Through these three great but different intellectuals, the *école de Milan* pointed to three different paths: Verri, who developed from a centralising plan for reform to constitutionalism; Beccaria, who never entirely rejected the Utopia that continued to colour his reformism as an official; and lastly Carli, who remained convinced that politics consisted of adjustments and cautious provisions rather than of radical reform.

After the death of Maria Theresa (for whom Frisi composed an oration that was a touching balance between expectations and achievements),[14] and the coming to power of Joseph II, the one-time group of Lombard reformers had reached the end of their period of greatest creativity in a climate of widespread and general unease. We see in his correspondence that Verri even reverted to the ideas of his father, to the point of looking for a political solution which would pay more attention to local autonomies. But routine had not dulled his creativity as can be seen not only in his *Osservazioni sulla tortura* but also in his letters to his brother and the *Ricordi alla figlia*.[15] But the example of the *école de Milan* was to yield other fruit. As well as the dialogue established with physiocratic Tuscany, where for example Marco Lastri recognised the greatness of Verri's *Meditazioni sull'economia pubblica* in the pages of the new series of the *Novelle letterarie*, there was also contact with the Piedmontese Giambattista Vasco, author of *La pubblica felicità nei possessori di terre proprie* who, as master of a new generation of Piedmontese intellectuals, did not forget the education in the ideas of the Enlightenment he had received in Milan. And a new generation was coming up, whose development can be exemplified by that of Giuseppe Gorani.[16] From the physiocracy of what is perhaps his most important book in the area of political reform, *Il vero dispotismo*, which aimed to force the hand of 'Josephism', reconciling it with freedom, the restless and adventurous Gorani was to follow a career as pamphleteer which led him to Jacobinism. For this he was to be harshly criticised by the old, lucid and vigilant Pietro Verri.

NOTES AND REFERENCES

The best reference work for the *école de Milan* is: Venturi F. (ed.) (1958) *Riformatori lombardi piemontesi e toscani*. Ricciardi, Milan–Naples. See also Venturi, F. (1969–84) 'La Milano del *Caffè*', in *Settecento riformatore*. Einaudi, Turin, vol. I. For P. Verri see: Valeri, N. (1937) *Pietro Verri*. Mondadori, Milan. See also: Verri, P

(1964) *Del piacere e del dolore ed altri scritti di filosofia e di economia.* Ed. De Felice, R. Feltrinelli, Milan; Verri, P. (1983) *Manoscritto per Teresa.* Ed. Barbarisi, G. Serra e Riva, Milan; *idem, Osservazioni sulla tortura.* Ed. Barbarisi, G.. Serra e Riva, Milan. For Beccaria see Venturi, F. *Riformatori lombardi.* op. cit., vol. III pp. 3–213; Beccaria, C. (1965) *Dei delitti e delle pene,* ed. Venturi, F. Einaudi, Turin; Zarone, G. (1971) *Etica e politica nell'utilitarismo di Cesare Beccaria.* Istituto italiano per gli studi storici, Naples; Maestro, M. (1973) *Cesare Beccaria and the Origins of Penal Reform.* Temple University Press, Philadelphia. See also: Beccaria, C. *Edizione nazionale delle Opere di Cesare Beccaria.* Gen. ed. Firpo, L: (1984), I, *Dei delitti e delle pene,* ed. Francioni, G., with Firpo, L. *Le edizioni italiane di Dei delitti e delle pene;* Beccaria, C. (1984), II, *Scritti Filosofici e letterari,* Ed. Firpo L., Francioni, G., Gaspari, G. Mediobanca, Milan. On *Il Caffè* see: Romagnoli, S. (1960) *Il Caffè.* Feltrinelli, Milan. See also: Ricuperati, G. (1976) 'Giornali e società nell'Italia dell'Ancien Régime (1668–1789)', in various authors, *La stampa italiana dal '500 all '800,* ed. Castronovo, V. and Tranfaglia, N. Laterza, Bari, especially pp. 191–228. On A. Verri see: Cicoira, F. (1982) *Alessandro Verri.* Patron, Bologna.

1. Neri, P. (1750) *Relazione dello stato in cui si trova l'opera del censimento universale del ducato di Milano.* Milan.

2. Verri, P. (1964) *Del piacere e del dolore ed altri scritti,* ed. De Felice, R. Feltrinelli, Milan, p. 118.

3. See Venturi, F. (ed.) (1958) *Riformatori lombardi, piemontesi e toscani.* Ricciardi Milan-Naples, pp. 419–80;   Apih, E. (1973) *La formazione culturale di G. R. Carli.* Deputazione di storia patria per la Venezia Giulia, *Trieste.*

4. *See: Venturi, F. (1970) Utopia e riforma nell'Illuminismo.* Einaudi, Turin.

5. See: Beccaria, C. 'Storia e dibattiti in Europa', in *De delitti e delle pene,* ed. Venturi, F., op. cit., pp. 111–660.

6. See: Lay, A. (1973) *Un editore illuminista: G. Aubert nel carteggio con Beccaria e con Verri.* Accademia delle Scienze, Turin.

7. See: Venturi, F. *Dei delitti e delle pene,* op. cit,. pp. 164–77. This is followed by the reply of A. and P. Verri, pp. 178–86.

8. Ibid., pp. 186–7.

9. See the beautiful edition of *Il Caffè,* ed. Romagnoli, S., (1960). Feltrinelli, Milan.

10. Ibid, p. 287

11. See: Venturi, F. (1979) 'Le avventure del generale Henry Lloyd', in *Rivista storica italiana,* pp. 369–433.

12. Published for the first time in *Collezione dei classici italiani di economia politica* (1804). Milan.

13. Carli, G. R. (1778) *L'Uomo libero.* The quotation is in Venturi, F. *Riformatori lombardi,* op. cit., p. 462.

14. Frisi, P. (1981) *Elogio di Maria Teresa imperatrice,* ed. Barbarisi, G. Sormani, Milan.

15. See: Verri, P. (1983) *Manoscritto per Teresa,* ed. Barbarisi, G. Serra e Riva, Milan.

16. See the section in Venturi, F. *Riformatori lombardi,* op. cit., pp. 479–560.

CHAPTER NINETEEN

Jurisdictionalism and Enlightenment: Cosimo Amidei (dates uncertain) and Carlantonio Pilati (1733–1802)

In the same period that saw the intellectuals of Lombardy producing a creative response to problems of economics, law and ethics, there was also a marked increase in tension with the Church. To a certain extent the economic and institutional reforms, as well as those of the taxation system, had created areas of conflict. The local clergy and the Roman Curia had resisted the *catasti* organised or planned by the Italian states, defending their exemptions and immunities and often providing a spearhead for other groups against this type of reform. Thus in the 1750s the Italian states had done no more than reach a compromise whereby only the most recently acquired properties of the Church were taxed. Benedict XIV had encouraged such a compromise through the Concordats, but the problem of how to free for sale the vast number of encumbered Church properties was still unresolved. As with the nobility and its *fidecommessi* and *maggiorascati*, so in this case the attack was concentrated on the mortmains, those properties left to the Church with the provision that it could enjoy the income from them but that they could not be sold. Concerning justice, the existence of the right of sanctuary was questioned by many. This tension began to affect other areas too, hitherto little touched in the jurisdictional debate, particularly church censorship and the control exercised by the religious orders, and the Jesuits in particular, over secondary and university education.

From the late 1750s, some ten years after the death of Giannone in the citadel in Turin, the news of events in Portugal, where Jesuits had been condemned and expelled, caused a chain reaction in Italy and Europe which greatly accelerated the states' offensive, involving intellectuals, state officials and religious orders. The French *parlements* were the first to take up the attack on the Jesuits in Bourbon territory. They found immediate and enthusiastic allies in the *philosophes*. There was considerable agreement among the leading contributors to the *Encyclopédie* about the Jesuits and their pedagogical ideas and, for example, the plan for the reform of education put forward by La Chalotais. Not only Voltaire but also Diderot and d'Alembert were drawn into this fight which, because of the family connections between the Bourbons, had considerable political repercussions.

Once the Jesuits were expelled from France, those of Parma and Naples were not long in following. A lively and often ferocious series of pamphlets stirred up Italian public opinion, with Rome, Naples, Florence, Venice, Parma and Milan the focal points of the storm. From the Bourbon courts, which were directly involved, the debate spread to Tuscany where the arrival of Leopold in 1765 revived an ecclesiastical policy which had begun to flag after the energetic beginnings of the Regency, and to Habsburg Lombardy, as well as awakening the dormant jurisdictionalistic traditions among the intellectuals and state officials of Venice. One only has to think of the success of a text like Francesco d'Aguirre's *Del diritto di asilo*, purporting to be published in Florence but in fact published in Venice in 1763 and attributed to various authors including Pompeo Neri. In fact the Sicilian d'Aguirre had written it in the 1720s when he was in the service of Victor Amadeus II. More remarkable and significant was the revival of the great jurisdictionalists, from Sarpi, to whom Francesco Griselini dedicated an important monograph in 1760, to Giannone.[1] After the 1723 edition of Giannone's *Istoria civile* it had appeared only in foreign translations starting with the Geneva anthology of 1738. But in the 1760s Venice and Naples reclaimed the author, re-examining not only the *Istoria civile* but also the *Opere postume*. Various intellectuals tackled biographies of Giannone, including Michele Vecchione, Michele Torcia and particularly Leonardo Panzini. Panzini had been able between 1766 and 1768 to read first the *Regno celeste* and then the complete *Triregno*, and his life of Giannone was the most complete and well thought out expression of the revival of jurisdictionalism guided by Tanucci. Genovesi too became closely involved in this new current and shortly before his death he drew up a new plan for the schools that would replace those run by the Jesuits. He also called for the abolition of the chair in decretals which related to canon law and was harmful and opposed to the law of the State.

The most important books, however, on the problem of the relationship between Church and State flowered in areas not directly involved in the Bourbons' anti-Jesuit offensive, where there was the possibility of a more considered discussion of the subject. Such was the anonymous work which appeared in 1768 under the title of *La chiesa e la repubblica dentro i loro limiti*, and which is now fairly certainly attributed to a Tuscan, Cosimo Amidei. In the introduction to the first edition there are explicit references to the conflict between the Bourbon court in Parma and the Holy See, and in the second, of 1783, these are referred to, a year before the author's death, in the new climate of Leopold's reforms and particularly of Josephism. Though of modest background, Amidei had been able to attend the Faculty of Law in Pisa, though not without great hardship, in the years immediately following the first reforms of Gaspare Cerati. A degree in law opened the door to a career in administration. A friend of Giuseppe Pelli whose unpublished *Effemeridi* provide an interesting reflection of what was read, thought and discussed in intellectual circles in Florence, Amidei has not only left few traces of himself but also, 'through philosophical laziness', few written works.

Two works are basic to an understanding of his ideas on the 'boundaries' of Church and State. The first is Rousseau's *Contrat social* (1762), which had been widely read and reprinted in Tuscany, and the second Beccaria's *Dei delitti e delle pene* (1764). To these can perhaps be added Verri's *Meditazioni sulla felicità* (1763). These works have in common not only Rousseau or the fact that the publisher, Aubert of Leghorn, was involved in each case, but also their utilitarianism, their *économique* point of view as in their theories of pleasure and pain. Besides being influenced by Rousseau, so much so that he was accused of plagiarism, Amidei was especially impressed by Beccaria who made him see the Church–State relationship in a new light. His reading of *Dei delitti e delle pene* gave rise to a correspondence, unfortunately incomplete, which bears witness to not only his admiration for Beccaria's work but also his determination that it should not remain an abstract proposal but that it should become the programme for those in government. He also read Muratori and Giannone, writers who were 'worthy of trust and who had laid the foundations of the problem which he intended to confront'. But Amidei's work shows other influences too – Montesquieu, Hume, Helvétius, Voltaire, the *Encyclopédie* and d'Alembert. His writing was polemical, consisting in large part of quotations, its originality lying in Amidei's insistence on approaching the jurisdictionalist tradition from the point of view of a *philosophe*, always keeping in the forefront the utilitarianism of the *école de Milan* and Rousseau's contractualism. And, through Mirabeau and his work on taxes, there were elements of physiocratic influence which were to become more marked in later works, particularly the *Mezzi per diminuire i mendichi*.

The result was a passionate plan for reform which adapted themes and ideas from contemporary European thought to a revival of traditional jurisdictionalism. There was no trace, however, of the materialistic ideas of d'Holbach's circle. This was not an area which concerned Amidei, and similarly he had not followed Rousseau in his attempt to formulate a new personal religion which was so essential a part of his thinking. Amidei was more concerned to determine limits, fight abuses and affirm the precedence of the sovereign State over the Church. But if the aim of the State was earthly happiness and that of the Church the preparation for the life to come, it was necessary to come to terms with all those areas where the Church had usurped powers belonging to the State. So far Amidei remains within the tradition of jurisdictionalism. What is new is not only the idea that the prime task of the State is the public good, but particularly that sovereignty is based on a pact which, by involving the general will, precedes any other decision. This was the starting-point for a renewed discussion of the Concordats. These agreements on exemptions and immunities for the possessions and the persons of the clergy, inasmuch as they were harmful to the public good, involved the will of a single person and could be corrected by the sovereign understood as the interpreter of the general will.

Another element that this work had in common with other jurisdictionalist writings of the time (in Venice for example), was the attempt to evaluate in quantitative terms (using the techniques of political arithmetic which were spreading through Tuscany, as can be seen from the periodicals) the harm done by ecclesiastical exemptions and immunities. Here Amidei tackled in a realistic way two problems that economists, in Italy and Europe, had raised more than once – the harm caused by ecclesiastical celibacy and the right of sanctuary. Concerning the first, Amidei showed that the statistics given by Johann Peter Süssmilch did not indicate a large difference in the number of marriages between Catholic and Protestant countries. In fact, Amidei asserted, following Hume, the growth of population was proportional to the development of trade and agriculture.[2] Therefore, unlike the Scot Robert Wallace, who in 1753 had maintained that the population of the ancient world had been the greater, he was convinced 'that the modern population must exceed the ancient'. From this he drew two important conclusions. The first was that in a society like the one in which he lived, dominated by inequality, privilege and a distorted system of production, as was apparent from the *maggiorascati*, *fidecommessi* and *latifundia*, celibacy was almost a benefit to the State. The second was the assertion that only by changing the system of production, creating new jobs and dividing up unused properties could celibacy be effectively reduced.

On sanctuary Amidei basically repeated the same argument. He understood all the reasons for its abolition given by the jurisdictionalists, collected and transformed by Beccaria, but he was reluctant to eliminate it, although it was an obstacle to the preservation of order, before there was a reform of a vindictive judicial system which allowed no rights to the presumed guilty and which could cruelly punish the innocent. His section on the censorship of books did not merely reflect the laws in existence in Tuscany or the provisions on the point of appearing in the Habsburg areas substituting state censorship for ecclesiastical censorship, but also proposed, for non-religious books, a measure of freedom of the press 'because this will be of considerable profit to the State'. The 1783 edition was to stress (in an additional note inspired by Helvétius) the view that books were also and primarily commodities and therefore the man of letters was a producer of wealth – a view held by those, like Guido Rucellai, who had inspired the law of 1743.

Amidei's later works, *Discorso filosofico politico sopra la carcere dei debitori* published in 1770 and *De' mezzi per diminuire i mendichi* presented to the *Accademia dei Georgofili* in 1770 and published in 1771, give us an interesting picture of how intellectuals viewed and at the same time urged on Leopold's reforms. In his defence of debtors, for whom the law prescribed harsh imprisonment, Amidei brilliantly combined utilitarian arguments, Beccarian humanitarianism, Rousseauian contractualism and an increasingly strong espousal of physiocratic theories in order to defend the freedom to contract debts. This work by Amidei, which was reprinted with a commentary that was full of reservations by Giambattista Vasco, went some way at least along the road which, starting with the debate on the right to punish, was leading to a questioning of property as a natural right. This was not Amidei's direct intention. He was satisfied by reforms and in the 1783 edition he referred triumphantly to Leopold's edict of 26 October 1782 which took into account what the author had written ten years before. But behind this reformism there were points that contradicted the defence of property – not only his belief in equality, or his support for the cause of the debtors against that of the creditors, but particularly his belief in the right to subsistence, several times reaffirmed as a natural and primary right. His *De' mezzi per diminuire i mendichi* clearly reveals these ideas and here the physiocratic approach is combined with a marked emphasis on the right of the State to intervene in the anachronistic forms of ownership which ultimately limit economic development and the social well-being particularly of the peasants, the only true producers. Thanks to the work of Venturi and the edition by Antonio Rotondò, there is revealed in Amidei's work an unsuspected wealth of ideas and the revival of Tuscan jurisdictionalism. Perhaps his limitation (or rather, his tactic) was the concealing of so many new ideas in the technical and rather cold language of jurisdictionalism.

These same problems were posed by another author who lacked Amidei's caution and whose work, as Venturi has written, was to initiate the most intense period of reform. This was Pilati and his plan *Di una riforma d'Italia*. Carlantonio Pilati came from Trent,[3] a border area and one with a confused identity, divided between the traditions of the Counter-Reformation, the cautious enlightened experiments in Rovereto, the influence of the Habsburgs and the resistance of Venice and the rest of Italy. Pilati's ideas must inevitably have been influenced by the situation of Trent itself, an ecclesiastical principality now firmly integrated into the Habsburg sphere. But the intellectuals of Trent could look for German culture not only to Vienna, Innsbruck and Salzburg but also, as in the case of Pilati, to the great German universities[4] which were seeing an important revival in the human, natural and social sciences. The German world also represented Protestantism and its spiritual values. Pilati's radicalism was the result of all these elements. He looked in one direction to the ideas of the Italian and French Enlightenment, and in the other to all that was most progressive in Habsburg reformism, to the ideas that were leading to Josephism. He was then able to compare these two elements with what he had observed in the German world as a student in Leipzig and Göttingen, a period that was to be formative in his development. Before becoming a teacher at the Trent *liceo* in 1764, he taught at Göttingen.

Pilati's first work, of 1764, is of interest because, if nothing else, it shows us what he was reading and thinking. It was something of a scholarly exercise as can be seen from the title: *L'esistenza della legge naturale impugnata e sostenuta da C. A. Pilati*. The first section is in fact a presentation of the theories of those – Hobbes, the libertines and the free-thinkers – who had attacked the idea of a natural law. What is striking in this first part is that though it purports to explore the ideas of his adversaries, in fact it contains some of the most fundamental ideas to be found in Pilati's later work: the exaltation of reason and experience as opposed to nature; the role of education according to what he had learned from Helvétius; and the instrumental character of all religions. Above all there is the acceptance of the ideas of Helvétius which were an important point of departure for the future author of the *Riforma d'Italia* and which were further confirmed by his next work, *Ragionamento intorno alla legge naturale e civile*, dedicated to the Duke of Brunswick.

The Curia immediately condemned Pilati's first book which had been translated into German in 1767. In Trent, where Pilati was at the centre of a group which read Febronius (then translated into Italian)[5] and sought out avidly unorthodox books (including those by d'Holbach attacking Christianity), life was becoming increasingly insecure. As soon as the *Riforma d'Italia* was published in early 1767, Pilati chose to leave his teaching job to seek that fame as a *philosophe* which this book seemed to predict. In August 1767 he was in Holland from where he wrote to his friend Francesco Stefano Bartolomei, saying that he had managed to get a copy of *Le christianisme dévoilé* and other books by the d'Holbach circle. Holland was not a fortuitous choice: not only was it 'the centre of all European negotiations, where congregate the most able subjects of all the foreign powers', but also the home of the great publishers of that radical Enlightenment to which he felt drawn and a place where he could launch his political and intellectual ideas on a European market. He received an offer from the Portuguese court of a post under Pombal. He enjoyed the protection of the Dutch minister, Benting, and it was probably through him that he could have become counsellor to the King of Denmark, Christian VII. He preferred, however, to move to Chur in Switzerland, where he could count on a friend like Christian Wenking, who translated his first work into German. Bartolomeo De Felice, who was to be the greatest publisher and populariser of ideas of the eighteenth century working from Berne and Yverdon, like Pilati chose the border region between Switzerland, Germany and Italy. This one-time monk and colleague of Genovesi at Naples University had published two series of periodicals, *L'estratto della letteratura europea* and the *Excerptum totius literaturae*. Pilati too thought a periodical could be a way to spread his ideas which drew inspiration not only from those of the *Encyclopédie*, Verri, Beccaria and the Lombard school, but also from the new trends in the German world.

Published in 1767, Pilati's greatest work was entitled not only *Di una Riforma d'Italia* but also *Ossia dei mezzi di riformare i più cattivi costumi e le più perniciose leggi d'Italia*. The repetition is deliberate and underlines the character of the work: a manifesto, a militant tract. It is addressed to the princes of Italy, without distinction between monarchies and republics. He looks first at the confrontation between Church and State which developed during the 1760s, but his approach is neither jurisdictionalist nor 'technical' as was Amidei's. Indeed, in the fullest edition of 1770, Pilati cruelly mocks Amidei for his passages on ecclesiastical celibacy and the right of sanctuary, treating him more as a champion of the Curia.

Pilati's reform of Italy cannot be confined within the moderate and technical limits of jurisdictionalism. It goes straight to the heart of the problem, calling for a reduction of the secular clergy, the abolition of the monastic orders, the confiscation of the Church's wealth and the setting up of state-controlled seminaries to provide the priests needed and train them in their job as public servants. It is clear that many of Pilati's ideas are drawn from

Febronianism and foreshadow Josephism. They strike deeply at civil society and its organisation. Pilati proposes that not only should all immunities and ecclesiastical jurisdictions be abolished but also that church property bound by *fidecommessi* and mortmains be restored to the State and put up for sale. The whole edifice built up since the earliest days of Christianity and based on the credulity and weakness of the first Christian emperors should be torn down by enlightened rulers. Roman law and canon law are the two fundamental props of the old order, which the reforms would wipe out; a system based on injustice, violence, abuse of power, deceit and insecurity. If the mark of political radicalism is republicanism, then Pilati fits ill into this mould in the sense that his proposal seems to care little what system of government is to carry it out. What does concern him is to show that the power of the ecclesiastics is disastrous both for republics and monarchies.

What gives this work its particular vibrancy and originality, and not only in the section on religion, is Pilati's profound awareness of the difference between the Italian states and those parts of Europe, including France, which had experienced the Reformation. It is tempting here to see Pilati almost as a crypto-Protestant, whose attack on the Church sounds like the voice of a dissenter who had embraced another faith. In fact for Pilati religion is not a matter of faith or theology. His comparison with the Protestant world is entirely pragmatic and concrete. Religion remains an important force capable of providing a moral code for society and one which, if it does not conflict with civil life and the State, is of great use. Protestantism, in its different forms, emerges as the variety of religion which most nearly approaches this ideal. Catholicism could become such an ideal, but only after a thorough reform, implying its complete transformation, and the sacrifice not only of its wealth but also of all the power acquired in the course of time over state and civil society. Pilati is deeply convinced that Protestant England, Holland and Germany are superior to Catholic Italy, not because the different forms of Protestantism are, from the religious point of view, more true than Catholicism, but because the ethics and the philosophy of Calvinism, Lutheranism and Anglicanism are closer to those of the *philosophes*. What for others remains a purely jurisdictional matter, becomes here the starting-point for a different and fairer society, where Montesquieu's dreams of liberty and Beccaria's longing for social justice can be realised. But the obstacle to be removed is the massive presence of a Church which not merely accumulates wealth taken from the State and society, but which brings with it a set of values incompatible with a rational world.

It is on these values that Pilati concentrates his most radical attack, even at the cost of filling his work with digressions and sudden changes of direction, to the detriment of the clarity and effectiveness of his thesis. Basic to his work is tolerance, understood in the broad sense of freedom of conscience and the rejection of all forms of inquisition. Several times in the volume we find echoes of Bayle's belief that a society of superstitious people is more harmful to the State than a society of atheists. The State and its sovereign are urged to adopt a firmly anti-aristocratic stance, since the clergy and the nobility, with their anachronistic institutions and their potential for violence, represent the greatest obstacle to change.

His arguments impressed his contemporaries and in 1769 an edition was published in Rimini under the title of *Italia riformata*, consisting of only Chapters 13 and 14, and which was reviewed by the *Journal encyclopédique*. The militancy of the work is particularly evident in the last three chapters of the 1770 edition, not only because there it is stated that 'now is the moment to liberate Italy from the tyranny of prejudice and superstition', or because it tackles in the most radical way the problem of ecclesiastical immunities, but above all because the central ideal of the work is intellectual reform, and the changes which are needed in educational institutions and more generally in cultural attitudes. In part Pilati is again drawing on Helvétius in his discussion of the importance of education and the necessity of state involvement in creating a new type of social conditioning which would take account of a *philosophique* moral code, but we are also hearing the first Italian voice to enter the debate on secondary and university education opened by La Chalotais, taken up by Genovesi and Paciaudi, which was to involve Gorani and Carli and which was linked to the crisis of the Jesuit system and the need to create a new type of public education.[6]

Pilati's contribution came from his own international experience, his knowledge of German education and particularly of the changes which were leading the great German universities to a system of knowledge no longer based on theology, church history, canon law and Roman law, but on history, geography, statistics, economics – the sciences of the state. He described with great accuracy developments in education, not only in France or England but also in Germany, giving the first clear information of that great cultural transformation which was to earn the professors of Göttingen the title of 'masters of Germany'. The *Riforma d'Italia* was an immediate European success. Voltaire was enthusiastic about it and it prompted him to write two pamphlets on the themes of Chapter 13. Inevitably it was also attacked, both by the Church and by the moderate jurisdictionalists like the Venetian Contin.

A similar storm greeted a small work of 1768, *Riflessione di un italiano sopra la chiesa in generale sopra il clero sì regolare che secolare sopra i vescovi e i pontefici romani e sopra i diritti ecclesiastici de' principi precedute dalla Relazione del regno di Cumba e da riflessioni sulla medesima*, which resembled the *Riforma*. Indeed, a summary of its ideas is contained in the last chapter of the second edition of 1770 of the *Riforma*. The description of events in Cumba, an imaginary country in that 'immense stretch of land lying between the Empire of China and the kingdom of Portuguese Brasilia', belongs – without any great originality – to that genre of Utopian literature popular in the eighteenth century. It was designed to demonstrate the destruction wrought in an innocent and pagan kingdom by the arrival of Catholic missionaries, and particularly Jesuits. This was an excuse for a fierce attack on the religious orders, their system of education, their parasitism and social harmfulness. But if all this, already said by Giannone whom Pilati follows, was true, what remedies were available to princes who had the interest of their states at heart?

Pilati reveals the limitations of the solutions so far produced. To bring the religious orders under the discipline of the bishops risked making the latter more powerful and even the eventual decision to reduce the different orders to just a few was an inadequate remedy since it left their power and their vices intact. The only effective solution was to abolish, gradually but firmly, all the religious orders. Looking at the Church as a whole, Pilati emphasised its purely spiritual task. It was precisely this purely religious character of the first Church, looking back to the teachings of Jesus and the Apostles, which revealed how much of an abuse were the claims to immunity and jurisdiction, not to mention the wealth, of the modern Church. The very meaning of excommunication, which was not a punishment but separation from the communion of the faithful, the breaking of a contract, had been turned on its head by councils and popes and used for unacceptable ends, to hit at sovereigns or state officials who opposed ecclesiastical abuses. In the relationship between Church and State, Pilati saw an unresolvable contradiction. Convinced that the Church should be subject to the same rights and obligations as any other private society, he accepted in principle its rules and hierarchies, as long as they were compatible with civil society, but on the other hand, in order to prevent the Church's abuse of power, he maintained that the State was more or less obliged to intervene to avoid the selection of people 'harmful to the State'. Dealing finally with the problem of immunities and church property and jurisdictions, Pilati looks back to Giannone, maintaining that a situation had come about whereby there were more clerics than there were faithful making up the true Church. By removing itself from secular jurisdiction and co-ordinated by the new hierarchies culminating in the pope, the clergy had little by little 'created a state within a state'.

The years in Chur were the most productive and important of Pilati's intellectual life. As well as the *Riflessioni* and the play *Il matrimonio di fra' Giovanni* (1768), he turned to journalism, taking as models *Il Caffè* and the *Estratto della letteratura europea* which since 1766 had been published in Milan. Thus was born the *Corriere letterario* which lasted some eighteen months and established a link with German culture, the French *Encyclopédie* and the two most important branches of the Italian Enlightenment in Lombardy and in Naples. In the summer of 1769, Pilati left Chur. He hoped for a while to be able to represent Denmark at the Neapolitan court where he dreamed of restarting the *Corriere letterario*. But relations with Naples were not so simple. Tanucci knew and admired Pilati's intellectual activities and Pilati had praised Tanucci's reforms in his *Riforma d'Italia*. It seems probable that the ideal, reforming minister to whom the *Riflessioni* were dedicated was Tanucci himself who in 1768 was leading the anti-curial campaign, involving the best minds of the day. The fall of the Danish minister Bernsdorf and the end of the period of reform in Denmark brought an end to this hope. Pilati's journey towards the Bourbon court was halted at Ferrara and Pilati found refuge in Venice where he frequented for some time the circle of Andrea Tron, the patrician who shared his reformist ideas. But not even this powerful protector was able to save him from the state inquisitors. As had happened thirty-five years earlier with Giannone, he was arrested on the night of 30 December 1769 and taken to the state boundary. He was expelled permanently, on pain of death.

Thus ended the most creative period of Pilati's life. Through the influence of Joseph II he was able to return to Trent, but his restless nature drove him to travel again around Europe, always searching for a role but becoming an increasingly marginal figure in the courts, the diplomatic service and even in European cultural circles. His attempt to turn historian was a failure. His *Storia dell'impero germanico e dell'Italia dai tempi carolinghi alla pace di Westfalia* was dropped after 1772, having got no further than the death of the emperor Henry V. It is probable that Denina's successful *Rivoluzioni d'Italia* (1769–70) took away his readers and thus his desire to continue with it. In 1782, with *L'Histoire des révolutions arrivées dans le gouvernement les lois et l'esprit humain après la conversion de Constantin jusqu'à la chute de l'Empire de l'occident*, he reconfirmed his Giannonian vision of civil and religious history in the early years of Christianity. Now close to the Austrian Freemasons and Adam Weischaupt's circle of Bavarian *illuminati* Pilati spent his last years between Trent and Vienna representing local interests to the Habsburg administration. Favourable to the French Revolution, particularly after the fall of Robespierre, he was to have close contact with the Cisalpine Republic, while his play *Il matrimonio di fra' Giovanni*, printed in 1789, was performed in Milan in 1796 when the new mood of anticlericalism and republicanism was awakening hopes of the realisation of those religious and intellectual reforms which he had written of thirty years before. He died in 1802, now far removed from the events that were taking Italy into the new Europe of Napoleon.

NOTES AND REFERENCES

On the background to Amidei and Pilati see Venturi, F. (1969–84) 'La chiesa e la repubblica dentro i loro limiti', in *Settecento riformatore*, vol. II. Einaudi, Turin.   See also: Amidei, C. (1980) *Opere*, ed. Rotondò, A. Giappichelli, Turin.   On Pilati, as well as the relevant sections in Venturi's *Settecento riformatore*, vol. II, see: Rigatti, M. (1923) *Un illuminista trentino del secolo XVIII Carlo Antonio Pilati*. Vallecchi, Florence.

Two areas which are insufficiently covered in this book are, firstly, that of anti-Enlightenment Catholicism and, secondly, Freemasonry. For the first see: Prandi, A. (1966) *Religiosità e cultura nel '700 italiano*. Il Mulino, Bologna (which gives proper space to men like Adeodato Turchi, Daniele Concina, Sigismondo Gerdil, Antonino Valsecchi and Giammaria Ortes);   *idem* (1975) *Cristianesimo offeso e difeso*. Il Mulino, Bologna;   Torcellan, G. F. (1969) *Settecento veneto e altri scritti storici*. Giappichelli, Turin.   The section dealing with Ortes was also published as a monograph: Torcellan, G. F. (1969) *Un économiste du XVIIIe siècle Giammaria Ortes*. Droz, Geneva, Paris.   On Freemasonry there is no work dealing with Italy comparable with: Roche, D. (1978) *Le siècle des Lumières en province. Académies et académiciens provinciaux*

1680–1789. Mouton, Paris–The Hague. See: Francovich, C. (1974) *Storia della massoneria in Italia dalle origini alla Rivoluzione francese*. La Nuova Italia, Florence. See also: Trentafonte, F. (1984) *Giurisdisionalismo, Illuminismo e Massoneria nel tramonto della Repubblica Veneta*. Deputazione di Storia patria per le Venezie, Venice.

1. See: Ricuperati, G. (1980) 'Pietro Giannone: bilancio storiografico e prospettive di ricerca', in various authors, *Pietro Giannone e il suo tempo*, ed. Ajello, R.. Jovene, Naples, vol. I, especially pp. 205–11; Chiosi, E. (1980) 'La tradizione giannoniana', in ibid., vol. II, especially pp. 765–88.

2. On Hume in Italy see: Baldi, M. (1983) *David Hume nel Settecento italiano: filosofia ed economia*. La Nuova Italia, Florence. Strangely, this work refers only once to Amidei, ignoring the work of Venturi and Rotondò's introduction to Amidei's *Opere*.

3. See: Donati, C. (1975) *Ecclesiastici e laici nel Trentino del Settecento 1748–1763*. Sansoni, Florence.

4. See: Marino, L. (1975) *I maestri della Germania. Goettingen 1770–1820*. Einaudi, Turin.

5. (Hontheim, J. N.) (1765) *Justini Febronii jureconsulti de statu ecclesiae et legitima potestate romani pontifici*. Bullioni (in fact, Venice).

6. See: Ricuperati, G. and Roggero, M. (1977) 'Educational policies in eighteenth-century Italy', in *Studies on Voltaire*, CLXVII pp. 223–69.

CHAPTER TWENTY

The Enlightenment in the Mezzogiorno and the crisis of the *ancien régime*: the school of Genovesi, Pagano (1748–99), Filangieri (1752–88)

It is not easy to summarise the events in southern culture in the years between the death of Antonio Genovesi (1769) and the French Revolution. Genovesi's legacy was undoubtedly of the greatest importance for men like Francesco Longano, Traiano Odazzi, Giuseppe Maria Galanti and Domenico and Francesco Antonio Grimaldi, to mention only the most famous of his pupils. Galanti had tried, after the death of his master, to give a first account of his contribution to the world of ideas with his *Elogio di Genovesi*. Voltaire praised the work, recognising the continuity of enlightened ideas developing from one generation to the next. Genovesi's influence is clear in the work of Galanti, Odazzi, Longano and Domenico Grimaldi. They share an interest in the problems of society in the Mezzogiorno and a desire to focus an analysis of the problems on the land itself, in order to understand the obstacles in the way of economic development which made the poverty of the peasants intolerable.

The ills of the South, which Genovesi had begun to describe and sought to heal with a robust, optimistic empiricism, were analysed with more detail in the works of his disciples. They discussed, for example, the disproportionate distribution of wealth, feudal oppression, the loss to the property market of lands tied by mortmains and *fidecommessi*, the parasitical extraction of revenue, the lack of investment, the absence of productive social classes and the limitations of the intellectual bourgeoisie. The legal class in particular, destined to live a marginal and subordinate existence, is described in its impotence in the pitiless *Testamento forense* by Galanti.[1] After Domenico Grimaldi's *Saggio di economia campestre per la Calabria Ultra* of 1770, and shortly before Longano's description of the Molise, there appeared Galanti's *Nuova descrizione storica e geografica delle Sicilie* which was the fullest and most important example of this type of research.

It is worth examining the context, both southern and European, in which this work was conceived. Galanti had tried to compensate for the weakness of the book market in the South, which survived predominantly on the trade in foreign books, by turning editor and instigator of cultural enterprises. From the first his models were Hume, Robertson, Voltaire and Giannone. He was attracted particularly to general history, going beyond the standard models (such as the *Universal History* and the work of Thomas Salmon, both of which were translated in Venice and Naples) which had for the most part been conceived before the appearance of the great historiography of the Enlightenment. Galanti's sixteen-volume *Storia filosofica e politica delle nazioni antiche e moderne* was no mere translation of Millot but included pieces from Voltaire, Condillac, Robertson, Hume and Chastellux. Particular attention was paid to the feudal problem. (Galanti had edited Robertson's *History of the Reign of the Emperor Charles V.*) The title of Galanti's work was an indication of its relationship to a work that was to become essential reading for a whole new generation of southern intellectuals, Raynal's *Histoire philosophique et politique*.

In the area of geography too Galanti had looked to new developments such as the work of Anton Friedrich Büsching, whose *Neue Erdbeschreibung* had begun to appear in translation (as *Nuova geografia*) in Florence and Venice in 1773. But both the translator of the Florence edition, Joseph Jageman, and the Venetian editor, Antonio Zatta, who had unscrupulously reprinted the Florence version, had realised the need to do something about the section on Italy which Büsching had described without first-hand knowledge. Galanti, after providing many supplementary passages for the Lausanne edition of 1776, decided to fill the gap with a *Nuova descrizione storica e geografica dell'Italia* (1782), in which, by co-ordinating information from different correspondents, he tried to construct an overall, informed picture of the political, social and economic situation in Italy. Shortly before this he had published a *Descrizione dello stato antico ed attuale del Contado del Molise*, where history and geography were more noticeably used to support a proposal for reform of obvious Genovesian inspiration. This was the beginning of a first-hand exploration of the situation in the Mezzogiorno that lasted for over a decade and which was brought together in the four-volume *Nuova descrizione storica e geografica delle Sicilie* of 1787–91.

This work documented a decline to which all the dominant groups had contributed – the Church, the barons and the viceroys who represented distant and greedy governments. The laws, the courts and the jurists had done the rest. The result was clear to see: a backward and primitive agriculture, the absence of industries, the demographic crisis and a social ideology which compelled those with talent to enter the parasitical professions rather than taking up productive activities. Anyone acquiring wealth tried to join the ranks of the nobility, preferring income to production. This analysis was not without political consequences. On 8 March 1781, Galanti was nominated Visitor of the Kingdom so that the ills of the provinces could be brought to the notice of the capital. In the same period he was a member of the commission on fiefs which was to try and find ways to abolish feudal institutions. His plans and hopes were destroyed by the definitive step backwards taken by the Bourbon government. In 1794 those who opposed his activities succeeded in obtaining his suspension, which was to be permanent. The French Revolution and the events which followed it transformed the great *illuminista* into an enlightened conservative who was to remain essentially distant from all that which in his own programme could have been carried out by the Revolution and particularly its heir, the new world of Napoleon. Galanti had often referred in his work to Giannone and Vico. He felt a bond with the first, though he believed him to be to some extent a victim of that legalistic approach which he was to criticise in his *Testamento*. Towards the second he had never managed to free himself of a certain mistrust, born of the fact that he found Vico too 'metaphysical'. But it was not from Vico and Giannone but from Genovesi that he dated the intellectual revival of the Mezzogiorno.

It is interesting to see, however, how in Naples in the last decades of the century Vico became once again an important influence for a group of intellectuals which formed around the periodical *Scelta miscellanea*. One of these was Francesco Antonio Grimaldi who graduated in law in Naples and thus was probably also a pupil of Genovesi as was his brother Domenico. He was chiefly interested in philosophy and history and was to encounter Vico in the course of writing his *Riflessioni sopra la disuguaglianza tra gli uomini*, published in 1779–80 as one of the most sophisticated European reactions to the theories of Rousseau[2] and egalitarian ideas in general, including Morelly's *Code de la Nature*. Inequality was part of man's condition from the moral as well as the political and social points of view. Conversant with Boulanger, Helvétius and d'Holbach, whose view of Vico had influenced his own reading, as well as the English philosophers, Grimaldi had sought to construct a new non-Utopian history of human society. Vico had started from man's interests, needs and passions, which were the motive force in his philosophy of history, even if he had then got bogged down in metaphysical speculation. Grimaldi too started from this point, though bearing in mind the comments of writers like Helvétius and D'Holbach.

Vico was again an important influence in Grimaldi's *Annali del regno di Napoli*, his last and most complex history of the South, where he deals with the problems of the wild, barbarous and civilised states. Vico was his guide (with Gibbon and Ferguson) to understanding the passage from one social form to another, the growth of needs, the role of the passions and the desire for independence, freedom and achievement. The *Annali* picked up where Giannone's work had left off but added something new. There was the same sympathy towards the barbarians and to a jurisdictionalist point of view, which came through even more strongly in the conclusion of the book written by the abbé Cestari who finished the book after Grimaldi's death. But there were also important differences. Giannone's *Istoria civile* was the history of a state and particularly of its capital from which came the power and the laws. The *Annali* was a history divided into many parts describing the not always peaceful succession of different civilisations – native, Greek, Carthaginian and Roman – in southern Italy.

Francesco Mario Pagano, who was to be another member of the *Scelta miscellanea* group studying under Genovesi, had also discovered Vico, through Gerardo de Angelis, a friend of the author of the *Scienza Nuova*, who had passed on to the young man his interest in poetry, myth and the primitive world. Pagano belonged to that group of intellectuals which had formed around the Di Gennaro and Grimaldi brothers, much influenced by Freemasonry and which was also frequented by Gaetano Filangieri. When Pagano published his most important work, the *Saggi politici*, in 1783, he already knew both Grimaldi's *Riflessioni sopra la disuguaglianza* and the first part of Filangieri's *Scienza della legislazione*. Pagano's reading of Vico, especially of the first edition, was strongly influenced not only by Boulanger, Buffon and d'Holbach, but also by Grimaldi. The Vico that he used to reconstruct the 'civil course of the nations', that is 'their beginning, development and decline', was a Vico (as was Grimaldi's) reconciled with a materialist vision of the world, inspired by Newton's mechanistic universe – as interpreted by Boulanger, Buffon and d'Holbach. Such a reading of the *Scienza Nuova* influenced the whole of Pagano's second essay which deals with the savage state and the origin of the family, where the first ideas of nobility led to force and violence, which were accompanied by courage and beauty, thus distinguishing the plebeians as the weak and inferior. The barbarians, who were closest to this savage state, confirmed, with their bellicose ideologies and disdain for manual work, this division between noble and servant, between victor and vanquished. In dealing with the subject of progress beyond the Middle Ages and the evolution of civil societies, Pagano touched on the great theme of the century, the right of property, defending it against more communistic solutions, using arguments from Locke.

In his *Saggi politici* Pagano follows Genovesi, but also looks back to precedents in Vico and arguments which can be compared with Hume, presenting an apologia for the middle class and, while leaving it unclear whether he prefers a republican or monarchical political system, he attempts to show that the social rise of the plebeians was more rapid in a monarchy than in an aristocratic republic. The last two essays are devoted to the decline of nations and restate, in the light of Vico and Robertson, not only the particular and inevitable nature of the feudal system, but also present a positive judgement on the barbarians. As Grimaldi wrote too, when the barbarians took over a world that was by then corrupt and depopulated, although they destroyed illustrious monuments from the past, in fact they became part of a by now inevitable decline and perhaps prevented an even more serious regression which might have returned Italy to the savage state. Dealing with events in the Mezzogiorno and the problems inherited from the past, Pagano saw in the medieval Norman and Swabian kings the beginning of revival. But the model that Roger II of Hauteville and Frederick II had before them was the Byzantine monarchy and, as a result, their laws reflected 'the ferocity of the despotism of a decadent nation'. The Angevins, as Giannone had taught, 'called by the pope, supported by the barons', brought about feudal society.

This had been opposed by the generous Aragonese, who had, however, failed to prevent the kingdom falling into the hands of foreigners and becoming a province. To its internal problems (a protracted feudalism, with a large part of the land occupied by ecclesiastic benefices) were thus added all the elements of a bad administration, and subordination to a political system which cared little about trade or industry.

This was the inheritance from the past, which still oppressed the present 'national' situation. Pagano divides the social classes in the Mezzogiorno into four groups: feudal landowners, ecclesiastics, the jurists, and the plebeians. The latter, poor and oppressed, had had 'to support through the centuries the immense colossus formed by the first three classes'. The jurists, acting as mediators and having eaten away at the wealth formerly owned exclusively by nobles and ecclesiastics, had initially had a positive effect on social development, but as they began to use their professional education for the acquisition of power, instead of acting as reformers they had put their own interests first, encouraging a formalistic culture and the spirit of contentiousness. The move from being a province of Spain or Austria to a 'national state' in 1734 had been an important turning-point, but the work was not complete. The central feature, a Code, was lacking. The first edition of the *Saggi politici* ended by expressing a hope for reform, in the knowledge that failure would mean catastrophe for society.

Although, like Grimaldi, Pagano's reading of Vico was distorted by Buffon, Boulanger and d'Holbach, there were differences too. In Grimaldi the attack on equality as preached by Rousseau tended to stress the historical necessity of inequality and the process of formation of the noble élite. Pagano, by contrast, took a less static view of history and recognised the possibility that non-aristocratic classes might take over the leadership of the country. This provoked a remarkable response in Italy, in Europe and especially in Naples. Pietro Napoli Signorelli's review of 1785 in the *Giornale enciclopedico* of Naples revealed the split taking place among the followers of Vico. The future author of *Vicende della cultura napoletana* defended the orthodox Vico, whom it was possible to reconcile with Catholicism and the views of the anti-Enlightenment, against the materialistic Vico, the follower of the 'catastrophe theory', presented by Pagano. Freemasonry was to play an important role in this debate. Vico's symbolism, his revived Platonism and even his obscurities lent themselves to the arcane mysteries of the sect, still in the process of evolving its own language. The traditionalist Signorelli reacted similarly against this treatment of Vico.

In the years immediately preceding the French Revolution, Pagano returned again to penal law and the need for its reform in his *Considerazioni sul processo criminale* (1787). Following in Beccaria's footsteps he worked on this subject for a decade, resulting in the posthumously published *Della ragion criminale*. Appointed advocate of the poor in the Maritime and Admiralty Tribunal in 1789, in the same year he was to write a passionate appeal in favour of free trade and against the restrictions of the *annona*, *Ragionamento sulla libertà di commercio del pesce in Napoli*, where arguments drawn from the libertarian tradition were added to a recognition of the ills that had by now become intolerable. The second edition of the *Saggi politici* emphasised Pagano's radicalism. It is significant that the references to Francesco Antonio Grimaldi have disappeared. If nature and history did not show the equality dreamed of by Rousseau, yet equality was an unquenchable human aspiration. The ideal of justice, first found in Plato, was beginning to be equated with democracy. The privileges of the nobles appeared increasingly shocking and unacceptable. The chapters praising Bourbon reformism and expressing the hope that from it there would result a change in the society of the Mezzogiorno have also disappeared. Pagano was set on a path which was to lead to Jacobinism. He was among the intellectuals who attempted to carry out these ideas in the Parthenopean Republic and for which he was condemned to death in 1799.

It is interesting to speculate in what direction Gaetano Filangieri would have developed if his life had not been cut off so early, even before he had completed his great work. His links with Pagano were very close for more than fifteen years. Born in 1752, he had met Pagano in 1770 when he had attended his lectures on ethics at Naples University. From then on their friendship continued to grow. Both were close to Francesco Antonio Grimaldi, and frequented the Di Gennaro brothers' circle. In 1782 Pagano dedicated the first of his 'political' tragedies *Gli esuli italiani* to Filangieri. The latter had enthusiastically quoted the *Saggi politici* in his *Scienza della legislazione*. Both members of the English-rite masonic lodge, in 1786 they experienced the impact of the hermetic world of the North. Friedrich Münter introduced them to the ideas of Weishaupt's *Illuminati* which Pagano, Zurlo, Jerocades and Tommasi had enthusiastically espoused. It seems from his letters that Filangieri opposed them in the name of the English rite. Affectionate and concerned, Pagano wrote to him that the temple was by now in ruins and that a hand 'both merciful and cruel will give it the *coup de grâce*, in order to rebuild it',[3] referring obviously to Münter's visit. It was the Freemasons of the English-rite lodges, including Pagano and Tommasi, who, on 20 September 1788, were to commemorate Filangieri's premature death. Tommasi has left a detailed and unusual memoir of the rites:

It was a very moving occasion. The gathering was large. Tears and sorrow could be seen on every face. The lodge was decked in black. The portrait of the deceased faced the East and was festooned with garlands of cypress and flowers, surrounded by many lights. It was placed on a mound where lay the square, the level, the compasses and the other masonic instruments . . ..[4]

Filangieri's *Scienza della legislazione* is the most far-reaching document of that decade which culminated with the French Revolution. What strikes the modern reader is its unity, comparable to only a very few other eighteenth-century works, and to these he refers constantly: Vico's *Scienza Nuova*, Montesquieu's *Esprit des lois*, Rousseau's *Contrat social* and Schmid's *Principes de législation universelle*. Filangieri attempted, through the science of legislation, to set up a complete model of society, changing, directly or indirectly, the fundamentals of social life. His book is thus the most successful of the plans for society which we also find in Pagano's *Saggi politici* and, in part at least, in Grimaldi's work. As with these two authors, the central problem to be resolved was the relationship between democracy and freedom. Although he does not quote them, Filangieri too always had in mind Grimaldi's objections to the Rousseauian myth of equality. Although it represented a profound need in man, it was not possible to build a model society on such a premiss. Like Pagano in both the first and second editions of his *Saggi*, so too Filangieri had avoided the trap of the conservatism implicit in this pitiless demolition of equality. Unlike Pagano he sought a solution which moved increasingly towards democracy. Filangieri's proposal thus is the most important attempt of his day, not only in Italy but also in Europe, to rationalise the society of the *ancien régime*. It was an ingenious plan, not without voluntarism, to avoid the catastrophe which he saw looming on the horizon.

Where does Filangieri stand in relation to Italian and European thought? He had already begun to think about legislation and reform at the time when the most intense phase of Bourbon anticlericalism was coming to an end. From this cultural and religious background, Filangieri had been introduced to important new ideas through his master De Luca and his uncle, Bishop Serafino Filangieri, both exponents of that regalistic and enlightened episcopacy, most famous among whom was Francesco Serrao. Filangieri was to retain these influences, transforming them, partly in the light of Habsburg and Josephine models, into a civil religion, a fundamental moral code which would make the State and society one, linking legislation to customs and usage. His work had matured during the hopes and then disappointment of the Tanucci period, when the influence of Maria Carolina had aroused expectations of more reforms, and under the influence of Joseph II's policies which were now coming to the attention of intellectuals and politicians. He was well aware that great changes were taking place internationally. He was writing at the time of the American Revolution and, along with the majority of European intellectuals, his sympathies were on the side of the patriots. The struggle between the colonies and the mother country represented for him a blow for international democracy, liberty and brotherhood against tyranny. England was no longer that country depicted in Montesquieu's *Esprit des lois*. The revolt of the colonies had brought to light the problems and limitations of a society that, after the Seven Years War, had emerged as the dominant economic and colonial power.

In the 1780s, Filangieri saw the crisis of this hegemony, which had resulted in the Bourbon states led by France and Holland aligning themselves on the side of the Americans. Although supporting the Americans' cause, because it was a just one, and convinced after 1780 of their eventual victory, nevertheless Filangieri accurately pointed out the contradiction and shortsightedness in the attitude of the European powers, particularly Spain and Portugal, which possessed immense American empires. The victory of the colonists and the resulting independence for the former English colonies would have serious consequences in South America. Europe would lose, sooner or later, all its colonies. Filangieri's radical pacifism was looking for another solution, based on the acceptance by England (given her reputation for civilised behaviour and importance in the fields of philosophy, science and politics)[5] of the colonists' basic demands. They should be allowed the same political and fiscal rights as the inhabitants of the mother country as well as economic and commercial rights.

In his diagnosis of the ills of Europe, Filangieri saw clearly the problems of France where reformism was reaching a crisis after the fall of Turgot. He saw too the difficulties of Spain and Portugal notwithstanding the reforms of Charles III and Pombal, for the basic situation based on colonialism and the exploitation of foreign resources which had brought about the ruin of the Spanish and Portuguese economies had remained unaltered. In his *Scienza della legislazione* he noted the slow and dignified decline of Holland whose prosperity was based on trade, but which in the eighteenth century was beginning to reveal the limitations of this type of development, which lacked a solid basis in production and agriculture despite the efforts of its industrious inhabitants, who were being increasingly hard pressed by competition with France and England.

Filangieri saw too the potential of Russia, of its westward moves and its strategies in the Mediterranean. The Russia that he admired was not that of the autocratic Peter the Great who had wanted to impose a Western model on his country, forcing it to accept habits, techniques and fashions which remained foreign or which unnecessarily outraged its most deep-rooted traditions, but rather the Russia of Catherine, whose *Nakaz* (1767) shone out as, theoretically at least, an example of the correct path to follow. This Semiramis of the North had tried to adapt for her own vast country all that was best and most profound of the European Enlightenment. It was this (and not power politics) that indicated how the balance in Europe was moving eastwards and it was there that the reforms of Frederick II and Joseph II were being enacted. Filangieri does not say much about these two sovereigns who are partly subsumed into the figure of Catherine II.

There were two criticisms, however, that he felt impelled to make. First, as a result of his belief in free trade, he was implicitly opposed to protectionism and the control of the economy. Second, concerning militarism, which he saw as the reverse or evil side of all reformist policies, Filangieri was opposed to all armies not only because of his strong support for the pacifist ideals of eighteenth-century philanthropy, or for economic reasons since armies were a hindrance to policies of reform, but also because they were inimical to his ideal society, where arms were only for defence in which all patriotic citizens would participate. He draws a radically different political map of the world with the developed centres – France, Holland and England – in crisis, taking account of the emergence of Russia (which had momentarily raised hopes of freedom for Greece) and particularly putting into perspective the situation of North America as the new home of liberty and democracy. It was Raynal who, in his searing though contradictory attack on the West and its slave-based colonialism, was to place a question mark over Europe and its relationship to the other continents.[6] This was the beginning of a more than superficial interest in extra-European geography and history.

Africa appeared as a continent enfeebled by the plundering of Arabs and Europeans who robbed her not so much of wealth as of men, that most precious and irreplaceable resource of society. Asia showed two contrasting faces: on the one hand India with its inflexible caste system and its world of petty sovereigns so reminiscent of feudalism, on the point of being conquered by the French and especially the English; on the other, China, which a well-established eighteenth-century tradition, from Doria to the physiocrats and to Raynal, saw as a political, economic and social alternative to the West. China appeared a peaceful, more populous state than any in the West, and one which had developed its agricultural economy to the extent of feeding a population incomparably larger than that of all the European states put together, allowing a thriving trade and exquisite craftsmanship. Economic self-sufficiency, based on the development of agriculture, was possible without the expansionist, conquering spirit which seemed to be the cancer of the West. But China struck Filangieri also as a model of legal despotism, to use the physiocratic term. There was not only the sovereign who ensured respect for the law, preventing the big landowners from abusing their power over the peasants, but also an able and rational bureaucracy which guaranteed the enforcement of the law even in the most distant provinces of the Empire. Religion and morality offered a fascinating example of that co-ordination between legislation, customs, the ethical code and religion which Filangieri hoped to realise through Christianity (refined by masonic ideology). The mandarin was an example of the intellectual and interpreter of the law – the philosopher-bureaucrat, that Filangieri had found in the southern tradition of Doria, Gravina and Vico. He was the holder of Plato's *jus sapientioris*, transformed in Filangieri's version to *philosophe*.

This understanding of the great changes afoot in Europe and outside lies at the heart of Filangieri's thought. His new 'science' included politics, economics, law, education and religion. With a geometric precision, redeemed and transformed by a vigorous and emotional language, Filangieri constructed his idea of society in a framework of reformism, Utopianism and a consciousness of the approaching crisis. Inevitably he was influenced by Montesquieu whom he aimed to continue and develop, advancing from the 'spirit' (*esprit*) to the 'rules', to establish a practical science of legislation. He had to take into account a *corpus* of political doctrines that were by now far more complex than those available to the great French scholar. Along with the ideas on liberty and the role of the intermediate bodies between absolutism and the people, there had also emerged, in a pragmatic work of Western political thought such as the *Contrat social*, a theory of democracy, challenging contemporaries with all its revolutionary implications and all its unresolved problems. Even law had been transformed, as can be seen in a short book like *Dei delitti e delle pene* – so full of new values and a new vision of the world – and so too the idea of nature.

Between Montesquieu and Filangieri stand two important figures: Boulanger and Buffon. Through them it had been possible to interpret Vico's philosophy of history in a naturalistic way. The Newtonian universe had definitively ousted that of Descartes, providing a view of the world that was less mechanistic and more organic. Most importantly, Filangieri was writing at a time when economics was becoming a science. He looks not so much to Adam Smith's *Wealth of Nations*, published in 1776, as to all the theoretical assumptions from late-mercantilism, to Genovesi, to physiocracy and the critical realism of Galiani. He found the first great synthesis of what was becoming 'classic' economics in Pietro Verri's *Meditazioni sull'economia politica*. Indeed it was through this text that Filangieri was able to make the link between legislation and economics. Another of Filangieri's contributions, missing in Montesquieu, was the development of the discussion on education and its content, which had exercised all the great men of the European Enlightenment.

Although Filangieri was convinced, like Montesquieu, that the nobility as an intermediary between absolute power and the people had a role in protecting freedom, he was totally opposed to the system which had guaranteed to the feudal nobility privileges, powers and the defence of their property. Thus when speaking of economics he writes against *maggiorascati* and every type of right of primogeniture, while when speaking of justice he feels forced to attack every form of jurisdiction not subject to state control. This was a subject discussed at the time throughout Europe, in works like Boncerf's *Les Inconvénients des droits féodaux*,[7] which had sparked off a similar debate to that stimulated in Naples by the publication of the *Scienza della legislazione*. Genovesi had prepared the way, fighting for the freedom to sell fiefs and attacking the economic consequences of the retrogressive institutions which were (together with ecclesiastic land tenure) the chief cause of the South's backwardness. Filangieri could not fail to see the complete contradiction between a modern concept of law and the survival of a system where the administration of justice was, as in most states of the *ancien régime*, shared between the feudal landowners and the magistrates. This was particularly true in the Mezzogiorno: 'A remnant of the old feudal government leaves criminal jurisdiction with the barons. This prerogative, of which they are extremely jealous, is the first link in that long chain of disorders which combine to destroy our civil liberty . . .'[8] Though a noble and of an ancient feudal family, he did not hesitate to act against his own class interests. Feudal jurisdictions and in general all the rights connected with the fief were incompatible with a modern society.

This was an area for resolute measures. But how then could he reconcile this view with the view of the nobility as an intermediary body acting as an instrument for potential freedom and a protection against the despotic logic which could be implicit in absolutism? Filangieri's solution was complicated and contradictory. He wanted to separate the functions of the nobility from feudalism, eliminating the latter but not the former, with the feudal landowners as a separate body possessing distinctions but essentially without privileges. Only despotism could get rid of all distinctions. Even in a democracy, despite the desire for equality, there would emerge what Filangieri called, in a happy and apt phrase, a 'nobility of opinion'. This was particularly true in monarchies, where 'the constitution of the government does not require political equality'. The type of society that Filangieri believed to be most suitable for the South, and perhaps more generally for the countries of Europe, was still a monarchy, but a modernised monarchy, whose absolutism would be rationally limited not only by the law but also by the magistrates who executed it, the latter being competent and esteemed public officials.

This compromise with monarchy (and particularly with the continued existence of the nobility), albeit with reduced powers, shows up very clearly in the section where Filangieri is obliged to accept a diversification of punishments according to social class, starting from the idea that the nobles were much more sensitive than the plebeians to punishments which touched their honour. Beccaria's rigorously egalitarian system is here somewhat muddied by Filangieri. On the matter of the death penalty too Filangieri's compromise with monarchy leads to his being less radical and principled than Beccaria. The programme for education (in Book IV) contains elements of all these ideas. In line with his rejection of equality and following a social stratification based on a schema of nobility, bourgeoisie and urban or rural proletariat, Filangieri describes a system of public education that would from the very start encourage the social virtues of each group. His model contained an inherent dichotomy in that it was based on the division of the nobility and bourgeoisie on one side from the workers on the other, according to their future work, intellectual or manual.'I would from the start divide the people into two classes. In the first I include all those who serve or could serve society with their hands, in the second those who serve it with their talents.'[9] The first class, of workers, would receive an elementary education, controlled by local magistrates, which would be public and free and geared towards teaching solid vocational skills, whether in trade or agriculture.

Filangieri's plan was analytical, providing for both the educational and vocational content and also for the methods for encouraging in these future artisans and peasants not only manual ability but also the physical and moral strength to convert them if necessary into soldiers. A Utopian aspect of this plan was Filangieri's proposal that the money spent by the European states on mercenary armies be redirected to education. The abolition of professional soldiers would result in an improvement in the education of the community and would prevent offensive wars. The country's own militia would suffice for defence, recruited from the workers and peasants, educated to be patriotic and strengthened by a civic and physical upbringing. Here, as in Machiavelli, the reference to Ancient Greece and Rome is clear. The education of the lower classes would last for thirteen years and end at the age of seventeen when, after a solemn public ceremony, intended to impress itself on the minds of the youths, they would pass to adulthood and take up the trades they had learned, along with solid moral, religious and civil values. Such a system should remain flexible, allowing, through a system of study grants, the movement from this type of education to the other, of those who appeared exceptionally gifted.

His plan for this second class and their higher education was equally detailed and complex. Here Filangieri's point of view was all too realistic, in the sense that he aimed to make theoretical learning coincide as far as possible with the possession of wealth. His model in this case was English society where a good education cost so much that it was the almost exclusive monopoly of the monied classes. Suspicious of the semi-educated (with a contempt that was by now typical of the late Enlightenment), Filangieri asserted that 'the country that most abounds in errors is the one where it costs the least to succeed in a literary career'. This ease not only produced intellectuals without employment, but also deprived the 'productive classes' of energy without returning any benefit.[10] The education of the upper class was to take place from the age of five, in special colleges that would provide a solid basis in professional and political theory. Nobles and rich bourgeois would have to learn how to live together and cast off mutual prejudices. The curriculum, following the epistemological ideas of the day and particularly Helvétius, was designed to stimulate the four basic faculties of the intelligence: perception, memory, imagination and reasoning.

Filangieri's ultimate aim was clear – to bring about a change in public opinion. His understanding of the new and complex power of public opinion, this invisible 'tribunal', 'more powerful than the magistrates and the laws, the ministers and the kings', with which intellectuals and governments now had to reckon, was unusually profound. Public opinion in fact 'shows us that sovereignty resides constantly and truly in the people and that they will not allow it to be exercised whether it be left in the hands of many or a single person, of a senator or a king'.[11] But in order to act positively and to involve the majority in the decisions of an enlightened government or to stimulate reforms, public opinion needed a free press, an inalienable right which cannot be taken away without causing irreparable damage to society. An unrestricted free press would be able to correct the very errors which might arise from it.

Book V of this work, unfinished and merely sketched, deals with the laws concerning religion. The author was aware of approaching a subject that was not just delicate but which would give rise to attacks and suspicions no less serious and certainly more insidious than those caused by his antifeudal stance. There are three very interesting elements in this section which even stylistically differs from the preceding books, almost as if the author, conscious of the difficulty of the subject, felt the need to amass proofs and explanatory footnotes, which are absent in the previous books.

The first is his reference to Vico and Boulanger (or rather to an interpretation of Vico which resembles that of Grimaldi and Pagano) to explain the relationship between religion, civil society and State in strictly historical terms. Accepting the idea of a progression from a primitive polytheism to a more evolved monotheism, Filangieri uses the category of barbarism to describe the time when an insufficiently developed civil and moral code encouraged a theocracy, a form of government where the sacred served to strengthen a still hazy idea of justice. The emergence from barbarism had allowed, as in Greece and Rome, a plurality of religions: one for the masses, one for the government and one for the philosophers. The first was still polytheistic and embellished with the poets' fables, 'which are the first theologies of the nations', the second was based on ritual and civil ceremonies and the third capable of correcting the most superstitious aspects of the first.

The second unusual element is Filangieri's obvious desire to force revealed religion to coincide – in an age of reason such as the West now knew – with civil religion, in complete harmony with the values of law, ethics and customs. Fanaticism and irreligion were two extremes still capable of threatening a true religion.

The third element is closely related to the first two and is the description of a method to bring about a change of religion so as to allow the legislator to adjust it to the requirements of justice, policy and morality. These are astonishing pages, not only because they describe a logical, rational and pure religion which he wished to introduce into the sectarian world of the eighteenth century, but above all because they are presented almost without apology, as a justification for the intervention of Freemasonry, that society of wise men who in the name of a higher ideal of justice and reason wished to change even Catholicism into a 'civil' religion.

Filangieri had been correct in anticipating fierce attacks on his book from the nobility and the clergy. The first four books had come out between 1780 (I and II) and 1783 (III and IV). The debate between Giuseppe Grippa, a moderate pro-aristocratic reformist, Michele Torcia, a supporter of Filangieri's ideas and Salvatore Pignatelli, an apologist for feudalism, was very fierce and dragged on even after Filangieri's death.[12] Nevertheless, the *Scienza della legislazione* met with great success both in Italy and Europe. In 1787 Filangieri was invited to join the *Consiglio delle Finanze*, the new body typical of the brief but intense period of reform in the southern kingdom and in which were involved also, after his death, not only Galanti but also Melchiorre Delfico and Giuseppe Palmieri. The *Scienza della legislazione* was and remained an essential work in the battle against feudalism until the famous work by David Winspeare. And this was probably not the most important aspect of this thought-provoking work which, through Benjamin Constant's *Commentaire* of 1822, was to play once more an important role in the advance from the ideas of the Enlightenment to those of a liberal constitutionalism.

NOTES AND REFERENCES

For monographs and anthologies of Galanti, Longano, the Grimaldi brothers, Pagano and Filangieri see: Venturi, F. (1962) *Illuministi italiani*, vol. V, *Riformatori napoletani*. Ricciardi, Milan–Naples. See also: Galanti, G. M. (1969) *Della descrizione geografica e politica delle Sicilie*, eds Assante, F. and De Marco, D. Esi, Naples;

Rainone, A. (1968) *Il pensiero economico di G. M. Galanti*. Naples; Galanti, G. M. (1970) *Memorie storiche del mio tempo*, ed. De Marco, D.; Galanti, G. M. (1981) *Giornale di viaggio in Calabria (1792)* ed. Placanica, A. Società editrice napoletana, Naples. On D. Grimaldi see: Sisca, A. (1969) *Domenico Grimaldi e l'Illuminismo meridionale*. Pellegrini, Cosenza. On F. A. Grimaldi see: Giarrizzo, (1981) *Vico, la politica e la storia*. Guida, Naples, pp. 211ff. On Pagano see: Solari, G. (1963) *Studi su Francesco Mario Pagano*, ed. Firpo, L. Giappichelli, Turin. On Filangieri see: Cotta, S. (1954) *Filangieri e la scienza del governo*. Giappichelli, Turin. See also: Maestro, M. (1976) 'Filangieri and his "Science of Legislation"', in *Transactions of the American Philosophical Society*, N. S. vol. LXVI, pt 6; Goggi, G. (1976) 'Diderot, Raynal e Filangieri: uno studio di fonti', in *Giornale storico della letteratura italiana*, CLIII, fasc. 483, pp. 381–418;   *idem* (1980) 'Ancora su Diderot, Raynal e su altre fonti della "Scienza della legislazione"', in *La Rassegna della letteratura italiana*, a. LXXXIV, fasc. 1–2, January–August, pp. 112–60; Becchi, P. (1986) *Vico e Filangieri in Germania*. Jovene, Naples.

1. See the facsimile edition of the 1806 Venice edition: 1977 Bibliopolis, Naples.
2. See: Rota Ghibaudi, S. (1961) *La fortuna di Rousseau in Italia (1750–1815)*. Giappichelli, Turin. On the influence of Montesquieu see: Ambri Berselli, P. (1960) *L'opera di Montesquieu nel Settecento italiano*. Sansoni, Florence; Rotta, S. (1971) 'Montesquieu nel Settecento italiano', in *Materiali per una storia giuridica*, ed. Tarello, G. Il Mulino, Bologna, I, pp. 108–12.
3. See the undated letter in Venturi, F. (1962) *Riformatori napoletani*, vol. V of *Illuministi italiani*, Ricciardi, Milan–Naples, pp. 935–6.
4. See: Tommasi D. (1788) *Elogio storico del Cavalier G. Filangieri*. Raimondi, Naples. On Tommasi see: Feola, R. (1977) *Dall'Illuminismo alla Restaurazione. Donato Tommasi e la legislazione delle Sicilie*. Jovene, Naples.
5. See: Venturi, F. (1969–84) *I grandi stati dell'Occidente*, vol. IV, pt I of *Settecento riformatore*. Einaudi, Turin, pp. 3–202.
6. Ibid., pp. 371–7.
7. See: Mackrell, J. Q. C. (1973) *The Attack on 'Feudalism' in Eighteenth-century France*. Routledge and Kegan, London–Toronto.
8. See: Filangieri, G. (1806) *La scienza della legislazione*. Santini, Venice, vol. III, book III, Ch. XVII, pp. 193–210. See also: Ch. XVIII, Appendice all'antecedente capo sulla feudalità, pp. 210–30.
9. Ibid., vol. V, book IV, pp. 14 ff.
10. Ibid., vol. VI, book IV, p. 4.
11. Ibid., vol. VII, book IV, pp. 108ff.
12. See: Villani, P. (1968) 'Il dibattito sulla feudalità nel Regno di Napoli dal Genovesi al Canosa', in various authors, *Saggi e richerche sul Settecento*. Istituto italiano per gli studi storici B. Croce, Naples, pp. 252–331.

CHAPTER TWENTY-ONE

The intellectuals and the State in the crisis of the *ancien régime* in Piedmont

The Savoyard states had undergone an extraordinary process of reform in the first half of the eighteenth century. Here even from the cultural point of view, the role of civil society had been subordinated to that of the State and its institutions. The university and secondary schools had absorbed the greater part of the local intelligentsia and most of the products of a press which could not match that of Venice or Naples, and even less that of Tuscany. But the cautious humanistic education provided by the Piedmontese educational institutions was not without significance, for it provoked an independent, and to some extent creative, reaction. The life of Giuseppe Baretti illustrates this. After completing his studies in Turin, Baretti went to London and became a teacher of Italian in the circle of Samuel Johnson. This contact with English public opinion and its openness and lack of prejudice prompted Baretti, on returning to Italy, to start the periodical *La Frusta letteraria*, which was a successful combination of literary journal and propagator of information to a wider public. It is not hard to detect in Baretti's lively prose traces of those anti-Enlightenment ideas that he must have acquired in Turin from the Barnabite Sigismondo Gerdil, opponent of Locke, Newton and Montesquieu and subsequently of Rousseau and d'Holbach.

Carlo Denina too had been influenced in the same direction as is clear from the Catholic reformism of his first works, but he differs from his master in his lively curiosity about the ideas of the Enlightenment, apparent in both his *Discorso sopra le vicende della letteratura* (1761) and in the *Parlamento otta-viano*, a periodical somewhere between the *Spectator* and the *Lettres persanes*. These two works are remarkable for the international influences they contain, such as was to be found in court and diplomatic circles. Through these had passed such men as David Hume (who had read in Turin the proofs of *L'Esprit des Lois* published in Geneva), Louis Dutens, who edited Leibnitz and later wrote memoirs full of nostalgia for Turin, Edward Gibbon, John Wilkes, the Portuguese ambassador De Souza and the Neapolitan Domenico Caracciolo. Through Dutens Denina was put in contact with the Scottish writers and as a result of his introduction to that developing culture felt compelled to change the second edition of his *Discorso* which was the first example of a summary of the history of culture and its development from the beginnings, deriving from Voltaire and Yves Goguet.

Denina (1731–1813) was to be an important figure in Piedmontese cultural life. Born in Revello, a farming village in the Saluzzese, of a poor family, he gained entry to the university thanks to the *Collegio delle Provincie*. After a period teaching in secondary school and following the success of his *Rivoluzioni d'Italia*, he was awarded the chair of Italian eloquence and Greek language at Turin University. The *Rivoluzioni d'Italia* was a 'general history' of the peninsula, previously attempted only by the Humanists Carlo Sigonio and, in the early eighteenth century, Muratori. Denina acknowledges a great debt to the latter, particularly on matters of scholarship. Muratori, still imbued with the theological spirit, provided material for a philosophical history of Italy in the style of Voltaire, Hume, Gibbon and Robertson. As in his previous work, the *Discorso sulle vicende della letteratura*, Denina was much indebted to Montesquieu for his categories of greatness and decadence, causation and theory of climate. He had taken from contemporary historians (Varillas, Vertot, d'Orléans and others) the term 'revolution' as a synonym of change, applying it to very long periods and composite areas. It was a history of Italy which aimed to draw on what was best in historiographical tradition, from Machiavelli and Guicciardini to Muratori and Giannone, presenting it from a moderate but firmly jurisdictional point of view, not without Gallican influence.

This book revived interest in Piedmontese culture. It answered a need sorely felt at this time, when hopes of reform and the clash between Church and State led many intellectuals to question the identity, history and specificity of the Italian states. Pietro Verri had encouraged his brother Alessandro to finish and publish his planned *Storia d'Italia*. The appearance of Denina's history caused Alessandro to lose all interest in this work which remained unpublished. Pilati too stopped working on his history of Italy and the Empire, which had been overtaken by Denina's *Rivoluzioni*, so that the latter remained the only work of its kind in the second half of the eighteenth century.

In the 1770s much was changing. A good illustration of this is the *Discorso sopra l'arte istorica* of 1773 by Francesco Galeani Napione. This young intellectual who was to become a typical representative of the Savoyard service nobility, in considering the problems of how and what history to write, while using all the methodology of the Enlightenment, showed his preference for a 'universal' or global history of his own country. He developed this idea in 1788 (though it was not published until 1791) in his discussion of the history of Piedmont which appeared, significantly, as an appendix to *Dell'uso e dei pregi della lingua italiana*.[1] Denina too had had a go at 'Savoyard history' with a general reconstruction of the history of his state to replace that by Samuel Guichenon. Then he wrote a *Histoire de Victor Amédée II* in an attempt to imitate Voltaire's *Siècle de Louis XIV*. In these projects too he had understood the climate of the 1770s, more interested in looking at the different branches of regional culture and society than in large general themes. The *Bibliopea*, a book on the art of rationally constructing books, was indicative of Denina's desire to set himself up as mentor of the Savoyard intellectuals who were emerging in the leading academic institutions.

It was however his *Dell'impiego delle persone* which he had started to have printed in Tuscany (thus outside the State of Savoy) which unleashed the opposition of the conservative clergy who objected to his moderate reformism and his proposals for civil revival. By publishing outside the country without permission he had violated the censorship laws and, deprived of his chair, he was confined for a while in Vercelli. This unpleasant experience was certainly the reason for his decision to leave Piedmont and to enter the service of a sovereign like Frederick II who appeared to have a greater appreciation of culture and intellectuals. Denina was assisted in this decision both by his knowledge of the diplomatic world and by the network of contacts which linked the members of the Turin *Société Royale* with the great academies of Europe. Indeed, it was Saluzzo, future organiser of the Academy of Sciences, who suggested Denina for Berlin. Here he was to publish that *Geschichte Piedmonts* which was the fruit of his ideas on the history of Savoy and which he rewrote in Napoleonic times as *Storia dell'Italia occidentale*.

The presence of Denina in Berlin should be seen not so much as an exile or a search for freedom as a comfortable niche for a cosmopolitan intellectual. He was there during that period of intense relations between Piedmont and Prussia that, from the cultural point of view, resulted in the discovery of the German world. There is precise evidence of this in the *Lettere brandeburghesi* from Denina to his friends of the *Accademia Sanpaolina* and in the success of his other works from his *Prusse littéraire* to the biography of Frederick II.

While Denina was pursuing his historical and linguistic studies in Berlin, in Piedmont there took place a remarkable development in the field of both the arts and sciences. In 1757 the *Société Royale* was founded in the house of the Marquis Angelo Saluzzo di Monesiglio. This led to the creation of the Academy of Sciences which became a public institution in 1783. This group of intellectuals brought Turin into the world of the great European academies, of Paris, London, Berlin and St Petersburg. The noble members, like Saluzzo and Ludovico Morozzo, were army officers with close links to the school of artillery, which was a centre of scientific and technical innovation. Then there were the university professors, disciples of the physicist Giambattista Beccaria, including Giuseppe Luigi Lagrange, Francesco Cigna and Carlo Allioni. The presence of a gifted doctor and surgeon like Ambrogio Bertrandi, a man of wide European culture, showed the importance of the links with the university, reformed by Victor Amadeus II. This group of scientists, aristocrats and military engineers published, between 1759 and 1773, that *Miscellanea philosophica-mathematica*, then the *Mélanges de philosophie et de mathématique*, with which men like Euler, d'Alembert, Bernouilli and Condorcet were linked. In 1775 the group launched another project of scientific popularisation with the translation of the *Scelta degli opuscoli*, a Lombard periodical which, in the Turin edition, included many local additions.

In the field of the humanities, the *Accademia Sanpaolina* was formed, meeting in the house of the Count Bava di San Paolo, whose members included Count Francesco Galeani Napione, Count Robbio di San Raffaele, the abbé Valperga di Caluso and Count Tana. Count Vittorio Alfieri also frequented it, reading one of his tragedies there, as did visiting foreigners, including August Ludwig Schlotzer, as Denina relates in his *Lettere brandeburghesi*. This group was particularly interested in Italian history and language. It was in this environment that Napione developed the ideas contained in his *Dell'uso e dei pregi della lingua italiana* of 1791. The choice of Italian as the language of culture meant giving up the bilingual tradition of the State of Savoy and recognising Piedmont as a country on the frontier but Italian for all that and part of Italian culture. Napione's ideas coincided with those of Muratori in his choice of the cultivated, written language of the courts and the law rather than the spoken language of Tuscany. This was the language which should be used for a history of the country which would be of use to the citizen and particularly to the state official. In 1782, a year before the foundation of the Academy of Sciences, a group of young aristocrats, led by Felice di San Martino and Prospero Balbo, founded a new academy, the *Filopatria*, which differed from the other more in generation than in ideology. The *Filopatria* too was open to young intellectuals from the professions and universities, united by their desire to pursue with greater energy and clearer aims the discussion of the history of their country. They were, through Balbo, influenced by many of Vico's ideas, in the discovery of a philosophy of history which differed from that of Voltaire, while their interest in the primitive world came from the work by Court de Gibelin. Felice di San Martino tried in the early stages to introduce matters of economics and reform. Verri and Pilati were discussed. The *Accademia Filopatria* produced (and some of its members contributed to) the *Biblioteca oltremontana*, the most lively periodical not only in Piedmont but in all Italy, at least in the years leading up to the French Revolution.

The appearance of this journal would be incomprehensible without first taking a look at the two Vasco brothers[2] who were certainly the most important and cosmopolitan intellectuals active in Piedmont in the years of the crisis of the *ancien régime*. Francesco Dalmazzo and Giambattista Vasco came from an ancient aristocratic family. The former was born in Pinerolo where his father was intendant, in 1732. After completing his law studies he had lived in Mondovì where he gave early evidence of his originality and independence. In 1765 we find him corresponding with Rousseau to whom he sent his *Suite du Contrat social*, conceived as a development of Rousseau's ideas and a contribution to the fight then being waged by the Corsicans for freedom and independence. He had tried to reconcile what he had learned from Rousseau with the idea of monarchy. A year later he defended Pietro Verri's *Meditazioni sulla felicità* (and, by implication, Beccaria's *Dei delitti e delle pene*) against the attacks of Facchinei. His first published work, *Delle leggi civili reali*, was produced in Milan by Galeazzi in 1766 during his enthusiastic collaboration with the *école de Milan*. Although defending, with the help of

Montesquieu, the role of the nobility in a monarchy, F. D. Vasco came down decisively against *fidecommessi*, *maggiorascati* and generally against the other remnants of a feudal society. Through Rousseau he had become an enthusiastic follower of Beccaria.

His ideas did not remain purely abstract but led him to intervene actively on behalf of the Corsicans. He tried to gather together from Mondovì and Liguria men and weapons for the uprising. Denounced, he had to flee into exile, but in 1768 he was arrested in Rome and imprisoned in Ivrea. This led him to an important reassessment of the fundamental values of the Enlightenment, democracy and liberty. Once again he felt the need to write a commentary on a major work. This time he chose Montesquieu, whom he had begun to translate, as far as the twenty-eighth book, comparing his ideas with those of Rousseau on democracy and the general will. Meanwhile his imprisonment became less harsh in the last years of the reign of Charles Emanuel III. From Mondovì he saluted the new sovereign Victor Amadeus III in his *Saggio analitico sul commercio dei grani* which showed his inclination, influenced by physiocracy, towards free trade. Contributing to the *Biblioteca oltremontana* was his way of re-entering the cultural life of Piedmont, after the years of prison, exile and suspicion. But precisely for this reason, although contributing to his brother's fight for enlightened ideas, his role in the periodical was limited to problems of law and justice, and in 1790 he published his *Saggio filosofico intorno alcuni articoli importanti di legislazione civile*.

The real protagonist of the *Biblioteca* between 1787 and 1789 was Giambattista Vasco, Francesco Dalmazzo's younger brother by one year, and, like him, educated in Victor Amadeus II's reformed law faculty. After his studies, in 1751, he had entered the Dominican order with the name of Tommaso, obtaining a degree in theology in 1758 at Bologna, thus becoming a lector in his order. After a stay in Genoa, Vasco was recruited (not without misgivings on the part of the minister Bogino) as professor of theology at Cagliari University where the State of Savoy was attempting to introduce its new educational model. He was to teach the new course in scholastic dogma and ecclesiastical history laid down by the ubiquitous Gerdil, who proposed St Thomas's *Summa theologica* as a guide. For a reader of Montaigne, Descartes, Spinoza, Leibnitz, Condillac and the authors of the *Encyclopédie* this was not an easy task. Very soon his courses began to annoy Bogino who forced him to resign before the end of 1766. His brother, Francesco Dalmazzo, had tried to introduce him into the Lombard circle, recommending him to his friends in the *école de Milan*, but the conspiracy, his flight and subsequent arrest had caused Verri and Beccaria to lose interest in these dangerous Piedmontese admirers and followers. Nevertheless, Giambattista Vasco managed to move from Genoa to Cremona, where he met one of the contributors to *Il Caffè*, Count Giambattista Biffi, and through his contributions to the Lombard periodicals, first the *Estratto della letteratura europa* and then the *Gazzetta letteraria*, not only did he manage to overcome Verri's lingering doubts, but he emerged definitively as a reformer and particularly an economist.

The first result was *La felicità pubblica considerata nei lavoratori di terre proprie*, which was a response to a question set as a competition by the Economic Society of St Petersburg in 1767, and published in Brescia by Rizzardi (the first publisher of *Il Caffè*) in 1769. This work had many original features distinguishing it from other contemporary works on this subject. While starting from the physiocratic idea that the true basis of wealth is the land, Vasco drew consequences from this idea which to a great extent are the opposite of those of the *économistes*. He was interested not in the productivity that could result from large properties, the investment of capital and the use of a waged workforce, but in the opposite; in the involvement in the property of the largest possible number of peasants or small landowners. His ideal was not a strict equality, but a society governed by a rational distribution of the land which would unite a peasant class to the State, to its laws and to its defence. In comparison with his brother, Giambattista seems less concerned with the problems posed by Montesquieu. His anti-feudal stance gives by implication a role to the nobility as an intermediate body. In a rational state (monarchy or republic) with good laws and a proportionate system of taxation, with the conscious support of a broad social base, self-sufficient because productive, there would be no necessity for either the machinery of public charity (and thus the legacies to hospitals and pious institutions) or the presence of an intermediary body capable of resisting absolutism.

Thus, although Vasco shared many of Pietro Verri's ideas, whereas Verri's point of view remained that of a wealthy landowner, utopia and reform come together to great effect in Vasco's plan. For the countries that had land available for distribution (like Russia and America) the course to pursue was that of an agrarian law that, on the one hand, would guarantee to the greatest possible number of peasants ownership of land and, on the other, would avoid the re-formation of concentrations of land. His proposal for countries where the land was already unequally distributed was rather different. Here direct intervention was not possible, but legislation, preventing those who had excessively large amounts of property from acquiring more, by adjusting the systems of inheritance, taxation and assistance to all those wanting to become small producers would in the long run manage to achieve the same result. This work represents the moment when Vasco was closest to the idea of a democracy of small producers and artisans not so distant from the ideals of Rousseau and from what d'Holbach was formulating in the years preceding the Turgot experiment. Vasco did not leave the two fundamentals, wealth and freedom, to the mercy of economic freedom and the whims of production and the market. Like Mably, he dreamed of a state which could deal with excessive inequality by various strategies, from agrarian laws to milder provisions. But the objective, ultimately, was one and the same: to ensure liberty not through the resistance of an intermediate, rich, powerful and independent body, but through the support of a broad-based class of small producers, in the framework of a society that could benefit not only the place of consumption (the city) but also the place of basic production (the country). Even if this essay did not win the competition, its fame in Italy and Europe was so great that the 1770 Lausanne edition of the winning text – by Béardé de l'Abbaye – also contained a translation of Vasco's work.

Having moved to Milan and become the most active contributor to first the *Estratto* and then the *Gazzetta letteraria*, both published by Galeazzi, Vasco aspired to the chair in economics that had been created for Beccaria. In order to obtain it he wrote *Della moneta*, published in Milan in 1772. This work examines not only the debates of the 1750s but also the later ideas of G. Rinaldo Carli, Pompeo Neri and other European contemporaries which considered France's dramatic financial problems. Vasco emerges decidedly on the side of free trade. The State should as far as possible consider money as a commodity and confine itself to setting a reasonable rate between the different metals, starting with copper which was less subject to fraudulent debasement. He envisaged a new type of monetary system which would abolish all types of restriction and accentuate the view of money as a commodity.

After the publication of this work, even if he was not offered the chair, Vasco was made public censor, without pay. He was at the same time the chief contributor to the *Gazzetta letteraria*, a successful weekly journal printed by Galeazzi. Through his reviews it is possible to trace the development of his political ideas which moved from the early influence of Rousseau towards English constitutionalism, as introduced to Europe through Holme's *Constitution d'Angleterre*. The failure of his hopes for a more secure post in Lombardy and difficulties with his colleagues who distrusted his intellectual freedom and considered him an interloper, caused him to return to Piedmont where the death of Charles Emanuel III had meant not only the removal of Bogino, 'mortal enemy' of the Vasco family, but also the beginning of new freedom and hope for the intellectuals in the Savoyard state.

These were 'the years of obscurity', as a recent biographer has put it, when Giambattista, who had left holy orders, prepared the way for his difficult re-entry into the cultural world of Piedmont, concerning himself now with technical problems in the field of agriculture and silk production. He kept up his contacts with the Lombards, particularly Biffi and Carlo Amoretti, secretary of the Patriotic Society where Pietro Verri was an influential member. He collaborated with the Department of Finance, writing memoranda on the *catasto* and on taxes. Shortly before he had written the essay on mendicancy and the ways to eradicate it, which was not to be published until 1790 after recognition from the *Société Patriotique* of Valence in the Dauphiné. This work began from the basic idea that the wealth of a nation was the same as the product of its land and its industry. The population tends to adapt itself to the means of subsistence. If, for any reason, either the agricultural or industrial product is cut off, a part of the population will become beggars. If Vasco was still reflecting a situation where the most serious problem was that of agricultural land, since industry was not sufficiently developed to absorb the workforce deprived of work in the country, it is interesting to note, however, how he sees agricultural and industrial problems as being equally the cause of mendicancy. A second (less direct) cause was taken from physiocratic theory. The fall of prices for agricultural goods affected not only the people involved in the agricultural holding, from the owner to the labourers, but also trade and industry which no longer received part of the income produced from the land. The third cause Vasco saw (using the arguments of free trade) as lying in the guild system, and in the mechanisms for the defence of privileges which the trades upheld against the freedom of work.

As for remedies, Vasco proposed that the wealth of charitable institutions and hospitals should be pooled in a general office for charitable works, managed by the State and taken away from private individuals and religious foundations. The task of the office would not only be to ensure a better use of resources, but also to prevent casual and fortuitous assistance. Vasco's plan suggested that not only should the labour of those who were disabled or partially unable to work be employed as much as possible, but also that those unproductive categories of people who crowded into the cities should be kept as far as possible in the country in convenient centres, rationally distributed. A free labour market would thus be able to absorb a large proportion at least of the unemployed. On work and the guilds he put forward the ideas that he was to develop in 1789 in response to a problem set by the Verona Academy in his *Delle università delle arti e mestieri*, which looked back to Turgot's experiment and quoted directly and approvingly from Adam Smith.

The *Biblioteca oltremontana* in its most important stage (between 1787 and 1789) is quite incomprehensible if one ignores the role played by this great economist and reformer, who had managed to eradicate the memory of the turbulent events in his life and that of his family to the extent of being awarded a small pension for his services by the Department of Finance. For a short time, he was a focus for some of the young men of the *Filopatria* and particularly Felice di San Martino, and the members of the Academy of Sciences. As well as his prestige as a thinker, his first-hand journalistic experience in Lombardy was important. The *Biblioteca oltremontana* represented the most authoritative voice of that group of scientists, engineers and doctors – many from the aristocracy – who were to contribute to the Academy of Sciences, founded in Turin in 1783. Giambattista was the writer of the greater part of the periodical, Felice di San Martino the most enthusiastic follower and to some extent the link with the *Filopatria*, while Giambattista's brother Francesco Dalmazzo confined himself to writing on matters of law and justice. Making use of the relatively greater freedom in academic circles, the review was able to discuss in surprising depth the problems of a European culture feeling the effects of the crisis of the *ancien régime*. The political and economic theories of the late Enlightenment were passionately compared and analysed. The *Biblioteca*'s desire to be *oltremontana* (looking beyond the Alps) was a deliberate reaction to the conservatism and parochialism of the *Accademia Sanpaolina* and which were apparent too in the *Filopatria*.

The question of enlightened absolutism, with reference particularly to Frederick II, Joseph II and Leopold, was its first objective. What were the reforms which would justify a concentration of power such as happened in these states and societies, which would make a monarchy acceptable and even preferable? A second question arose from Turgot's failure and the crisis among the *philosophes*. Siding always with the most radical solutions, the review followed attentively the debate on the public debt, the convocation of the States General and the conservative role of the *Parlements* that claimed to be the same as the two Chambers in England. Giambattista Vasco was able to show that this claim was entirely unjustified. The English model (known through Holme) was òne which related to a complex mixed society which had to a great extent solved those problems that were becoming (after the failure of demands for reform) ever more acute in France. Nor was it the England described by Montesquieu, for from being the home of freedom it had become the enemy of freedom in the American colonies. Through Raynal, the review (dominated at this time by Vasco) followed the *philosophes'* violent denunciation of the despotism, exploitation and slavery that Europe had extended to all corners of the world. It was a situation which could not endure.

In 1789 Giambattista Vasco was co-opted into the Academy and drawn ever deeper into the technical problems of reform. His brother ceased to contribute. The *Filopatria* took firm control of the review and made it its own. The change was neither painless nor insignificant. Felice di San Martino for example drifted gradually away from the *Filopatria* which expanded eventually to include even the most eminent men of the *Sanpaolina*. The *Biblioteca*, now significantly no longer *oltremontana*, turned its attention increasingly to matters of local history, literature and erudite studies. The contributors were intellectuals like Giuseppe Vernazza and Napione, with their dignified but essentially conservative and anti-Enlightenment scholarship.

The rumblings of revolution and their repercussions in Piedmont rapidly changed the climate which had permitted this short but important period in the life of the *Biblioteca*. In 1791 Francesco Dalmazzo was arrested for publishing a *Saggio politico* suggesting a constitutional solution to the problems in France. This work, the culmination of the ideas of a lifetime, was deemed a threat to the Crown and the author was taken to Ceva and the prison which had once housed Giannone. A few months later Giambattista fled to Milan where he was to publish his last work, *L'Usura libera*, in response to a problem posed by Joseph II. But Lombardy too was no longer the land of *Il Caffè* and a free press. A weary and disheartened attempt to take up again his old career as a journalist caused the censor to intervene. After his brother Francesco Dalmazzo had died in the castle at Ivrea, Giambattista was to return to Piedmont to the home of the Marquis d'Incisa, the aristocrat who had always been his friend and protector and who, in 1796, was to bury him in the family tomb.

In the early 1790s Turin University was closed. The Academy of Sciences, whose transactions came to an end in 1793, was no longer the centre of new plans and hopes. Even the *Biblioteca* was closing, producing among its last publications Vincenzo Monti's *Basvilliana*, thus opening the way to counter-revolutionary ideas. For some of the young Piedmontese intellectuals who had shared the hopes of men like the Vasco brothers, Saluzzo and Morozzo, this last crisis of the *ancien régime* meant making the leap from Enlightenment to

Jacobinism. This was the path chosen by the historian Carlo Botta, pupil of Carlo Tenivelli. The latter, a member of the *Accademia dei Filopatridi* and the *Accademia degli Unanimi*, defender of Victor Amadeus II's educational reforms and a secondary-school teacher in Moncalieri, was shot as a Jacobin in 1797 – a sign of the gravity of the crisis in an intellectual world which only a few months before had been spilling over with ideas for reform.

NOTES AND REFERENCES

The basic reference works, flawed by a 'nationalist' point of view, are: Calcaterra, C. (1935) *Il nostro imminente Risorgimento*. SEI, Turin; idem (1941) *I filopatridi*. SEI, Turin; idem (1943) *Le adunanze della Patria società letteraria*. SEI, Turin. On Baretti see: Jonard, N. (1965) *Giuseppe Baretti*. Clermont-Ferrand. On Denina see: Venturi, F. (1958) *Riformatori lombardi piemontesi e toscani*. Ricciardi, Milan–Naples, pp. 699–753. See also: Negri, L. (1933) 'Un accademico piemontese de' Settecento: C. Denina', in *Memorie accademia delle scienze di Torino* series 2, vol. LXVII. On Vasco, as well as the sections in Venturi, F. op. cit., pp. 755–879, see: Venturi, F. (1940) *F. D. Vasco*. Droz, Paris; Vasco, F. D. (1966) *Opere*, ed. Rota Ghibaudi, S.. Fondazione Einaudi, Turin; Marocco, G. (1976) *Giambattista Vasco*. Fondazione Einaudi, Turin. On the scientific Enlightenment see: Ferrone, V. (1984) 'Tecnocrati, militari e scienziati nel Piemonte dell'Antico Regime, Alle origini della Reale Accademia delle Scienze di Torino'. In *Rivista storica italiana*, 2, 1984, pp. 414–509; various authors (1985) *I primi due secoli dell'Accademia delle Scienze di Torino*. Accademia delle Scienze, Turin. On Sardinia see: Ricuperati, G. (1986) 'Il riformismo sabaudo settecentesco. Appunti per una discussione'. In *Studi Storici*, 1.

1. Turin, 1791.
2. See: Venturi, F. (1969–84) *Settecento riformatore*. Einaudi, Turin, IV, pt ii, pp. 1036ff.

PART SIX

Historians and the Italian Enlightenment (Giuseppe Ricuperati)

CHAPTER TWENTY-TWO

The *ancien régime* and the Italian Enlightenment: a historiographical problem

The reconstruction of the eighteenth century and its possible historiographical interpretations began simultaneously with the events themselves. Pietro Giannone's *Istoria civile del regno di Napoli* (1723) provided a key to an understanding of the first decades of the century which, when expanded with notes and additions (which appeared in successive editions, in French in 1742 and in Italian in 1753), was to remain for a long time the standard work. Giannone touched on several essential problems, which lay outside the limited confines of his book – the oppressive role of the Church, the decline of Italy during the centuries of Spanish domination, the recovery of recent times, the phenomenon of Habsburg reformism and the necessity for energetic jurisdictional action. He reveals a certain longing for a 'national' state in the South, such as was to come about after 1734 under the Bourbons. The jurisdictional debate of the 1760s which re-examined previous thinking in the light of a new economic, social and cultural viewpoint, resulting in a decisive return to Giannone, was to reaffirm the ideological and interpretative consistency of his work.

Muratori's *Annali d'Italia* (1744–49) with its neo-Ghibelline point of view was more reflective and analytical. In the same years that the old Modenese priest was writing for the next generation his manual on reform and 'the public good', he was also tracing a peaceful picture of the 'civil' history of Italy, where not only military events were arranged systematically, but also the different types of reformist policy emerging from Piedmont, the Habsburgs and the Bourbons. He concluded the work in the hope that peace, after the War of the Austrian Succession, and enlightened Catholicism embodied in a figure like that of Benedict XIV would bring about ever greater possibilities for collaboration, fostering man's rational capacity to change the world.

There was also a school of historiography that, unlike the Giannonian and Muratorian schools which were both linked in different ways to Imperial jurisdictionalism and therefore called neo-Ghibelline, could be termed neo-Guelph. We find this in the history of Italy and Europe during the War of the Spanish Succession written by the Marquis Francesco M. Ottieri, of which one part was published in 1728 while the rest was stopped by Imperial opposition so that the work was only completed in the 1750s.[1] Ottieri overturned the previous points of view. In a belated reply to Machiavelli, he praised the pacifying role of the papacy, the only institution with the strength to oppose the greed of the great powers.

Another source deserving mention represents a fascinating source of information about the individual states, drawn almost from life, but transformed into historiographical form. This was the *Storia dell'anno*, a periodical publication, which came out with exemplary regularity from 1737 to 1811 and which, drawing on the gazettes, narrates the chief events of the time, in Italy and abroad, from 1730. Behind this enterprise, part newspaper and part aid to contemporary history, there were, not surprisingly, historians like Innocenzo Montini, influenced by Muratori, and journalists like Girolamo Zanetti, Giovanni Efis and Domenico Caminer.

Alongside these rather uncritical chronicles, with little interpretation or analysis to distinguish one period of Italian history from another, there were also foreign travellers' impressions which were immediately followed by the defensive or argumentative reactions of the Italians. In a lengthy chapter of the recent *Storia d'Italia* entitled 'L'Italia fuori d'Italia', Franco Venturi tellingly reconstructs the slow change in the image of Italy in the eighteenth century, and reveals the layers of prejudice and falsification (or at least foreign viewpoints) that registered many of the traditional limitations of the situation in Italy but usually failed to grasp the overall vitality and ability to change that was emerging.[2] With Mabillon, Addison and Charles de Brosses the long-enduring picture of Italy as a museum of archaeological ruins, more interesting for its past than its future, was steadily reinforced, with only little variation. It was for this attitude that Giuseppe Baretti, writing from London, could justifiably criticise Samuel Sharp and his description of Italy (1767), even if Baretti's own point of view was also basically opposed to the new values of the Italian Enlightenment and much closer to the sardonic and essentially conservative attitude of Tobias Smollett.

The attitude of young English travellers was chiefly conditioned by the Grand Tour mentality, with its conventions and rituals. This was true even for a man like Edward Gibbon who was to draw the inspiration for his greatest work from the ruins of Rome. But the travels of the scientists and agronomists were to be different. One only has to think of names like Jean Lalande, John Symonds and Arthur Young. The scientists saw an enlightened Italy that was not only developing and seeking links with international centres, but which also had its own rich individuality. The agronomists turned away, almost brutally, from the monuments of the past to look at the present economic situation and particularly the changes taking place in Lombard agriculture.

A properly historiographical attempt at an evaluation of events in Italy in the eighteenth century was made by Carlo Denina in the original conclusion to his *Rivoluzioni d'Italia*, and then in an additional Book XXV written between 1792 and 1793 and published in 1793 in the third Venice edition of the work under the title of *Italia moderna*. It is interesting to compare the conclusion of Book XXIV, *Riflessioni sopra lo stato d'Italia dopo la pace di Utrecht*, written in the 1760s, with what Denina was writing during the period of the French Revolution. In the first, having examined very critically the Habsburg government of the Mezzogiorno, Denina envisages the transformation to a national state under a reforming prince, surrounded by 'very able' ministers. He comments on the somewhat passive tranquillity of the Papal States and the Venetian Republic and on the reforms in Tuscany, first under the energetic Regency and then with the arrival of Leopold. He gives a brief description of the importance of the change of regime in Lombardy, the reforms affecting Parma and the flourishing revival in Piedmont. Like Muratori twenty years before, Denina, encouraged by the optimism of the 1760s, concluded his work with a cautious, pacifist proposal for reform: development of the population; an attack on excessive inequality; opposition to unbeneficial crops; an attack on an indiscriminate increase in the wealth of the clergy and on ecclesiastical celibacy; development of education; pursuit of peaceful policies.

Book XXV gives a summary of the events of 1713 to 1792, thus dealing with a period of what was for him 'modern' or contemporary Italy. Although very compressed, the picture painted by Denina revealed many of the fundamental problems of Italian and European history: the strengthening of Piedmont under Charles Emanuel III and then Victor Amadeus III; the enormous international significance of the suppression of the Jesuits; the turning of Catherine II's Russia towards the Mediterranean; Maria Theresa's reforms and those, even more radical, of Joseph II. His description of the demographic, economic, social and productive situation showed how the different Italian states varied in development, with the North (Piedmont and Lombardy) more densely populated and active, central Italy (especially Tuscany) roused by reform and thus beginning to develop and the Mezzogiorno, rich in problems, population and potential. The high population of Naples was seen by Denina as a positive factor, as for the rest of Europe. He commented how Naples had the same relation to the State as London had to England, that is, with a tenth of the population of the kingdom. By contrast, the delay in the introduction of reforms was noticeable in the Papal States and particularly in the Roman Campagna which (after a rich and glorious past) was one of the most depopulated parts of Italy.

If, from the point of view of productivity and work, Italy had no reason to envy other countries, so also was it true for her arts and sciences. Referring to Voltaire and his famous introduction to the *Siècle de Louis XIV*, Denina argued that Italy was not in decline 'as some foreign travellers would have us believe', and that the Italian eighteenth century was the equal of the 'famous centuries of Augustus, Leo X, or Urban VIII and Galileo . . .'.[3]

Denina's description is certainly informative, even if it concentrates on institutions sometimes to the detriment of the aims of the militant Enlightenment. It was more a perceptive review of developments, even at a local level, than an analysis of groups and political and intellectual proposals.

Thinkers for and against the Enlightenment are dealt with in the same way, in so far as importance is given more to the quantity and variety of ideas than to their quality and political significance. Thus in Lombardy his attention is drawn not to the *Accademia dei Pugni* and *Il Caffè* but to the decorous and moderate enlightened ideas of Parini. Pietro Verri is not even mentioned whereas Gian Rinaldo Carli is, whose sceptical detachment from reform had by now matured. In compensation, Mantua, the city of Bettinelli and Andrés, is compared to Weimar 'where there dwell in comfort Wieland, Goethe, Herder, Bertuch and other famous German writers'.

The State of Savoy merits a chapter to itself, 'a part of Italy that in the preceding three centuries had given signs of having emerged from barbarism'. His version of events in Piedmont, entirely centred round the reforms of Victor Amadeus II, including those of education, reveals very clearly the link between these reforms and the intellectual liveliness of the second half of the century, expressed not so much or solely in university life but through literary and scientific academies, of which the Academy of Sciences was the centre and most important result both in Piedmont and in Europe. Developments were taking place not only in the sciences, and chemistry in particular, but also in literature, as could be seen from the example of the greatest living tragic poet, Vittorio Alfieri.

In conclusion, Denina touches on the many questions which were to remain unanswered and which appeared sometimes in the attacks of foreign observers. Above all, he sought an answer to the question of why, despite Italy's development, there was so much emigration of intellectuals and craftsmen, resulting in a severely unbalanced society. This emigration affected the countries that were most densely populated. More difficult to answer was the accusation that Italians lacked patriotism, compared with, for example, the English and the French, particularly 'when these two nations were competing for trade and influence in the general affairs of the globe'. Denina's response was that patriotism is born of national rivalry, and that virtue 'which for politicians is merely valour and boldness, is nurtured amidst wars: in peace it inevitably languishes and dies'. In the face of the threat of the French Revolution, Denina still saw in Rome and its international role a centre to inspire identity. But once again it would be an enlightened, reforming Christianity, renouncing earthly riches, which would reach out to bring about a pact with the State to ensure the public good. In this sense he was already answering one of the questions which was to reappear more than once in the historiography of the Risorgimento – the significance of the lack of a Protestant Reformation in Italy. Through reform and enlightened Catholicism, eighteenth-century Italy could – Denina optimistically maintained – carry out all that was most positive in the Reformation but without losing the values of Catholicism.

The years when Denina was finishing his *Rivoluzioni d'Italia* saw a profound change in the cultural influences underlying the eighteenth-century view of history. Italian literature could not ignore the great European upheaval of the French Revolution and then, particularly, the rise of Napoleon. The very concept of literature was changing, no longer being seen as knowledge (as in the works of Tiraboschi or Andrés). A new concept was emerging, that of the civil and moral consciousness of a people. Paul Hazard[4] has shown that some of the values of Italian Romanticism were to come about as antitheses, as a resistance to the ideological as well as political pressures of the *Grande Nation*. Here the rediscovery of Vico played an important role, for through Vincenzo Cuoco and Foscolo he became a 'national' author.

Naturally the Vico discovered by the early Romantic intellectuals was no longer the Vico of Francesco Mario Pagano and Gaetano Filangieri, a Vico interpreted in the light of the radical Enlightenment, influenced by Buffon, Boulanger and d'Holbach and providing an esoteric language for southern Freemasonry. Nor was it the orthodox Vico of Pietro Napoli Signorelli, author of *Delle vicende della cultura napoletana*. It was a Vico measured against the philosophies of Romantic history, compared with Edmond Burke, Mme de Staël and Schlegel. It was a Vico who was to have a long but subterranean existence until once again rediscovered for Europe (not without the assistance of Italian emigrants) by Michelet.

It cannot be said that this Vico provided an overall picture of the Italian eighteenth century. A more fruitful line of inquiry is the link with Lombard culture, which had remained more faithful in general to the values of the Enlightenment, as expressed by Pietro Verri, *Il Caffè* and the *école de Milan*. Here not only is the continuity of values from the *philosophes* to the nineteenth century more clearly perceptible, but we also find a fundamental contribution to the reconstruction of political and economic thought in the eighteenth century. This was the fifty volumes of the *Scrittori classici italiani di economia politica*, collected by Baron Pietro Custodi. He was a pupil of Pietro Verri, one of the young intellectuals who had understood Verri's clear development from the ideas of the Enlightenment to those of constitutionalism. A political writer and politician, a radical in the period of transition between Cisalpine Republic and Napoleonic regime, Custodi took advantage of his authority as an official to make this collection of the classics of Italian political economy, printed in Milan during the first fifteen years of the nineteenth century and which were to be an essential point of reference for Ferrara's *Biblioteca degli economisti*. Indeed, for the political and economic ideas of the eighteenth-century authors (who make up the majority) Custodi's collection was to continue to be of great importance.

If new editions were printed of, and monographs written about, authors like Genovesi, Verri and Beccaria it was thanks to Custodi that notice was also taken of one particular Italian thinker of the eighteenth century whose bitter and lucid realism remained unaffected by his contemporaries' rationalistic Utopias. This was Giammaria Ortes who, because of Custodi's book, earned a mention in Karl Marx's *Capital*. And Custodi's collection holds other surprises. Even today it is essential for anyone studying Giambattista Vasco. While his brother Francesco Dalmazzo, thanks to the biographical and explanatory essay by Franco Venturi, can be read in an accurate edition, Giambattista, who was probably the more important thinker, is still awaiting a complete edition and must still be read in Custodi's collection. But to give an idea of the complexity of the work of Verri's one-time pupil and old friend, it should be said that Custodi did not confine himself to publishing only the most famous works. He also carried out the first analytical research on the *Biblioteca oltremontana* for the whole of the period (1787–89) when it was run and mostly written by Vasco. Thus we can see not only the evolution of Verri's theories, but also his campaigning and journalistic side.

While Custodi was completing his work on the texts of the Enlightenment, in Lombardy Giambattista Corniani was offering another approach to the eighteenth century in his *Secoli della letteratura italiana dopo il suo risorgimento*, published in 1804–9 and dedicated to Francesco Melzi d'Eril. There were two eighteenth-century predecessors for Corniani's work, that by his compatriot Gian Maria Mazzuchelli and that by Girolamo Tiraboschi.[5] Thus he felt the need to justify, particularly with respect to the second of these, the difference in his approach, which was less scholarly in emphasis but which stressed the historical context in which the author was writing. In fact, his division of history into epochs (nine, from the eleventh century to the mid-eighteenth century) does not fit very convincingly with the individual descriptions of the authors, who are allotted to their historical period in a way which is too mechanical and has too little justification. The ninth epoch, which begins with the satirical poet Girolamo Gigli and ends with Carlo Goldoni, contains merely a list of biographies with few and uncertain attempts at internal classification. The work was carried on by Stefano Ticozzi. He attempted to give an account of the second half of the eighteenth century, thereby revealing that the idea of literature as knowledge was not entirely dead. The biographies, some of which follow Corniani's plan, do not, in their subdued uniformity, give us any sense of the culture of the eighteenth century.

A similar project was attempted by Camillo Ugoni, a man of letters and patriot from Brescia and friend of Ugo Foscolo. In 1818 he had suggested to the academy of Brescia that he should resume and complete G. M. Mazzuchelli's *Scrittori italiani*. A little later he decided to follow Corniani's plan and write the biographies of the Italian intellectuals of the second half of the eighteenth century. Inevitably he looked back to Tiraboschi's model. But he departed from it more widely and markedly than did Corniani. He may have followed the system of writing a history not of literature but of the writers themselves, but his attempt to reconstruct the individuality and subjectivity of each writer was his own development. He thus gives us, right from the first draft (*Della letteratura italiana nella seconda metà del sec. XVIII*, 3 vols, Brescia, Belloni, 1820–22), a more comprehensive result, influenced not only by his links with the 'Conciliatore' group, but also with the contemporary works of Ginguené and Sismondi. In 1855 this first draft was republished in Turin in *I secoli della letteratura italiana dopo il suo risorgimento. Commentario di G. B. Corniani colle aggiunte di C. Ugoni e S. Ticozzi e continuato fino a questi ultimi giorni*, edited by Francesco Predari.

Ugoni, who had been in Switzerland, Germany, Paris and London as a political refugee, continued with this work, encouraged too by his contributions to Michaud's *Biographie universelle*. The work, which was published in four volumes in Milan between 1856 and 1858 immediately after Ugoni's death under the same title, *Della letteratura italiana nella seconda metà del secolo XVIII*, is, and was seen to be by contemporaries, for the most part different from the first draft, not only in its choice of biographies, but also in its maturity and sophistication.

The diffuse history of eighteenth-century Italian literature, written by Antonio Lombardi between 1827 and 1830 in eight volumes, on the other hand, is a feeble imitation of the erudite tradition of Tiraboschi. The abbé Lombardi had collaborated with Tiraboschi and succeeded him as librarian in the Este library in Modena, writing a eulogy of his friend and master in 1796. In his introduction Lombardi explained the differences from his master's work which he had to introduce, but stated that he intended to follow the latter's model of a history of literature rather than one of writers. Lombardi's plan was rather mechanically derived from that of Tiraboschi: general history, princely patronage, cultural institutions (universities and academies) and lastly science. The latter was described analytically according to the following plan: theology, philosophy and mathematics, natural history, anatomy, medicine and surgery, civil and canon law. This was followed by *belles-lettres* and arts, with a remarkably long chapter devoted to history. The profiles of the historians, starting with Muratori, are presented without any order, whether chronological, topographical or of importance. The majority are of scholars, along with profiles of Muratori, Tiraboschi and Angelo Fabbroni. After a chapter on translators (particularly of the classics), Lombardi turns to Italian and Latin poetry and the study of grammar, rhetoric and eloquence. The final chapters are dedicated to archaeology, philology and scholarly studies and an attempt to evaluate the arts (painting, sculpture, architecture and music). Although providing a wealth of information, Lombardi's work reveals all the defects of an erudite method that, on the one hand, while wishing to retain for literature its eighteenth-century character of encylopaedic culture, was unable, on the other, to endow intellectual events with any importance, whether individual or collective.

In considering the picture of the eighteenth century held by the nineteenth, another Italian exile, Francesco Saverio Salfi (1759–1832), deserves a mention. He was in Paris between 1815 and 1832 where he was a friend and collaborator of Pierre Louis Ginguené. He published, with the French critic, the correspondence of Ferdinando Galiani (1818). After Ginguené's death in 1816, Salfi completed this important work with his *Resumé* that was to be translated several times into Italian. He was also an active contributor to the *Revue encyclopédique*.

In his *Eloge de Filangieri*, Salfi sought to make better known an author who had already attracted the attention of Benjamin Constant in 1822. As a journalist and friend of the great historian Michelet, Salfi was also at the centre of the upsurge of interest in Vico which was to lead not only to Michelet's translation, but also to Giuseppe Ferrari's book on *La mente del Vico* (1837). As a historian of literature, Salfi divided the chronological span, from the beginnings to his own day, into seven periods, stressing, in the sixth period (1675–1775), the French influence on genres and writers. It is interesting that he describes the Enlightenment, both in literature and more generally in civil history, as finishing very early, in the period which is now seen as the time of the crisis of the *ancien régime*. In this context, Vico is called 'the most original writer of his age'. The pre-revolutionary decades, the years of the Revolution and the first decades of the nineteenth century are seen as integral parts of a single period, the seventh, that of the writer himself.

A neo-Ghibelline point of view dominates two histories of literature which precede the important work of Francesco De Sanctis. One is by the Neapolitan patriot Luigi Settembrini, closely linked, even on the emotive level, with the eighteenth-century tradition of Giannone, Filangieri and Pagano, and the other, the more scientific *Storia delle belle lettere in Italia* (Florence, 1844), by Paolo Emiliani Giudici.

The themes of civil reform and economic discussion which were already to be found in the work of Carlo Botta and Pietro Colletta, both of whom had close links with the Enlightenment, reappear in Cesare Balbo. With his work, according to Walter Maturi, we see the beginning of a new evaluation of the eighteenth century reacting in turn against the dismissive attitude of the reactionary press which had dominated at the time of the Restoration. Balbo published his *Storia d'Italia* in Turin in 1830 and a *Sommario della storia d'Italia* in 1846. In the latter his attitude to the eighteenth century antici-pates a liberal and monarchical view of the Risorgimento, an attitude intended to create a historical validation for Savoyard political leadership, pledged to the principles of a moderate constitutionalism. As a result he saw enlightened despotism as a positive experience, but one which was held back by absolutism. He minimised the importance of Austrian reformism and placed great stress on the territorial expansion of the House of Savoy, its intentions towards other Italian territories, its entry into the diplomatic arena of the great powers and the progressive Italianisation of culture and politics in Piedmont. Balbo's Catholic and moderate stance places him among the neo-Guelph writers who emerged in the years of the Restoration and who aimed to eradicate the secular, anti-curial and enlightened tradition in Italian history, putting forward in its place the idea of the continuity of Catholic culture and of the positive role of the papacy including its historical support for the moderate elements of the Risorgimento.

In the nineteenth-century debate between the neo-Guelph and neo-Ghibel-line schools of history, attitudes to the eighteenth century were fundamental for this was the time when jurisdictionalism, in new guises, became once again a central question, and when the first radical criticism of the Church and its powers had appeared. Thus the ideas and personalities of the eight-eenth century became involved in the historical and political debate even when it tackled the question of the Lombard conquest – one of the chief subjects of debate in the first decades of the nineteenth century. In his *Discorso sopra alcuni punti della storia longobardo in Italia* (Milan, 1822), Alessandro

Manzoni attacked the view which linked Machiavelli to Muratori and Giannone and which saw the Lombards as the defenders of the unity between State and society against the destructive power of the papacy. Later, in 1840, in *Storia della colonna infame* he contributed to neo-Guelph historiography and to moderate thought an acute critique of the ideas of the Enlightenment, bringing the discussion, which had been at the very heart of the struggle of the Enlightenment against religion and institutions, within the sphere of personal morality and the private relationship between the individual and Providence.

There was in Lombardy also the tradition which, following the teachings of Melchiorre Gioia and Giandomenico Romagnosi, sought to make a secular and progressive link between the Enlightenment and the ideas of the early nineteenth century and the beginnings of European positivism. The most important figure in this movement was Carlo Cattaneo, the inspiration of the periodical *Il Politecnico* which consciously looked back to *Il Caffè* and its battle for a cultural renewal. In *Notizie naturali e civili della Lombardia* (first edition, Milan, 1844), Cattaneo provides an interesting and succinct picture of Lombard society in the eighteenth century, which reflects the views held by Pietro Verri on Maria Theresa's reforms, those of Gian Rinaldo Carli on the *catasto* and those of the English traveller Arthur Young on the Lombard countryside.

A move to transcend this neo-Guelph or neo-Ghibelline historiography comes with the work of Giuseppe Ferrari. His cultural background was similar to Cattaneo's, and with him he had spent his early career as a contributor to the *Annali universali di statistica* which owed so much to the enlightened ideas of Gioia and Romagnosi. Having gone to Paris, his book on Vico contributed to the European discovery of the Neapolitan philosopher. A republican federalist, sympathetic to French Utopian socialism, Ferrari gave a new view of the secular and enlightened currents in eighteenth-century Italian history. In his *Histoire des révolutions d'Italie* (published in Paris, in 1856–58, and translated into Italian by the Treves publishing house in Milan in 1870–72) he supported the idea of a 'Ghibelline' Risorgimento, hostile to Savoy and anticlerical, whose roots could be found in the Habsburg reformism of Maria Theresa, Joseph II and especially Leopold and in the ideas of the French Enlightenment.

As well as this work, which though full of shrewd observations is not without certain hasty generalisations, Ferrari's *Corso sugli scrittori politici italiani* (Milan, 1862), which in the last section deals with the eighteenth century, deserves a mention. He wished to review the church–state struggle as it had concerned various great intellectuals, whom his work helped to make better known. He was interested particularly in Radicati di Passerano and Giannone. He stressed Radicati's choice of a radical rejection of the Church, that 'conspiracy organised against the good of all men', but also his inability to find a way to 'attempt a real struggle against papal power'. In this struggle Giannone is the chief protagonist. Ferrari questions Giannone's image as an orthodox jurisdictionalist and, basing his argument on Giannone's unpublished works, particularly the *Triregno*, shows clearly where Giannone's criticisms of the Church become criticisms of Catholic spirituality. His method, based on a comparison of religions, is promoted to a 'new science'. Setting aside the question of Ferrari's value as a historian following the harsh criticisms of Croce, countered by Gioacchino Volpe and the recent reassessments of Giuseppe Berti and others, his work was an attempt, in many ways successful, to provide a secular and anti-Savoyard interpretation, in which the age of Enlightenment is given the central role that the most assertive theses of neo-Guelph historiography had tended to deny it.

In the same vein of political and pro-Enlightenment thought, which remained in the minority throughout the century, are the studies which Pasquale Villari published as an introduction to the works of Cesare Beccaria (Florence, 1854) and Gaetano Filangieri (Florence, 1864). Giacomo Racioppi's biography of Antonio Genovesi (1871) deserves to be mentioned too, not only as one of the best general books on the author of *Lezioni di commercio*, but also as a successful attempt to portray the meaning and particular nature of the southern Enlightenment. It was not Vico, who seemed isolated from the problems and the men of his time, but Giannone, Genovesi and Filangieri who were for Racioppi the central figures in the struggle for reform and enlightened ideas, which he went on to link with all that was best and most progressive in the events of his own age. In his work we see re-emerging, behind Genovesi, figures like Celestino Galiani, reformer of the university and, particularly, Bartolomeo Intieri – men whose important role in the origins of the southern Enlightenment has been emphasised in recent years. Remarkable too is Racioppi's attempt to grasp the sense of events, problems and tragedies, like the 1764 famine which had been discussed by Genovesi. Racioppi's work, so closely linked to a tradition which did not attempt to conceal its roots in the Enlightenment, together with the work of other important authors like Samuele Cagnazzi and Ludovico Bianchini (who wrote on, respectively, statistics and finance), ushered in a period of positivist studies which were to look back to, among others, Bartolomeo Capasso and Michelangelo Schipa.

An important turning-point in the development of Italian historiography, even if it does not include a specific interpretation for the eighteenth century but covers the long period from the end of the Middle Ages to the nineteenth century, is the work of Francesco De Sanctis. Even in the early writings of 1842–44 (collected in *Purismo, illuminismo, storicismo* by A. Marinari, Turin, 1975), De Sanctis had thrown new light on the Enlightenment, seeing in Voltaire the beginning of a new historiography, based on the study of the customs and character of different nations, while in the doctrine of the *philosophes* he saw a free critique of 'religious, political and moral principles', which in France, in his opinion, had developed into a destructive scepticism but which in Italy had stimulated a lively moral and civil reform. His Giobertianism of those years led him to emphasise the continuity of Tridentine Catholicism despite the new values of the Enlightenment; but it did not prevent him from stressing the positive elements in eighteenth-century thought which for him had become constructive forces for civil progress with Catholic mediation.

After the publication of his *Storia della letteratura italiana* in 1870, De Sanctis's ideas developed further as a result first of the influence of Hegelianism and then of European positivism, together with the maturing of his democratic and liberal convictions in politics. The French Revolution, the ultimate consequence of the political movement of the eighteenth century, became the crucible for the liberal and democratic movements of the following century. In his book De Sanctis put forward as well as a 'democratic' evaluation of the eighteenth century, a reconstruction of the past where the unifying protagonists are society, its aspirations and its social movements. This work goes beyond literary history to provide authoritative support for that positivistic direction in which Italian historical research was moving.

Historical research underwent many changes during the nineteenth century. History was establishing itself as a separate discipline, with its own centres for study and debate. The profession of historian was becoming recognised. Indicative of this development was the setting up, in almost all the capitals of the Italian states and, after Unification, in the chief cultural centres, of *Deputazioni di storia patria*. Alongside these were born the first reviews of regional history, while in the universities chairs in history were created. This flowering of historical studies, even if initially scattered and chiefly academic in character, led to many discoveries about the past and a new look at research on the eighteenth century. The influence of the 'positivist' school of history demanded investigations into the character of society, into the structure of states and into economic problems, while helping to remove history from the literary confines which held it. A good example of these new historiographic interests can be found in Carlo Tivaroni's *Storia critica del Risorgimento italiano* (Turin, 1888–97) in nine volumes, the first of which is devoted to the history of Italy before the French Revolution. The State, social classes, finance, economic movement and culture are the elements which make up this analysis, in which we have a foretaste of historiographical problems that were to become of great importance. The work is presented in a narrative framework which, as Walter Maturi[6] has said, is influenced by a desire to reconcile opposing interpretations. One has only to look at the treatment of the crisis of the Venetian Republic, which Tivaroni sees as resulting from the structure of the institutions and their system of representation; or his discussion of the significance of Habsburg policies and the existence in them of that Catholic reformism just then being discovered by the German historians; or his analysis of the State of Savoy, which he sees as united but conservative, jurisdictionalistic but lacking in ideological freedom; or finally his treatment of the southern baronacy and its restraining effect on the reform movement.

In the fervour of historical study, which reached a climax between Unification and the last decade of the nineteenth century, the eighteenth century did not receive much attention compared to classical antiquity, the Middle Ages or the Renaissance. It was rather in the context of the crisis of positivist historiography that an interest in eighteenth-century economic and social history began to emerge. These were the historians of the school which Croce has called 'economico-juridical'. It had inherited from positivism a concern for the material factors in history, but in rejecting the presumed neutrality of the historian and a view of erudition as an end in itself, it reveals the influence of historical materialism whether in Antonio Labriola's mature interpretation in the second of his essays *Del materialismo storico, dilucidazione preliminare* (1896), so influential among young historians, or in the more distortedly reductionist interpretations.

Linked with this current in historiography came a new interpretation of the eighteenth century which brought to the surface problems of society and economy, reconstructed political history in terms of the history of the ruling classes, analysed the clash between Church and State in all its implications and studied the impact of the reforms of the ruling princes. This was an important lesson in methodology and discipline, where the differing ideological viewpoints on which a great part of nineteenth-century historiography had been based lost much of their importance. Instead there was a beneficial return to the facts, and the discovery of new areas for research. Some of this research is an essential reference point even today – for example the works by Giuseppe Prato on economic life in Piedmont or Salvatore Pugliese on economic and financial conditions in Lombardy in the eighteenth century. Other research on Lombardy was carried out by Alessandro Visconti and Silvio Pivano, while Luigi Einaudi studied the finances of Savoy and Niccolò Rodolico and Antonio Anzilotti Tuscany at the time of the Regency and Leopold. In these same years Michelangelo Schipa, a historian of great erudition and sympathetic to positivism, tackled again all the problems of southern society in the modern age, making a contribution to our knowledge of the political and institutional life of the Kingdom of Naples which is still relevant today. The economico-juridical school did not become definitive in historiography, developing as a methodology for only a brief period, between the beginning of the twentieth century and the First World War. Placed at a parting of the ways between the decadence of the philological method, which failed to confront problems historically, the emergence of Marxism (soon however vitiated by the schematism of an evolutionary interpretation) and Croce's answer to the crisis of positivism, the economic-juridical school proved unable to develop that potential for historiographical reform which had been present in its beginnings.

The reactionary solution to the crisis of the post-war period, represented by Fascism, corresponded with a division in the intellectual ranks of the economico-juridical school. Ettore Rota took up a nationalistic position which tended to oppose positivist methodology; Gioacchino Volpe, with greater intellectual astuteness, turned to a historiographical eclecticism which in fact supported the cultural policy of the regime; while Anzilotti moved towards Croce's ideas without losing sight of the importance of economic and institutional matters. Liberal historiography was to some extent inspired by Anzilotti's methodology; it both fuelled the opposition to Fascism, as in

Guido De Ruggero's *Storia del liberalismo europeo* (1925), and, in the years of the consolidation of Fascism, also opposed the nationalistic trivialisation of the eighteenth century in the works of several historians close to the regime. These tensions can be seen in the work of Carlo Morandi, a one-time pupil at Pavia of Anzilotti and Ettore Rota, from his first book *Idee e formazioni politiche in Lombardia dal 1748 al 1814* (Pavia, 1927) which saw in the eighteenth-century Enlightenment the origins of modern liberalism.

In the same year Giulio Natali published, with the Vallardi press in Milan, *Il Settecento*, a large work of immense erudition which is still useful today, though it fails to come to grips with the problems of the period. An immense storehouse of people, facts and book titles, though coming alive only in the sections on 'customs' (which even so are superficial and conventional), Natali's *Settecento* tried to draw attention to a century that the author believed, with some reason, to have been unjustly neglected. Taking issue with Gabriel Maugain (*Etudes sur l'évolution intellectuelle de l'Italie de 1657 à 1750 environ*, Paris, 1909) who had grasped all the connections between the new historical and scientific advances of the second half of the seventeenth century and the Enlightenment, Natali made an explicit break at the year 1748, the year of Aix-la-Chapelle, which in his opinion ushered in 'the age of the reforming princes', 'the age of our second Renaissance'. His work contains frequent nationalist allusions and assertions of an independent Italian culture, and a dislike of the Enlightenment, which he describes as 'a dogmatic, uncritical, anti-historical philosophy' only redeemed when it moderates its polemical side and becomes, as in Italy, the instrument for reform. These and other central elements put it in the category of the nationalist historiography which was coming back into favour at the time. The same author declares explicitly: 'many Italians repeat that the eighteenth century is, even in Italy, the century of French philosophy. I have more faith in those of our historians who can be called nationalists who see a single original and indigenous line in the development of our thought.' Jurisdictionalism and Jansenism become 'a distant preparation for one of the most remarkable aspects of the national Risorgimento', that is, the defeat of the temporal power of Rome.

These words by Natali show a tendency present in the Italian historiographic tradition which came to the fore during the Fascist period, when the origins of the Risorgimento were sought in the eighteenth century. With the nationalist historians there returned all the hostility to the French Revolution and to the Enlightenment so typical of reactionary historiography, now given new life by a pro-Savoyard view of the Risorgimento. The reforms were interpreted as direct action to reinforce the State; the territorial expansion of the House of Savoy became the central point of the history of the eighteenth century in that it prefigured national unification; all references to a supposed national feeling in Italian intellectuals of the eighteenth century were stressed as being precursors of the Risorgimento; even economic progress was emphatically seen as being the work of a bourgeoisie laying the foundations for the political unity of the State. The most prominent interpreter of this view of the eighteenth century was Ettore Rota, who as early as 1911 had published an inquiry into the Habsburg period in Lombardy in which he depreciated the importance of the reforms of Maria Theresa and Joseph II with a political animosity which betrayed the anti-Austrian sentiments pervading Italian historiography since the Risorgimento. *Le origini del Risorgimento*, published by Vallardi in 1938, was the culminating point of this nationalist interpretation of the eighteenth century. In this book the culture of a century – which in reality had known an intense exchange of ideas with Europe – is confined within national boundaries, and the culture of the eighteenth century is reduced to the expectation of national unity, centring on a Piedmont already aware of its historic mission.

The distortions which could result from such a dynastic and openly ideological history can easily be imagined. Not surprisingly, the task of writing the entry on 'The Age of Reform' in the Italian Encyclopaedia (*Treccani*, edited by the philosopher Giovanni Gentile) was given to Rota on the suggestion of Gioacchino Volpe. In 1936 in the *Rivista storica italiana* Volpe had written a long article entitled 'Principi di Risorgimento nel '700 italiano' where, with a historical perceptiveness foreign to Rota, he put forward the thesis of the eighteenth-century origins of the Risorgimento, supporting it with arguments which, on the one hand, proposed again the role of the House of Savoy as a catalyst, albeit more in terms of the organisation of the State and political culture than as a military power, while, on the other, it relied on a generic 'national and unified consciousness' which emerged in the eighteenth century. Less narrow and rhetorical than Rota's writing, Volpe's article put an authoritative seal of respectability on nationalistic historiography.

Restrictions on free expression and a skilful manipulation of the tools of historical research to assist the aspirations of the regime together favoured an official historiography that was very responsive to Fascism's need for self-justification. The Savoy-biased, anti-Enlightenment, Italo-centric interpretation of the eighteenth century was an essential part of this. It resulted in a cultural provincialism which smoothed out any problems in research and aimed to prevent comparisons with European culture. Thus it was not surprising that a book like P. Hazard and H. Bédarida's *L'Influence française en Italie au XVIIIe siècle* (Paris, 1934) which placed eighteenth-century Italian culture in a European context, subordinate to France, was completely ignored, even in its limitations, by the official historiography.

The beginnings of a revival of studies on the Italian eighteenth century can be attributed to the influence of Piero Gobetti and his *Risorgimento senza eroi* (1926). This work – whose author was not a professional historian – looked back to the revisionism of Ferrari and Alfredo Oriani and to the concretism of Gaetano Salvemini, in order to give a broader base to his concept of a 'liberal revolution'. The Risorgimento had taken place, but because it was led by a state like that of Savoy, which since the eighteenth century had silenced or exiled its intellectual heroes like Radicati, Giannone, the Vasco brothers and Vittorio Alfieri, it had shown from its birth a moral weakness that was to manifest itself after Unification as a failure of democracy, which was to leave it an easy prey for Fascism. It is a political book, harsh and peremptory, which failed to please a historian like Adolfo Omodeo. Yet little more than a decade later he had come to understand perfectly the political and civil value of the historiography which developed from this first attempt. A comparison in the light of later historiographical developments of two texts like that by Piero Gobetti of 1926 and the more general *Politica del '700* by Antonello Gerbi, published in 1928 and inspired by Gaetano Mosca and Benedetto Croce, shows clearly the role that the neo-Enlightenment ideas of the young Piedmontese political thinker played in anti-Fascist circles. Gerbi – following Croce – still sees the eighteenth century as the mould for a richer nineteenth century. What interests him is the pre-Romanticism to be found in the eighteenth century.

The important European historiography of the Enlightenment was able to progress beyond this attitude in the 1930s[7] seeking an interpretation that the authoritarian irrationalism of the political regimes of the day (Fascism in Italy, Falangism in Spain and Nazism in Germany) seemed to have destroyed. Gobetti played an important part in this direction, not only as the originator of a liberal-socialist programme which was to inspire the anti-Fascist movement *Giustizia e Libertà*, but also because he had identified in the radical and reformist ideas of the Italian eighteenth century the beginnings of a political and ethical movement which merited study. And this was the road followed by one section of the anti-Fascist historians who not only opposed the rhetorical and nationalistic aspects of the eighteenth century but also found in the ideas of a neo-Enlightenment a focus for opposition to the Fascist regime.

The most important book in this vein was by Luigi Salvatorelli, who deserves the credit, according to Maturi, for having rediscovered the Italian Enlightenment. His *Pensiero politico italiano dal 1700 al 1870* (1935) not only explicitly went beyond the national events of the State, re-establishing as a historiographic criterion the dialectic between them and the rest of civil society, but also related the two centuries through the threads linking the ideas of the eighteenth-century Enlightenment and the democratic doctrines of the nineteenth. Salvatorelli, one of the most active collaborators with Gobetti and the 'liberal revolution', continued this link with the Enlightenment through the pages of the Turin review *La Cultura* published by Einaudi.[8] Other works of the later 1930s also show the influence of Gobetti, including the biography of Pietro Verri by Nino Valeri (1938) and Franco Venturi's book on F. D. Vasco (1940), one of Gobetti's 'heroes'. In the previous year Venturi had published his *Jeunesse de Diderot*. There was a growing interest in the culture and economic history of the eighteenth century, involving scholars differing in ideological outlook like Carlo Morandi, Franco Valsecchi, Raffaele Ciasca and Luigi Dal Pane. Schipa's southern tradition of scholarship was revived, in the shadow of Croce, in important works by Nino Cortese, Ernesto Pontieri and Fausto Nicolini.

It is not easy to summarise in these few pages Croce's attitude towards eighteenth century history.[9] From the philosophical point of view Croce stressed Romanticism rather than Enlightenment. Vico, even though he lived in the first half of the eighteenth century, is seen by Croce as a precursor of Romanticism and idealistic historicism. And it was this Croce who inspired Gerbi's work. While this was to be an essential feature of Croce's thought, yet his political and historiographical battle was to lead him to rediscover topics which had been greatly developed in the eighteenth century – politics, the idea of liberty, history as thought and action – categories which were to be widely used by men who would follow different paths from his, such as Salvatorelli, De Ruggero and Omodeo. This can be seen as far back as 1925 with his *Storia del regno di Napoli* where a link is made between the reform movement and later liberal developments.

After the second World War much new research on the eighteenth century emerged. The change in the cultural and political climate led to the need for a complete review of previous interpretations. Contact with other schools of historiography which had been excluded by the cultural autarky of the Fascist regime meant that new areas of research were opened up, while the writings of Antonio Gramsci were an important influence giving rise to a Marxist historiography. The Crocean school was less keen to tackle the subject of eighteenth-century history and there is no doubt that the historiographical reassessment of the eighteenth century, which is one of the most innovative aspects of historical studies since the war, had first to come to terms with Croce's negative view of the Enlightenment, whose ideas he considered to be anti-historical, abstract and unphilosophical. At the same time it is true that the young Croce's research into Neapolitan culture, republished in 1945, and his book on the history of the Kingdom of Naples were of the utmost value to young historians. One has only to think of the importance of a book like *Il Risorgimento in Sicilia* (Bari, 1950) by Rosario Romeo, which starts with the eighteenth century. At the same time studies of the regional history of the eighteenth century were becoming more frequent, as a result of the re-alisation that the states of the *ancien régime* were separate constitutional and political units, with their own individual social contexts.

Notwithstanding the reassessment of the Enlightenment carried out by both the Marxists, encouraged by the cultural policy of the Italian Communist Party, and by the exponents of what Maturi calls 'radical' historiography (for example the youthful studies by Venturi on the origins of the *Encyclopédie* and on F. D. Vasco), it was not easy, in the early stages at least, to renew the overall image of the Italian eighteenth century. This is clear from the first volume of Giorgio Candeloro's *Storia d'Italia*, inspired by Gramsci, which began to appear in 1956, and whose title is still *Le origini del Risorgimento*. The basic body of knowledge, still ultimately dependent on the research of the economico-juridical historians and their followers, was resistant to a Marxist interpretation, even one as flexible as that of Candeloro and which was to produce valuable results in the later volumes. Franco Valsecchi's *L'Italia nel Settecento* (Milan, 1959) with a political-diplomatic point of view, was also more a useful summary of the state of studies in the past than a stimulus to new research.

In the late 1950s, the eighteenth century became once more the centre of historical interest. Historians of different tendencies devoted studies often of outstanding value to it, including Venturi's book on Radicati di Passerano (1954), Marino Berengo's on Venetian society in the late eighteenth century (1956), Guido Quazza's on the reforms of Victor Amadeus II (1957), Mario Mirri's article on Leopoldine reformism published in the review *Movimento operaio* in 1955 and the early studies of Rosario Villari and Pasquale Villani. Their points of view differ and so do the subjects discussed, but these works have one thing in common – the attempt to re-enter that society, to link ideas with forces (as Quazza aptly wrote) and to look at eighteenth-century reforms from the point of view of the aspirations and objectives of the protagonists. In 1954 Venturi published in *Rassegna storica del Risorgimento* a kind of manifesto where he defined the lines of his research as developed through the years with an exceptional coherence and depth. His volumes in the series *Illuministi italiani*, published by Ricciardi, and his numerous articles which have appeared in the *Rivista storica italiana* paved the way for the first volume of *Settecento riformatore* (1969). The long task of documentation took shape in a reconstruction of the Enlightenment and the Italian reform movement from the beginning of the eighteenth century to the years of the famines, the connecting thread being the ideas of reform which spread over Italy and Europe. These ideas were rooted in history, revealing situations and the men who seized and manipulated them, revealing societies and states reacting and adapting in different ways not only to international policies and events often affecting them, but also to economic recovery and the possibility of reform. In 1976 the second volume of *Settecento riformatore* came out, which, carrying on from volume I, analyses the fight for the secularisation of the State, of society and of culture through which the reform movement had to pass so as to be able to continue, after the mid-1760s, with its economic and civil programme.

The third volume of this great work is called *La prima crisi dell'Antico Regime, 1768–1776.* Here Venturi further extends the limits of Europe, to Russia, Bohemia, Poland, Denmark, Sweden and Greece, to analyse that constant exchange of ideas between Italy and the Continent which is the central theme of his *Settecento riformatore.* He shows the first and inevitable breakdown of the old social and political balances in Europe. The emergence of Catherine II's Russia, the rebellions and battles in the East, the peasant revolts, starting with the very serious one of Pugachev in Russia, the famines, the crisis of the republican states and the eventual halting of the reform movement – these are the main themes of this volume which, in comparison with Volume I, makes great and important use of a source hitherto little used, either by Italian or other historians. This was the gazette, and other journals – the means for absorbing and modifying in public opinion political notions stirred up by outside forces. In the first two volumes, he used contemporary periodicals to a great extent, but chiefly to create a context of debate around important books. In Volumes III and IV we have not so much or only the learned or critical journal (which implies a very individual political and cultural voice) but also the gazette with its impersonality and ephemeral nature which nevertheless registers events, reactions and changes. The transformation of Italian society between 1776 and 1789 is analysed in the light of what was happening in America, of what reactions the American Revolution had provoked in Great Britain, of the crisis and evolution of the reforming countries of Europe – most notably Portugal after Pombal, France after Turgot and Spain with Floridablanca. The second part of Volume IV shows how Italian public opinion (connected to, though different from that of Europe) reacted to the changes in eastern Europe. Italy is described as a prism, through which 'to take apart, reassemble and analyse the political system penetrating from beyond the Alps and over the seas . . .', an Italy attracted, 'not without detachment, by the political events being acted out elsewhere, from Jefferson's America to Catherine II's Russia . . .' (IV, 1, p. xiv). In the fifth volume Venturi plans to concentrate on Italy and the reforms set in motion by the European states present in Italy and influenced by the theoretical ideas of the Europen Enlightenment.

Venturi's historiographical venture cannot easily be categorised. It contains many references to past historians like the Gobetti of *Risorgimento senza eroi*, Salvemini, Croce, Chabod and to contemporaries like Carlo Dionisotti. His is a history of ideas, which looks for proofs and references in society, stressing the creative function of men rather than the more nebulous political management of the ideas themselves.

Many historians have followed a method of historiography close to that of Venturi, often prompted by suggestions in his books, and they have contributed to our knowledge of different aspects of eighteenth-century reformism, with works such as that on the ruling class in Venice (Torcellan), the political biography of Francesco Maria Gianni, the minister and architect of Leopold's reforms (Diaz), the ideas of Ferdinando Galiani (Diaz and Guerci), the Parma of Du Tillot and Condillac (Guerci), the effects of the Enlightenment on the Republic of Genoa (Rotta), the figure of Pietro Giannone and the cultural reforms of Victor Amadeus II (Ricuperati) and the ideas of the Neapolitan reformers (Galasso). Prominent among these for his studies on the Italian and European Enlightenment is Furio Diaz, whom M. S. Anderson considers with reason to be, with Venturi, one of the chief figures in this area of research. In the essay which opens the collection *Per una storia illuministica* (1973), Diaz gives a very full and thought-provoking account of the relationship between contemporary reformism and a study of the Enlightenment.

That Marxist historiography made great strides after the war is explained by many factors, among which were the regaining of political democracy which allowed the free circulation of ideas, the substantial numbers of intellectuals close to the socialist and communist left and the publication of Gramsci's *Quaderni del carcere* containing his ideas on Italian history. At the same time, the majority of Marxist historians who concerned themselves with the modern period showed a willingness to take into account other historiographical approaches, not immediately consistent with Marxism, such as that of the *Annales* or of the more general economic and social historiography of France and England. An early product of this revival, where several currents merged in a historiography concerned chiefly with the economic and social bases of history, was the book by Marino Berengo on Venetian society at the end of the eighteenth century (1956). The relationship between Venice and the mainland, closely analysed, not only renewed the history of the State and society, but also opened up new areas for research – on the history of the rural areas, on urban society and on culture and cultural institutions. Thus also Quazza's book of 1957 combined different elements, an interest in political history, diplomacy and institutions and the lesson of the great Piedmontese economic historians, like Giuseppe Prato and Luigi Einaudi, in order to attempt a reconstruction of a state and a society at a moment of great political and social dynamism. Zangheri's studies of 1961 are a more consistent result of research which aimed to understand social relationships in a period of transition through the extent and movement of property.

Other historians (Porisini, Rotelli) dealt in those years with similar problems. There were also the innumerable studies on economics and labour by the indefatigable Luigi Dal Pane who had trained as a historian in the 1930s. An essay published in 1955 in *Movimento operaio* by Mario Mirri is important for its re-evaluation of the traditional view of Leopold's agrarian reforms. Previous historians, like Anzilotti and, more recently, Imberciadori had judged them in over-optimistic terms and without following up the implementation of the intended reforms. After him Giorgio Giorgetti perfected the study of the relationship between landowners and peasants in the Tuscan countryside in the eighteenth century, examining the effects of the *mezzadria* system, the results of the reforms of Gianni and the grand duke and the capacity of the great landowners to resist them. Research on economic history in Lombardy, the product of different historiographic traditions, has increased our knowledge of the structures of society. Among such studies are those of Mario Romani, Bruno Caizzi and Cafagna's Marxist-influenced essay of 1959.

Much work, following various methodologies, has been done on the economic history of the Kingdom of Naples, including Ruggero Romano's book of 1951 on trade (which follows the model of the historiography of the *Annales*), the books by Rosario Villari and Pasquale Villani, the research of Maurice Aymard and the later studies inspired by his work, and, most recently, the work of Augusto Placanica on eighteenth-century Calabria and Paolo Macry on the grain trade. Both Villari and Villani were concerned to go beyond ethico-political historiography, but they became increasingly aware that the economic and social context could not be understood apart from individuals, ruling groups and reforming intellectuals. Villani's *Mezzogiorno tra riforme e rivoluzioni*,[10] in the 1973 version, can be seen as the most considered result of an approach which combines French and English economic and social historiography with a Marxist outlook. This is rather different from Venturi's approach, more concerned with social structures than theoretical awareness, but which includes an analysis of intellectual rationalisations and political designs.

The third volume of Einaudi's *Storia d'Italia* (1973), which deals with the period from the early eighteenth century to Unification, reflects these developments in historiography. They are apparent too in Stuart Woolf's succinct summary of political and social history at the beginning of his large work for the English-speaking public, *A History of Italy (1700–1860)* (London, 1979). Alberto Caracciolo has attempted a picture of Italian economics, drawing on some fifteen years of valuable research. Venturi provides a useful excursus on the view of Italy put forward by European travellers, while Nicola Badaloni offers a history of culture according to a system whereby he attempts to link ideas to social values.

Research on the history of the Church, currents of religious thought and the role of religion in the different social groups, has been carried out by historians who, though starting from a Catholic point of view, have rejected traditional constrictions and limitations, to move towards a more concrete political, civil and social history of religion. Among them are Ettore Passerin d'Entrèves, Gabriele De Rosa, Romeo De Maio and Alfonso Prandi. An important work, tackling some of the problems of the history of eighteenth-century Catholicism (including the papacy of Benedict XIV, Muratori's religion and the relationship between Leopold and the Jansenism of Scipione de' Ricci), is Mario Rosa's *Riformatori e ribelli nel Settecento religioso italiano* (Bari, 1969). Of great interest is the ambitious project, co-ordinated by Alberto Vecchi, to publish the letters from Muratori's correspondents, thus complementing the correspondence of this great man published by Campori in the first decade of this century.

Legal history, which has traditionally chiefly concerned itself with the Middle Ages, has also made a valuable contribution to our knowledge of the institutions and juridical and political ideas of the eighteenth century, in the studies of Giovanni Tarello, Giuliana d'Amelio, Corrado Pecorella, Raffaele Ajello, Ugo Petronio and Mario Cattaneo. Ajello, particularly, by extending his concept of legal history to embrace the political history of institutions and social groups, has emerged as one of the central figures in the present-day reconstruction of the situation in the Mezzogiorno in the eighteenth century.

It is difficult to evaluate the most recent offerings. This ground has in any case been covered in the small volume *Immagini del Settecento in Italia* (1980) which provides a general balance of the work of the last few decades of historians, church historians, historians of literature, philosophy, science, law, foreign literature, economics, music and language. From it emerges a complex historiographical picture, with, in different areas, including that of the cultural institutions of the *ancien régime* (journals, schools, academies, professional bodies), the accent chiefly on social history. In relation to the picture drawn by Furio Diaz for political historiography and by Paolo Casini for the history of science, the most strikingly original work is, however, that of a young scholar, Vincenzo Ferrone, in his recent *Scienza, natura, religione. Mondo newtoniano e cultura italiana nel primo Settecento* (1982). He has had the courage to return to the origins and development of the Italian eighteenth century, looking at the scientific models and the political and religious ideologies implicit within them. The result is an original, complex and thought-provoking book which also has implications for the later eighteenth century.

It not only shows what developments and general results can come from such a full history of culture and ideas, but is likely to be long talked of, and not only in Italy.

Ferrone takes Rome at the end of the seventeenth century as his starting point. From Rome came both the repression of the Inquisition and a new interest in science. In comparison with Naples, Padua, Bologna and Florence, Rome appears as the centre of a new and fruitful spirit of enquiry that was not only scientific but also religious and ethical. It was linked with enlightened Catholicism which, early on, had been influenced by the rationalism of the Anglican theologians and their 'Newtonian ideology' (see below).

The prime mover of this new mood was Celestino Galiani. His work and his fight against the *veteres*, even influential figures like Doria and Vico, was of the greatest significance for the origins of the southern Enlightenment, showing the way from the theories of the natural sciences to those of the social sciences. In the face of the vitality of Galiani's ideas, the collapse of the radical Enlightenment, as represented in Italy by Radicati and Giannone, and whose scientific models were either out of date or non-existent, was, according to Ferrone, inevitable. But towards the middle of the seventeenth century – and just at the moment when the papacy of Benedict XIV seemed to be opening up new possibilities – enlightened Catholicism too began to turn back towards the Newtonian tradition, losing its bite. This was to have important consequences for the development of the Italian Enlightenment.

Some of the influences on Ferrone are clear: the Venturi school; the English-speaking school of the history of science (particularly Margaret Candee Jacob who has introduced not only new descriptions such as 'Newtonian ideology' but who has particularly brought out the importance and diversity of the radical Enlightenment in Europe); a thorough knowledge of the history of Italian philosophy, of Eugenio Garin, Paolo Rossi and Paolo Casini; the work of Raffaele Ajello on not only the juridical world of the South but also on institutions, classes and ideologies. The result is a picture of early eighteenth-century Italy and her relations with the rest of Europe which is comprehensive, consistent and largely new. Ferrone is to be applauded for re-examining, in two stimulating articles on the origins of the Academy of Sciences in Turin[11], the significance of the reign of Victor Amadeus III and the role of the scientific Enlightenment in Italy and Europe at the time of the crisis of the *ancien régime*.

Another influence on new research has been the desire of the different regions to discover and reconstruct their past. Alongside the history of ideas in Italy in a European setting as presented by Venturi, the *Storia d'Italia* edited by Ruggero Romano and Corrado Vivanti for Einaudi (Turin), the breaks and continuities of Italian history which are discussed in the *Annali*, we now have not only a large number of regional and town histories, but also the *Storia d'Italia*, edited by Giuseppe Galasso (for UTET). This history deals with the *ancien régime* by providing an analytical reconstruction of events in the old Italian states. One of the most recent and convincing contributions to this work is that of Carlo Capra on eighteenth-century Lombardy in the volume on the Duchy of Milan from 1535 to 1796, which appeared in 1984.

The region of Emilia Romagna is producing the ambitious *Cultura e vita civile nel '700*, involving since 1979 not only academics from the universities of Bologna and Parma, but also from other regions and universities of Italy. This project has raised problems. Can the ideas of the eighteenth century be separated so neatly into regional areas[12] which in some cases, such as that of Emilia, are very new? In the eighteenth century this area was divided, both politically and culturally, into the Legations, the Farnese Duchy (later Bourbon) and the Este Duchy. In fact, the first results of this project have shown that fears of the emergence of an inward-looking local history are excessive if not groundless.

The usefulness of such research which, instead of starting simply from the traditional idea of the cultural unity of Italy, delves deeply to find not only local details but also the links between different centres and outlying areas which made up the political, social and cultural geography of the Italy of the *ancien régime*, can be seen particularly in, for example, the results of the conferences on Maria Theresa held in 1980 under the aegis of the region of Lombardy in Mantua, Milan and Pavia. The proceedings of these have been published by Il Molino in 1982 under the title *Economia, istituzioni, cultura nell'età di Maria Teresa* and edited by A. De Maddalena, E. Rotelli and G. Barbarisi. Although very variable in type and extent, these articles give a new and rich picture of the history of Lombard society and its relationship with Vienna and Habsburg models. The first section deals with economic history and is composed chiefly of detailed local studies or a categorisation of previous studies, including such subjects as the *catasto*. The two successive volumes on, respectively, ideas and institutions (the latter understood in its broadest sense, including the functioning of power, social structures and the mechanisms of the state concerned with finance and administration), contribute much that is important and new.

Another conference was held in Naples in 1981, entitled *I Borboni di Napoli e i Borboni di Spagna*. The proceedings have been published by Guida, edited by M. Di Pinto, in 1985. They give an interdisciplinary historical view, with contributions from political, social, legal, institutional, and cultural historians and historians of philosophy, resulting in a new picture of the Bourbon model and its application in southern Italy, Sicily and Spain. It was a subject which it would have been difficult to approach from a purely local point of view, and the result has been particularly successful (see especially the more general essays by A. Maravall, A. Elorza, R. Ajello, F. Renda and G. Giarrizzo).

The proceedings of a conference held in Trent in 1984 at the Italo-German Institute, with the significant title of *Il Trentino fra Sacro Romano Impero e antichi stati italiani* and edited by C. Mozzarelli and G. Olmi (Il Mulino, Bologna), provide another important example of the emergence of not only a local and specific dimension, with its economic, social and institutional characteristics, but also of the coming together of contacts, communications and cultural relations which only in a situation of collaboration between the

Austro-German and the Italian world could be examined so broadly. This ecclesiastical principality, crossroad of so many cultures and home of a complex figure like Carlantonio Pilati, and its 'secular' opponent, Rovereto, whence arose, by no coincidence, the debate on magic and reason, are related, on the one hand, with Vienna and the neighbouring Austrian areas and, on the other, with the Habsburg models being established in Naples, the world of Lombardy and Tuscany and more generally with events influencing Italy, such as in the case of the relationship between Firmian and the Parma of Du Tillot and Paciaudi.

This new 'regional' history, which Mozzarelli and Olmi justify in their brief but illuminating introduction, seeks, even in the title, to avoid shorter and 'easier' titles such as 'The Trentino between Austria and Italy', in order to highlight the Trentino's position as a frontier area, the extremes of which are only comprehensible in the context of an *ancien régime* consisting of multi-national survivals and small, fragmented Italian states.

This method should be applied to a greater extent in other areas. The history of the State of Savoy in the eighteenth century, for example, is now inconceivable without taking into account, on the one hand, the centre which gradually excluded, even linguistically, areas such as Nice, Aosta and Savoy or transformed a distant area such as Sardinia, and, on the other hand, the growth of 'frontier' histories which cannot be defined as local and which raise fascinating and creative problems for a reconstruction of the state and society of Savoy, freed once and for all from the myth of the origins of the Risorgimento. The most obvious, but not the only, example can been seen in Jean Nicolas's important work on eighteenth-century Savoy[13] which has restored to the transalpine world, so closely linked to the State of Savoy, that identity which Lucien Febvre, at the beginning of this century, gave to a frontier area like the Franche Comté – a service which Fernand Braudel then rendered so abundantly for the entire Mediterranean area.

The history of Italy as a historiographical problem[14] as was understood, from their differing perspectives, by Denina and Cattaneo, is today more than ever a history, for the whole of the eighteenth century, of cities and areas subdivided into much smaller areas than simply North, South, Centre or the islands. Their cultural identity, not easily perceived or recreated in the framework of a unified reconstruction, can be better approached (as in Carlo Dionisotti's project[15] – and this is broadly adopted in the recent *Letteratura italiana* published by Einaudi and edited by Alberto Asor Rosa) by means of a geography which, together with history, can restore to every area its original voice and individuality.

NOTES AND REFERENCES

There is no one work with deals with the historiography of the eighteenth century. See: Carpanetto, D. (1980) *L'Italia del Settecento. Illuminismo e movimento riformatore.*

Loescher, Turin. Although Diaz and Venturi are mentioned in Anderson, M. S. (1979) *Historians and Eighteenth Century Europe 1715–1789*, there is no section devoted to the historiography of Italy in particular. The following works may be helpful: Maturi, W. (1950) 'Gli studi di storia moderna e contemporanea', in various authors, *Cinquant'anni di vita intellettuale italiana. Scritti in onore di B. Croce*, eds Antoni, C. and Mattioli, R., s.a. I, pp. 246ff; the contributions by Quazza, G., Villani, P. and De Rosa. L. (1970) in *La storiografia italiana negli ultimi venti anni*. Marzorati, Milan. Quazza's essay was republished as a single work in 1971, *La decadenza italiana nella storia europea*. Einaudi, Turin; various authors (1980) *Immagini del Settecento in Italia*. Laterza, Bari.

The following are just some of the works which indicate the change of interpretation of the last forty years: Candeloro, G. (1956) *Storia dell'Italia moderna* I, *Le origini del Risorgimento 1700–1815*. Feltrinelli, Milan; Valsecchi, F. (1959) *L'Italia nel Settecento. Dal 1714 al 1788*. Mondadori, Milan; Venturi, F. (1969–84) *Settecento riformatore* (in 4 vols). Einaudi, Turin. This latter is the realisation of a plan of research described in Venturi, F. (1954) 'La circolazione delle idee', in *Rassegna storica del Risorgimento*, fasc. 3–4, pp. 203–22. From this resulted also the great anthologies *Illuministi italiani*. See vol. III, Venturi, F. (1958) *Riformatori lombardi, piemontesi e toscani*. Ricciardi, Milan–Naples; vol. V, ed. Venturi, F. (1962) *Riformatori napoletani*; vol. VII, eds Venturi, F., Giarrizo, G. and Torcellan, G. F. (1965) *Riformatori delle antiche repubbliche, dei Ducati, dello stato pontifico e delle isole*. See also: Diaz, F. (1973) *Per una storia illuministica*. Guida, Naples.

See also two recent foreign contributions: Woolf, S. (1979) *A History of Italy. 1700–1860. The Social Constraints of Political Change*. Methuen, London; Jonard, N. (1979) *Le siècle des Lumières en Italie*. L'Hermès, Lyons.

1. Ottieri, F. M. *Istoria delle guerre avvenute in Europa e particolarmente in Italia per la successione della Monarchia di Spagna*. Rome, vol. I 1728, vols II–IV 1756–57.
2. Venturi, F. (1973) 'L'Italia fuori d'Italia', in various authors, *Storia d'Italia* III, *Dal primo Settecento all'Unità*. Einaudi, Turin, pp. 987–1481.
3. See: Denina, C. (1979) *Le rivoluzioni d'Italia*, ed. Masiello, V. UTET, Turin, p. 1319.
4. Hazard, P. (1910) *La Révolution Française et les lettres italiennes*. Paris.
5. On literary histories see: Getto, G. (1981) *Storia delle storie letterarie*. Sansoni, Florence.
6. Maturi, W. (1962) *Interpretazioni del Risorgimento*. Einaudi, Turin.
7. Ricuperati, G. (1974) 'P. Hazard e la storiografia dell'Illuminismo', in *Rivista storica italiana*, a. LXXXVI, fasc. II, pp. 372–404.
8. Turi, G. (1980) *Il Fascismo e il consenso degli intellettuali*. Il Mulino, Bologna, pp. 193ff.
9. Cotroneo, G. (1970) *Croce e l'Illuminismo*. Giannini, Naples.
10. The first draft, significantly different from the 1973 version, dates from 1962. See also Villari, R. (1961) *Mezzogiorno e contadini nell'età moderna*. Laterza, Bari.
11. Ferrone, V. (1984) 'Tecnocrati militari e scienziati nel Piemonte dell' Antico Regime. Alle origini della Reale Accademia delle Scienze di Torinol', in *Rivista storica italiana*, a. xcvi, fasc. II, pp. 414–509.
12. Prosperi, A. (1983) 'La ragione nei confini di una regione?' in *Quaderni Storici*.
13. Nicolas, J. (1978) *La Savoie au 18e siècle*. Maloine, Paris, 2 vols.
14. Galasso G. (1979) *L'Italia come problema storiografico*. Utet, Turin.
15. Dionisotti, C. (1967) *Geografia e storia della letteratura italiana*. Einaudi, Turin.

Maps

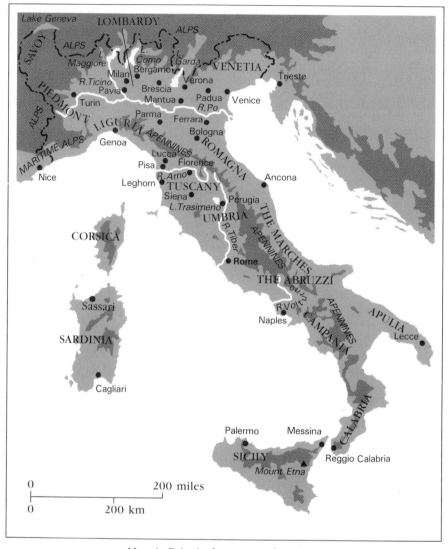

Map 1. Principal towns and regions

Map 2. Political divisions during the eighteenth century

Index

Abbaye, Béardé de l', 304
Abetone, 52
Abruzzi, 4, 25, 26, 30
Academies
  Academy of Sciences, 121, 300, 301,
    305, 306, 313
  Arcadia, 83–5, 87, 88, 89, 129
  Moscow Academy, 87
  Naples Academy of Science, 129
  Physiocratic Academy, 213
  Verona Academy, 305
Accademia
  degli Investiganti, 79, 80, 81, 90, 106
  degli Oziosi, 99, 100, 101, 253
  degli Unanimi, 307
  dei Filopatridi, 307
  dei Fisiocritici, 79
  dei Georgofili, 130, 213, 215, 254, 276
  dei Lincei, 78
  dei Pugni, 94, 261, 262, 265, 266
  dei Quirini, 87
  dei Trasformati, 260
  del Cimento, 79
  del Concili, 79
  delle Scienze, 99
  Filopatria, 301, 305, 306
  Medinaceli, 82, 90, 96, 100, 106
  Sanpaolina, 300, 301, 305, 306
Acta eruditorum, 79, 81, 89, 103, 109
Adda, 37, 52
Addison, Joseph, 264, 311
Adige, 37
Adriatic, 10, 52, 147
  coast, 68
  plain, 17, 25

trade in, 198, 199
Aegean, 68
Africa, 11, 12, 292
agriculture, 4, 5, 6, 19, 22–32, 37, 41,
  45, 46, 47, 49, 51, 254
  improvements, 50, 57, 67, 155, 201,
    215
  Muratori on, 134
Agrigento, 4
Agro Pontino, 197
Agro Romano, 30, 46, 197
Aguirre, Diego d', 92, 129
Aguirre, Francesco d', 92, 93, 114, 121,
  129, 145, 149, 150, 259, 274
Aix-la-Chapelle, Treaty of, 127, 151,
  175, 187, 188, 189
Ajello, Raffaele, 187, 329, 330, 331
Alembert d', 254, 264, 266, 273, 275,
  300
Alessandria, 140
Alfieri, G. A., 115
Alfieri, Vittorio, 301, 313, 323
a livello, x, 52, 177, 214–15
Allioni, Carlo, 300
allivellazione, x, 214–15, 218
Althann, Cardinal d', 108, 148
alzamento, x, 251
Amalfi, 36
Amelio, Giuliana d', 329
America 12, 99, 135, 212, 216, 226,
  291, 303, 306
  revolution, 290
Amidei, Cosimo, 210, 217, 220, 273,
  274–7, 278
Amoretti, Carlo, 304

Amsterdam, 34, 35, 83, 118, 125
ancien régime, 4, 49, 54, 64, 132, 145,
    146, 154, 155, 182, 188, 204, 206,
    221, 223, 234, 236, 239, 242, 267,
    268, 269, 270, 293, 298, 310
    crisis of, 284, 298, 301, 305, 306,
    317
    historiography of, 310–32
Ancioni, Giambattista, 87
Ancona, 8, 16, 34, 35, 72
    free port, 195
Anderson, M. S., 327
Andrea, Francesco d', 107
Andrea, Gennaro d', 98, 99
Andrés, Juan, 313, 314
Argelati, Filippo, 250
Angelis, Gerardo de, 287
Anglicanism, 279
Annali d'Italia, 130, 132, 310
annona, x, 15, 17, 23, 24, 25, 63, 167,
    170, 200, 213, 214, 234, 236, 237,
    245, 256, 288
Antwerp, 12
Anzilotti, Antonio, 321, 322, 328
Aosta, Valle d', 141, 206
Apennines, 25
    passes, 52
appalti, 71
Apulia, 17, 27, 35, 36, 43, 46, 238
architecture
    Florence, 14–15
    Naples, 18
    Palermo, 18–19
    Rome, 15–16
    Turin, 8
    Venice, 9–10
Arezzo, 14
Argento, Gaetano, 106, 107, 109, 181
Ariani, Agostino, 82
Aristotle, 82, 90, 153
Arno, 13
arrendamenti, x, 65, 185, 187, 192 n2
arrendatori, x, 65, 185
Asia, 292
Asor Rosa, Alberto, 332
Astigiano hills, 32
Atlantic, 141
Aubert, Giuseppe, 213, 264, 275
Augustine, Saint, 219
Aulisio, Domenico, 106

Austria, 59, 89, 126, 127, 140, 147–9,
    151, 179, 187, 188, 189, 195, 197,
    199, 202, 211
    Empire, 11, 61, 98, 141, 146, 187,
    194, 269
    Freemasons, 282
    in Genoa, 203
    in Lombardy, 146, 259, 260
    in Naples, 146, 180, 184, 185
    in Sicily, 146
    Leopold succeeds Joseph, 221
    regime, 9, 57, 63, 65, 91, 158–78
    see also Vienna; Habsburg Empire
Austro-Sardinian invasion, 177
Avella, 36
Avellino, 36
Aymard, M., 4, 27, 29, 36, 38, 42–4,
    45, 328

Bacchini, Benedetto, 79, 89, 91
Bacon, Francis, 80, 102, 108, 254
Badaloni, Nicola, 329
Balbo, Cesare, 317
Balbo, Prospero, 301
Ballerini brothers, 125, 130, 131
Banco di San Carlo, 148
Bandini, Sallustio, 169, 170, 213
Bank of Sant'Ambrogio, 161
Bank of Santa Teresa, 161
Barbarisi, G., 331
Baretti, Giuseppe, 264, 265, 298, 311
Baroni, Clemente, 132
Bartolomei, Francesco Stefano, 298
Bava di San Paolo, Emanuele, 301
Bavaria, 242, 282
Bayle, Pierre, 79, 89, 106, 116, 122,
    127, 279
Beccaria, Cesare, 213, 220, 226, 259,
    262–4, 265, 266, 269, 270, 271, ·
    275, 276, 278, 279, 288, 294, 301,
    302, 304, 314, 319
Beccaria, Giambattista, 300, 302
Bédarida, H., 323
Belforte, circle, 104
Bellettini, A., 39
Belloni, Girolamo, 15, 197
Beloch, J., 4, 7, 39
Beltrami, D., 45
Bencini, F. D., 93, 94, 114
Benedict XIII, 193

Benedict XIV, 48, 129, 130, 134, 151, 171, 184, 193, 194, 195, 196, 197, 252, 273, 310, 329, 330
Benting, 278
Berengo, Marino, 49, 198, 326, 328
Bergamasco, the, 37
Bergamo, 126, 161
Berlin, 300
Berne, 266, 278
Bernouilli, J., 300
Bernsdorf, 281
Bertenstein, Protocol of, 159
Berti, Giuseppe, 319
Bertola, Giuseppe Ignazio, 18
Bertolini, Stefano, 212
Bertrandi, Ambrogio, 300
Bertuch, 313
Bettinelli, 313
Bianchi, Isidoro, 266
Bianchini, Francesco, 90
Bianchini, Ludovico, 319
Biblioteca napoletana, 80
Biblioteca oltremontana, 301, 302, 305, 306, 315
Bibliothèque italique, 89, 109, 112, 124
Bibliothèques (Dutch), 81, 91
Biella, 52, 144
Biffi, Gian Battista, 262, 265, 302, 304
Biscardi, Serafino, 81
Boccaccio, Giovanni, 85
Bochat, Louis de, 112, 124
Bodin, Jean, 108
Bogino, Giovan Battista, 155, 205, 206, 302, 304
Bohemia, 226
Bologna, 16, 36, 71, 72, 80, 90, 91, 92, 193, 194, 199
    population, 16
    region, 48, 195
Boncerf, Pierre-François, 293
Boncompagni, family, 15
Bonneval, Alexandre, 110
Borelli, Giorgio, 67
Borghese, family, 15
Borromeo, family, 89
Bosquet, Marc-Michel, 112
Bossuet, Jacques-Bénigne, 89
Botta, Carlo, 307, 317
Botta-Adorno, Antonio, 170, 174, 212
Bottari, Giovanni Gaetano, 88, 128, 131, 196

Boulainvilliers, Henry, 114
Boulanger, N. A., 104, 286, 287, 288, 293, 295, 314
Bourbon, 15, 91, 93, 107, 236, 273
    conquests, 150
    courts, 274
    Europe, 243, 290
    Italy, 179–91, 194, 310
    policy, 263
    reformism, 121, 149, 289, 290
        compared with Habsburg reformism, 240
    return to Naples, 151
    rule, 101, 175, 285
    State, 100
bourgeoisie, 15, 19, 51, 54, 55, 56, 57, 58, 64, 68, 71, 72, 73, 152
    of Amsterdam, 125
    in Filangieri, 294, 295
    of Naples, 147, 240
    in Pagano, 287
    of Savoy, 142, 143
    of Tuscany, 215
Bovara, Giacomo, 231
Bower, Archibald, 109
Boyle, Robert, 112
Bozzolo, 189
Brandenburg, 87
Braudel, Fernand, 332
Brenckman, Hendrick, 89
Brescia, 126, 264
Bresciano, the, 37
Broedersen, Nicola, 125
Broggia, Carl'Antonio, 122, 134, 135, 185, 250
Brosses, Charles de, 311
Bruno, Giordano, 80
Brunswick, duke of, 278
Buffon, G., 104, 287, 288, 293, 314
Bulferetti, L., 69
Buonafede, Appiano, 104
Burke, Edmund, 314
Burlington, Lord, 124
Burnet, Gilbert, 81, 89
Büsching, Anton Friedrich, 285
Butel-Dumont, George-Marie, 255

Cadiz, 34
Caetani, family, 15
Cafagna, Luciano, 328

Caffè, Il, 94, 132, 153, 226, 259, 262, 264–6, 270, 281, 303, 306, 314, 318
Cagliari, 8
  university, 206, 302
Cagnazzi, Samuele, 319
Caizzi, Bruno, 37, 328
Calabria, 4, 25, 36, 238, 239, 246
Caloprese, Gregorio, 84, 90, 99
Caltanissetta, 4
Calvinism, 81, 89, 112, 116, 118, 279
Cambridge, 125
Caminier, Domenico, 311
Campanella, Tommaso, 80
Campania, 46
Campiani, M. A., 93, 114
Campo Formio, Peace of, 124
Campomanes, 204
Campori, Matteo, 329
Candee Jacob, Margaret, 109, 330
Candeloro, Giorgio, 325
Cantelli, Jacopo, 80
Capasso, Bartolomeo, 319
Capasso, Nicola, 88
Capitanata Foggia, 4
Capra, Carlo, 50, 232, 234, 330
Capua, Leonardo di, 80, 101, 106
Caracciolo, Alberto, 51, 329
Caracciolo, Domenico, 187, 241, 244–7, 298
Caravita, Filippo, 104
Caravita, Nicolò, 82
Carli, Gian Rinaldo, 50, 131, 132, 167, 262, 264, 265, 270, 280, 304, 313, 318
Carpio, marquis del, 99
Cartesian, 80, 88, 101
  physics, 111
Cary, John, 255, 269
Casale, 141
Casini, Paolo, 329, 330
Castro, 30
Catania, 4
Catanzaro, 36
catasto, x, 50, 65–6, 150, 154, 160, 215, 273, 304, 318
  Milan, 161–4, 233, 259, 260
  Naples, 186, 187, 190
  Piedmont, 205
  Venice, 200
Catherine II of Russia, 220, 291, 312

Catholicism, 80, 93, 100, 123, 131, 165, 166, 279, 280, 288, 296
  edict of tolerance, 229
  enlightened, 116, 117, 121–2, 128, 129, 130, 132, 310
  in Denina, 298
  reformism (in Maffei), 125
Cattaneo, Carlo, 318, 329, 332
Cava dei Tirreni, 36
Cavaliere, Giuseppe, 149
Celesia, Pier Paolo, 203
Cerati, Gaspare, 92, 93, 94, 122, 128, 129, 169, 212, 274
Cerda, Luis de la, duke of Medinaceli, 82
Cestari, Gennaro, 286
ceto civile, x, 63, 81, 82, 91, 99, 102, 107, 108, 245
Ceva, 112, 306
Chabod, F., 327
Charles II of Spain, 82, 103, 140
Charles VI, Emperor, 10, 34–5, 60, 103, 108, 127, 129, 141, 160
Charles of Bourbon (later Charles III of Spain), 18, 19, 61, 65, 103, 112, 117, 149, 151, 172, 179–88, 237, 243, 253, 254, 291
  in Naples, 179–88
  returns to Spain, 237
  victory over Austrians, 179
Charles Emanuel II, 142
Charles Emanuel III, 117, 118, 143, 146, 193, 204–6, 259, 302, 304, 312
Chastellux, F. J., 285
Chiesa e la repubblica dentro i loro limiti, La, 210, 274
Chigi, family, 15
China, 135, 292
Choiseul, E. F., 191
Christ, *see* Jesus
Christian VII of Denmark, 278
Christianity, 82, 100, 124, 313
  and magic, 132
  in Filangieri, 292
  in Giannone, 110–11, 113
  in Pilati, 282
  in Radicati, 116
Christina of Sweden, 83
Chur, 278, 281
Church, 23, 71, 84, 100, 107, 110, 111, 112, 113, 115, 123, 125, 130, 140,

141, 150, 159, 160, 163, 165, 171,
173, 273
careers in, 72
Dutch, 219
in Duchy of Milan, 224, 225,
228–30, 259
in Galanti, 285
in Genovesi, 257
in Giannone, 310
in Modena, 176, 178
in Naples, 180, 181, 182, 183, 184,
187
in Papal States, 193
in Parma, 188, 189, 190
in Sardinia, 206
in Tuscany, 210, 212, 217, 219
urban expansion of, 7
Church and State, 81, 108, 117, 146,
148, 155, 165, 171, 173, 274
in Amidei, 274–7
in Milan, 228, 229, 230
in Piedmont, 299
in Pilati, 278–81
in Tuscany, 218
see also jurisdictionalism
Ciampini, Giusto, 78, 79, 83, 84
Ciasca, Raffaele, 324
Cigna, Francesco, 300
Cipolla, G. M., 39
Cirillo, Pasquale, 173
Cisalpine Republic, 282, 314
city-states, 7, 9, 68, 72, 202, 203
Clarke, Samuel, 253
Clement XI, 92, 93, 108, 129
Clement XII, 16, 151, 171, 182, 193,
194, 195, 196
Clement XIII, 48, 164, 165
Colbert, J. B., 99, 133, 256
Collegio delle Provincie, x, 93, 146, 299
Colletta, Pietro, 317
Collins, Anthony, 118
Colloredo, 149
Colonna, family, 15
Comacchio, 91, 175
Como, 52
Comune (Florence), 70
Concina, Daniele, 125, 132
Concordat, 273, 275
with Milan, 162, 163
with Naples, 184, 186, 187

with Savoy, 93, 121, 145
Condillac, E. B. de, 154, 189, 285, 302,
327
Condorcet, Antoine de Caritat, Marquis
de, 300
Conforti, Francesco, 88
Consiglio politico, 124, 125
Constant, Benjamin, 296, 316
Constantinople, 11, 34
Constitutions (of Piedmont), 145, 146
Contegna, Pietro, 91, 107, 148, 182, 186
Conti, Antonio, 112
Contin, Antonio, 280
Contrat social, 275, 289, 292
Corio, Giuseppe Gorini, 132
Cornelio, Tommaso, 80
Corniani, Giambattista, 315
Corriere letterario, 281
Corsica, 11, 226, 301, 302
uprising, 202, 203, 204
Corsini, family, 122, 195
Corsini, Lorenzo, 102
Cortese, Nino, 324
Cosenza, 36
Cosimo I (Medici), 70
Cosmi, Giovanni Agostino de', 247
Coste, Pierre, 99
Council of Spain, 103
Council of State (Savoy), 143
Council of Ten (Venice), 67
Counter-Reformation, 6, 19, 78, 83, 114,
152, 154, 171, 191, 194, 198, 218,
219, 230, 277
countryside, 22–32
Coyer, G. F., 134, 255
Craon, Marc Beauvan de, 169, 170
Cremona, 302
Crescimbeni, Gian Maria, 84, 129
Cristiani, Beltrame, 163
Cristoforo, Giacinto de', 81, 90
Croce, Benedetto, 101, 319, 321, 324–5,
327
Crusca, x, 85
anti – , 265
Cuneo, 142
Cuoco, Vincenzo, 314
Curia, 63, 78, 79, 81, 82, 83, 84, 108,
148, 151, 165, 168, 171, 179, 182,
184, 189, 190, 194, 195, 196, 219,
273, 278

Custodi, Pietro, 314, 315
Cybo, Maria Teresa, 175
Cyprus, 34

Dal Pane, Luigi, 324, 328
Danckelmann, 87
Dangeul, Plumard de, 255
Danio, Amato, 81
Dante, 85, 86
Danube, 158
Davanzati, Domenico Forges, 88
De Antiquissima Italorum Sapientia, 96, 100, 101, 106
decurionato decurioni, 59
De Felice, Bartolomeo Fortunato, 266, 278
Dei difetti della giurisprudenza, 173
Dei delitti e delle pene, 220, 226, 262–4, 270, 275, 292, 301
deism, 106, 154
Deleyre, Alexandre, 189
Delfico, Melchiorre, 242, 296
Delille, Gérard, 26
Della moneta, 250–3
Della pubblica felicità, 93, 132–6, 250, 252
Dell'impiego del denaro, 130
De Luca, Luca Nicola, 290
De Maddalena, Aldo, 38, 42, 46, 47, 331
De Maio, Romeo, 329
Denina, Carlo, 264, 265, 282, 298–301, 311–13, 332
Denmark, 281
De Rosa, Gabriele, 329
De Ruggero, Guido, 322, 325
De Sanctis, Francesco, 317, 319–20
Descartes, 80, 90, 99, 100, 101, 106, 121, 122, 293, 302
De Soria, Gualberto, 203
De Souza, 298
De Thou, J. A., 108
De' tributi, 135
De Witt, Jean, 81
Diaz, Furio, 216, 327, 329
Diderot, Denis, 252, 266, 273, 324
Di Gennaro, brothers, 287, 289
Di Gennaro, Giuseppe Aurelio, 88
Dionisotti, Carlo, 327, 332

Di Pinto, M., 331
Discorsi (Machiavelli), 98, 116
Discours (Radicati), 115, 116, 118
Dominicans, 218
Donati, Claudio, 56, 57
donativo, x, 206
Doria, family, 15
Doria, Paolo Mattia, 81, 96–100, 101, 106, 112, 121, 124, 130, 183, 243, 253, 292, 330
Dragonetti, Giacinto, 257
Duni, Emanuele, 104
Dutens, Louis, 298
Du Tillot, Guillaume, 189, 190, 191, 327, 332

East, 147
ecclesiastics, 15, 19
    in Duchy of Parma, 190
Edict of Constantine, 111
educational reforms
    Duchy of Milan, 228, 230–1, 270
    in Filangieri, 293, 294–5
    in Genovesi, 257
    in Pilati, 280
    Naples, 243–4
    Parma, 191
    Piedmont, 298
    Venice, 202
Efis, Giovanni, 311
Einaudi, Luigi, 73, 141, 321, 328
Elorza, A., 331
Emanuele Filiberto, 8
Emilia, 46
Emilia-Romagna, 28, 30
emphyteusis, x, 26, 27, 29, 30
Empire, *see* Austria
Encyclopédie, 129, 213, 254, 264, 265, 266, 273, 275, 278, 281, 302
England, 10, 19, 22, 41, 42, 47, 49, 81, 83, 89, 98, 99, 103, 109, 112, 116, 117, 124, 130, 135, 140, 142, 144, 147, 152, 154, 176, 212, 256, 257, 269, 280, 290, 291, 292, 312, 313
    critical reviews, 128
    culture, 129
    education, 295
    philosophers, 286
    physiocratic theories, 214
    political system, 124, 126, 304, 306

Protestant, 279
trade, 11, 52, 186
views on Italy, 298, 311
enlightened absolutism, 100, 210, 211,
223, 227, 241, 243, 305
Enlightenment, 46, 66, 83, 86, 93, 115,
123, 124, 128, 132, 145, 154, 155,
163, 177, 182, 187, 189, 191, 206,
210, 217, 220, 227, 228, 250, 252,
253, 302, 306
European, 293
French, 201, 204, 277, 318
in Denina, 298
Italian, 123, 213, 277, 310
late Enlightenment, 295, 305
Lombardy, 259, 273
Naples, 250
'radical', 109, 110, 118, 132, 278,
314
Russia, 291
southern, 238, 239, 241, 242, 254,
261, 284–96
Enna, 5
Esmandia, Michele d', 150
Esprit des Lois, 124, 131, 136, 196, 289,
290, 298
Essai politique sur le commerce, 135
Essai sur les moeurs, 124
Este, dynasty, 175
Duchy, *see* Modena
Este, Ercole d', 175
Este, Francesco d', 175
Este, Francesco III, 175
Este, Rinaldo d', 175
Estratto della letteratura europea, 266, 278,
281, 302, 304
Euganian hills, 32
Eugene, Prince, 109, 110
Euler, L., 300
Europe
population, 2–5, 7
trade, 11, 12, 23
Evans, R. J. W., 224
Excerptum totius literaturae, 278

Fabbroni, Angelo, 212, 316
Facchinei, Ferdinando, 264, 301
famine, 4, 17, 25, 156, 182, 206, 213,
236, 245, 256
Fano, 194

Fardella, M., 90
Farnese, Elizabeth, 151, 179, 180, 188
son (Philip of Bourbon), 151, 187,
188, 189
Farnese, family, 30, 79, 91, 188
Febronianism, 164, 201, 229, 279
Febronius, 278
Febvre, Lucien, 332
Felloni, G., 35
Ferdinand, Archduke of Milan, 232
Ferdinand IV of Bourbon, 237, 238
Ferdinand, Duke of Parma, 189, 191
Ferguson, Adam, 286
fermiers, 28
Ferrara, 71, 281
Ferrara, Francesco, 314
Ferrarese, the, 175
Ferrari, Giuseppe, 316, 318, 323
Ferrone, Vincenzo, 329–30
feudalism, 23, 28, 30, 154, 159
domains, 12, 194
families, 17, 19, 162
fiefs, 26, 32, 60, 62, 64, 70, 72, 73, 83,
285, 292
Filangieri on, 296
Genovesi on, 256, 257, 293
in Lombardy, 58, 60
in Milan, 234
in Naples, 181, 184–5, 237, 238,
239, 242, 245, 246
in Papal States, 71
in Piedmont (Savoy), 72, 73, 141,
143, 206
in Sardinia, 206
in Sicily, 246–7
in South, 62, 66, 284
in Tuscany, 70, 215
jurisdiction, 174, 176, 186
lords, 22, 56, 180
nobility, 123
Pagano on, 287, 288
Vasco on, 302
Vico on, 103
fidecommesso, xi, 23, 24, 41, 71, 115, 134,
148, 154, 174, 256, 267, 270, 276,
279, 284, 302
Filangieri, Gaetano, 104, 153, 239, 240,
242, 244, 257, 284, 287, 289–96,
314, 316, 317, 319
Filangieri, Serafino, 290

Filicaia, Vincenzo, 90
Finale, 12
Firmian, Carlo di, 163, 164, 165, 230, 231, 332
fiscali, xi, 148, 167
Fiume, 10, 35
Flanders, 49, 55
Florence, 8, 12, 14, 19, 31, 52, 70–1, 79, 80, 81, 90, 122, 127, 128, 154, 156, 168, 171, 174, 190, 211, 212, 213, 219, 254, 264, 274
Fogliani, Giovanni, 246
Folch de Cardona, A., 110
Fontanini, Giusto, 90
Forbonnais, François Véron de, 254, 255
Foscarini, Marco, 199
Foscolo, Ugo, 314, 315
Fraggianni, Nicola, 107, 182
France, 10, 11, 12, 22, 79, 81, 83, 89, 92, 98, 99, 103, 109, 133, 134, 141, 142, 144, 145, 147, 152, 154, 161, 175, 176, 179, 188, 191, 202, 256, 269, 273, 274, 279, 280, 290, 291, 292, 304, 306, 313
culture, 129
Freemasonry, 242
government, 11
monarchy, 72
physiocratic theories, 214, 216
Regency, 115
revolutionary, 206
State, 124
Francesco III (d'Este), 175, 176, 177
Francis Stephen of Lorraine, 166, 170, 171, 174
Frederick II, 133, 291, 300, 305
Frederick II (of Swabia), 287
Freemasons, 104, 123, 130, 170, 171, 242–3, 282, 287, 288, 289, 296, 314
free thinkers, 106, 109, 110, 112, 118, 130, 277
free trade, 50, 52, 200, 213, 234, 241, 255, 256, 271, 288
Filangieri on, 291
Vasco, F. D., on, 302
Vasco, G., on, 304, 305
French Revolution, 12, 221, 230, 234, 282, 286, 288, 289, 312, 313, 317, 320
Fréret, Nicolas, 114

Frisi, Paolo, 132, 262, 264, 265, 270, 271
Friuli, 31
Frusta letteraria, 264, 298
Furio, Antonio, *see* Maffei
Futa, 52

gabellotti, 28, 43
Galanti, Giuseppe Maria, 239, 242, 257, 284, 285, 296
Galasso, Giuseppe, 327, 330
Galeazzi, Giuseppe, 266, 301, 304
Galiani, Celestino, 92, 93, 94, 99, 104, 114, 121, 123, 128, 129, 148, 182, 184, 196, 253, 269, 271, 319, 330
Galiani, Ferdinando, 104, 122, 187, 197, 237, 242, 244, 250–3, 256, 293, 316, 327
Galileo, 79, 80, 243, 312
Gallican, 92, 114, 117, 128, 194, 229, 243, 299
Garelli, Pio Nicolò, 109, 110, 129
Garfagnana, 175
Gàrin, Eugenio, 330
Garofalo, Biagio, 90
Gassendi, Pierre, 80, 106, 111
Gatti, Antonio, 90
Gazzetta letteraria, 302, 304
Gazzetta veneta, 264
Gee, Joshua, 255
Geneva, 81, 89, 112, 114, 123, 124
Genoa, 6, 8, 11, 12, 19, 34, 35, 37, 52, 55, 68–9, 85, 98, 160, 179, 190, 202–4
uprising in, 12, 174, 203
Genovesi, Antonio, 93, 104, 122, 155, 187, 239, 240, 241, 242, 243, 250, 253–7, 261, 269, 270, 278, 280, 284, 285, 286, 287, 293, 314, 319
Gentile, Giovanni, 323
Gerbi, Antonello, 324, 325
Gerdil, Sigismondo, 136, 265, 298, 302
Germany, 12, 81, 87, 89, 103, 204, 226, 278
culture, 277, 281, 300
Freemasonry, 242
Protestant, 279
universities, 277, 280
Ghibelline (neo-), xi, 91, 125, 132, 151, 175, 194, 310, 317, 318

Gianelli, Basilio, 81

Gianni, Francesco Maria, 212, 214, 216, 217, 327, 328

Giannone, Pietro, 91, 93, 102, 104, 106–113, 115, 116, 118, 121, 123, 124, 125, 128, 130, 148, 181, 182, 188, 237, 240, 243, 244, 257, 263, 273, 274, 275, 280, 281, 282, 285, 286, 299, 306, 310, 317, 318, 319, 323, 327, 330

Giarrizzo, Giuseppe, 331

Gibbon, Edward, 286, 298, 299, 311

Gibelin, Court de, 301

Gigli, Girolamo, 315

Ginguené, Pierre Louis, 315, 316

Gioberti, 319

Gioia, Melchiorre, 318

Giorgetti, Giorgio, 40, 41, 51, 328

Giornale de' Letterati, 78, 79, 81, 84, 123, 128, 264

    (Pisa ed.) 129

Giornale enciclopedico, 288

Girfoni, 36

Giudici, Paolo Emiliani, 317

giuspubblicismo, xi, 152, 153

Giusti, Luigi, 164, 166

Gobetti, Piero, 323, 324, 327

Goethe, 313

Goguet, Yves, 299

Goldoni, Carlo, 315

Gonzaga, family, 140, 141

Gorani, Giuseppe, 271, 280

Göttingen, 277, 280

Gournay, Vincent de, 255

Gozzi, G., 264, 265

Gramsci, Antonio, 325, 327

Grand Tour, 311

Gravina, Gian Vincenzo, 84–8, 90, 92, 93, 94, 98, 114, 122, 124, 129, 145, 243, 292

Great Britain, *see* England

Greece, 291

Gregoria, Rosario, 247

Gregory XIII, 15

Grendi, E., 69

Greppi, Antonio, 161, 166

Grimaldi, brothers, 287

Grimaldi, Costantino, 90, 107, 131, 148, 182, 242, 257

Grimaldi, Domenico, 284, 286

Grimaldi, Francesco Antonio, 104, 242, 257, 284, 286, 288, 289, 290, 295

Grimani, Francesco, 92

Grippa, Giuseppe, 296

Griselini, Francesco, 200, 201, 274

Groppello, 142

Grotius, 96, 100, 101, 102, 103, 107, 108, 124, 130

Guastalla, 151

    Duchy of, 188

Guelph (neo-), xi, 91, 98, 189, 190, 310, 317, 318, 319

Guerci, L., 327

Guevarre, Andrea, 144

Guicciardini, Francesco, 107, 108, 299

Guichenon, Samuel, 299

guilds, 19, 36, 52, 70, 71, 186, 305

    in Milan, 234

    in Savoy, 144

    in Venice, 201

Gustav of Sweden, 220

Habsburg

    court, 91, 121

    Duchy of Milan, 223–34, 259

    Empire, *see* Austria

    in Barcelona, 110

    in Florence, 71

    -Lorraine, 158–78

    possessions in Italy, 110, 140

    reformism, 101, 146–50, 240, 310

    regime, 32, 50, 59, 60, 61, 65, 91, 98, 108, 276, 277

    Spain, 140

    see also Austria; Vienna

Hague, the, 83

Halle, 87

Harrach, von, 61, 103, 160

Haugwitz, Friedrich-Wilhelm, 159

Hazard, Paul, 314, 323

Hegel, 320

Helvétius, 210, 240, 252, 262, 263, 275, 276, 277, 280, 286, 295

Herder, 313

Hesiod, 85, 86

Historia literaria, 109

historiography, 34, 38–44, 54, 310–332

Hobbes, 88, 97, 277

Hohendorf, baron, 109, 110

Holbach, Paul Henri, Baron d', 104, 252,

253, 266, 275, 278, 286, 287, 288, 298, 303, 314

Holland, 10, 19, 22, 81, 83, 87, 89, 92, 98, 99, 103, 117, 118, 123, 125, 126, 130, 135, 142, 147 186, 216, 226, 269, 278, 279, 290, 291

Holme, 304, 306

Holy Office, *see* Inquisition

Holy See, 91, 163, 274
see also Rome; Church

Holy Years, 15

Homer, 85, 86, 103

Huet, Pierre Daniel, 86

Hume, David, 255, 256, 275, 276, 285, 287, 298, 299

Hungary, 175

Huyssen, Heinrich von, 87

Hydra mystica, 84, 88

illuminista, xi, 50, 166, 226, 239, 241, 243, 260, 286

Imberciadori, 328

Impiego del denaro, Sull', 125, 131, 132, 250

Incisa, marquis d', 306

India, 135, 292

industry, 9, 11, 12, 16, 17, 19

Innocent XII, 87

Innsbruck, 277

Inquisition, 81, 82, 112, 113, 115, 116, 117, 123, 130, 165, 171, 183, 184, 191, 218, 219, 244, 246, 264, 282

institutions, 54–74, 140–56, 158–78, 179–91, 193–207, 210–21, 231–3

intellectuals, 78, 276, 298, 301
in Duchy of Milan, 225, 227, 234, 260
in Naples, 240–3
in Tuscany, 211

Intieri, Bartolomeo, 99, 122, 250, 253, 254, 319

Istoria civile del regno di Napoli, 91, 104, 107, 108, 109, 112, 125, 188, 274, 286, 310

Istoria filosofica, 82

Italian economy
eighteenth century, 45–74
seventeenth century, 22–44

Italian language, 146, 243, 244, 254, 301

Ivrea, 113, 302, 306

Jacobins, 88, 230, 243, 257, 271, 289, 307

Jageman, Joseph, 285

Jansenism, 88, 100, 114, 125, 129, 130, 132, 164, 189, 194, 214
in Duchy of Milan, 225, 228–30
in Naples, 243–4
in Tuscany, 217–19

Jerocades, Antonio, 289

Jesuits, 84, 90, 93, 100, 109, 110, 114, 117, 125, 128, 129, 145, 175, 190, 191, 201, 230, 238, 243–4, 247, 257, 273, 274, 280, 312

Jesus, 81, 281
in Giannone, 110–11

Johnson, Samuel, 298

Joseph II, 56, 58, 60, 61, 136, 166, 167, 170, 207, 216, 217, 221, 269, 270, 271, 282, 290, 291, 305, 306, 312, 318

Josephism, xi, 224, 225, 227, 229, 230, 271, 274, 277, 279, 290

Journal des Sçavants, 78, 79, 81, 88

Journal encyclopédique, 129, 280

Junta, 65, 165
for the *catasto* (Milan), 149, 161, 162, 163, 167

jurisdictionalism, xi, 106, 108, 110, 114, 117, 128, 129, 145, 147, 148, 151, 153, 155, 159, 164, 165, 170, 171, 175, 176, 178, 181, 182, 183, 184, 187, 188, 189, 190, 191, 194, 196, 198, 199, 201, 257, 273–81, 317
Duchy of Milan, 231
in Bogino, 205
in Denina, 299
in Giannone, 310
in Grimaldi, 286
Naples, 240, 243, 253
Sicily, 247
Tuscany, 214, 217, 218, 219

Justi, 164

Juvara, Filippo, 8

Kaunitz, count, 159, 164, 165, 228, 230, 231, 270

Keralio, Auguste de, 189

Klingenstein, Grete, 228

Labriola, Antonio, 321
La Chalotais, 257, 273, 280
Lagrange, Giuseppe Luigi, 300
Lalande, Jean, 311
Lama, Bernardo, 92, 93, 114, 121
Lambertenghi, Luigi, 262, 265
Lambertini, Prospero, see Benedict XIV
Lami, Giovanni, 127–9, 197, 212, 264
Lancisi, Giovanni Maria, 90
Lastri, Marco, 212, 271
latifundia, xi, 22, 25, 26, 27, 27, 237, 276
Law, John, 37
Lazio, 30, 71
Leclerc, Jean, 81, 91, 96, 99, 253
Leghorn, 7, 8, 11, 12, 13, 14, 16, 34, 35, 52, 71, 129, 170, 203, 213, 264, 266
Leibnitz, 89, 91, 101, 109, 124, 298, 302
Leipzig, 79, 81, 87, 89, 277
Leo X, 312
Leopold of Habsburg, 15, 51, 71, 136, 170, 210–21, 234, 274, 276, 305, 312, 318, 328, 329
Lettres Persanes, 115, 264, 298
Levant Company, 10
libertarianism, 201
Liber Nobilitatis genuensis, 69
libertines, 277
Liguria, 5, 31, 202, 203, 302
    coast, 11
    territories, 12
Lisbon, 34, 195
    earthquake, 204
Lloyd, Henry, 266
Locke, John, 93, 99, 100, 106, 121, 122, 123, 154, 216, 217, 251, 253, 256, 287, 298
Lodoli, Carlo, 199
Lombardi, Antonio, 316
Lombardy, 2, 5, 11, 32, 37, 40, 42, 43, 46, 49, 50, 51, 52, 57–61, 94, 112, 140, 149, 176, 177, 178, 218, 306, 311, 312, 313
    census, 121, 200
    Enlightenment in, 259–271, 281
    illuministi, 211
    school, see *Milan, école de*
    under Maria Theresa, 158–167

under Maria Theresa and Joseph II, 223–34, 274
Lomellina, 46, 140
Lomellini, Agostino, 203, 204
London, 7, 34, 37, 83, 109, 116, 117, 123, 124, 125, 226, 298, 300, 311, 312
Longano, Francesco, 239, 242, 257, 284
Longo, Alfonso, 262, 265, 270
Lorraine
    House of, 16, 151, 179, 194
    government, 122
    Regency, 71, 129, 158, 167–78, 211
    rulers, 13, 15, 210
Louis XIV, 83, 88, 91, 98, 99, 133, 136, 141, 147, 189, 207
Louis XV, 189
Lucania, 4, 25
Lucca, 19, 55, 129, 179, 204
Lucretius, 85, 86
Lunigiana, 12
Lutheranism, 279
luxury
    in Beccaria, 269
    in Galiani, 251–2
    in Genovesi, 255, 256
    in Muratori, 134, 135
    in Verri, 269
Luzzatto, Gino, 35
Lyons, 37, 52, 242

Mabillon, Jean, 79, 81, 89, 311
Mably, 303
Machault, 254
Machiavelli, 86, 96, 97, 98, 107, 108, 113, 116, 117, 130, 133, 134, 136, 260, 263, 294, 299, 311, 317
Macry, Paolo, 328
Madrid, 12, 151, 188, 190, 195, 237
    see also, Spain
Maffei, Scipione, 56, 91, 92, 98, 122, 123–8, 130, 131, 132, 199, 250, 252, 262
Magalotti, Lorenzo, 90
maggiorascato, xi, 134, 267, 276, 293, 302
magic, 131–2
Magliabechi, Antonio, 79, 80, 81, 90
Maiello, Gennaro, 88

Malebranche, Nicolas de, 100, 112, 114, 121, 122
Mamachi, T. M., 132
Mandeville, Bernard de, 255
Manifesto, 115
Mantovano, the, 46
Mantua, Duchy of, 15, 140, 162, 313
Manzoni, Alessandro, 317
Maranon, Marco, 150
Maravall, A., 331
Marches, the, 28, 30, 72, 194, 196
Marchese, A., 149
Marchetti, Alessandro, 90
Maremma, 13, 30, 169–70, 213
Maria Amalia, 189
Maria Carolina, 238, 290
Maria Christina, 221
Maria Theresa, 10, 50, 61, 66, 92, 109, 136, 158–67, 175, 178, 200, 211, 271, 312, 318, 331
Marinari, A., 319
Marinoni, Giovanni Giacomo, 150
Marseilles, 11
Marsham, John, 86
Marsili
  circle, 80
  family, 89, 92
Marx, Karl, 314
Mascov, Gottfried, 87, 88
masons, *see* Freemasons
Massa, Duchy of, 12, 175
masseria, 27
Massime, 98
Maturi, Walter, 317, 320, 324, 325
Maugain, Gabriel, 322
Maurists, 79, 81, 128
Mazarin, cardinal, 99
Mazzei, Filippo, 212
Mazzocchi, Alessio, 88
Mazzuchelli, Gian Maria, 315
Medici
  Cosimo III de', 14
  Duchy or State, 13, 14, 70, 151, 168, 172
  Gian Gastone de', 14, 167
  properties, 188, 194
  see also Tuscany
Medici, Luigi, 241
Medinaceli, Luis de la Cerda, 82
Meditazioni sulla economia politica, 266, 293

Meditazioni sulla felicità, 260, 261, 262, 264, 267, 275, 301
Mediterranean, 141, 147, 238, 291, 312
Mélanges de philosophie et de mathematique, 300
Melchiorre, Bartolomeo, 132
Mellarède, Pierre, 143
Melon, François, 100, 134, 250, 252, 256
Melzi d'Eril, Francesco, 315
Memmo, Andrea, 199
Mencken, Johann Burckard, 81, 87, 99, 103
mercantilism, 134, 147, 154, 155, 159, 164, 178, 186, 251, 252, 254, 255, 256, 293
  in Naples, 240
  in Savoy, 144
  in Vienna, 146
merchants, 10, 11, 13, 16, 19, 64, 69, 204, 238
  English, 13, 19, 34, 70, 186
  French, 13, 16, 19, 34, 70, 186
Messere, Gregorio, 85
Messina, 5, 7, 8, 19, 34, 186, 246
Metastasio, Pietro, 88, 92
mezzadria, xi, 25, 28, 29, 30, 31, 52, 213, 214, 215
mezzadro, xi, 28, 29, 48, 213, 214, 215
Mezzogiorno, *see* South
Michaud, 316
Michelet, Jules, 314, 316
middle classes, *see* bourgeoisie
Migliavacca, Celso, 125
Milan, 2, 7, 9, 12, 15, 16, 35, 50, 52, 57, 59, 61, 66, 73, 89, 154, 156, 190, 199, 266, 270, 274, 282, 304, 306
  école de, 213, 262, 264, 266, 269, 271, 275, 278, 301, 302, 304, 314
  patricians, 58, 59, 60, 61
  Senate, 59
Milan, Duchy of State of, 15, 37, 42, 45, 46, 85, 140
  Habsburg reforms in, 149, 151
  Under Joseph II, 223–34
  under Maria Theresa, 223–34, 158–67, 170, 175, 217
Milanese, the, 45

Millot, 189, 285
ministero togato, xi, 63, 65, 81, 82, 107, 148, 237, 246
Miolans, 112
Mirabeau, marquis de, 270, 275
Miro, Vincenzo de, 149
Mirri, Mario, 51, 326, 328
Miscellanea philosophica-mathematica, 300
Modena, 36, 79, 80, 89, 90, 112, 123, 128, 134, 154, 179, 199, 217
    Duchy of, 15, 85, 158, 174–7
    Este Duchy, 15, 91, 176
    Este Library, 316
moderni, 96, 99, 100, 253
Modica, 7
Molise (the), 4, 238, 284
monarchy
    in Doria, 97–8
    in Filangieri, 294
    in Radicati, 117
Mondovi, 7, 142, 301, 302
money, 250–3
    in Verri, 267
Monferrato, 140
Monforte, Antonio, 90
Monregalese, the, 142
Montaigne, Michel, 302
Montalto, 30
Montealegre, marquis of Salas and, 180, 181, 186
Montelatici, Ugo, 254
Montesquieu, 97, 114, 115, 124, 131, 136, 154, 196, 210, 240, 250, 254, 261, 262, 263, 275, 279, 289, 290, 292, 293, 298, 299, 302, 303, 306
Montfaucon, 89
Monti, Vincenzo, 306
Montini, Innocenzo, 311
Morandi, Carlo, 322, 324
Morea, 34
Morellet, André, 264, 266
Morelly, 255, 286
Morgagni, G., 92
Morozzo, Ludovico, 300, 306
Mosca, Gaetano, 324
Moscow, 87
Mozzarelli, C., 331, 332
Mugnano del Cardinale, 36
Münter, Friedrich, 289
Muratori, Ludovico Antonio, 88, 89–92,
    93, 114, 122–3, 125, 127, 128, 129, 130, 131, 132–6, 145, 153, 155, 164, 166, 173, 175, 196, 212, 219, 226, 250, 252, 253, 254, 257, 262, 263, 265, 275, 299, 301, 310, 311, 312, 316, 317, 329
Musschembroek, Pieter van, 253
Muti, family, 15

Nakaz, 291
Napione, Francesco Galeani, 299, 301, 306
Naples, 7, 8, 12, 15, 16, 17, 20, 34, 36, 62–6, 73, 79, 80, 81, 83, 88, 89, 91, 92, 93, 98, 99, 101, 104, 106, 107, 108, 109, 121, 122, 128, 147–9, 151, 153, 154, 156, 173, 175, 179, 190, 195, 196, 213, 236, 237, 240, 241, 242, 286, 288, 312
    Enlightenment in, 250–7, 281
    illuministi, 211
    university, 129, 244, 254, 257, 274, 278, 289
Naples, Kingdom of, 4, 61, 85, 172, 217, 236–47, 251, 312
    Bourbon, 112, 149, 179–88
    Regency, 237
Napoleon, 282, 286, 313, 314
Natali, Giulio, 322
Nazari, Francesco, 78
Necker, Jacques, 247
Neri, Pompeo, 150, 155, 161, 162, 163, 169, 170, 173, 212, 213, 215, 259, 271, 274, 304
Neri, Venturi, 173
Netherlands, see Holland
Newton, 82, 93, 99, 100, 101, 106, 112, 121, 122, 154, 169, 250, 287, 293, 298, 330
Niccolini, Antonio, 128
Nice, 9, 11, 141, 142, 143, 144
Nicolini, Fausto, 324
nobility, 54–74, 82, 97, 141, 151, 152, 154, 296
    in Filangieri, 293, 294, 295
    in Galanti, 285
    in Genoa, 11
    in Genovesi, 255
    in Milan, 162, 228, 232–3, 259
    in Modena, 176

in Naples, 180, 181, 182, 238, 245
in Pagano, 289
in Piedmont, 102, 142, 143, 205
in Pilati, 280
in Rome, 15
in Trieste, 11, 19, 23, 40, 41, 42, 51
in Tuscany, 168, 173, 174, 215
in Vasco, 302, 303
in Venice, 11, 200, 203
Nola, 36
Nouvelles de la république des lettres, 79, 81, 89, 122
Novelle letterarie, 127–9, 212, 264, 271
Nuzzi, 15

Odazzi, Traiano, 270, 284
oligarchies, 10, 22, 28, 55, 56, 57, 58, 60, 66, 67, 68, 72, 159, 163, 198
Olmi, G., 331, 332
Omodeo, Adolfo, 324, 325
Oneglia, 9, 11
Opuscoli, 122
Oriani, Alfredo, 323
Orient, *see* East
Origines iuris civilis, 85–7
Orlandi, Giuseppe, 253
Orleans, d', 299
Ormea, 115
Orsi, Giangiuseppe, 90
Orsini, family, 15
Ortes, Gianmaria, 200, 314
Osservazioni letterarie, 123, 127
Ottieri, Francesco M., 310, 311
Ottoman
empire, 110, 186
government, 11
see also Turkish
Oxford, 124

Paciaudi, 191, 280, 332
Padua, 2, 68, 80, 90, 91, 92, 126, 131
Pagano, Francesco Maria, 104, 257, 284, 287–9, 290, 295, 314, 317
Paglierini brothers, 131
Pagnini, Giovan Francesco, 211, 212, 250
Palermo, 4, 7, 8, 18–19, 34, 246
Pallavicini, Gian Luca, 61, 155, 160–3, 164
Palmieri, Giuseppe, 296
Palmieri, Matteo, 96, 242

Panzini, Leonardo, 113, 274
Paoletti, Ferdinando, 211
Paoli, Pasquale, 226
papacy, 71, 72, 98, 311
Papal States, 5, 15, 16, 45, 48, 71, 85, 91, 151, 179, 189, 193–7, 312
Parere sull'incertezza della medicina, 80
Parini, Giuseppe, 260, 313
Paris, 7, 83, 92, 112, 114, 123, 124, 125, 128, 187, 190, 194, 226, 252, 264, 300
Parlamenti, 56
Parlamento ottaviano, 264, 298
Parma, Duchy of, 15, 46, 79, 85, 90, 91, 140, 151, 175, 179, 180, 187, 188–91, 217, 274, 312
Parthenopean Republic, 241, 289
Pascoli, Lione, 15, 195
Passarowitz, Peace of, 34
Passerin d'Entrèves, Ettore, 329
Passionei, Domenico, 88, 128
patriciate, 7, 123, 124, 198
in Amsterdam, 125
in Bologna, 72
in Florence, 70, 71
in Lombardy, 55–61
in Lucca, 204
in Milan, 159–62, 166, 167, 224, 231, 232–3
in Naples, 241
in Venice, 62, 66, 126, 199, 201, 202, 203, 204
Patriotic Society, 225, 265, 304
Paul III (Farnese), 15, 188
Pavia, 7, 58, 230
university, 166, 230
peasants, 6, 15, 22–32, 49, 58, 62, 132, 162, 237, 239, 241
education for (Milan), 231
in Amidei, 277
in China (Filangieri), 292
in Filangieri, 294
in Milan, 162
in Savoy, 143–4, 156, 205, 206
in Sicily, 244, 247
in Tuscany, 170, 215
in Vasco, G., 303
Peccorella, Corrado, 329
Pelli Bencivenni, Giuseppe, 212, 217, 274

Pembroke, Lord, 124
Pensabene, 149
Perequazione, xi, 142, 143, 204
Perlongo, Gaetano, 149
Pescia, 31
Peter the Great, 87, 133, 291
Petrarch, 85
Petronio, Ugo, 232, 329
Petty, William, 251
Philip V, 141, 151, 180, 254
Philip of Bourbon, 151, 187, 188, 189
Philosophic Dissertation upon Death, 118
Philosophical Transactions, 78, 88
physiocrats, 154, 170, 187, 204, 211,
    212, 213, 214, 216, 247, 252, 256,
    267, 268, 269, 270, 271, 275, 276,
    277, 292, 293, 302, 303, 304
Piacenza, Duchy of, 15, 151, 187, 188
    see also Parma
Piazza, xi, 63, 245
Piedmont, 5, 8, 36, 37, 40, 45, 46, 48,
    51, 52, 57, 92, 93, 114, 115, 121,
    122, 129, 141, 143, 151, 183, 187,
    193, 197, 202, 271, 298–301, 302,
    304, 306, 310, 312, 313
    plain of, 32
Piedmontese, 194
    court, 118
    nobility, 9
    provinces, 9
Pignatelli, Francesco, 84
Pignatelli, Salvatore, 296
Pilati, Carlantonio, 273, 277–82, 299,
    301, 332
Pinerolo, 141, 143, 301
Pisa, 14, 128, 129, 168, 169, 170, 212,
    220, 264
    university, 274
Pisano, the, 31
Pistoia, 14, 31, 218
    Synod of, 219
Pitteri, Francesco, 87, 112
Pius VI, 48, 197
Pivano, Silvio, 321
Placanica, Augusto, 328
plague, 2, 4, 8, 9, 10, 11, 12, 15, 16,
    17, 19, 27, 39
Plato, 96, 99, 100, 131, 288, 289, 292
podestà, 58
Poland, 126

Pombal, 278, 291
Poni, Carlo, 28, 36
Pontieri, Ernesto, 324
Pontine Marshes, 48
Pope, Alexander, 113
popes, 193–7
    Benedict XIII, 193
    Benedict XIV,.48, 129, 130, 151,
        171, 184, 193–7, 252, 273, 310,
        329, 330
    Clement XI, 92, 93, 108
    Clement XII, 16, 151, 171, 182,
        193–6
    Clement XIII, 48, 164, 165
    Gregory XIII, 15
    Leo X, 312
    Innocent, XII, 87
    Paul III, 15, 188
    Pius VI, 48, 197
    Sixtus V, 15
    Urban VIII, 78, 312
population, 2–20, 39, 69
Porisini, Giorgio, 328
Porta, Giambattista della, 80
ports, 6, 34–44
    Ancona, 16, 195
    free ports, 10, 11, 12, 16, 19, 195,
        203
    Genoa, 11
    Leghorn, 11, 13, 71
    Marseilles, 11
    Messina, 19
    Naples, 17, 64
    Nice, 11
    Oneglia, 11
    Trieste, 10–11
    Tyrrhenian, 12
    Venice, 9, 11, 203
Portugal, 135, 154, 196, 204, 273, 278,
    290, 291
Po
    valley, 9, 15, 29, 31, 32, 42, 46, 47,
        48, 51, 55, 71, 141, 197, 199
    river, 52, 195
    states of, 15
Praesidios, 140, 188
Pragmatic Sanction, the, 127
Prague, 158
Prandi, Alfonso, 329
Prato, 52, 218, 219

Prato, Giuseppe, 37, 141, 321, 328
Predari, Francesco, 315
Prince, The, 98, 116
Progymnasmata physica, 80
Protestantism, 276, 277, 279
Prussia, 226, 300
Pufendorf, Samuel, 87, 96, 102, 103
Pugliese, Salvatore, 46, 321
Pyrenees, Treaty of, 140
Pyrrhonism, 101, 102, 130

Quadruple Alliance, 141
Quazza, Guido, 326, 328
Querini, Angelo, 199

Racconigi, 36
Racioppi, Giacomo, 319
Radicati di Passerano, Alberto, 106,
    113–18, 121, 318, 323, 326, 330
Ragion poetica, 85–7
Ramazzini, Benedetto, 80, 90
Rastatt, Treaty of, 141, 143, 149
Ravennate, the, 71
Raynal, Guillaume-Thomas, 285, 291,
    292, 305
'refeudalisation', 23, 40–2
Reformation, 279, 313
Regency Council, 170, 171
Reggio, 176
Reggio Calabria, 246
Regolotti, 93, 114
religion, in Filangieri, 295–6
Renda, F., 331
Reno, valley, 197
republic, in Doria, 97–8, 100
Rialp, Perlas, di, 110
Riccardi, Alessandro, 107, 108, 109, 123,
    128, 148
Ricci, Scipione de', 219, 329
Richecourt, 168–9, 170, 171, 173, 174
Richelieu, 99
Ricuperati, Giuseppe, 327
Riflessioni sopra il buon gusto, 90, 91, 130
Riforma d'Italia, 277–281
Risorgimento, 265, 313, 317, 318
Rivoluzioni d'Italia, 282, 299, 311, 313
Rizzardi, 303
Robbio di San Raffaele, Benvenuto, 301
Roberti, Gaudenzio, 79
Robertson, William, 285, 287, 299

Robespierre, 282
Rodolico, Niccolò, 321
Roger II of Hauteville, 287
Roggero, Marina, 93
Roma, Joseph, 92, 93, 114
Romagna, 30, 194
Romagnosi, Giandomenico, 318
Roman Campagna, 312
Romani, Mario, 328
Romano, Ruggero, 36, 38–40, 42–3,
    328, 330
Romanticism, 314
Rome, 7, 8, 15–16, 35, 71, 78, 79, 80,
    83, 84, 85, 88, 90, 91, 92, 93, 107,
    108, 113, 114, 115, 122, 128, 129,
    131, 151, 165, 171, 175, 182, 186,
    195, 274, 313
Romeo, Rosario, 325
Rosa, Mario, 329
Rosenberg, count de, 212
Rossi, Paolo, 330
Rota, Ettore, 321, 322, 323
Rotelli, E., 328, 331
Rotondò, Antonio, 277
Rotta, S., 327
Rousseau, Jean-Jacques, 210, 213, 217,
    220, 240, 261, 262, 263, 264, 267,
    269, 270, 275, 276, 286, 288, 289,
    290, 298, 301, 302, 303, 304
Rovereto, 131, 277
Royal Society, 78, 81
Rucellai, Giulio, 170, 171, 212, 214,
    218, 276
Russia, 87, 133, 238, 291, 303, 312
Russo, 242, 257

Sabbioneta, 189
Sabina, 30
Saggi politici, 287, 288, 289, 290
St Petersburg, 300, 303
Salento, 25
Salernitano, the, 36
Salfi, Francesco Saverio, 316–7
Salmon, Thomas, 285
Saluzzo di Monesiglio, Angelo, 300, 306
Salvatorelli, Luigi, 324, 325
Salvemini, Gaetano, 323, 327
Salzburg, 277
San Marino, 197, 204
San Martino, Felice di, 301, 305, 306

San Severino, 36
Santisteban, count of, 180
Sapienza, 78
Sardinia, 5, 114, 140, 205–6
Sarpi, Paolo, 107, 108, 112, 116, 117, 171, 201, 263, 274
Sassari, university, 206
Savoy, 5, 9, 12, 37, 51, 141, 206
Savoy (State of), 8, 72, 73, 85, 112, 113, 114, 116, 140, 141–6, 173, 179, 193, 204–7, 298–300, 302, 304, 313
    court, 113, 136
    House of, 57, 73, 92, 121, 183
    Victor Amadeus II, 73
Sbaraglia, Giambattista, 90, 110
Scelta degli opuscoli, 300
Scelta miscellanea, 104, 286, 287
Schio, 36, 52, 200
Schipa, Michelangelo, 319, 321, 324
Schlegel, Friedrich, 314
Schlötzer, Ludwig, 301
Schmid, 289
Scienza chiamata cavalleresca, 56, 123
Scienza della legislazione, 289, 291, 293, 296
Scienza nuova, 100, 102–4, 130, 287, 289
Scottish writers, 298
Secchi, Pietro, 265
Selden, John, 102, 103
Sella, Domenico, 58
Senate
    Milan, 149, 165, 166, 230, 232, 233, 259
    Nice, 141
    Piedmont, 141
    Savoy, 141
    Venice, 67, 126, 201, 202
Sereni, Emilio, 40–1, 46
Serenissima, la, see Venice
Sergardi, Ludovico, 84
Sergio, Carlo Antonio, 88
Serrao, Francesco Andrea, 257, 290
Serrao, Giovanni Andrea, 88, 242
Settembrini, Luigi, 317
Seville, 12
Sforza, family, 57
Sharp, Samuel, 311
Sicilian Interdict, 92
Sicilies, Kingdom of the Two, 5, 17,

179, 187
Sicily, 4–5, 12, 26, 27, 28, 34, 35, 43, 46, 48, 85, 91, 114, 140, 149, 236, 238, 239, 241, 244, 245–7
Siena, 7, 14, 168, 170, 174
Signorelli, Pietro Napoli, 288, 314
Sigonio, Carlo, 299
Sismondi, 315
Sixtus V, 15
Smith, Adam, 50, 266, 268, 293, 305
Smollett, Tobias, 311
Smyrna, 34
social classes, 54–74
Società patriottica, see Patriotic Society
Société Patriotique (Valence), 304
Société Royale, 300
Society of Jesus, see Jesuits
Solaro di Breglio, Roberto, 104
Sommaria, 65
Sonnenfels, Joseph von, 164, 226
South, the, 2, 4, 8, 17–19, 22, 25–8, 36, 41, 45, 46, 48, 61, 62, 80, 96, 140, 148, 151, 179, 180, 236–47, 257, 284, 285, 296, 310
    Denina on, 312
    Filangieri on, 293, 294
    Pagano on, 287, 288, 289
South America, 291
Spain, 11, 12, 32, 59, 98, 99, 135, 141, 147, 154, 179, 187, 189, 196, 202, 204, 243, 256, 269, 290, 291
Spanish
    Bourbon, 61
    domination, 7, 57, 59, 60, 63, 65, 83, 89, 98, 99, 101, 108, 140, 158, 168, 180, 194, 195, 260, 310
    Empire, 83
    in Naples, 62, 238
    in Sicily, 149
    monarchy, 12, 69, 238
Spectator, 264, 265, 298
Spinelli, archbishop, 253
Spinelli, Troiano, 99, 250
Spinoza, 80, 99, 101, 106, 110, 111, 116, 302
Staël, Mme de, 314
State, 7, 54–74, 82, 100, 164, 274, 298
    absolute, 206, 230
    Duchy of Milan, 228, 230–2

in Genovesi, 256
in Muratori, 133
Savoy, 298, 299
Tuscany, 215–16
State and Church, 81, 107, 108, 155,
    164, 165, 166, 171, 172, 176
in Amidei, 274–77
in Pilati, 278, 279
Milan, 229, 230
Naples, 181–4, 187, 245
Parma, 189
Tuscany, 210, 218
Steele, Richard, 264
Storia dell'anno, 311
Storia d'Italia, 38
Süssmilch, Johann Peter, 276
Switzerland, 52, 55, 278
Symonds, John, 311
Syracuse, 5

Tana, Agostino, 301
Tanucci, Bernardo, 155, 181, 182, 187,
    188, 237, 238, 240–5, 252, 257,
    274, 281, 290
Tapié, Victor L., 226
Tarello, Giovanni, 329
Tartarotti, Girolamo, 123, 131, 262
Tavanti, Angelo, 211, 212, 215, 250
tax farming, 142, 160–1, 166, 167, 172,
    178, 200
in Duchy of Milan, 232, 260
in Tuscany, 214
Telesio, Bernardino, 80, 88
Tenivelli, Carlo, 307
Tertullian, 111
Thomas, Saint, 302
Thomasius, 87, 164
Tiber, 195
Ticino, river, 151
Ticozzi, Stefano, 315
Tindal, Matthew, 118
Tiraboschi, Girolamo, 175, 314, 315, 316
Tivaroni, Carlo, 320
Toland, John, 109, 110, 111, 112, 113,
    118
Tolfa, 12
Tommasi, Donato, 289
Toppi, Nicola, 80
Torcellan, G. F., 327
Torcia, Michele, 274, 296

Toulouse, 92
towns, 2–20
trade and manufacture, 5, 10, 11, 12, 13,
    17, 23, 34–44, 49, 51, 52, 70, 134,
    144
Genovesi on, 254–5
Naples, 185–7
Papal States, 197
Tuscany, 211, 213–4
Venice, 200
traders, *see* merchants
Trapani, 4
Trent, 163, 277, 278, 282
Trevisan, Bernardo, 90
Trieste, 10, 11, 19, 34, 38
Triregno, 106, 110, 113, 116, 274, 318
Troisi, Vincenzo, 88
Tron, Andrea, 199, 202, 281
Turgot, 291, 303, 305, 306
Turin, 5, 6, 7, 8, 14, 15, 19, 73, 85,
    88, 91, 92, 104, 112, 113, 114, 115,
    116, 121, 130, 145, 146, 151, 187,
    206, 298, 299, 300, 306
Turkey, 34, 87, 135, 147, 168, 175
Turkish
army, 110
Empire, 10
Wars, 10
Turrettini, Jean Alphonse, 109, 112, 124
Tuscany, 5, 12, 13, 14, 16, 28, 31, 36,
    46, 51, 52, 55, 83, 122, 128, 129,
    156, 163, 175, 176, 179, 188, 196,
    197, 264, 271, 275, 276, 277, 300
Denina on, 312
Grand Duchy of, 85, 91, 151, 211
language of, 301
Regency, 134, 158, 167–74, 218
under Leopold, 210–21, 274
Tyrrhenian, 11, 12, 17, 34, 129, 175
coast, 25
plain, 25, ports, 13

Ugoni, Camillo, 315, 316
Ulloa, Bernardo de, 254, 255, 256
Umbria, 31, 71
Unification, 151
Universal History, 285
universities
Bologna, 16
Cagliari, 206, 302

German, 277
Naples, 93, 104, 106, 121, 148, 244, 254, 278, 289
Padua, 202
Parma, 191
Pavia, 58, 166, 230
Piedmont, 85, 88, 91–4, 104, 114, 121, 129, 145–6, 150, 205, 206, 299, 300, 306
Pisa, 94, 122, 129, 161, 169, 212, 220, 274
Sassari, 206
Urban VIII, 78, 312
Urbino, 30, 194
usury, 125, 130, 196, 252
Utrecht, Dutch Church of, 219
Utrecht, Treaty of, 140, 141, 144
Uztariz, 254, 256

Valdarno, 31
Valdichiana, 31
Valdinievole, 31
Valenza, 140
Valeri, Nino, 324
Valle Caudina, 26
Valletta, Giuseppe, 81, 90, 99
Vallisnieri, Antonio, 80, 90, 91
Valperga di Caluso, Tommaso, 301
Valsecchi, Franco, 324, 325
Valsesia, 140
Van Swieten, 226
Varillas, 229
Vasco, Francesco Dalmazzo, 301–2, 305, 306, 314, 323, 324, 325
Vasco, Giambattista, 266, 271, 276, 301–6, 314, 315, 323
Vecchi, Alberto, 329
Vecchione, Michele, 274
Venetian
    mainland, 37
    nobility, 10, 11
    plain, 31, 200
    Republic, 5, 37, 49, 55, 91, 124, 126, 176, 312
Veneto, 2, 9, 31, 32, 36, 37, 40, 45, 46, 48–9, 52, 67, 68, 125, 126, 199
Venice, 2, 7, 9, 10, 16, 34, 38, 56, 66–8, 73, 90, 91, 98, 112, 122, 124, 131, 147, 179, 197–202, 274, 275, 277, 281

Ventura, Francesco, 182, 186
Venturi, Franco, 166, 185, 190, 236, 241, 242, 277, 311, 314, 324, 325, 326–7, 328, 329, 330
Venturini, Salvatore, 177
Vercelli, 46, 47, 300
Vernazza, Giuseppe, 306
Vernet, Jacques, 89, 109, 112, 123
Verona, 10, 32, 67, 92, 123, 126
Veronese, 37
Verri, brothers, 113, 153, 155, 259
Verri, Alessandro, 173, 262, 265, 266, 299
Verri, Gabriele, 173, 259
Verri, Pietro, 50, 132, 166, 173, 213, 226, 227, 259–62, 263, 264, 265, 266–70, 271, 275, 278, 293, 299–301, 302, 303, 314, 315, 318, 324
Vertot, René-Aubert, 299
veteres, 96, 99, 100, 101, 106, 121, 253
Vicenza, 32, 37
viceroyalty
    Austrian, 107
    Naples, 61, 62, 63
viceroys
    Austrian, 18, 24, 64, 65
    d'Althann, 108, 148
    del Carpio, 99
    de la Cerda, 82
    Harrach, 61, 103, 148
    Spanish, 18, 20, 99
    Visconti, 148
Vico, Gennaro, 93, 103, 104, 121
Vico, Giambattista, 81, 85, 88, 91, 96, 99, 100–4, 106, 130, 253, 286, 287, 288, 289, 292, 293, 295, 301, 314, 316, 317, 318, 319, 324–5, 330
Victor Amadeus II, 8, 73, 91, 92, 93, 114, 115, 116, 117, 133, 141–6, 150, 151, 173, 174, 204, 205, 207, 263, 274, 300, 302, 307, 313, 327
Victor Amadeus III, 206, 302, 312, 330
Vienna, 10, 87, 88, 92, 93, 106, 109, 110, 111, 112, 121, 123, 128, 147, 151, 277, 282
    court, 63
    see also Austria
Vigevano, 46
Villani, Pasquale, 4, 240, 326, 328

Villari, Pasquale, 319
Villari, Rosario, 326, 328
Virgil, 85
Visceglia, M. A., 36
Visconti, Alessandro, 321
Visconti, family, 57
Visconti, Giuseppe, 262, 265
Visconti, viceroy, 148
Vita civile, 96, 98, 99, 100
Vivanti, Corrado, 330
Volpe, Gioacchino, 319, 321, 323
Voltaire, 100, 124, 154, 189, 210, 257, 263, 273, 275, 280, 284, 285, 299, 301, 312, 319
Voyage en Italie pendant l'année 1789, 50

Wallace, Robert, 276
War
    of the Austrian Succession, 8, 15, 127, 132, 159, 175, 186, 187, 188, 194, 202, 205, 310
    of the Polish Succession, 8, 15, 112, 122, 141, 148, 150, 151, 175, 194, 195, 259
    of the Spanish Succession, 5, 8, 9, 11, 13, 15, 18, 87, 91, 114, 140, 143, 205, 310

Seven Years, 159, 163, 174, 202, 204, 223, 259, 290
Wealth of Nations, 50, 266, 293
Weimar, 313
Weishaupt, Adam, 282, 289
Wenking, Christian, 278
Westphalia, Treaty of, 140
Wieland, 313
Wilkes, John, 298
Winspeare, David, 257, 296
Wolff, C., 164
Woolf, Stuart J., 45, 329
Woolston, Thomas, 118

Young, Arthur, 31, 50, 311, 318
Yverdon, 266, 278

Zaccaria, Francesco Antonio, 125, 175
Zanetti, Girolamo, 311
Zangheri, Renato, 40, 41, 328
Zanon, Antonio, 200
Zatta, Antonio, 285
Zeno, Apostolo, 91, 110
Zenobi, B. G., 72
Zurich, 37
Zurlo, A. C., 289